ART GUIDE / NEW YORK

About the Author

A. L. Chanin is widely known as staff lecturer at New York's Museum of Modern Art since 1946, as the conductor of courses in art appreciation for the Museum's Institute for Modern Art and as a popular lecturer to private organizations.

During the 1930's, Mr. Chanin was himself a painter. He studied at the celebrated Barnes Foundation in Merion, Pennsylvania, and in 1934 he received a Barnes Fellowship to continue his scholarship at European museums. In the 1950's, Mr. Chanin was the author of a weekly column of art criticism and a contributor to *Art News, Arts Digest,* the *New York Times Sunday Magazine, The Nation* and other periodicals. More recently he has been assembling material for art guidebooks, of which this volume is the first in a series.

Art guide /

NEW YORK

A. L. CHANIN

 HORIZON PRESS   NEW YORK

Number One in the series of World Art Guides/
Published by Horizon Press, 156 Fifth Avenue, New York.

Composition by Howard O. Bullard.
Printed in the United States of America
by The Comet Press, Inc.

To my wife, Margit

Permissions to reproduce works of art appearing in this book are kindly granted by:

Courtesy of the Metropolitan Museum of Art, Bequest of Benjamin Altman, 26-27, 38, 53-54, 56-57, 60-61, 66   Anonymous Fund, 12   Anonymous gift, 7, 19   Gift of Samuel P. Avery, 118   Jules S. Bache Collection, 2-3, 5, 25, 28, 37, 41, 48, 59, 63, 79   Gift of Julia A. Berwind, 20   Gift of Harry Payne Bingham, 35, 87   Bequest of Lizzie P. Bliss, 139 Gift of Mary Cassatt, 134   Collection of Stephen C. Clark, 115   Gift of Erwin Davis, 94   Bequest of Theodore M. Davis, 6, 99   Dick Fund, 75   Bequest of Mrs. David Dows, 127   Bequest of Michael Dreicer, 23   Bequest of Isaac D. Fletcher, 89   Fletcher Fund, 21-22, 32, 47, 76-77, 80   Michael Friedsam Collection, 65   Friends of the Museum, 62   Gift of Edward J. Gallagher, Jr., 150   Gift of Robert Gordon, 9-10   Bequest of Maitland F. Griggs, 1 Bequest of Mary Stillman Harkness, 29-30   Bequest of Edward S. Harkness, 40, 72   Gift of Frederick H. Hatch, 125 Gift of Mr. and Mrs. Ira Haupt, 57   H. O. Havemeyer Collection, 42-43, 49, 58, 86, 88, 90, 92-93, 95, 97, 102, 104-109, 111   Arthur H. Hearn Fund, 137, 155   George A. Hearn Fund, 135, 147, 152-153   Gift of George A. Hearn, 126, 130, 132   Gift of Henry Hilton, 116   Bequest of Collis P. Huntington, 67   Morris K. Jesup Fund, 117, 124, 151 Kennedy Fund, 4, 8, 16-17, 31   Samuel D. Lee Fund, 136 Leland Fund, 15   Bequest of Samuel A. Lewisohn, 69, 103, 110, 112, 114   Gift of Henry G. Marquand, 36, 68 Gift of J. P. Morgan, 11, 24   Munsey Fund, 13-14, 78 Bequest of Helen Swift Neilson, 64   Gift of William Church Osborn, 91, 96, 98, 100, 113   Bequest of Herbert L. Pratt, 120   Alfred N. Punnett Fund, 133   Rogers Fund, 18, 34, 38-39, 44-45, 70, 85, 128   Gift of Mrs. Russell Sage, 121 Bequest of Gertrude Stein, 52   Alfred Stieglitz Collection, 140-141, 143-145, 147, 149   Samuel D. Lee Fund, 136 Bequest of Cornelius Vanderbilt, 73,   Bequest of William K. Vanderbilt, 71   Gift of Miss Louise Floyd Wickham, 123 Wolfe Fund, 50, 81-84, 101, 122, 129, 131.

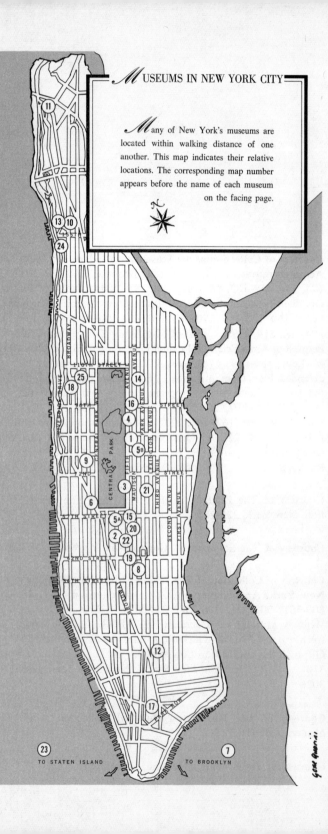

M USEUMS IN NEW YORK CITY

M any of New York's museums are located within walking distance of one another. This map indicates their relative locations. The corresponding map number appears before the name of each museum on the facing page.

TO STATEN ISLAND

TO BROOKLYN

CONTENTS

HOW TO USE THIS BOOK

The format of this book has been designed to make its use as convenient as possible. It is divided into three parts:

1. Detailed discussions of outstanding paintings in the major museums. These are divided into seven sections, each devoted to one of the larger museums. Each section opens with an introduction which includes transportation directions, museum hours (these are subject to change), admission fees (if any), etc., and a brief history of the museum, indicating its areas of greatest strength. The discussions themselves are preceded by numbers which refer to the reproductions, thus allowing the reader to relate the text to the appropriate painting with minimal difficulty. The works encompassed are chiefly oil and tempera paintings, though pastels and watercolors are included when these media form a major part of the expression of important artists, as with Degas or John Marin. At the end of each section appears a brief list of major sculptures, intended only as a sampling of the museum's sculpture collection.

2. A checklist of smaller museums. This section includes the same information on transportation, hours, etc., along with briefer descriptions of the nature of the institutions and lists of their most important art works.

3. Biographies and evaluations of the artists. These are listed alphabetically and include significant facts about the artists' lives, phonetic pronunciations where necessary and brief critical evaluations of their work as a whole. Immediately below each artist's name appears a list of the New York City museums in which his important work is represented. Some of the museum names appear in boldface; the numbers which appear immediately after these indicate that the artist's major works are discussed, under the same numbers, in the museum sections.

NOTE: The order in which the paintings are listed under each museum is roughly chronological and generally, though not always, according to "school" or style—e.g., Italian or Dutch, Impressionist or Cubist. The sequence in which the paintings appear in the text is roughly approximate to the sequence in which they may be seen in the museum, but an exact sequence is impossible due to frequent changes made by the museum staffs. The reader who is not familiar with the layout of a given museum would be well-advised to obtain a copy of the floor plans which several museums make available.

Not all the paintings discussed in this guide are always on view. Some may be removed temporarily to make way for a special exhibition, while others may be on loan or undergoing restoration.

INTRODUCTION

This book has been written to guide the viewer toward a greater enjoyment of the incredibly rich store of art treasures housed in the museums of the City of New York. Its detailed discussions of those works the author considers especially significant—from a 14th Century Duccio panel in the Frick Collection to a 20th Century satire by Jean Dubuffet in the Museum of Modern Art—are intended for those who are interested in more than an aimless stroll through museum galleries. I have attempted, first, to direct the museum-goer to the finest of the thousands of works on view, allowing him to "look over" the collections in advance and decide which paintings interest him most and which places he will want to explore in an afternoon, a day or over a prolonged period. My second aim was to increase the viewer's insight into and pleasure in these works by clarifying the essential aspects of their compositions and supplying some of the stories behind them which give them more immediate relevance to us.

The plan, scope and method of the book grew out of my twenty-odd years of experience in public lectures directly before the paintings discussed. Since New York City's museums contain such exceptional abundance, particularly in the art nearest to us—that of the later 19th Century and the 20th—the task of selection and exclusion is not an easy one, especially if a balance is to be struck between the achievements of earlier centuries and those of our more recent, and still controversial, candidates for immortality. Inevitably, many outstanding names are missing, either because the city's museums still lack important examples, or because space limitations demand that a choice be made among certain styles or among equal or near-equal achievements.

Words and reproductions are, of course, no substitute for the experience of direct contact with works of art. This volume is offered, therefore, not to take the place of museum visits, but as a guide for the museum visitor *while looking* at the paintings.

In gathering most of the background, historical data and similar information which went into the preparation of this volume, I have been aided tremendously by various museum publications. I am especially indebted to several of the highly informative catalogues published by the Metropolitan Museum of Art—*A Catalogue of Italian, Spanish and Byzantine Paintings*, by Harry B. Wehle, Curator of Paintings; *A Catalogue of Early Flemish, Dutch and German Paintings*, by Harry B. Wehle, and Research Fellow Margaretta Salinger; *A Catalogue of French Paintings XV-XVIII Centuries*, by Charles Sterling, Curator of Paintings at the Louvre—and to various articles in the splendid Bulletins published by the Metropolitan.

For data on the second half of the 19th Century, John Rewald's two books—*A History of Impressionism* and *Post-Impressionism: from Van Gogh to Gauguin*, both published by the Museum of Modern Art—were invaluable. Equally helpful—in fact, essential—for the sections on 20th Century art were the many Museum of Modern Art publications, especially *Masters of Modern Art*, edited by Alfred H. Barr, Jr., *Matisse: His Art and His Public*, by Mr. Barr, and the long list of comprehensive exhibition monographs for which the Museum of Modern Art's Publications Department is famous.

Another outstanding source was the remarkable—and beautiful—twelve-volume edition of *An Illustrated Catalogue of the Works of Art in the Collection of Henry Clay Frick*, with an introduction by Sir Osbert Sitwell, published by the Pittsburgh University Press. For the Whitney Museum, compact, factual exhibition monographs, such as *John Sloan*, by Lloyd Goodrich, the Museum's Director, and *American Art of Our Century*, by Mr. Goodrich and John H. Baur, the Whitney's Associate Director (published for the Whitney by Frederick A. Praeger), were most helpful. The handsome *A Handbook to the Solomon R. Guggenheim Collection* provided factual material on the paintings in that institution.

Museums without comprehensive catalogues, such as the Brooklyn Museum and the Gallery of Modern Art, compensated with the knowledge and helpfulness of their staffs.

I also want to record my gratitude to the staffs of all the museums for help in compiling photographs. In this respect I owe extra thanks to Pearl L. Moeller of the Museum of Modern Art.

And finally, for the inevitable chores of editing, typing and retyping, I am grateful to my editor, Joseph Focarino, to Barbara Rex and Dorothy Knowles and, especially, to patient Margit Chanin.

ART GUIDE / NEW YORK

THE MUSEUMS

THE METROPOLITAN MUSEUM OF ART

Fifth Avenue at 82nd Street.   TR 9-5500

Hours: Mondays through Saturdays 10-5; Sundays and holidays 1-5. Free.

Transportation: Fifth Avenue Buses 2, 3 and 4 to 82nd Street; Madison Avenue Bus to 82nd Street; 79th and 86th Street Crosstown Buses to Fifth Avenue. Lexington Avenue IRT to 86th Street.

Talks: Free gallery talks Tuesdays, Thursdays and Fridays at 2:30. Equipment for receiving 45-minute recorded tours available for 50¢ until 3:45. Free lectures and film showings Sunday afternoons in the Grace Rainey Rogers Auditorium. Subscription lectures (and concerts) throughout the year.

Special collections: Costume Institute (exhibits of clothing and accessories). Junior Museum (wide range of exhibits, programs and facilities for children). Thomas J. Watson Library, Print Study Room and Textile Study Room (exhibits and research facilities; primarily restricted to scholars and Museum members). The Cloisters (see separate listing).

Sales and loans: Art and book shop; main entrance. Art lending collection, photographic reference collection and collection of photographs and slides for sale; main floor rear.

Restaurants: Cafeteria (lunch Mondays through Saturdays 11:30-2:30, Sundays 12-3; coffee hour Saturdays 3-4:30, Sundays 3:30-

4:30); main floor. Junior Museum Snack Bar (Mondays through Fridays 10-10:45 and 12:40-4:30; Saturdays 10-4:30; Sundays 1-4:30); ground floor. Both closed holidays.

Parking: Entrance at south end of building (Mondays through Saturdays 9:30-5:30; Sundays 12-5:30; holidays 12:30-5:30). Charge: $1.

Calendar of events: Mailed monthly on request at no charge.

The Metropolitan is the most comprehensive museum in the Western Hemisphere and one of the most encyclopedic in the world. Its collection includes about one million art objects spanning some 5,000 years. The roster of its departments indicates the variety of treasures it houses under one roof: American Paintings and Sculpture (including furniture and silver in the American Wing); Arms and Armor; The Costume Institute; Drawings; Egyptian Art; Medieval Art (including the Cloisters); Musical Instruments; Near Eastern Art; Prints; Renaissance and Post-Renaissance and European Art Other Than Painting.

The museum was conceived not in New York, but in Paris. At a July Fourth dinner in 1866, John Jay, minister to Germany and grandson of the great Supreme Court Chief Justice, declared that it was "time for the American people to lay the foundation of a National Institution and Gallery of Art," and that "the American gentlemen . . . in Europe were the men to inaugurate the plan."

That same year, a provisional committee was organized in New York. On Washington's Birthday, 1872, the Metropolitan opened with a rather feeble collection in a converted dancing academy and stables at Fifth Avenue between 53rd and 54th Streets. The next year, it moved into a mansion on East 14th Street. In 1880 it settled permanently in what was then almost suburban territory on the border of Central Park. The original two-story brick building—now the West Wing—was conceived in part by Calvert Vaux, who was also a designer of Central Park. The present main building, facing Fifth Avenue, was designed by a celebrated builder of mansions, Richard Morris Hunt and his son Richard Howland Hunt. A mixture of Roman, Classic and Renaissance motifs, the building was completed in 1902 and acclaimed a masterpiece of contemporary architecture! (The rough blocks of stone over the facade's four pairs of columns were intended for sculptural groups representing Egyptian, Greek, Renaissance and modern art; the sculptures have never been commissioned.) Flanking wings were added in 1905, 1910 and 1916 by McKim, Mead and White. The American Wing was added in 1924; its walls include the marble facade of the United States Bank, an old Wall Street building torn down in 1915.

In addition to its more than 3,000 paintings, a few of the Museum's highlights include: the only Egyptian tomb on this continent; the world's largest collection of Cypriot sculpture; a room from a villa at Boscoreale, a town destroyed during the 79 A.D.

eruption which annihilated Pompeii; an entire 16th Century Spanish patio; stained glass windows; the gold, enamel and pearl Rospiogli Cup ascribed to Cellini; a 1721 pianoforte built by Cristofiori, the Florentine inventor of the instrument; a Chinese ceremonial bronze wine vessel over 5,000 years old; rare Persian illuminated manuscripts and rugs; an almost complete set of Degas sculptures; and an abstract sculpture of the sun by the contemporary American Richard Lippold, made with some 2,000 feet of 22-karat gold wire.

Note: A floor plan of the Museum is available free at the lobby information desk.

Italian Painting

SASSETTA
• **1. The Journey of the Magi.** (Date uncertain)   Sassetta shows the Three Kings, accompanied by courtiers, jesters and a pet monkey, setting out on their journey to the stable where the Christ Child lies. The composition is based on the lively diagonals of the criss-crossing hills and the procession, and the balancing horizontals of the distant town and the formation of cranes (symbols of vigilance and loyalty). The artist delights in stylized figures, gay costumes and graceful horses. Particularly decorative passages occur in the dark, slender legs of the bottom two horses against the grey rocks, in the prancing white charger above them and in the red tunic and billowing blue cloak of its rider. The placement of the Star of Bethlehem beneath the procession indicates that this panel was once part of a larger painting in which the Nativity was shown below. An Adoration now in Siena is assumed to be the missing lower portion.

TURA, Cosimo
• **2. The Flight into Egypt.** (About 1470)   In this little painting filled with drama and spiritual intensity, Tura interprets a passage from St. Matthew: "The Angel of the Lord appeared to Joseph

1

2

in a dream, saying, arise, and take the young child and his mother, and flee into Egypt . . . for Herod will seek the young child to destroy him. When he arose, he took the young child and his mother by night, and departed into Egypt." Crisp and sharp, Tura's line elaborates the surface, expressing form and action and giving vitality to the figures and landscape. The Virgin's movement toward St. Joseph establishes a rhythmic relationship between the figures. The ass (searching the barren ground for water or grass) unites the two with the circular movement of its neck. A horizontal motif, repeated across the base, gives stability to the active movements. Against a tonality of blues and greens, the scarlet of St. Joseph's cloak stands out dramatically—a sudden shift of harmony which adds a prophetic and emotional note to the scene.

CRIVELLI, Carlo

• **3. Madonna and Child.** (About 1470-73) In this exquisitely formal and symmetrical picture, the surface glows with the lacquer-like quality of fine tempera painting. The Madonna functions as part of the vertical design, while horizontal motifs appear in the balustrade, the folds of the lilac panel and the fabric in the foreground. The gold embroidery on the blue mantle and the halos of the Child and the Madonna harmonize with similar patterns and forms repeated throughout the picture. The decorative objects surrounding the figures are not only integral parts of the structure, but symbols familiar to cultured Christians in Crivelli's time. The apple signified sin, evil and death in the Garden of Eden. The fly symbolized sin and redemption when it appeared in pictures of the Virgin and Child. The gourd was taken as a prefiguration of the Resurrection. Birds meant winged souls—the spiritual as opposed to the material; the goldfinch, fond of thistles and thorns, alluded specifically to Christ's crown of thorns and His Passion. Indeed, almost every object and every color in this picture and others like it contains symbolic significance. The Virgin's sky-colored mantle referred to Heaven and Heavenly love. Violet, the color of the Child's cushion, represented truth, passion and suffering. White was innocence of soul and deep red repre-

3

4

sented Christ's martyrdom. The halo was a symbol of God's light. (Only Christ's halo contains a cross.) The pearl symbolized salvation and sometimes Christ's admonition, "neither cast ye your pearls before swine." The bramble represented the purity of the Virgin and living trees symbolized life. The signature reads "Opus Karoli Crivelli Veneti"—"The work of Carlo Crivelli of Venice."

BOTTICELLI, Sandro

• **4. Three Miracles of Saint Zenobius.** (About 1505)   Born of noble parents, St. Zenobius (334-424) was converted to Christianity by a tutor and eventually became Bishop of Florence. Botticelli shows three of his miracles in one painting. At left, the Saint stops a funeral procession and restores a dead man to life. In the center, he revives a messenger who was killed accidentally while bringing him sacred relics. At right, St. Zenobius takes holy water to St. Eugenius, who then crosses the piazza and restores a dead relative by sprinkling him with the water. The corpses in the coffin, apparently the sacred remains of martyrs, were once painted over, and were revealed only recently by cleaning. Through the spotting of color and the insistent motif of plunging figures, the three separate groups are integrated into an indissoluble whole. The floating pennants play an important role in connecting the central group with that on the left. At right, as the figures surge dynamically toward the edge, diagonal steps restore the composition's equilibrium in a daring countermovement. The precise geometric order of the buildings adds stability to the sway of the figures, while the stress on line and precision lends variety to the arrangement. A serene landscape balances the tense action.

GHIRLANDAIO, Domenico

• **5. Francesco Sassetti and His Son Teodoro.** (About 1468-70) A partner in Lorenzo de Medici's bank in Lyons, Francesco Sassetti commissioned Ghirlandaio to paint frescoes for his family chapel in Santa Trinità in Florence, as well as family portraits like this one. Sassetti and his son are effectively contrasted against

5

6

the distant view of an inlet. The emphatic curve of the father's dark purple skull cap and the slope of the hill at left relieve the straight dark edge at the top of the painting and the green ground. Against the dominant note of Sassetti's red doublet, Ghirlandaio contrasts the delicate forms of the child's curving hair and the decorations of his tunic.

BELLINI, Giovanni

• **6. Madonna Adoring the Sleeping Child.** (Date uncertain) The emphasis on line, contour and dry color mark this picture as belonging to Bellini's early period, when he was influenced by his brother-in-law Mantegna. Delicate, yet majestic in the firm moulding of her robe, the Virgin looms gracefully against a pale sky. The Child's contours find echoes in the robe and cloak and winding landscape. A dark pillow accentuates the Child's head and provides a keystone for the colors of the landscape. The low horizon gives the Madonna monumental height and scale. (The thin, scraped blues are due to faulty cleaning and restoring in the past.)

MANTEGNA, Andrea

• **7. Adoration of the Shepherds.** (About 1460) In a painting which amalgamates trends old and new, the landscape demonstrates the Renaissance's growing interest in spatial perspective, while St. Joseph's classical posture and the design of his garment's folds reflect Mantegna's passion for antique sculpture. The shepherds (like the landscape) also reveal the artist's keen eye for blunt realism. Compressed within a sweeping, rhythmic movement, the monumental figures are arranged in a stately pyramid design which starts with St. Joseph, reaches its apex with the Madonna (heightened by the cherubs and the rocky structure above her head) and concludes with the shepherds. A distant hillock toward the right echoes the triangle of the rocky ledge in the foreground. Patterns of enamel-like color unify the picture. St. Joseph's yellow acts as an important balance on the right, and his reds are related to the red of the Virgin, the cherubs and the shepherds' sleeves. The blue of the Virgin's cloak forms a strong center.

CARPACCIO, Vittore

• **8. The Meditation on the Passion.** (About 1505-10) The dra-

7

8

matic, trance-like mood of this painting is unusual for Carpaccio. In fact, the picture was attributed to Mantegna for centuries, until photographic studies revealed Carpaccio's signature underneath a covering of paint; a forged Mantegna signature is still faintly visible at lower right. Two figures balance Christ: Job, the Old Testament patriarch who personifies poverty and unshakeable faith, sits at right, while at left is St. Jerome, with the lion he befriended in the desert. Job sits on a block inscribed in Hebrew with "My Redeemer liveth" and the number "19", perhaps a reference to the chapter of the Book of Job in which the phrase occurs. The Hebrew on Christ's throne reads: "With a Cry" and "Israel . . ." The composition centers on the ruined Renaissance throne. At left, its elaborate back fills the space diagonally between St. Jerome and Christ. At right, its color relates with the reddish flesh of Job. The landscape begins ruggedly at left, then falls away to a panoramic vista. On both sides, lavish details blend into the background. A mellow color tone flows over figures and landscape, diffusing lines, contours and volumes.

PIERO DI COSIMO

• **9. A Hunting Scene** and • **10. The Return from the Hunt.** (About 1485) The meanings of these two pictures are obscure. The noted art scholar Panofsky suggests the plausible explanation that they are part of a series showing the growth of civilization through the control of fire, a story told by the Romans and recounted in Piero's time by Boccaccio. *A Hunting Scene* shows primitive men and beasts fighting each other before man has learned to control and use fire; the forest burns unchecked. *The Return from the Hunt* symbolizes the lessening of violence as man learned the art of building, indicated by the rough boat; in the far background, game still flee into the water to escape fire. In *A Hunting Scene* the embattled figures are spaced in a rhythmic pattern of alternating light and dark around an inverted triangle which starts in the spread of foliage across the top and narrows down through the centaur with the club and the foreground trees. The fallen figure at right demonstrates Piero's fascination with two new pictorial resources: the mastery of anatomy, and the dramatic design possibilities of foreshortening and perspective. *The Return from the Hunt* stresses sinuous contours. The mountain,

9

figures, slender tree and boat are coordinated through shapes and lines that flow like a long horizontal wave. These panels were among the first pictures given to the Museum. They are among its rarest Italian paintings.

RAPHAEL

• **11. The Madonna and Child Enthroned with Saints.** (About 1504-05)   Painted when the artist was barely twenty-two, this precocious performance is weakened only by a tendency toward sweetness. The infant St. John is shown adoring the Child. At left, St. Catherine, her oval face so typical of Raphael, holds the wheel of her martyrdom. (She was killed in a torture device of wheels armed with points and saws.) St. Peter holds the gold and silver keys of Heaven and Hell. At right, St. Cecilia, patron of music, wears a crown of pink and white roses. St. Paul leans on a sword as he reads the Holy Book. In the lunette above, God the Father is flanked by angels. Raphael employs a traditional symmetrical composition, centered on the throne and figures, but the vigorous rendering of Sts. Peter and Paul shows the impact of Leonardo da Vinci and Michelangelo, whose work Raphael had just seen in Florence. Among the most charming elements are the intricate designs formed by the contours of the garments, and the intervals of soft blue between the green bandings and Sts. Catherine and Cecilia. The vista of sky and the glimpse of Raphael's native Umbria show the artist's brilliant feeling for spatial design as a setting for frontal groups. The historian Vasari wrote that Raphael painted this altarpiece "for the nuns of St. Anthony of Padua; in it the infant Christ is on his mother's lap, fully clothed, as it pleased those simple and pious ladies that he should be. . . . This work is full of devout feeling and is held in great veneration by the nuns." In the 17th Century the nuns sold the altarpiece and its panels, part by part. The altarpiece itself passed on to the family of the Princes of Colonna of Rome, who sold it in 1802 to the King of Naples. In 1910, J. P. Morgan acquired it for $484,000; his son gave it to the Metropolitan.

• **12. The Agony in the Garden.** (About 1504)   Within a small panel at once delicate and dramatic, poignant and restrained,

10

Raphael creates a monumental composition picturing the hours
before Jesus' capture as described in the Gospel of St. Mark: "And
they came to a place which was named Gethsemane and He saith
to His disciples 'Sit ye here, while I pray' . . . . And He cometh,
and findeth them sleeping." Amidst the drowsing disciples, Christ
is emphasized by the sky and by the slender trees which endow
the landscape with its lyrical quality. The hillock at right flows in
a diagonal that merges with a sleeping disciple. At left, the pose
of the lower youth extends and underlines the diagonal of Christ's
robe. This panel, one of five originally set in the base of the altarpiece, was sold by the nuns of St. Anthony to ex-Queen Christina
of Sweden, then living in Rome. Subsequent owners included a
Cardinal, two Princes, a Duke, Samuel Rogers (a minor poet
and friend of Wordsworth and Byron), Baroness Burdett Couts
(a friend of Charles Dickens, who advised her on charitable projects, including a home for rehabilitating prostitutes) and Clar-
ence Mackay, head of International Telephone and Telegraph.
In 1932, the panel was bought by the Museum and reunited with
the altarpiece after a lapse of almost three centuries.

TITIAN
- **13. Alfonso d'Este, Duke of Ferrara.** (About 1522-23)   Alfonso d'Este (1486-1534), third husband of Lucrezia Borgia, defied
Renaissance aristocratic convention by working as a blacksmith,
carpenter and armorer and becoming an expert on the employment of artillery. Titian alludes to this by placing the Duke's hand
proudly on a cannon. The design represents a typical Venetian
portrait scheme: a dark figure emerging softly from an almost
equally dark background, but with strong light accentuating face
and hands. (This portrait tradition reaches from Giorgione
through Veronese, and is given further distinction by artists as
diverse as Rubens, Rembrandt, Cézanne and Soutine.) Despite
fading and what appear to be extensive restorations, the original

12

grandeur of Titian's work is still evident. The Duke's shrewd features form the apex of an asymmetrical pyramid. The relationship of the three golden flesh notes suggests movement within the calm scheme of the composition. The cannon defines a horizontal base. A sumptuous sleeve concludes the right side of the design with a rich chord of color.

● **14. Venus and the Lute Player.** (About 1562-65)   One of a series on the theme of reclining Venuses, this vision of love, dance and music belongs to Titian's last years. The painting is either unfinished or deteriorated, and consequently weakened—particularly when the dry surfaces are compared to the lush landscape—yet it remains a grand composition. The flesh of the nude sings out against dark fabric. Massive, richly-colored hangings open on a vast, idyllic vista. The intricate by-play of the curtain enriches the composition at right, where its folds become a radiating design pivoting toward the head and shoulders, and at top left, where it relates to the pose of the lute-player, his cloak and the neck of the lute. In the landscape, the painting's finest moment, Titian's brush flows with masterly ease. Broken touches of color shimmer in the clouds and trees. Interwoven bands and veils of color glow with gold and silver. The pool, the dancing figures, the grove and the towering mountains palpitate with light.

13

1

1

TINTORETTO

- **15. The Miracle of the Loaves and the Fishes.** (About 1544-47) Tintoretto portrays the miracle in which Jesus, preaching in the desert, fed five thousand followers with only five loaves and two fishes. Christ is shown taking one of the loaves from a boy and giving it to St. Andrew. The canvas is a blend of Biblical theme, Venetian pageantry and majestic grandeur. The composition is based on a parallel succession of curving, horizontal masses. A restless force is generated from the core by the dance-like swirl of the two central figures; encircling masses undulate about them, each unit balanced and contrasted with another. The groups in the left and right foreground direct the eye into the center, while in the far background a white-robed host establishes a stable balance. The rendering is exceptionally free. With its theme of the feeding of multitudes, this painting may have been intended for a charitable institution; some scholars consider the robed figures to be almshouse inmates.

- **16. Doge Alvise Mocenigo Presented to the Redeemer.** (About 1577-84) From August of 1575 to July of 1577 a great plague raged in Venice, claiming some 50,000 victims including the aged Titian. In 1576 Doge Mocenigo pledged a temple to the Redeemer if the plague would cease; in 1577 the temple was begun by the famous architect Palladio. Tintoretto shows the vow taking place in a loggia overlooking Venice. Three related groups are set against architecture, sky and water. Christ's whirling robe (framed by angels), His movements and the child musician below Him direct the eye toward the kneeling Doge. The Doge's robe and the stairs link his figure to the rhythmic grouping of the Saints at right. They, in turn, direct the eye back to the center. The foreground serves as a stage for the majestic confrontation. Luminous color, terse and robust handling and the play of light against dark keep the painting pulsating. The Doge, dead at the time of this painting, was sketched in from an earlier Tintoretto portrait. In the left foreground is the lion of St. Mark, patron Saint of Venice. Photographic studies show that the Saint himself was originally included, but was painted out—perhaps because his figure was too imposing in relation to Christ's; more water and

16

steps were added to fill his former space. The figures at right are probably St. John the Baptist (holding his attribute, a lamb), St. Augustine or St. Louis (the Doge's name-sake), St. John the Evangelist, and St. Gregory, patron of the Doge's family. Some scholars identify the third figure as St. Roch, a 14th Century religious who nursed plague victims; in 1485, Venetians had stolen his body from France and brought it to their city. This painting is a preliminary study for a mural in Venice's Ducal Palace. The study once belonged to the English art critic John Ruskin, who bought it in Italy for a mere 50 napoleons—less than $200.

VERONESE, Paolo

• **17. Mars and Venus United by Love.** (About 1576-84) Some scholars believe this painting represents the adoption of Hercules by Juno, since passing a man's hand through a woman's garment is an ancient adoption rite, and the gesture of pressing milk is a symbol of a nursing mother. Others consider the offering of milk to signify Chastity transformed by Love into Charity, and the horse, held back by Cupid, to be passion restrained. Still others consider the theme to be martial force nourished by beauty. Although not important to the enjoyment of the painting as a work of art, the various interpretations illustrate the obsession with classical allusions and elaborate symbolism of Veronese's time. In this sumptuous work, the main moments occur in the bending form of Mars and the counter-movement of Venus. Her pearly skin is opposed by his ruddy face, muscular arms and gleaming armor and the design of his cloak's heavy folds. As Mars' back slopes toward Venus, it becomes part of a continuous line that starts with the large brown leaves above and continues in three parallel contours: the left arm of Venus, the edge of the ruined wall and the torso of the faun. There are some weak spots: the elbow and the hand of Venus seem flat and wooden, the face of the goddess overly pink and the horse stilted. This may be the result of retouching, or the picture may have been worked on by assistants.

17

CARAVAGGIO, Michelangelo
• **18. The Musicians.** (About 1594) Made when the artist was about twenty (and probably commissioned by his first important patron, Cardinal del Monte) this painting combines a classical theme with the beginnings of Caravaggio's characteristic treatment of detail, light, color and character. The four youths are linked in a rhythmic interplay centering on the boy tuning the lute. The back of the singer at right and the white drapery curve to meet the red folds, while the book of music gracefully establishes an undulating diagonal. The shoulder of the boy at left continues the direction of the main figure's robe. Caravaggio almost flattens features and muscles (foretelling Manet); his handling of flesh is broad and cool. At lower left appears a typical Caravaggio still life of fresh grapes, wet with dew. For some 300 years, this painting was lost—known only from contemporary descriptions. In the 1940's, a retired British Navy surgeon visiting a small town found it, covered with centuries of dirt and repainting, and bought it for under $300. After cleaning, it was found to be the long-missing masterpiece.

TIEPOLO, Giovanni Battista
• **19. The Glorification of Francesco Barbaro.** (Date uncertain) To honor Francesco Barbaro (1398-1454), who won fame for his defense of Brescia against the Milanese, his descendants commissioned this ceiling painting for the Barbaro Palace in Venice. The enthroned leader holds the Venetian baton of a condottiere— a professional military leader—while his left arm rests on the Lion of Brescia. Above, Fame blows a trumpet, a winged Victory holds a laurel crown and Plenty carries a cornucopia. In the foreground is Prudence, the serpent on her arm embodying Wisdom. The statuette signifies the Arts. In Tiepolo's charmingly theatrical portrayal, the tiers of figures, painted as if seen from below, seem buoyant and air-borne. At lower left, a figure directs the eye to the hero, who is seated on a ruined cornice floating on clouds; vividly silhouetted against a semi-circular formation of golden orange, her dark blue dress is a link to the other blues. This painting once belonged to Stanford White, whose firm designed the two Fifth Avenue wings of the Metropolitan Museum. In 1906 White was shot and killed at the old Madison Square Garden in a sensational murder-scandal revolving around the show-girl Evelyn Nesbitt.

20

GUARDI, Francesco

• **20. Fantastic Landscape.** (About 1780) This grand and spacious composition is divided into two simple horizontals: ground and sky. At left, the perspective of the wall and the arch shifts diagonally toward the center. Space is further accentuated by the drifting arrangement of receding figures. The deepest charm of the painting is in its tone and handling. At once rugged and delicate, the strokes glide smoothly but emphatically over forms. The water, almost breathed onto the canvas, is cool and glistening against the stones of the quay. The building is painted lightly and firmly, the figures created by rapid, expressive strokes.

Flemish Painting

VAN EYCK, Hubert (attribution)

• **21. The Crucifixion** and • **22. The Last Judgement.** (Date uncertain) Van Eycks are rarities in museums, and these two panels —rich in action, pattern and color, and rendered with masterly finesse—are among the finest examples of Flemish art in America. *The Crucifixion* starts with the mass of mourners at bottom. Their cloaks and colors merge them into a single monumental group, balanced by the green-robed Magdelene, whose anguished gesture directs the eye upward to the soldiers and horsemen. The white of the headdress and trimmings among the mourners reappears in the horsemen, notably in the ermine edge of the robe at center. The horsemen and the circle of figures form a freize at the feet of the climactic crosses. A blue sky provides a symbolically peaceful contrast. *The Last Judgement* is based on the Apocalyptic Book of St. John the Evangelist. Words of St. Matthew appear across Christ's robe—"Come, ye Blessed of my Father"—and at the sides of the Archangel—"Depart from me, ye cursed, into everlasting fire." Christ the Judge is attended by the Virgin and St.

21   22

John. Angels carry the instruments of the Passion and blow trumpets. Below the throne, the Twelve Apostles sit in glory, while virgin martyrs welcome the elect to Heaven. The bishops, cardinal and monks represent the Church, and the richly-dressed figures stand for temporal power. Between Heaven and Hell, the earth and sea give up the dead. St. Michael stands astride Death. The damned are separated from the just not only by placement, but by their sharp contrast to the calm of the upper group. The wings of the skeleton both divide and unify the lower and upper halves. Above Death, the orderly design of wings and robes conveys a sensation of forms suspended in space. Inscribed on the frame of *The Crucifixion* is a passage from Isaiah beginning "And the Lord hath laid on him the iniquity of us all." On the *Last Judgement* appear these words, among others: "And death and hell delivered up the dead which were in them" and "I will also send the teeth of beasts upon them, with the poison of serpents of the dust." In the early 1840's, a Russian envoy to Spain bought these two panels, together with a central panel, from a Spanish convent. The central panel, *Adoration of the Magi,* was stolen and has never been found. In 1845, the collector bequeathed the remaining two to the Hermitage Museum in St. Petersburg. They were sold by the Soviet government in 1933.

VAN DER WEYDEN, Rogier

• **23. Christ Appearing to His Mother.** (About 1440-45)   According to legend, after His Resurrection Christ first appeared to His mother. She is shown here interrupted in her reading of a devotional book, while the background telescopes time by depicting the Resurrection itself. Van der Weyden achieves a taut, powerful effect through variations in scale and the contrasting colors of the two key figures. Christ's crimson and blue mantle, with its intricate convolution of folds, and the Virgin's robes, spreading out at the base, give their forms dominion over the complex Gothic architectural elements. They gesture rigidly, as if re-enacting a dramatic pantomime—a stylization closer to the Medieval approach than to the realism emerging in the artist's time. The eye is led from the frontal plane of the main figures, through a series of receding planes and on to the distant horizon. The movement is accelerated by the perspective of the bench, the tiles and the winding road and hills. The surface is gem-like, and the two figures especially seem hewn from beautifully-colored stone. On the lower capitals in the arch appear St. Mark (right) and St. Paul (left). Above them are scenes from the later years of the Virgin's life. The scroll carried by the angel reads: "This woman fulfilled all things triumphantly, therefore a crown was given unto her." Along the Virgin's mantle is the Magnificat, the expression of humility she spoke on her visit to her cousin Elizabeth. On the capitals in the background are Old Testament themes believed to prefigure the Resurrection: David and Goliath, Daniel in the lion's den and Samson. This panel formed the right wing of a triptych bequeathed by Queen Isabella of Spain, patron of Columbus, to the Royal Chapel of the Cathedral of Granada in 1504. The Queen's father had received it as a gift from Pope Martin V.

• **24. The Annunciation.** (About 1460-64)   The Annunciation is described in the Gospel according to St. Luke: "And the Angel came in unto her, and said, 'Hail, thou that art highly favored, the Lord is with thee; blessed art thou among women . . . thou shalt conceive in thy womb, and bring forth a son, and shalt call his name Jesus.' " The eye is immediately charmed by this painting's enamel-like lustre, the firm yet delicate grace of its figures, the striking color patterns and the dramatic space. The Angel and the Madonna, placed asymmetrically, are framed by a compressed perspective rising steeply from foreground to window to courtyard. The Angel's icy blue wings link the interior with the sky. Despite the elaborate pattern of the Angel's vestments, the Madonna retains dominance through the intensity of her blue mantle, the red of her bodice and the sharp contours of her hair. The emphatic geometric edge of her mantle is set off by the magnificent design of planes and angles in the folds of the bed. The lilies symbolize purity and the candle may signify Christ. An enclosed garden is a Medieval symbol of the Virgin. The peacock, indicated in the Archangel's wings, is a symbol of immortality. On the window and in the rug are the arms of Ferry de Clugny, a Chancellor of the Order of the Golden Fleece, who about the time of this picture became Bishop of Tournai, Rogier's birthplace.

CHRISTUS, Petrus
• **25. Portrait of a Carthusian.** (1446)   Polished realism and exquisite handling fuse here in a memorable portrait. In the dramatic background, dark red merges slowly into flame. Flemish visual fidelity is evident in details like the fly on the painted

24   2

frame. The fly, a symbol of sin, may signify the monk's triumph
over, or battle with, sin. Since a halo is used only for saints, this
one may have been added later, though some scholars believe
the portrait represents Dionysius the Carthusian, a monk revered
in his time as blessed.

MEMLING, Hans

● **26. Tommaso Portinari** and ● **27. Maria Portinari.** (About
1472)   Tommaso di Folco Portinari (1432?-1501), a prominent
Florentine and a descendant of a brother of Dante's Beatrice,
worked for the Medici bank in Bruges, then one of Europe's
great port cities. The ambitious financier, with the Pope as partner, once attempted to corner the supply of alum; when his plan
failed the Medici had to abandon their Bruges bank and Tommaso returned to Florence. At thirty-eight, Tommaso married
the fourteen-year-old daughter of a wealthy Florentine family
living in Bruges—Maria Bandini-Baroncelli. She became the
mother of his ten children. Two years after their marriage, these
companion portraits were painted. Tommaso's sensitive portrait
excels in firm but delicate modeling. Flesh tones are rich against
the dark doublet and dark brown hair. The simplified color
scheme gives intensity and power to the structure of the head
and the strong, meditative face. While retaining the soberness
and dignity of her husband's portrayal, Maria's painting is enriched and varied by her more elaborate costume. The slant of
her conical hennin and the silken veil hanging from it frame the
refined oval of her head. Her square neckline is contrasted against
the V-curve of the white fur collar. The veil also acts as intermediary between background and luminous flesh. In the year of
his marriage, Tommaso commissioned Memling to paint *The
Passion of Christ,* in which he and his bride appear. Tommaso is
also seen near the Archangel in a Memling *Last Judgement.*
About 1476 Tommaso commissioned Hugo van der Goes' masterpiece *The Adoration of the Shepherds,* one of the greatest

6   27

Flemish paintings, in which an older Maria is shown with their eldest daughter and Tommaso with their two sons; Maria wears the same rich necklace and fur trimmings which appear in this Memling.

• **28. A Lady with a Pink.** (Date uncertain)   Holding a pink flower—a symbol of betrothal—the figure is elongated to conform with the narrow confines of this beguiling portrait. The vertical is subdivided horizontally by the wall and the foreground ledge. The curves of the arch, the trees and the headdress and even the somewhat angular curve of the left hand lend elegance to the design. The red velvet gown is a resonant note in a warm-toned harmony crowned by the bright blue of the sky.

DAVID, Gerard

• **29. The Archangel Gabriel.** (About 1520)   Gabriel's billowing robes and bluish wings glow against fireplace, window seats, casement and paving tiles. The colors of the vestments contain something of the pastel nuances of the tiles, while the crisp white lines repeat the slender columns of the fireplace; these relationships establish a symbolic as well as compositional link between God's chief messenger and the everyday domestic setting. The Archangel wears an alb, a white, lined tunic which recalls the robe of mockery that Herod placed on Christ and symbolizes purity and eternal joy to the redeemed. About the alb is a cope (a large cape), the most sumptuous of ecclesiastical vestments. The sceptre indicates sovereignty. On the cope are inscribed Alpha and Omega, the first and last letters of the Greek alphabet: " 'I am Alpha and Omega, the beginning and the ending,' saith the Lord, 'all which is and which was, and which is to come, the Almighty.' " A fragment from St. Luke also appears: "The power of the Most High shall overshadow thee. . . ."

• **30. The Virgin of the Annunciation.** (About 1520)   With its intensity, its magnificent orchestration of blues and its masterly

28

2

rendering of folds, this panel is a gem of late Flemish art. From the deep blues of the Virgin's robe and the bed-covering (with its slow-paced, beautifully designed rhythm of folds) to the dark browns, all is sombre. Mary's pale, luminous face is totally absorbed as she receives the divine message. The dove in the golden circle is a symbol of the Holy Ghost. The auriole above Mary's head signifies her sanctity, the lilies her purity. The Rosary is a form of devotion to Mary. Blue is the color of Heaven, of Heavenly love and truth. Brown symbolizes renunciation of the material world.

BOSCH, Hieronymus

• **31. The Adoration of the Magi.** (1490?)   Considered among the earliest surviving paintings by Bosch, this composition is serene and stately compared to his later demoniac pictures. The setting—the walls and towers of a roofless castle—provides a stage of deep space. The Virgin establishes a strong center, her deep blue glowing in isolation. Around her, figures are spotted in an almost formal order. The red of the kneeling King is echoed throughout the composition, even to tiny, distant figures. The colors are delicate, the contours interestingly varied. A delightful element is introduced in the curved folds of the canopy being spread by four young angels. The droll earthiness of Bosch's later work is hinted at in the two shepherds who peer in, warming themselves over a fire. The ox and the ass, which warmed the Christ Child with their breath, show that even the humblest creatures were present at the Nativity and recognized the Babe as Son of God. In the far left background appears an imaginary Jerusalem.

PATINIR, Joachim

• **32. The Penitence of St. Jerome.** (Date uncertain)   The three panels are linked into a unified sweep of land and sea. A high perspective gives the broad panorama drama, and the landscape

31

is bathed in clear atmosphere. The central panel shows the penitent St. Jerome beating his breast with a stone as he prays. Behind him the artist illustrates an ancient legend: After the Saint had won the friendship of a lion by removing a thorn from its paw, his fellow monks demanded that the lion work for its daily food. The Saint set it to guard an ass that brought wood, but the ass was taken by robbers and sold to a passing caravan of merchants. The monks accused the lion of having devoured his charge until the lion saw the caravan returning and brought the ass back to prove his innocence. Patinir shows the merchants praying for forgiveness, while the lion once more stands proudly on guard. The left wing shows the Baptism of Christ by St. John, and the right wing depicts the Temptation of St. Anthony by demons.

BREUGHEL, Pieter, the Elder

• **33. The Harvesters.** (1565)   One of the rarest old masters in New York—if not the country—this painting is a fine example of Breughel's revolutionary fusion of landscape and figures. The striking composition is dominated by the mass of grain which cuts an abrupt diagonal across the canvas. Opposing this aggressive movement are the stable vertical and spreading branches of the pear tree. The languid twist of the tree trunk is in turn challenged by the pose of the exhausted sleeper and the rake and sheaf of grain leaning at angles beside him; the figure repeats in miniature the wheat's diagonal movement. The dark tree and foliage create a frontal plane which sets the grain back in space. Beyond the field and rolling landscape, a cool, airy vista flows to a distant harbor and a far horizon. All is united into an organized pattern of clear-cut areas. So subtly has Breughel controlled this unity that only prolonged examination reveals the forty or so figures—including swimmers, wagoners and children at play—which serve as links connecting point to point. *The Harvesters* is one of a famous series with which Breughel helped usher in landscape as an independent motif in great art. Of the original twelve pictures, representing the months of the year, seven have disappeared. When Vienna was looted by Napoleon's army in 1809, *The Harvesters* was probably among the pictures stolen. During World War I, it was sent to this country. In 1919 the Metropoli-

32

tan was able to buy the painting for $3,370—the Museum's biggest bargain—because the dirty, fly-specked picture was mistaken for a work by one of the artist's sons. Cleaning revealed that it was beyond the talents of Breughel's followers, and under a piece of wood which had been fastened to the canvas to make it fit the frame, Museum officials discovered the artist's signature and date still faintly visible.

RUBENS, Peter Paul

• **34. The Triumphal Entry of Henry IV into Paris.** (About 1631) King Henry IV of France (1553-1610), an ally of the Protestants, captured Paris from the embattled Catholic League in 1594. Rubens presents his entry into the city as an imperial Roman procession. The King, in a golden chariot drawn by four white horses, holds the olive branch of peace, as a winged Victory crowns him with victors' laurel. Francia—or perhaps the Roman war goddess Bellona—holds the reins. Apollo serenades the monarch as soldiers escort the chariot to a triumphal arch. Bound captives follow, and cheering groups watch in admiration. Such puffed-up glorification of royalty would be bombast in the hands of a minor painter, but Rubens pours into it power and dignity. A blend of pageantry, allegory and history, the small panel surges with irresistible action. Color is applied lightly, and brush strokes are as fluid as the swirling rhythms which animate the picture. Group links with group, space interval with space interval, to form an unbroken sweep. The central pyramid is balanced by sub-groups in the foreground at both sides. *The Triumphal Entry,* a sketch for one of twenty-one allegorical paintings depicting the lives of Henry and his Queen, Marie de Medici, was commissioned by Marie after the King's assassination. With the exception of Michelangelo's frescoes on the Sistine Ceiling, they constitute the most ambitious commission ever granted to one artist. The project was abandoned midway, however, when the Queen fled to Brussels.

• **35. Venus and Adonis.** (About 1635) One of the finest Rubens works in America, this composition of golden bodies in heroic dimensions breathes an air of Olympian grandeur. The painting retells the legend in which Venus, accidentally wounded

4   35

by the arrow of her son Cupid, fell in love with the handsome
Adonis. She implored him in vain to give up his passion for
hunting, and when he was killed by a wild boar the grieving goddess caused the anemone to spring up from his blood. Rubens
shows Venus and Cupid attempting to dissuade him from his
final, fatal hunt. A pyramid is established by Venus and Adonis,
with Cupid and his bow and quiver filling in the base. Beginning
at lower right, the eye follows the voluptuous body of the goddess to the arm of Adonis resting on her thigh, then to the arm
and spear which continue the movement into space. The turning
heads of the dogs direct the eye back into the picture. The canvas
glitters with a splendor of color. The bronze of Adonis, the
pearly sparkle of Venus and the shimmer of Cupid are set against
a background of deep purple, airy blue, gauzy white and rich
red. The colors are contrasted to heighten their symphonic richness, as in the greens against pinks which enliven Venus' flesh.
Venus and Adonis was given to John Churchill, first Duke of
Marlborough and an ancestor of Winston Churchill, to commemorate his 1704 victory over the French at Blenheim. Rubens was
the Duke's favorite artist, and in time he owned about seventy-
five pictures by, or attributed to, the master. More than thirty-five
were sold at auction in 1885, including three now in the Metropolitan: *Venus and Adonis, Atlanta and Meleager* and *Anne of
Austria* (now considered a workshop painting). This painting is
probably entirely by Rubens—unusual in a composition of such
size.

VAN DYCK, Anthony

• **36. James Stuart, Duke of Richmond and Lennox.** (Date uncertain)   Blacks and silver-greys establish the basic harmony of
this elegant portrait. The restrained richness is emphasized particularly in the lace collar, the embroidered star and the hose.
One of the most skillful passages occurs in the greyhound—
swiftly brushed in, taut, graceful and lithe. Van Dyck painted

36

several portraits of James Stuart, a cousin of King Charles I. Around Stuart's neck in this version hangs The Jewel of the Garter, known as The George. The Star of the Order is embroidered on the left shoulder of his cloak. The garter can be seen below his left knee.

• **37. Robert Rich, Earl of Warwick.** (Date uncertain)   Rich was a friend of Cromwell and a Puritan sympathizer during the English Civil War. He played a leading role in founding colonies in Massachusetts, Connecticut, Rhode Island and the Bermudas, and in 1643 became governor-in-chief of all English colonies. In this fine example of Van Dyke's suave court and society portraits, the artist revels in the splendor of surface appearance. Standing above a flurry of land and sea, the Earl has an air of dignity and command. The direction of his figure towards the right gives a supple movement to a mannered stance. The cloak becomes a counter-poise. Van Dyck exploits the glitter of the silver brocade and the richness of the cloak and gold-trimmed breeches. The armor on the ground lends depth and glowing highlights. Yet the Earl's sensitive features remain the focus of interest.

German Painting

DURER, Albrecht
• **38. The Virgin and Child with Saint Anne.** (1519)   A pyramid arrangement is given diamond-shaped angularity by the tilt of the Child's head and the line of the Virgin's hands. Rhythmic tension pulses between the figures. Modeling is firm, and clean-cut lines combine with light and shade. St. Anne's odd headdress frames the Madonna's face, while the Virgin's dark blue cuff is vital in underlining the base of the composition. Details like the fingers are masterfully drawn, supple and sensitive. The enamel-like color creates a sense of substance. A Dürer painting is a rarity in

39

America, and this one has an interesting story. In 1630 it was acquired from a Nuremberg wine merchant by Maximilian I of Bavaria, a collector of Dürer's work. It remained in the Royal Picture Galleries near Munich until the mid-19th Century, when, perhaps because it had become darkened with dust and varnish or perhaps because some ten copies of it were then in existence, it was included in an auction sale. The sale aroused strong criticism in Germany; though many authorities contended that the painting was not a genuine Dürer, arguments were published for several decades. Finally, in 1910, a scholar found documents relating to its acquisition by Maximilian, and later cleaning and study confirmed that this was, indeed, an original. The Metropolitan also owns the unfinished Dürer *Salvator Mundi*.

CRANACH, Lucas, the Elder

• **39. The Judgement of Paris.** (About 1528)   The legend of the Judgement of Paris is a favorite subject of many artists, and Cranach and his assistants painted it many times. Discord, angered because she was not invited to a wedding feast, threw a golden apple among the guests marked "for the fairest." The prize was claimed by Hera, wife and sister of Zeus; by Athena, goddess of wisdom; and by Aphrodite, goddess of love. To choose among them proved too delicate a matter even for Zeus, and he sent the three contestants, along with Hermes, messenger of the gods, to the handsome shepherd Paris, son of King Priam of Troy. Each goddess sought to influence the choice: Hera offered dominion over the earth, and Athena victory in war. But Aphrodite offered Helen, wife of King Menelaus, the most beautiful woman on earth. Paris gave the apple to Aphrodite, sailed for Greece and abducted Helen. Thus started the ten-year Trojan War. Cranach treats his subject with tongue-in-cheek whimsy. Paris, an armor-clad knight, looks up awkwardly as he appraises the ladies. The Apple of Discord is a crystal ball held by Hermes. The goddesses pose like coquettish mannequins, and behind them

40

is a German landscape with a castle on a cliff. The decorative mass of dark leaves forms a charming setting for the droll nudes. Their light flesh-notes are co-ordinated with the enormous plumes Paris wears, with the curvilinear horse (who seems rather pushed in as an afterthought) and with the flying cupid. The goddesses are linked in a sinuous movement. Rhythm is stressed by their poses and gestures, by the plumed hat of the center goddess, by Hermes' bizarre helmet and by the river and the rocky mountain. The landscape combines a Gothic love for realistic detail with Cranach's delight in patterns of contrasting colors and textures. On the rock in the right foreground appears Cranach's mark, a crown and winged serpent.

HOLBEIN, Hans, the Younger

• **40. Portrait of a Member of the Wedigh Family** (1532) Detail is keenly observed, yet subordinated to the general design. Set against a striking turquoise background, the sitter's dark cloak is balanced by the light green table cloth. In the skillful handling of the satin texture, Holbein creates variety through the quiet interplay of folds. Flesh is delicate; the eyes and mouth, the swell of the cheekbone and the soft line defining the edge of the hair are drawn with rare refinement. The identity of the sitter was discovered in 1887, when a German scholar observed that his ring and one in another portrait in the Berlin Museum both displayed the arms of the Wedigh family, Cologne merchants associated with London business ventures. Inscribed on the paper in the book is a motto from the Roman playwright Terence: "Truth breeds hatred." On the book-cover are the artist's initials, "H.H."

• **41. Dirk Berck of Cologne.** (1536) The sitter's half-length, full-front pose is balanced by the curtain, the cord and the red of the table. His lustrous silk cloak, with its marvelously executed sleeve, is set effectively against metallic green. The graceful opposing movement of the cord creates a symmetrical balance. The soft brown mass of beard, the flat cap (set at a slight angle) and the cut of the hair set off the flesh. Dirk Berck, a prosperous merchant and member of the historic Hanseatic League, lived in London in a neighborhood called the Steelyard, near London Bridge. The cartellino at left carries a Latin inscription from Virgil: "Some day it will be pleasant to remember." The letter is inscribed "To the honorable and noble Dirk Berck in London in the Steelyard—Consider the end."

Spanish Painting

EL GRECO

• **42. Cardinal Don Fernando Niño de Guevara.** (About 1598-1600) El Greco's most famous portrait is not only a technical tour-de-force, but a masterpiece of subtle characterization. At the time of its execution, the sitter was Archbishop of Toledo and Seville; shortly afterward he was to become Grand Inquisitor. As El Greco depicts him, his scarlet robes provide the immediate dramatic impact, the energy of their silken textures and dynamic folds heightened by a sweep of glittering white highlights. But the picture's nervous agitation soon becomes its dominant quality. The Cardinal's biretta slants disconcertingly off his head to the right. The contours of his costume sweep diagonally across the straight lines of the chair and the massive stability of the door. Even the tooling on the leather wall and the patterns of the marble floor add to the rhythmic animation. The Cardinal's thin face and pale flesh set off his incisive, appraising eyes, but it is in his hands—one hanging slackly, the other tensely gripping the arm of the chair—that El Greco offers perhaps the most remarkable insight of all. After the Cardinal's death, this painting was hung over his tomb in Toledo. Eventually a copy was substituted and the original was sold. The letter on the floor bears El Greco's true signature: "Domenicos Theotocopoulos made it."

• **43. View of Toledo.** (About 1604-14) The *View of Toledo*—one of the most familiar pictures in the world—is probably the greatest "portrait" ever painted of a city and perhaps the first major landscape in art. In a composition electric with emotion, the ground, sky and building swirl as restlessly as an ocean. Space recedes dramatically. The swaying foreground foliage appears as if lit by a giant floodlight. Hovering between the awesome sky and the whirl of hills and river, the cluster of buildings is bathed in an eerie radiance. At first, the painting appears to represent the city in a storm, but the presence of swimmers, strollers and horsemen moving about undisturbed raises a more interesting possibility: The flash of unearthly light and the dramatic rent in the sky above the buildings may symbolize the presence of God's spirit above Spain's Holy City. Such a moment of celestial drama

42

4

would be consistent with El Greco's theological concepts. Moreover, the same sky can be seen in a number of El Grecos without storms, and effects like the cloud-opening appear, though less climactically, in a number of his Crucifixions and portrayals of saints. The painting shows Toledo from across the Tagus River. At left is the Medieval castle of San Servando. On the crest rises the Cathedral. Nearby is the massive Alcazar Palace (which over three centuries later was held by Franco forces during a bitter Civil War siege). For compositional purposes, El Greco shifted the Cathedral and the Alcazar; he also eliminated an enormous hospital. El Greco lived in Toledo, Spain's ancient capital, from 1577 until his death thirty-six years later. Though the city's prosperity was declining as the court abandoned it for Madrid and its skilled Moorish weavers and Jewish merchants were expelled, Toledo was still Spain's religious and intellectual center. Mrs. Henry Osborne Havemeyer, a great benefactor of the Metropolitan, acquired the *View of Toledo* for a mere $14,000; at the same time, however, she paid almost four times as much for a far lesser painting, Pieter de Hooch's *The Visit,* also in the Metropolitan. The inscription reads: "Domenicos Theotocopoulos made it."

- **44. Adoration of the Shepherds.** (About 1608) A jagged diamond-shaped composition links the figures grouped around the Christ child. At lower right, St. Joseph's staff, foot and thigh form one side of the diamond, leading the eye to the Madonna. The drapery in her hand continues the movement on to the shepherds and around to the figures in green and reddish-brown. The composition is enriched by secondary elements like the position of the lamb (which forms the lower apex), the color and folds of the yellowish cloak, the succession of arms in the center pointing toward the Child, the green shirt at left (echoing Joseph's robe) and the accents of the muscular leg in the left foreground. Amid these rapturous figures, Mary and the Child retain dominance through the crimson of Mary's gown and the radiant fabric

about the Babe. The ruined vault forms a dramatic arch above
Mary and Joseph; Joseph's gesturing right hand leads the eye
beyond it to the Annunciation to the Shepherds. El Greco's color
is audacious in its sudden contrasts; orange and green, lemon
and glittering white blend in an eerie harmony, suggesting something supernatural even as they substantiate fabric and flesh,
stones and leaves. The lamb brought by the shepherds pre-figures
the sacrificial death of Christ, the Lamb of God. Flying cherubs
carry a scroll inscribed: "Glory to God in the highest. We praise
Thee, we bless Thee." When this painting was acquired for $23,-
000 in 1905, the purchase was assailed by many as bad judgement
and extravagance. The Metropolitan also possesses a smaller
variation of this theme, of about the same period.

• **45. St. John's Vision of the Mysteries of the Apocalypse.**
(About 1613)   There is no certainty about the theme of this
startling painting (one of its 19th Century owners even called it
Sacred and Profane Love), but it appears to be one of three pictures El Greco did for the Hospital of St. John the Baptist in
Toledo, and it may interpret this passage from the Book of Revelation: "And when he had opened the fifth seal, I saw under
the altar the souls of them that were slain for the word of God,
and for the testimony which they held. And they cried with a
loud voice, saying, 'How long, O Lord, holy and true, dost thou
not judge and avenge our blood on them that dwell on the earth?'
And white robes were given unto every one of them." Although
the painting is unfinished, it virtually sings out from the wall. The
wildly elongated figures, rhapsodic gestures and rich colors create
an effect of almost blinding spirituality. The giant figure of St.
John—a tempest of movement, color, brushstrokes, folds and
highlights—is more than dramatic, it is awesome. His head flings
up in astonishment, his arms stretch out to the sky. The drapery
on which he kneels—or is he rising?—is both a base for his figure and a link to the seven others who move rhythmically across

the canvas, their skins flickering with radiance and shadow, their muscles tensed. About them, draperies become bold color chords, fluttering as if charged with a fiery spirit. Flying cherubim intensify the sensation of tormented ecstasy. Small passages of missing or cracked paint have been restored by the Museum.

VELAZQUEZ, Diego Rodríguez

• **46. Christ and the Pilgrims of Emmaus.** (About 1620)   Velázquez depicts the passage in which St. Luke tells of the two disciples who met Jesus after the Resurrection. At first they did not recognize Him, but "it came to pass, as He sat at meat with them, He took bread, and blessed it, and broke, and gave to them. And their eyes were opened, and they knew Him." The moving story is portrayed quietly, even prosaically when compared to Rembrandt's radiant version on this theme, yet Velazquez' matter-of-fact approach has its own poetry, evoking the wonder of the moment without a wasted motion. The composition begins with Christ's robe and leads to His hand (with the understatement of an unobtrusive wound) as it holds the bread. The rose of the robe contrasts with an unusual blue, with the gold-ochre of the figure at right and with the greyish-brown of the third figure. The tablecloth, painted with a relish for its texture and weight, binds the three forms and areas together. The color relationship creates a slow movement into deep background space, and the rhythms of the figures follow a similarly restrained tempo. With the exception of the glow of Christ's robe, colors are austere and sober. This painting may have been done when the artist was about twenty-one, shortly before he became court painter to Philip IV.

ZURBARAN, Francisco de

•. **47. The Young Virgin.** (Date uncertain)   Each form in this strong and deeply religious picture is rendered with crystal clarity, yet all fit into a precise relationship around the sorrowing Virgin. Light and dark play major roles, as in the folds of the curtain and skirt and the blue of the girl's vest; they also give movement to a stable, symmetrical composition. The book and the folded hands signify the Virgin's devotion to prayer. The embroidery, work basket and scissors relate to a tradition that in her youth she spun and wove in the Temple of Jerusalem. The lily, emblem of purity, foretells the Annunciation. Roses, according to tradition, had no thorns in the Garden of Eden; in a picture with the Virgin, they often signify that she was "a rose without thorns," exempt from the consequences of the Fall of Man.

GOYA, Francisco

• **48. Don Manuel Osorio de Zuñiga.** (1784)   In Goya's early portraits, models are posed in the the prevailing fashionable mode of elegant rigidity, and paint is applied smoothly and thinly; yet in masterpieces like this, the artist injects new vitality into the traditional formula. The boy is painted with superb sensitivity, his silken garments set off by a marvelous frilled collar and sparkling white sash. His face is pearly-smooth. Dark, glowing eyes lend the skin an alabaster translucence—a technique, like that of the sash, which reappears in Manet and Renoir. The child's solemnity is undermined by his extraordinary collection of pets. All that is known of him appears on the canvas: his name and the year of his birth. The card in the pet magpie's beak is engraved with Goya's name. This painting belonged to Mme. Henri Bernstein, mother of the French playwright who included in one of his works the stage direction: "Over a settee a large picture by Goya: *The Child with a Bird.*" Under the terms of its bequest to the Museum, the painting is at present on view only during the summer.

• **49. Majas on a Balcony.** (About 1810-15)   In depicting flirtatious ladies (known in Spain as *majas*) and their escorts (*majos*) watching the life of the street from a balcony, Goya unites two disparate aspects into a masterful vignette: the men recall Rembrandt's broad masses, subtle space and brooding drama; but the sparkle of the girls' costumes is typical of Goya's vivacious handling and luminosity. The dash and staccato treatment of the girls and the light which bathes them almost foretell Impressionism. The dark cloaks and lowered heads of the men appear sinister, an effect heightened by the height of the wall behind them. The horizontal railing and the insistent vertical bars of the balcony establish a base for the curvilinear, flowing forms of the figures.

• **50. The Bullfight.** (Between 1810-20)   According to legend, Goya was a bullfighter in his youth. In any event, he was certainly an afficianado of bullfighting and sometimes even signed his name Goya des Toros—Goya of the Bulls. He did many paintings and etchings on the theme. In this composition, the horizontal line of seated figures at bottom forms the base of a straggling pyramid which reaches its apex where the partition

meets the far wall. Countering the partition is an energetic diagonal that flows from the group in the far right foreground to the
bull, the picador, the man standing by the wall and finally to the
toreadors on the other side. Lively color is handled economically.
Dabs of pigment mould shapes, inject nuance and convey vivid
action. Slashing strokes make the drawing fluent and expressive,
as in the sensation of bulk and strength in the bulls and the agility and tension in the toreadors.

PICASSO, Pablo

• **51. The Blind Man.** (1903)   This is a prime example of Picasso's Blue Period, during which he developed his first truly personal style. Pictures from these years are characterized by a
brooding melancholy and by gaunt figures bathed in blue; some
are weakened by sentimentality, but the best, like this one, capture authentic poignancy. The composition is eloquently simple
and monumental. The figure is drawn with convincing solidity
and sensitive characterization. The blue, used with resourceful
variations and restraint, fuses with a light which is ghostly and
wan, yet somehow harsh. Coupled with expressive drawing, the
blue suggests suffering, hunger and loneliness. The greenish tone
of the flesh, the ivory and brown nuances of jug and bread and
the umber color of the table provide telling counterpoints. This
painting and the Metropolitan's *Harlequin* of 1901 are the only
Blue Period Picassos in New York museums. *The Actor* of 1905,
also in the Metropolitan, represents the transition from the Blue
Period to the Rose Period.

• **52. Gertrude Stein.** (1906)   This celebrated portrait hints at
the dawn of a momentous new movement in art—Cubism. The
sitter's character is almost hypnotic. Her solid body is relaxed and
assured. Her hands rest lightly on her lap, glowing against the
dark umber of the dress. Strong and mask-like, her face contrasts
sharply with the muted colors and soft modeling of figure and
hands. While much in the painting reflects the late phase of
Picasso's gentle and romantic Rose Period, the face distinctly
betrays the artist's new interest in primitive art and early Iberian

sculpture and his first steps toward angular simplifications and well-defined planes. Within a year, this interest would develop into the first Cubist picture, *Les Demoiselles d'Avignon* (Museum of Modern Art). At this point, however, despite the stylization of the features Picasso still retains the personality of the sitter—grave and calm, vital and meditative. Gertrude and her brother Leo Stein were pioneer collectors of modern art. In her book on Picasso, Miss Stein related how she walked many times to his now-legendary ramshackle studio in the Rue Ravignon. Wearing her customary corduroy suit, she posed in a broken armchair while Picasso's mistress Fernande read to her. She posed eighty times, "and at the end, Picasso rubbed out the head. He told me that he could not see me any more and went off to Spain. . . . On his return Picasso painted the head without seeing me again, then he gave me the portrait. For me it is myself. It is the only representation of me that will always be myself." From 1906 to 1946, this painting hung in Miss Stein's famous salon. Bequeathed to the Metropolitan, it became the first Picasso oil to enter the Museum.

Dutch Painting

HALS, Frans

• **53. The Merry Company.** (About 1616)   With his relish for lively people, Hals captures a festive moment of Dutch life. His deft brush records fleeting expressions, shimmering garments and the very substance of the stein, bread, sausages and pigs' feet. The faces in the center background had been covered over at some time and were revealed only recently by cleaning. The elaborate detail of the girl's lace collar and embroidered stomacher and the overly-pink face of her companion mar somewhat the unity of the composition. At the time of this painting, Hals belonged to two clubs enticingly named The Branch of the Vine and Love

First of All. His initials, "F.H.", are painted on the stein.

• **54. Yonker Ramp and His Sweetheart.** (1623)   In this robust composition, frontal close-ups contrast boldly with the scale of the background figures and the fireplace—a juxtaposition which creates a vivid sensation of space. The dabs of paint on the face, the flash of white lines in the collar and the sparkle of the buttons on the doublet are typical of Hals. Yonker (meaning Lord) Ramp, whom Hals painted several times, was probably a well-known man-about-town.

TERBRUGGHEN, Hendrick
• **55. The Crucifixion with the Virgin and Saint John.** (About 1626)   A symmetrically arranged trio forms the base of this stark composition filled with tragic emotion. An unidealized Christ, tortured and emaciated, hangs limply on the cross. The pallor of His body is emphasized by the brown background and loin cloth, while streams of blood add a ghastly color note and deepen the somber mood. The cross is accentuated against the horizon, where the symbols of Golgotha—a skull and bones—encounter the touching image of splintered wood and a growing branch. The heavy, elaborately-draped figures of the Virgin and St. John take on monumentality against the darkening sky. This painting is said to have been found in a bombed church in London. Its appearance at a London auction caused a sensation.

RUISDAEL, Jacob van
• **56. Wheatfields.** (Date unknown)   This tranquil landscape is a variation on the motif Ruisdael painted often: a low horizon, curving road between ripe wheatfields, some figures, cottages, clumps of trees and a windy sky crossed by dramatic billowing clouds. The limited, subdued color evokes light and, somehow, a sense of the weather. Implicit in the low land and high sky is Ruisdael's characteristic emotional content—his mystic reverie on solitude amid vastness.

54

55

HOBBEMA, Meindert

• **57. Entrance to a Village.** (Date unknown) A typical Hobbema, this landscape is less poetic than a Ruisdael, but more faithful as a record of optical reality. Low-keyed colors and dark masses are poised against the fresh sky. Red roofs appear throughout the composition to relieve the generally cool tonality. A winding road leads into the center. Light and shadow fall in small, rhythmic patterns on road and fields. The luminous blue-and-pink sky communicates a sense of space continuing beyond the horizon. Hobbema blends solemnity with the picturesque.

REMBRANDT

• **58. The Gilder Herman Doomer.** (1640) This unassuming portrait is often bypassed for lesser but more spectacular pictures, yet its shrewd and sympathetic characterization rank it as a work of true poetry. Golden flesh is modeled by delicate shadow (as in the forehead, eye sockets and chin) and enriched by extremely sensitive lines (as in the beard and moustache). In a subtle play on space and solidity, the head merges almost imperceptibly with the hat, the neck with the ruff, the ruff with the muted red-brown coat. A simple composition leads the eye from darkened hand to ruff to the climax of glowing cheeks. Not an inch lacks inner light and richness. The effect is not of paint, but of color and form. Doomer was an Amsterdam gilder and framer whose son Lambert studied with Rembrandt at the time of this painting; Rembrandt's companion portrait of his wife is now in the Hermitage in St. Petersburg.

• **59. The Standard Bearer.** (1654) Avoiding the courtly swagger favored by Rubens and van Dyke, Rembrandt endows an elderly, anonymous standard-bearer with majestic dignity. The gold-embroidered sword-belt, the ostrich plume, the hand holding the glove and the subdued glitter of the rhythmic buttons provide striking contrasts to the dominant deep tones. The accessories co-ordinate to give a pyramid form to the figure; the slant of the staff forming one side and the buttons on the pantaloons and sleeves describing the other narrow in to the strong point of the face framed by plumes. The sword-belt and banner are insignia of the City of Amsterdam. Weak areas, most likely due to the ravages of time, occur in the lusterless white of the plumes,

the dry color under the chin and the airless space and relatively dull texture of the right background. This painting once belonged to Sir Joshua Reynolds.

• **60. Lady with a Pink.** (About 1668-69) Radiant light flows from face to flower to the hand on the lap. Despite Rembrandt's refusal to idealize the sitter's plain features, rich illumination gives them an air of inner spirituality. The head is accentuated by a luster of pearls, an earring and the white fabric about the shadowed neck. The horizontal of the picture frame behind the woman gives contrast to her gently curving figure. The picture-within-a-picture also helps define depth. Thin paint contrasts with rich encrustations to create variety.

• **61. Man with a Magnifying Glass.** (About 1668) The dimly-defined slope of the cloak, the hand and the contour of the left arm form a diagonal base. Golden flesh is firmly constructed in a face which dominates the dramatic space effects. The color of the hand provides a quiet echo. This portrait appears to be a companion to the *Lady with a Pink*. The sitter is unidentified, but the earring and glass suggest he was a goldsmith.

• **62. Aristotle Contemplating the Bust of Homer.** (1652-53) In what was to become one of the most sensational sales in history, *Aristotle Contemplating the Bust of Homer* was placed on auction at the Parke-Bernet Gallaries on November 15, 1961. Bidding began with $1,000,000. Within four breathless minutes, it had climbed to a record-breaking $2,300,000. The successful bidder was James J. Rorimer, Director of the Metropolitan, who is said to have signaled his final offer by moving his eyes to the right and fingering his lapel. The celebrated painting had humble beginnings. At a time when Rembrandt's commercial success was waning, Don Antonio Ruffo of Messina, Sicily, wrote him to commission a painting of "a philosopher." Ruffo was so pleased with the result that he paid 500 florins—about $8,000—and later

commissioned two more paintings, one of Homer and one of Alexander. (Their fate is uncertain.) In the picture which so delighted Ruffo, Rembrandt has created a majestic image of the soulful intellect, rapt in dream-like meditation, emerging from a background of brooding darkness. The picture represents Rembrandt's mature powers at their height—his splendid color, enthralling play of light and shadow, simplicity of massing and fusion of spirit with tangible reality. The dark mass of Aristotle's simple costume is relieved by the golden mantle over his arms and the glitter of the chain. Glowing light permits his figure simultaneously to emerge from the dim curtain behind him, yet melt into the deep space. His arms, the chair and the contour of the curtain link into a formation which curves across the canvas, trailing off slowly at lower right. The tablecloth and the books provide a balance of horizontal stability. The brooding face emerges as the climax of the composition. Features are painted as broad planes. The hair, beard and hat form a black halo and provide a link between cloak and mantle. The sleeves —a harmony of folds and planes—underline the main movement as they provide textural variety. Every form and color blends gently in flowing chiaroscuro. The bust of Homer—a version of which is preserved in Rembrandt's former studio—subtly echoes Aristotle's features. Aristotle wears a medallion showing his student, Alexander the Great, who was said to have carried a copy of Homer's *Iliad* annotated by his teacher. Thus three mighty ancients are brought together in this painting. The picture's history is fascinating and complex. It remained in the Ruffo family until 1743. In 1815 it appeared in London in the first major loan exhibition of old masters. In time it was acquired by the Frenchman Rudolphe Kann, who also owned the Metropolitan's *Lady with a Pink* and *Man with a Magnifying Glass*. In 1907 Joseph Duveen bought the Kann collection with a borrowed $5,000,000 and sold the *Aristotle* to Mrs. Collis P. Huntington, widow of a California railroad tycoon. The painting was inherited

by her son Archer Huntington, founder of the Spanish Museum, and hung in the library of his home on East 57th Street in New York along with two other paintings ascribed to Rembrandt, *Hendrickje Stoffels* and *Flora*. Archer Huntington gave the latter two to the Metropolitan but sold the *Aristotle* back to Duveen. In 1928, Duveen sold it for $750,000 to Alfred W. Erickson, an advertising magnate who controlled such enterprises as Congoleum, Bon Ami and Technicolor. With the 1929 stock market crash, Erickson resold it to Duveen for $500,000, but shortly before his death in 1936 he repurchased it for $590,000. It was after Mrs. Erickson's death in 1961 that the picture was placed on auction and acquired by the Metropolitan. When it was displayed in the Museum's Grand Hall, over 82,000 persons swarmed to see it on the first Sunday alone, and a clamor arose in the press over its great cost. Ironically, the *Aristotle* had been exhibited frequently within the preceding few decades without arousing unusual reaction. In this country it was shown in Detroit in 1930, in Chicago during the 1933 Century of Progress Exposition and in New York's Knoedler Gallery in 1940. It had even been at the Metropolitan once before—in a 1909 exhibition of Dutch masters.

TERBORCH, Gerard

• **63. Curiosity.** (Date uncertain) Out of the deep background, two figures emerge gradually, joined almost abruptly by a third. The detailed treatment of a satin dress and pink bodice acts as a counterbalance to the dark right side of the picture, while the dim gleam of the chandelier echoes the sheen of the dress. The letter-writer's blue and ermine jacket, the white kerchief and the spotting on the little dog create lively patterns. Rendering and story-telling are artfully subordinated to the general harmony of the picture. The title refers to the young maidservant, who leans over to see what the seated woman is writing.

2

63

STEEN, Jan

● **64. The Lovesick Maiden.** (Date uncertain)   Steen painted this
theme several times. The girl's "illness"—as indicated by the
Cupid above the door, the doctor's knowing grin and the distracted expression of the girl herself—is love, though the solici-
tous mother seems ignorant of the nature of the malady. The
open door, with its glimpse of a church, may suggest the girl's
desire to marry. The maiden's shimmering skirt (recalling Steen's
Merry Company, also in the Metropolitan) and the color notes
of her fur-lined jacket and red bodice act as center of both the
composition and the color organization. In his emphasis on
humor, facial expressions and the meticulous painting of details,
Steen sacrifices other elements. The color lacks light and substance; forms are placed loosely; light and dark are rather abrupt.

HOOCH, Pieter de

● **65. The Maidservant.** (About 1670-75)   In this charming
Dutch interior painting, de Hooch stresses space. The perspective
of the floor, the diminishing beams of the ceiling and the open
door with its glimpse of another room are key elements in creating depth. A frame of morning sunshine flooding in from an
unseen window surrounds the girl in an appealing pattern. The
slant of the checkered unit echoes the direction of the open door
and repeats the accent of the floor. The painting has probably
been cut off at the right; originally, as can be seen, de Hooch
portrayed the lady of the house in bed, chatting with her husband, who is dressing.

VERMEER, Johannes

● **66. Girl Asleep.** (About 1650-60)   The near-abstract architecture of this arrangement vies intriguingly with the manner in
which Vermeer has integrated its host of everyday objects. The
smooth, cool-toned background is opposed by the vigorous design and color of the Turkish rug on the table. The tilt of the
sleeping figure creates a balance between the contending forms

64   6

and colors. An especially striking organization occurs in the play of straight lines, flat surfaces and parallels at right. In the map, the half-open door, the table and picture in the room beyond and the lion-headed chair in the foreground, vertical plays against horizontal, dark against light and coolness against warmth. (The patterns would have delighted the much later Dutch master of geometric abstraction, Piet Mondrian.) Only the still life on the table detracts; it has been heavily repainted or retouched. Sold at auction in Amsterdam in 1696, this picture was entitled *A Drunken Maid-Servant Asleep Behind a Table.* Recently a more persuasive theme has been advanced: the cupid, letter and mask in the dim painting at upper left indicate that Vermeer intended to depict a girl saddened because her "unmasked" lover has proven false.

• **67. Lady with a Lute.** (About 1664)   Especially notable here are the concentration of broad forms and the emphatic contrasts of light and dark. The blue drapery and the chair almost blend with the tablecloth as a result of the pearly light that flows tranquilly behind them. In the glow from the window, the girl forms a link between the foreground and the rectangle of the map. The strong yellow on her sleeve contrasts effectively with the dark silhouette of the top of the chair.

• **68. Young Woman with a Water Jug.** (Date unknown)   Out of prosaic raw material, the artist has captured a hushed moment and suspended it in time. Each object, color and shape in this jewel-like painting is integrated into a deceptively simple composition. The main elements are two verticals—the casement window and the figure—and the horizontals of the table and map. They are varied by the curve of the arm opening the window and by the gleaming objects on the table. Color by color and form by form, the observer's eye glides effortlessly through the magnificent arrangement. The still-life area begins with the cool flesh color of the foreshortened hand and the brass jug, its shape brilliantly defined by broad planes. The jug and basin are en-

6   67

riched by colored reflections from the table and the chair. Completing the unit is the dusty-yellow and rose-pink jewel box, a foil to the fabric draped across the chair. Colors are not merely applied, but seem to come alive through harmony and the magic of light. The genius of Vermeer's composition becomes still more apparent when it is compared with interiors painted by other Dutch artists. Their compositions are relatively disjointed, their colors less luminous and individual. A disproportionate amount of their appeal is based on anecdote.

VAN GOGH, Vincent

• **69. The Arlésienne (Mme. Ginoux).** (1888)   One of van Gogh's most famous portaits, this composition derives much of its force from its sharp contours, areas of uncompromising poster-flatness (showing the influence of Japanese prints) and audacious harmony of color. As the figure leans to the left, the vividly-colored books swing the eye back toward the striking semi-circle of the table-top at right. "I have an Arlésienne at last," van Gogh wrote his brother Théo, "a figure slashed on in an hour . . . background pale lemon, the face grey, the clothes black, black, black with perfectly raw Prussian blue." Two years later, the artist stated: "What excites me the most . . . is portraiture, modern portraiture. I endeavor to do this . . . not through photographic resemblance, but through our impassioned aspects, using our science and our modern taste for color as a means of expression and of exaltation of character." This is one of several van Gogh portrayals of Mme. Ginoux, who managed a cafe in the building he lived in at Arles. Gauguin also painted her, and this portrait was strongly influenced by van Gogh's brief contact with him in Arles.

• **70. Cypresses.** (1889)   In 1889 van Gogh voluntarily entered an asylum for the insane in the former monastery of Saint-Rémy. That June, allowed to paint outdoors for the first time (often under guard), he finished *Cypresses* and wrote the following de-

scription to his brother: "I have painted two studies of cypresses, in that difficult bottle-green shade. . . . The cypresses are always occupying my thoughts. . . . They are as beautiful in line and proportion as an Egyptian obelisk. And the green has a quality of such distinction." "The trees in it are very thick and massive. The foreground, very low with brambles and brushwood; behind some violet hills a green and rose sky with crescent moon. The foreground especially is painted with thick clumps of brambles with touches of yellow, violet and green." Every inch of van Gogh's canvas ripples with animation. The glowing, thickly-textured pigment is, in the artist's word, "plastered" on. The trees undulate upward from the pulsating ground and flowing hillside, outlined against the spiraling lines of the moon and radiant color-swirls of the sky. Despite the turbulent surface, forms maintain substance and solidity. Van Gogh's pen-and-ink sketch for this painting is in the Brooklyn Museum.

British Painting

GAINSBOROUGH, Thomas
● 71. **Mrs. Grace Dalrymple Elliott.** (About 1770-80)   Daughter of a Scotch advocate and wife of a celebrated doctor, Mrs. Elliott was a great celebrity popularly nicknamed "Dolly the Tall." Among her admirers were the Prince of Wales, the Duke of Orleans and Lord Cholmondeley, in whose castle this portrait once hung. Such was Mrs. Elliott's reputation that English newspapers protested her pictures being exhibited alongside "ladies of rank." Any composition based on a tall figure shown full length in elaborate costume is almost certain to be more a portrait of the dress than the individual. Such is the case with *Mrs. Elliott,* but the painting is saved from aesthetic barrenness by the quality of its execution. Gracefully assimilating the van Dyke portrait

71

tradition, Gainsborough's painting is distinguished in its silken color, feathery handling and authentic charm. The grey-blue background enhances the gold and silver notes of the costume's folds and lends dignity and a frame of space to the figure. A touch of muted orange in the sky helps relate the low horizon to the central color motif. Gainsborough made several portraits of Mrs. Elliott, one of which is now in the Frick Collection. A Reynolds portrait of Mrs. Elliott's daughter, Georgiana Seymour, is in the Metropolitan.

LAWRENCE, Thomas

• **72. Elizabeth Farren, Countess of Derby.** (1790)   Elizabeth Farren, a famous comedienne who starred in such plays as "She Stoops to Conquer" and "A School for Scandal," married the Earl of Derby, founder of the famed Derby races. This painting of her made Lawrence famous almost overnight (though some newspapers sniffed at a fur-trimmed cloak and muff in a spring landscape). Nevertheless, it suffered the fate of most portraits—advice to the artist on how it could be improved. Miss Farren wrote Lawrence that "they tease me to death about this picture. . . . One says it is so thin in figure that you might blow it away; another that it looks broke in the middle. In short, you must make it a little fatter. At all events diminish the bend you are so attached to, even if it makes the portrait look ill." The changes were never made.

TURNER, Joseph Mallord William

• **73. The Grand Canal, Venice.** (1835)   Exhibiting Turner's fascination with radiant light, this picture also recalls the harbor panoramas of the artist's favorite, Claude Lorrain, and anticipates the late painting of Monet. Forms dissolve into luminous color, and marble almost melts into atmosphere. Ships, gondolas and figures provide dark punctuation between the soft sky and glistening water. Although the buildings verge on the ethereal, Turner—like Renoir many years later—retains enough substance

72

and quality to keep the scene from becoming sentimental or facile. In the left background are the Campanile and a glimpse of the Doge's palace. At right appears the Church of Santa Maria della Salute.

French Painting

LA TOUR, Georges de

• **74. The Fortune Teller.** (Before 1633)   This wry, quiet painting became the center of a storm of protest in 1960 when the French press discovered that a de la Tour—a national treasure—had been allowed to leave the country. Unknown until the late 1940's, *The Fortune Teller* was apparently discovered in a monastery and was acquired by an art dealer who outbid the Louvre with an offer of $28,000. Somehow it was cleared for export and sold to the Metropolitan for between $600,000 and $800,000. One of only twenty-odd de la Tours known—three of which, including one in the Frick, are in the United States—this is also one of the artist's few works showing a scene in bright daylight. The theme of the gullible youth was widely popular in the artist's time. De la Tour depicts a young gallant having his fortune told by an old Gypsy while three wily girls surround him, one to steal his purse and pass it to the ready hand of her companion, another to cut off a medallion he wears on a chain. An almost stolid frieze of figures is given liveliness and variety by the vivid pattern of the costumes and the rhythmically-linked gestures of arms and hands. At left, the arm of one girl swings across to the bottom line of the youth's tunic; the movement is picked up and completed at right by the arm of the old woman. An especially ingenious design occurs in the placement of four hands against the dark dress in right center. An almost trance-like quality of suspense is imparted to the calm action. The clear, luminous oval face of the girl at center recalls the coloring of Vermeer and Manet. The crone's dark wrinkled face seems still more aged set against her elaborate headdress.

POUSSIN, Nicolas

• **75. The Rape of the Sabine Women.** (1632-34)   Poussin portrays a legend taken from Plutarch's life of Romulus. The early

75

Romans, snubbed by the girls of more settled communities, decided to acquire wives by a ruse. They invited the Sabine tribe to a religious festival, at the height of which they seized their guests' daughters. Romulus is shown on a high podium raising his staff and mantle as a signal to begin the abduction. In this turbulent tableau, figures are posed as if in a climactic moment of ballet. The action starts in the foreground and recedes methodically into the far sky. At left, the woman being seized by a warrior guides the eye in a diagonal line all the way to the central triangle of swords; the line is repeated and balanced by the three struggling figures at right, while behind them fleeing figures form a dramatic counterpoint. The elderly woman and two children in center foreground unite these two major movements and establish a pyramid repeated and modified in the group at right. Striking colors bind the figures and accent the rhythmic pattern in their groupings. The blue of the abducted woman at left, for example, is echoed by a robe, then by the far warrior, then repeated in a sharper hue elsewhere throughout the painting and finally modified at the right. Stately buildings and a soft sky give the violence a serene setting. In Poussin's time, the Sabine legend was often painted as an allegory of marriage. This is the second of Poussin's two versions on the theme; the earlier work is in the Louvre. A Degas copy of the Louvre version is in the Gallery of Modern Art in New York.

• **76. The Blind Orion Searching for the Rising Sun.** (1658)   In Greek legend, the King of Chios kept postponing the promised marriage of his daughter to the giant Orion until Orion, in a drunken fit, seized and violated the maiden. The angry King blinded Orion in revenge, but an oracle told him he could regain his sight by reaching the rays of the rising sun. The god Hephaestus provided him with his servant Cedalion as a guide. Poussin shows Hephaestus pointing out the sun's direction to Cedalion, who stands on Orion's shoulders. Artemis, the moon goddess, gazes at the giant from rain clouds. (She had fallen in love with Orion, but was later tricked into fatally shooting him; grieved, she placed him among the stars, where he appears with his dog Sirius.) In a composition which breathes of Homeric majesty, the mountains, trees and clouds provide a dramatic setting for the awesome figure of the striding giant. Orion's movement, the

76

flow of mist behind him and the wide road guide the eye toward the center. Collateral movements occur in the shape of the mountains and in the clouds beneath Artemis. A dark mass of trees at left halts the dominant sweep and gives space and scale to the landscape. Subtle colors range from deep, dark chords to the luminous tints of the clouds and sky. In some versions of the legend, Orion signifies the circulation of water in nature. Hence, Artemis may here represent rain.

CLAUDE LORRAIN

• **77. Sunrise.** (About 1647) This pastoral idyll, painted delicately but firmly, glows with the light of the sun. An appealing effect is created in the pink sky and clouds, which act as foil to the dark masses of the trees. The ground shimmers, its bluish mass suggesting deep space. Shepherd, sheep and cattle heighten the serenity. Claude's basic goal was the achievement of serene, atmospheric landscapes evoking antiquity. This painting belonged to Sir Joshua Reynolds and to Sir Francis Cook, who also owned Poussin's *Rape of the Sabine Women.*

WATTEAU, Jean Antoine

• **78. Mezzetin.** (About 1718) Mezzetin, a standard pantomime character borrowed from Italian *commedia dell'arte,* was a valet who delighted in fooling his master and serenading sweethearts. In this painting Watteau frames the luster of his colorful striped silks against a cool, dark background. Rich paths for the eye occur in the subdued lights of ground, bench and wall, in the balancing of the wall against the graceful curve of trees at left and in the pinkish sky above the statue. The painting evokes a wistful mood without straining the picturesque aspects of the subject matter. *Commedia dell'arte* troupes were banned in France in 1697, perhaps because of a presumed insult to Louis XIV's mistress, but shortly before this painting Louis XV rescinded the prohibition. *Mezzetin* was bought at auction for about $500 by Catherine the Great of Russia and was in the Hermitage in St.

79

Petersburg until 1931, when the Soviet Government sold it, along with many other notable paintings.

● **79. The French Comedians.** (Date uncertain)   This glimpse of the French stage may be a satire on actors' declamations or simply a scene from a tragi-comedy. Watteau deftly manipulates a difficult grouping: figures arranged horizontally in a frontal close-up across the width of the canvas. The actors are linked in a rhythmic procession from the weeping girl at left to the second girl, to the foppish gallant; his legs form the apex of the triangle running from the weeping girl, to the center, to the man in the cloak, while the oncoming actor supplies the second half of a compositional pyramid. The arches and floor (which lend spaciousness to the compact frontal massing) and the white accents spotted from the sleeve of the first actress to the splash of the fountain act as unifying devices. Judging from an early engraving, portions of the top, bottom and sides of this painting have been cut off. The oil once belonged to Watteau's life-long friend and biographer, Jean de Julliene, who also owned *Mezzetin*; De Julienne, who became director of the Gobelin Tapestry manufactory, sold this painting to Frederick II of Prussia.

CHARDIN, Jean Baptiste
● **80. The Silver Tureen.** (About 1727)   This is an early example of Chardin's magic way with commonplace still-life objects. Fur, feathers, metal, fruit and stone blend artfully in an informal but firmly-constructed arrangement. Light contrasts subtly with dark; texture is varied; the surface is rich and appealing. Against the dark background rests the silver tureen, gleaming with a reflected light and crowned by a resonant orange. The dead hare, at once soft and solid, forms the apex of a shallow pyramid, while the apple helps establish a horizontal base and acts to counterbalance the diagonal line from the paw to the orange.

DAVID, Jacques Louis
● **81. The Death of Socrates.** (Completed in 1787)   In the most important example of Neoclassical painting in the United States, David depicts Socrates' last hour as described in Plato's "Phaedo." The philosopher's figure is emphasized by its isolation, gesture and the sheer physical space it occupies from outstretched foot to upraised hand. (As in most Neoclassical paintings, de-

80

clamatory gestures and theatrical poses weaken the drama of a
heroic theme.) Color is contained within neat contours, and
modeling and solidity are conveyed by sculpturesque shading. At
left, a deep arch opens on a recessed area which relieves the generally shallow space. Socrates was condemned to death in 339
B.C. for "corrupting the young" and for "impiety." In depicting
his taking of the poison hemlock, David consulted poets and his-
torians for factual and symbolic accuracy. Thus, beyond the arch
Socrates' wife and child are leaving at the philosopher's request.
At the foot of the couch sits Plato. A weeping jailor hands Socrates the cup of hemlock. Absorbed in a discourse on the immortality of the soul, the philosopher's hand hovers over the fatal
cup—a symbolic gesture scorning Death. Facing Socrates is either
Phaedo or Crito. The young man weeping and lamenting at right
may be "the excitable Apollodorus." Plato related that after his
chains were unloosened, Socrates sat up on his couch, rubbing his
leg, and discussed the principles of pain and pleasure; even this
element is evident in David's composition. On the bench beneath
Phaedo are inscribed an owl and an olive branch—symbols of
wisdom and victory—and David's signature. David was commissioned to paint *The Death of Socrates* by the young statesman
Michel Trudaine de la Sabliere. At the Salon of 1787, the painting brought David acclaim; Sir Joshua Reynolds called it "the
greatest effort of art since the Sistine Chapel." In 1794 de la
Sabliere was guillotined and the painting passed on to his sister-
in-law. In 1812, according to an anecdote, Napoleon attempted
to buy the painting for 60,000 francs but was refused.

INGRES, Jean Auguste Dominique

• **82. Odalisque in Grisaille.** (Date uncertain)   In Turkish, the
word "odalisque" means chambermaid, but in European painting
the odalisque represents the type of exotic harem beauty familiar-
ized by Ingres, Delacroix and Matisse. Grisaille is the name
given to paintings in shades of grey, often done to give figures the

83

appearance of sculpture; this work, the only known grisaille by Ingres, is a second version of his famous *Odalisque* in the Louvre. In the figure of the satin-smooth nude, the master of meticulous drawing subtly distorts anatomy—the head is made smaller, the thighs more rounded, the back lengthened—in order to heighten the sensuousness of the flowing contours. An undulating line runs almost continuously from the curtain at left across the figure to the crisp folds at right. The somewhat geometric folds of the drapery enhance the languid curves of the nude and her pillows, while the large area of background emphasizes the soft flesh. The face is a handsome translation of Raphael's classic Madonnas, yet the total effect is of discreet, icy voluptuousness.

• **83. Madame Leblanc.** (1823)   From the lively detail of the India shawl to the quiet simplicity of the dark background, this portrait is poised and serene. Ingres dwells on the relaxed flow of the figure, playing off a sober black silk dress against the light on the face, the expanse of throat, the flesh showing through the sleeves, and the bold notes of the shawl (echoed in the flowers). More than twenty existing drawings for this portrait testify to Ingres' pursuit of perfection.

DELACROIX, Eugène

• **84. The Abduction of Rebecca.** (1846)   This exciting painting was inspired by an incident in Sir Walter Scott's "Ivanhoe." Richard the Lion Hearted and Robin Hood had attacked the castle of the Norman Bois-Guilbert, in which Rebecca, the Jewish maiden who refused to adopt Christianity, was held prisoner. During the attack a fire started, and in the resulting chaos Bois-Guilbert seized Rebecca and rode off with her. Delacroix portrays the villain, at lower right, directing a Saracen slave to lift the fainting girl onto his horse. The composition is filled with furious rhythms, entwining forms and bursts of exotic color. Most notable are the horse, its mane and tail windswept, its

84

hoofs pawing the ground impetuously; the turbaned man on the saddle; the swooning girl engulfed by a winding robe; the gesturing horseman with his blowing cape; and the billowing smoke and fire. Typically Romanticist is the diagonal massing. The group centers on the horse. A dramatic counter-balance occurs as the rider leans inward, the girl falls forward, the second man turns toward the castle and the horse itself thrusts toward the left. The colors recall Veronese, particularly the reds in the saddle, straps and turbans and the deep blue of the dress. When this painting was exhibited in the Salon of 1846, Baudelaire wrote: "The admirable thing about *The Abduction of Rebecca* is the perfect ordering of its colors, which are intense, close-packed, serried and logical; the result of this is a thrilling effect."

COROT, Jean Baptiste Camille

● **85. Hagar in the Wilderness.** (1834-35)   When Abraham, the founder of Judaism, had a son by his Egyptian servant Hagar, his wife Sarah cast both servant and child into the desert. ". . . and she departed, and wandered in the wilderness of Beer-sheba. And the water was spent in the bottle, and she cast the child under one of the shrubs [and] said, 'Let me not see the death of the child.' And she sat over against him and lifted up her voice and wept. And God heard the voice of the lad; and the angel of God called to Hagar out of heaven, and said unto her, 'What aileth thee, Hagar? Fear not; for God hath heard the voice of the lad where he is.' " This early Corot is unusual in its large size and its combination of landscape with Biblical figures. Definition is sharp, color is lustrous and the canvas is filled with vivid sun and shade. Sky and trees are rendered with crystal-clear freshness. Space has the breadth of a Poussin or a Claude Lorrain. Clearly, Corot's primary interest was in portraying the landscape, which seems to be a composite of the countryside near the Sabine mountains north of Rome. The angel, mother and child seem almost superimposed on the scene.

• **86. The Sibyl.** (About 1870)   In Corot's lifetime, his figure paintings were known to only a few admirers. Today, these solidly constructed, masterfully simple pictures rank with his finest landscapes. Sibyls were legendary prophetesses, and Corot's title is only a poetic name for a study of an Italian model wearing laurels. In her freely-handled, robust figure, color defines only the essential planes—as in the face and the hand holding the rose—and the effect is almost sculptural. This painting belonged to Alfred Robaut, a friend of Corot who in 1872 photographed over six hundred of the artist's pictures—possibly the first use of the camera to frustrate the sale of forgeries.

COURBET, Gustave

• **87. The Girls of the Village.** (1851)   A 19th Century turning point in landscape painting, this picture was Courbet's first major oil after his epochal masterpiece *The Burial at Ornans*. A grim panorama of figures about an open grave, *The Burial* was branded as brutal, savage and Socialist. But with this sunny canvas, Courbet felt "I have made something gracious; everything they have found to say up to now will be useless." The composition is dominated by three broad horizontals—the sloping curve of the horizon; the green area of the valley; and the sinuous line formed by the bush, the girls and the cattle. The painting is remarkably fresh for a pre-Impressionist landscape. Clear, strong light is established by a cloudless blue sky and heightened by the pinks, whites and yellows of the girls' frocks and the red and blue of the child's dress. Despite its massive depth, the painting contains charmingly rendered details, as in the foreground leaves, the roughly-painted feet of the child and the feel of the fabric and light on the dresses. The picture recalls Courbet's simple credo, "I love the solid earth." It also evokes Cézanne's admiring comment, "what a tough wrecker of pigment!" and Zola's description of Courbet's pictures as "powerful canvases . . . as real as life and as beautiful as truth." Yet despite Courbet's confidence in this painting, his scoffers were still not appeased. When it appeared in the Salon of 1852, the writer Gautier condemned it as having "the air of a cook on her Sunday off . . . vulgar to people of good taste," and another critic jibed: "But the girls! My God! One can easily understand why they have sought this soli-

88   8

tary place! They are so ill-favored, so disgraceful." Nevertheless, the painting was purchased by the Comte de Morny, the bastard half-brother of President Louis Bonaparte. The three girls are Courbet's sisters: Zellie is handing a delicacy to the shepherd girl; Juliette (who later inherited all Courbet's property in a one-sentence will) holds a parasol; Zoë (who spent her last years in an insane asylum) is in yellow. The setting for this landscape, as for *The Burial*, is the valley at Roch de Dix Heures near Ornans, close to the Swiss frontier.

• **88. Woman with a Parrot.** (1866)   Courbet's model was probably Joanna Heffernan, an Irish girl who was Whistler's model and mistress. Whistler and Joanna met Courbet at Trouville. She posed for Courbet's *The Beautiful Irish Girl Combing Her Hair* (also in the Metropolitan) and for Whistler's famous *Symphony in White No. 1; The White Girl* (in the National Gallery, Washington). In its sheer physical substance and frank sensuality this canvas challenged the then-fashionable treatment of the nude as an ethereal or mythological creature. Despite a rather waxen surface typical of Courbet, the figure's flesh is imbued with life. The nude and the fabric contrast forcefully with the dark background and the glossy, warm-colored hair. The figure sprawls in a bold arc from the cascade of hair to the sloping edge of the divan. The upraised arm and parrot are color echoes of the hair and form a link with the curtain at right.

MILLET, Jean François
• **89. Autumn.** (Date uncertain)   Millet casts a brooding spell over this farm scene. Weather is almost tangible. Two main horizontals—the dark earth and a luminous sky animated with clouds —create a slow, stately rhythm, while the contrast between them adds to the feeling of dramatic space. The woman, trees, cart and red roof provide quiet accents, with wagon and tree treated as a broad mass. Millet creates dignity and monumentality through the relaxed tempo of the lines and the passages of brownish color.

DAUMIER, Honoré
• **90. The Third-Class Carriage.** (About 1865)   Daumier fills this commonplace scene with power and grandeur. His insight into character is as absorbing as that of Dickens, and the dignity of spirit in the figures recalls Rembrandt. Parallel horizontals— the row of travelers and the bare bench—serve as a background for the central pyramid of grandmother, daughter and drowsing boy. The shape of the old woman's shawl and hood accentuates the central design, as do subordinate elements like the boy's inward slant and spread legs and the inverted pyramid formed on the bench. The central group is also emphasized and complemented by a sequence of pyramid units formed by the shoulders and faces of the figures behind. With a few telling colors, Dau-

mier achieves a rich, varied effect. The green of the skirt, repeated lightly in the boy and in the back of the man at right,
becomes a foil to the warm tonality of the dominant browns and
reds. Bluntly drawn, the figures are almost chiseled out by light
and dark in an effect that adds dramatic variety and strong
rhythms, especially in the array of faces in the background. The
square lines left on this incomplete picture were aids used by the
artist in enlarging the drawing from his watercolor study to the
canvas.

MANET, Édouard

• **91. The Guitarist.** (1860) This early Manet recalls the dark
brown tonality of old masters, but many of its more impressive
passages announce the arrival of a master of realism. Especially
notable are the drawing of the hands, the fabric of the trousers
and canvas shoes, the fresh color of the bench and the still life at
lower right. Crisp handling and the suppression of dark shadows
heighten the intensity of the colors. The painting has vigor, directness and solidity. The acceptance of this historic work at the
Salon of 1861 represented Manet's public debut. In contrast to
the reception received by his later works, *The Guitarist* was acclaimed so enthusiastically that it was moved from an obscure
spot into a prominent position and given an honorable mention.
The adventurous among the Salon visitors were struck by its
luminosity and brilliant painting. (*The Guitarist,* in fact, made
Manet a hero to the young art rebels of his day; a group including the painter Fantin-Latour and the poet Baudelaire visited the
artist to pay their respects—and were astonished to find that he
was only twenty-eight.) But even the conservatives liked the
painting, possibly because the familiar and picturesque Spanish
costume veiled to some extent Manet's fresh approach. Thus
Gautier, who was later to jeer at Manet's masterpiece *Olympia,*
wrote: "Caramba! Here is a guitarist who does not come from
the Opéra-Comique. . . . Velázquez would have asked him for a

90

light to his pipe. . . . There is a lot of talent in this life-like figure, broadly painted in true color and with a bold brush." But future hostility was foreshadowed by another critic, who asked disdainfully what poetry existed "in the idiotic figure of this mule driver [or] in the onion and cigarette, whose combined odors have just perfumed the room! The brushstrokes, caked and plastered in, are like mortar on top of mortar." The sitter has been identified as Jerome Bosch, a dancer in a Spanish troupe then appearing at the Paris Hippodrome.

• **92. The Dead Christ with Angels.** (1863-64) Ardently dedicated to depicting the every-day world, Manet seldom showed a propensity toward the profoundly religious or, for that matter, the deeply dramatic. Viewed in relation to more conventional religious painting, this work seems only a study of a posed nude, devoid of mystic feeling; but seen as an attempt to rejuvenate an abused, if hallowed, theme, the picture's stoic calm and dignity offer a fresh vision touched with simplicity. The torso, with its broad forms, firm planes and accentuated contours, recalls Manet's famous nude *Olympia*. The winding folds of the shroud and the dark, billowing robes of the mourning angels provide a vivid counterpoint to the pallid flesh. The inscription on the rock refers to the twenty-second chapter of the Book of John, and the snake is an ancient symbol of original sin. Exhibited in the Salon of 1864, *The Dead Christ* aroused hostile criticism. One critic wrote, "We have never seen such audaciously bad taste, the negation of scientific anatomy, spoiled color, lampblack abused and applied to the face of the most beautiful of men, carried so far as by Manet in *The Dead Christ*." But a more perceptive critic wrote, "no doubt as a sort of gibe at the bashful admirers of discreet and tidy painting, *The Dead Christ* is terrifying to behold."

• **93. Mlle. Victorine in the Costume of an Espada.** (1863) The potentially mawkish theme of a girl posed as a bullfighter becomes arresting through Manet's fresh insights into color and

2

93

form. The dark costume silhouetted against a light background offers a novel reversal of the technique used by the old masters. By considerably reducing shadows and intermediary notes, Manet not only gives crisp dash to the girl's curvacious figure, but initiates an important approach in modern art—the suggestion of form without modeling. Vivid, almost revolutionary color effects occur in the brilliant contrasts: the head against dark hat, brown arena wall and lively scarf; the flat pink of the legs against the shadowed ground; the yellow under the sleeves against the pink cape. The sketchy bullfighters in the background recall Goya. This picture was painted in the year of Manet's masterpiece, *The Luncheon on the Grass*. Manet sent both, along with *Young Man in the Costume of a Majo*, to the Salon of 1863. They were rejected, as were some 4,000 other paintings. The outcry was so great that the Government decided to hold a Salon of the Rejected—a decisive event in modern art. Manet defiantly exhibited all three, thus linking them with one of the most dramatic moments of 19th Century art. The girl in the picture was Victorine Meurend, an artist and model who posed for some of Manet's most famous canvases, notably *Olympia, The Luncheon on the Grass* and the Metropolitan's *Woman with a Parrot*. She spent the 1860's in the United States and in her later years is said to have peddled drawings and died in poverty. Mrs. Henry Havemeyer, who gave the Metropolitan this picture, wrote that she and the artist Mary Cassatt bought it in New York without Mr. Havemeyer's having seen it. "I fear Mr. Havemeyer would think it too big. 'Don't be foolish,' said Miss Cassatt, 'It is just the size Manet wanted it, and that ought to suffice for Mr. Havemeyer.' "

● **94. Woman with a Parrot.** (About 1866)   Manet, like Velázquez, was often absorbed with the problem of painting a single figure in space. This is one of his finest solutions. The girl emerges emphatically from the dark background, her delicate pink heightening the striking contrast, yet Manet succeeds in avoiding

94

the effect of a cut-out or a pasted-on pattern. The glow of the simplified gown demonstrates exceptional skill in rendering light and fabric. The gown's hem, the decorative lemon and the base of the stand help establish a firm foreground for the composition, while the stand emphasizes the contour of the dress. The girl's meditative air adds a poignant charm to the masterful figure study. This painting was shown in the Salon of 1868 and was subsequently acquired by the collector Hoschedé for 2,000 francs. Hoschedé's widow later married Manet. In 1878 the picture brought only 700 francs at auction—about $250. Given to the Metropolitan in 1889, it was possibly one of the first Manets to enter any museum.

• **95. Boating.** (1874)   In one of Manet's most daring performances in the new style of open-air painting, the feeling of casualness and spontaneity is actually carefully contrived. The cropping of the boat on three sides, for example, gives a close-up effect. The eye is swung to the right by the triangle of sail, then returns to the left through the contour of the man's back, the blue dress and the curve of the stern. Brilliant light is a key element. Sunny colors, which underline the striking arrangement of the large units subdividing the canvas, demonstrate how tellingly a few pigments can be combined. Forms are flattened, simplified and handled with breezy spirit. In the girl's face, hat and veil, strokes are so agile and delicate that they seem flicked on effortlessly; yet they are a firm abridgement of subject matter. Not an orthodox example of Impressionism, this work does show Manet's alliance with the challenging new style—a style he himself had helped to initiate through his use of light, clear color and crisp strokes. A comparison with *The Guitarist* shows the enormous evolution of his art in two decades. *Boating* was painted at Argenteuil—a town on the Seine where Manet visited Monet and Renoir—in the year of the first exhibition of Impressionists. The man in the picture is believed to be Rudolf Leenhoff, Manet's brother-in-law and himself a painter. The girl is unidentified.

MONET, Claude
• **96. The Beach at Sainte Adresse.** (About 1867)   Crystal-clear light infuses water, sand and figures. Paint is applied broadly, detail is minimized and surface is flattened out in a manner re-

97

calling Manet. To catch the ripple of waves, Monet employs stubby, broken brushstrokes that anticipate the darting lines of later Impressionism. Figures, waves, boats and a magnificent procession of clouds are summarized with vivid clarity. This seascape was painted during a low ebb in Monet's life. The year before, his full-length portrait of his fiancée, Camille Doncieux, had aroused great interest at the Salon, but this year the Salon rejected his masterpiece *Women in a Garden*. Camille was pregnant and Monet was penniless. Asked for help, Monet's estranged father replied that he should leave Camille and stay with his aunt at Sainte-Adresse, a little town on the Channel coast near Le Havre. Monet agreed. When his son was born that July he was unable even to raise money for train fare to Paris to see the infant.

● **97. Le Grènouillère.** (1869)   One of the first true Impressionist paintings, this work marks a major advance in the portrayal of outdoor life. Strong light quivering over water is evoked through staccato brushstrokes in a vibrant pattern of contrasting colors. Color, rather than paint, is used to portray surface. The figures on the circular platform are merely bright jabs of pigment. Strong light all but dissolves the bathers. Painting has turned a corner, departing from rounded delineation and emphatic outlines and embarking on the dissolution of form through which the Impressionists would seek to capture quick-silver movement and changing color. In August of 1869, Monet joined Renoir at La Grènouillère ("The Froggery"), a rowdy resort on the Seine favored by boating parties. (Maupassant describes it in "Yvette.") Both artists painted rather similar compositions; in his version of this scene, Renoir even included the cloth draped over the side of the pavilion. Renoir wrote of this summer, "We don't eat every day, yet I am happy in spite of it, because, as far as painting is concerned, Monet is good company. . . . I do almost nothing because I haven't much paint."

● **98. Vétheuil.** (1880)   Here Impressionism reaches the high noon of its shimmering color and stress on soft air and light. Solid mass is transformed into gossamer webs of brushstrokes; edges melt into the delicate fabric of color. The direct frontal view is divided into three main horizontals: sky, land and water. Trees add a strong color note and a balance for the 12th Century church. Rhythmic, vibrating dabs of color in the water capture its light-reflecting movement. A boat provides the lone accent in a vista bathed in summer light. Monet had rented a house in Vétheuil, where he could work in solitude, and remained there until 1881. The Metropolitan possesses another Vétheuil view, and a winter version is in the Frick.

● **99. Rouen Cathedral.** (1894)   One of a famous sequence showing the Cathedral at different hours from morning to sunset, this canvas represents Monet's systematic attempt to catch momentary light effects, as opposed to the general illumination used in most paintings. The series gave him an opportunity to push color to extreme intensity and invent a kind of mosaic of jewel-like luminosity. Color almost annihilates solid stone through its iridescence. The Cathedral looms in a direct close-up, an effect magnified by the cropping off of the sides, top and pavement; as in Degas and Toulouse-Lautrec, the arrangement conveys the sense of a scene recorded instantaneously. The blue sky acts as a relief to the shimmering filligree of the Cathedral. Sunlight cascades brilliantly. Monet painted the Rouen series from a second-floor window across from the Cathedral. Between 1892 and 1894 he completed more than thirty variations. At times he almost abandoned the attempt: "I labor without advancing," he wrote, "searching, groping, ending up without much of anything, but at the point of being exhausted by it." When he finally exhibited twenty of the series in 1895, even some champions of Impressionism denounced them as non-aesthetic and dry, scientific inquiries which over-emphasized one element—color. In recent years, however, such Monets have found high favor, partly due to their anticipation of free-form abstraction.

PISSARRO, Camille
• **100. Hillside at Jallaise, Pontoise.** (1867) Desperately poor at the time of this landscape, Pissarro painted pictures on window blinds to support himself and his family. Within a year, however, this painting and another *View of Pontoise* would be accepted at the Salon of 1868. The diagonal edge of the trees at right provides a strong guide into the space area of the buildings. The line of the green shoulder of the road at left is echoed in the fields on the slope. Contrasts of dark and light add drama and variety, while the luminous sky enhances the solidity of earth, fields, houses and trees. Pontoise, a town near Paris, also lured Cézanne and Gauguin.

99

RENOIR, Pierre Auguste

• **101. Madame Charpentier and Her Children.** (1878)   Because
this portrait group was a commission he hoped would lead to
more work, Renoir compromised his rich creative gifts for commercial acceptability. Even at that, he surpassed the society portraitists at their own game—the depiction of likenesses and
charming, luxurious interiors. The key to the massing is the diagonal formed by the three figures and the still life at upper right.
A counterbalance is provided by the slant of the mother's dark
dress toward the girls. An interesting distribution of blacks enriches the composition, but it is in the myriad of colors—in the
girls' dresses, jeweled flesh and shoes, for instance—that Renoir
shows his true delight, and in the bamboo chair and the Japanese
screens that he becomes freest and most creative. Mme. Charpentier was the wife of a famous publisher who subsidized Zola
when the author was struggling in debt. In 1877 she organized
a salon which remained for some twenty years a center of
French art and politics; her guests included the Goncourt brothers, Flaubert, Manet and Degas. Mme. Charpentier saw to it that
this portrait was hung prominently in the Salon of 1878, where
her social position encouraged critics to praise it. Renoir's work
soon began to sell more rapidly. Pissarro wrote, "Renoir has a
big success at the Salon. I believe he is launched. So much the
better. Poverty is so hard." The Metropolitan acquired this painting at a Paris auction in 1907 for only $18,500. The first Renoir
to enter any American museum, its purchase was strongly criti-
cized; today it is among the Museum's most popular paintings.

• **102. By the Seashore.** (1883)   In paintings like this one, Renoir invests the fragile charm of the 18th Century French style
with his own vigor and rich, luminous color. The masterly composition appears casual and uncontrived, yet the young woman
is artfully framed by the wicker chair and the rich and varied
background of sea, sky and cliff. Her charming oval face, its delicate flesh tones accentuated by dark hair and bonnet, holds the
eye. The blue of her garments sings out against the yellow of the
chair, while her white collar-trim and the fabric she is crocheting
lend frothy, diaphanous notes to her solidly-painted figure.

100   1

Rhythmic, vibrant brushstrokes in the skirt, echoed in an opposite direction behind the chair, give the composition a firm base
from which the eye wanders off to explore the background. The
surface has a porcelain-like dryness and translucent glaze.

• **103. In the Meadow.** (1894-95)   Colorful and flowing as the
bouquet which forms its center, this painting distills Renoir's love
of sunlight and youthful beauty. Despite the soft handling, organization is carefully indicated: one line flows from the pink dress
past the girl in white to the trees; an opposing movement follows
the hat, the spottings of reds and greens, the arm on which the
girl supports herself and the diagonal line of the ground at left.
Alternating spots of light and shade, as in the clumps of grass,
undulate from foreground into soft distance. The shimmering
greens of the rolling meadow, the colors of the dresses and sun-
dappled hair provide rich accents.

DEGAS, Edgar
• **104. The Foyer.** (1872)   In one of his earliest ballet compositions, Degas uses the effective device of tilting the floor upward
to dramatize the space of a large room. Grand piano, dancers
and mirror form a diagonal which swings to the right, where the
dark rectangle of the door balances the mass of the piano and

103

105

restores an asymmetrical balance. Mirrored reflections deepen space. Walls and floors frame the fluffy white dresses, while the violinist's suit, case and hat serve as dark accents. A vertical band of light balances the piano's horizontality. Although everything is drawn with sharp clarity, the scene is softened by smooth light. The interweaving of the various poses and the renderings of individual character add great charm to the picture.

• **105. Dancers Practising at the Bar.** (1877) In an audacious expanse of space, graceful dancers balance the strong diagonals of floor, baseboard and practising bar. Accents in the costumes help restore equilibrium and keep the eye within the picture. Details like the second girl's ribbon, the pink of her dancing shoe and the leftward pull of the watering can act as asymmetrical balances. This painting belonged to Henri Rouart, one of Degas' best friends, an artist and collector who also pioneered in early refrigeration and automobile development. Rouart had first bought another Degas from a dealer, but the artist asked to borrow it for further work and eventually spoiled it. Degas offered his friend any picture in his studio in replacement, but when Rouart chose this one he wanted to "improve" it by painting out the watering can. Rouart refused and took the painting away. In 1912 this painting brought $87,000, the highest price that had ever been paid at auction for the work of a living artist. Present at the sale, an old, enfeebled and nearly blind Degas was sardonic when congratulated on the honor. He retorted with a comparison of a horse who wins the race but sees the jockey get the award.

• **106. The Rehearsal on the Stage** and • **107. Rehearsal of the Ballet on the Stage.** (About 1878-79) These two versions—the first in pastel, the second in oil—testify to Degas' passion for perfection. The differences are slight, but significant. In the pastel, for instance, the neck of the bass viol pulls against the movement of the ballerina seated in the foreground; the dancer at extreme left faces out of the picture, while the second girl's arm returns the eye inward; the scenery is a fluffy, colorful balance to the pink skirt in the foreground. In the oil, the necks of the two stringed instruments modify the swing in the first painting; illumination is more diffused and restrained; the play of tones and the balance of darks and lights is more sensitive. The vantage point

106

in both pictures seems high above the stage. Distance recedes obliquely through the row of four dancers at left. The viols link with the dance director, whose hands lead toward the two relaxed male figures seated far off watching the rehearsal.

• **108. At the Milliner's.** (1882)   In compositions like this pastel, Degas (and later Toulouse-Lautrec) created the illusion of having accidentally observed a passing scene. The spectator is brought into the picture much in the way a movie camera dollies directly in for a close-up. The eye is attracted by the contrasting colors of wall and floor, the upward direction of the floor and the placing of the mirror at right angles to the spectator, partly concealing the salesgirl. The flattened background colors and the placement of the figures recall Japanese prints. An intriguing moment occurs in the silhouetting of the mirror against the hourglass dress of the salesgirl. The muted orange, the blue floor, the dark brown mirror and the greyish-green in the dresses are enhanced by the lively notes of the hats. The artist Mary Cassatt posed for the figure of the customer.

• **109. Nude—The Toilet.** (About 1885)   "I show them," Degas once remarked of his nudes, "deprived of their airs and affectations, reduced to the level of animals cleaning themselves." Shortly before his death, he added, "I have, perhaps, too much considered woman as an animal.". Nevertheless, this pastel gleams with the shimmer of flesh, the glow of light and the texture of fabric. The couch functions as a diagonal opposing the two women, while the white cloth flows in unity with their figures. The nude's head, thrown back, is related to the body of the hairdresser, whose head is left out to add to the spirit of an unposed arrangement. To Degas, beauty lay in capturing specific, unidealized character. In this picture, the expressive hand on the hip, the breasts, the knees and the firm feet unmistakably depict a particular individual. The artist also sought to capture uninhibited, unselfconscious action, far removed from the polite poses

109

of the conventional studio nude, and to demonstrate the fresh effects that could be instilled into the commonplace. At the eighth and last Exhibition of the Impressionists, in 1886, Degas exhibited a series of pastels, including this one, under the deliberately dry catalog title: *A Series of Nudes of Women, Bathing, Washing, Drying, Rubbing Down, Combing Their Hair or Having it Combed.* Even some of Degas' admirers were displeased by these pictures; the novelist Huysmans deplored their "unmistakable strain of contempt and hatred."

CEZANNE, Paul

• **110. Still Life: Apples and Primroses.** (1890-94)   This lyrical canvas divides into two sharply-contrasted zones—the active table unit and the quiet wall. Linking them are the vase, flowers and dark curtains at right, which also provide a vertical balance. The table slopes upward to the right and also rises sharply into the wall at left, an altered perspective which dramatically intensifies depth; the effect is strengthened by the forms which move across the table, much as in a Cézanne landscape. The apples, which form a diagonal of connecting groups, play up the intricate folds of the tablecloth. Cool white is pitted against the sonorous notes of the fruit. Pink flowers echo the fruit, while green leaves strike a deep accent. The blue-green of the background, with its light and dark tints, acts as a quiet foil to the strong pattern of the leaves. Cézanne gave this painting to Monet, above whose bed it hung till his death.

• **111. Rocks—Forest of Fontainebleau.** (1894-98)   Boulders, trees and a touch of sky interplay in a crescendo of massive chords. Sky and foliage at the horizon provide stability as the rocks heave and pull against one another. The massing of forms is varied by the complex angles and planes with which the structures are defined, the rhythm of the brushstrokes and the alternating areas of light and dark. Foliage sweeps over the top zone in accord with the tensions established by the rocks. The color, almost abstract, is a personal harmony based on violets, greens, oranges and insistent gleams of subdued yellow; thinly applied, it nevertheless conveys weight. During the period of this landscape, Cézanne was slowly emerging into recognition. Two of his paintings entered the Luxembourg Palace when, after years of

110   1

stubborn legal opposition, the French Government was finally forced to accept at least part of the great Impressionist treasures left to the state by Gustave Caillebotte. And in 1895 a dealer was persuaded by Pissarro to give Cézanne his first one-man show.

GAUGUIN, Paul

• **112. I Hail Thee, Mary. (Ia Orana Maria.)** (1891)   Gauguin described this picture in a letter to a friend: "A yellow-winged angel points out Mary and Jesus to two Tahitian women. Mary and Jesus, also Tahitians, nudes dressed in pareus, a kind of flowered cotton which is wrapped as one likes, around the waist. In the background, somber mountains and blossoming trees. A dark purple road and an emerald green foreground. To the left, bananas. I am rather pleased with it." In this famous Gauguin, an exotic bouquet of patterns and shapes merges into a sumptuous ensemble. The monumental, simplified figure of Mary balances the flowers at left. The fruit on the altar, set against green grass, provides a colorful base and reflects the decorative patterns in the white flowers on Mary's costume, the orange-yellow on the blue sarong and the graceful curves of the leaves and flowers which partially conceal the angel. In the background, the pink sand, deep blue water and a dark mountain present striking color contrasts. The immobility of the figures recalls primitive art; the two Tahitians praying before Mary were in fact adopted from a photograph of a Javanese bas-relief showing the meeting of Budda and three monks. This is one of the first paintings Gauguin made in Tahiti, "the promised land . . . where for the people to live is to sing and to love."

• **113. Two Tahitian Women.** (1899)   These stately figures evoke a mood of idyllic tranquility. The girl at left, with her oval face and simplified torso, recalls Gauguin's ability to see in Tahitians the majesty of Greek goddesses. With statuesque calm, the two pose like archetypal symbols, their classic grace combined with the earthy strength of Polynesian maidens. Their flesh is framed

IA ORANA MARIA

113

and enhanced by the golden foliage and the blue and green of their costumes. Red and pink mango blossoms add vivid accents. The tilted head of the girl at right varies the similarity in the poses, while the neckline of her dress flows with gentle linear rhythm into the wooden dish of blossoms. Gauguin painted this canvas during his second stay in Polynesia. Working in an office, he wrote to France seeking fifteen persons who would subscribe 160 francs each for a painting.

SEURAT, Georges

● **114. An Afternoon at La Grande Jatte.** (1884-85)   This canvas is the last of about sixty studies for the huge and epochmaking *An Afternoon at La Grande Jatte* (Chicago Art Institute), the famous painting in which Seurat charted new paths beyond Impressionism and into the 20th Century. Figures are placed in an inflexible and stately array within the complex composition. The network of colors, which throb with the brightness of sun and the coolness of shade, saturates but fails to dissolve the interrelated forms. The wealth of subsidiary units is virtually, inexhaustible. The two monumental strollers at right form the pivot of the composition. Their verticality plays against three emphatic, depth-describing horizontals: the shaded foreground, the sunny central zone and the dark tree area at top. The strollers also lead the eye leftward across the picture toward the three seated girls, the woman with the child, the trombonist and the distant sailboat. A balancing diagonal runs from the reclining man in the red shirt, through the strollers and on to the seated figures and the colonnade of trees. In the center, the red parasol acts as the apex of a pyramid formed by the groups at left and right. La Grand Jatte, an island in the Seine near Paris, was a public park in Seurat's time.

● **115. La Parade. (The Side Show.)** (1887-88)   In this haunting poem to evening, Seurat immobilizes what must have been a scene of lively activity into an uncanny stillness. Stately and eternal, the figures recall an Egyptian frieze. Firm horizontal borders are established at top and bottom by the row of flower-like gas jets and the heads of the onlookers. These lines are repeated in the railing at left and the platform in the center, while vertical contrast is provided by the series of panels in the background, the tree trunk, the musicians, the mysterious trombonist, the boy and the master

114

of ceremonies. Enhancing the solemn balance are the asymmetry of the tree, the railing and the vertical plane to the right of the trombonist. The free, delicate movement of the branches opposes the rigidity of the railing below them. Space and depth gain vitality by being compressed into a shallow sequence of planes formed by the dark foreground, lighter middle ground and hazy background, a device which prefigures the flat treatment of space developed by the Cubists some two decades later. Cool and warm colors shimmer in the twilight, often in emphatic contrast. Delicate gold, orange and violet are strengthened by the firm massing of darker violets and blues.

MEISSONIER, Jean Louis Ernest

• **116. Friedland, 1807.** (1875) The story of 19th Century art is one of the almost inconceivable neglect of artists now considered great, while fame and fortune were showered on painters who are today either forgotten or remembered only as minor talents. Most works by these dethroned kings now reside in museum cellars, but the few occasionally put on view throw light on past taste and help build an understanding of the unprecedented overthrow of art reputations that took place in the first half of this century. A typical example is that of Meissonier. His fame in his day was such that one observer wrote, " 'Make room for the King,' still exclaim the critics in approaching his works. . . . Hailed as the most conspicuous artist of the French school [and] praised for the fact of his perfect technical skill, [his] accuracy of detail is such that his diminutive figures bear the magnifying lens with a result that excites wondering admiration." The lionized Meissonier was honored with medals and decorations by the governments of England, Holland, Belgium, Germany, Spain and Russia. The artist labored for some fourteen years on his commemoration of Napoleon's victory over Russian and Prussian armies on June 14, 1807. He even hired a troop of cavalry to gallop over a wheatfield so that he could study the result. To A. T. Stewart, the American merchant prince who bought the picture, he wrote, "I wanted to paint Napoleon at the zenith of

116

his glory. . . . The Battle of Friedland, already commenced, was necessary to add to the enthusiasm of the soldiers and make the subject stand forth. . . . The soldiers cry out to him that they are his, and the great chief, whose imperial will directs the masses that move around him, salutes his devoted army." "I am convinced, and I have a certain pride in the avowal, that it is one of those works the value of which will increase with time . . . what has been said [against it] will pass away; but the work itself will remain an honor to us both." Stewart paid $60,000 for the painting. At his death in 1887, it was auctioned off at a far higher price; people rose in homage as the picture was placed on the stand. It was later presented to the Metropolitan, and the Museum's catalog of the 1890's devotes several pages to it—but only a few sentences to its recently acquired Manets, *The Boy with a Sword* and *The Woman with a Parrot*. Manet reportedly said of this painting, "Everything in it is steel except the swords."

American Painting

COPLEY, John Singleton
• **117. Mrs. Sylvanus Bourne.** (1766) Vigorous in handling and forceful in design, this is a fine example of the rugged art which the precocious Copley evolved almost on his own—a style notable for its organization, vivid feeling and keen characterization. The sharply defined planes of the face and the folds of the dress give substance to the forms. Face, dress and chair are linked across the canvas by zones of light and shade and an emphatic line which reinforces the bold masses. Brown, green and white build up a harmony of restraint and richness. The sitter was the daughter of Colonel John Gorham and a descendant of early Cape Cod settlers; she lived in Falmouth.

117

1

PRATT, Matthew

● **118. The American School.** (About 1765)   Pratt's masterpiece plays on the recession of four figures from left foreground into center background, balanced at right by a fifth figure before an easel. Depth is accentuated by the green units at left, in the center and in the chair at right. The figure at right, silhouetted against the rectangle of the canvas, is especially arresting. Pratt depicts Benjamin West's studio school in London, a mecca for American painters. West is at left, discussing a drawing held by the smiling Pratt, one of his first pupils. The three others are unidentified. West, the first American-born artist to directly affect European painting, settled in London in 1760. He was court painter to King George III and succeeded Reynolds in 1791 as President of the Royal Academy.

ALLSTON, Washington

● **119. The Deluge.** (1804)   This eerie vision of the Biblical flood is the first major American painting to blend mysticism with romanticism. The carefully calculated design presents a repertoire of chilling images—storm, waves, heavy clouds, desolation, drowned corpses, writhing serpents and a howling wolf—but potential melodrama is avoided through restraint. A sense of dramatic space results from the effective use of dark tonal masses and the rhythmic and remorseless succession of oncoming horizontals. Painted in Paris, *The Deluge* may have been inspired by Poussin's *Deluge* in the Louvre, but Allston infuses his painting with a peculiarly American quality which almost seems to prefigure Poe.

MORSE, Samuel Finley Breese

● **120. The Muse—Susan Walker Morse.** (About 1835-37)   This facile, grandiose portrait emulates the splendor of van Dyck and the English portraitists. Handling is crisp and color shimmering; the dress is treated with special vivacity. Morse's last major painting, this oil was made shortly before he completed the first prac-

120

tical telegraph. A professor at the newly-founded New York University, Morse was then occupying the top room of a tower on Washington Square which would later become Winslow Homer's New York studio. Despite the artist's poverty, the picture is sumptuous and aristocratic, even to the stone urn and baluster. The sitter, Morse's oldest child Susan, is depicted at about seventeen. In 1844 she married Edward Lind, a Puerto Rican planter who later took a native mistress. Her son went to Paris to study painting and died there. While returning to New York after the death of her husband, Mrs. Lind either jumped or fell into the sea. This painting was shown in the Rotunda of the Capitol in 1837, at a time when Morse hoped to get an important art commission from Congress. In 1873 it was among the paintings in the Metropolitan's first loan exhibition.

COLE, Thomas

• **121. The Oxbow.** (1836) In one of Cole's first panoramic landscapes, foreground is dramatized by blasted trees reminiscent of Ruisdael. The oval line of the river gives novel variety to an expanse of fields, and a thunderstorm evokes a Byronic spirit. The umbrella at right, the sketchbox, the portfolio marked "T. Cole," and the presence of the artist's easel amid the solitude heighten the romantic feeling and provide scale by which to gauge the spaciousness of the landscape. The Oxbow is a scenic point on the Connecticut River near Northampton, Massachusetts.

HARNETT, William Michael

• **122. Music and Good Luck.** (1888) The initial delight of this beguiling painting stems from its masterly illusion of reality and the nostalgic charm of its subject matter. But it is in the complex harmonies of form and space that the still life achieves its true artistic power: the precision and sensitivity of the arrangement recall, surprisingly, fine Cubist compositions; verticals, horizontals and graceful curves are related and opposed as Harnett plays on projection and recession to create a counterplay of resolved

121

tensions. The dominant violin shape is framed by a rectangle established by the edge of the cupboard door at one end and the bow and hinges at the other. This design is echoed by the framework around the cupboard door, while the sequence is contrasted by the diagonal of the music sheet and the piccolo and even by the placement of the artist's calling card. Further enrichment is afforded by the shapes of the horseshoe and the padlock. Depth is stressed by accentuating the shadows and in such elements as the projecting nails and the tear in the sheet of music. Color is delicate and mellow. This is the only painting in which Harnett juxtaposed dark forms against a light background.

MOUNT, William Sidney

• **123. Long Island Farm Houses.** (Date unknown) Mount's most famous landscape rejects the bigness of the Hudson River School for a direct, intimate glimpse of country living. In its informal appeal, the picture recalls something of the vivid modern approach to landscape painting. Space is defined through the curving fence and the willow tree, which are contrasted with the straight lines of the buildings and a succession of horizontals from road to fence. A beguiling touch is the children's costuming, based on Civil War uniforms.

BINGHAM, George Caleb

• **124. Fur Traders Descending the Missouri.** (Before 1845) Bingham's most poetic and unusual scene of pioneer life on the Missouri River, this memorable frontier vision is achieved through the simplest of means. Its haunting mood results largely from the contrast of hazy space with the well-defined figures and the distant trees and shore. Sky merges with glossy water to form a romantic setting for the gliding dugout canoe. The bemused trapper and dreamy boy seem to float soundlessly in an isolated, mysterious world, an effect strengthened by the still silhouette of the pet—possibly a bear cub. The Missouri was at the time of this painting the main artery for the beaver and otter fur trade centered in St. Louis; beaver hats were going out of fashion, however, and the scene Bingham captures was about to vanish. In 1845 this painting and three other Binghams were among the prizes awarded in an annual nation-wide art lottery sponsored by the Art Union; the lottery was dissolved in 1851.

3   124

JOHNSON, Eastman

• **125. The Hatch Family.** (1871)   Johnson's tableau of a wealthy New York family in the age of colossal fortunes skillfully groups three generations—fifteen persons—against a backdrop of Victorian American splendor. The figures are deftly linked by gesture and pose. The color notes of their clothes act as contrast and relief to the vivid red curtains. High space lends a stage-like scale to the grouping. Clear, thin color and minimal modeling add an appeal of decorative charm. Alfrederic Smith Hatch, investment banker and railroad tycoon who later became president of the New York Stock Exchange, is seated at his desk. Mrs. Hatch leans against the mantelpiece. Second from the door is Frederick N. Hatch, who founded a famous mission in Water Street, and in 1926 gave this painting to the Metropolitan. The room is the library of the new Hatch home at Park Avenue and Thirty-Seventh Street. The artist received $1,000 for each of the fifteen faces. When the infant was born after the painting had been begun, Johnson was sent a telegram saying, "Another Hatch, another thousand."

INNESS, George

• **126. Peace and Plenty.** (1865)   One of the most famous 19th Century American landscapes, this early Inness transforms the grandiose style of the Hudson River School into a light-suffused, idyllic vista. The execution is coherent and strong; details, suppressed or modified to preserve breadth and simplicity, merge into a majestic pastoral of bounty. The composite landscape is as convincing as an actual view. Massive elms are the pivotal units, their solidity lending distance to the radiant sky. Sheaves of grain and minute figures serve to create an airy, spacious foreground, from which the fields flow off into a hillside hazy with the setting sun. Compared with Inness' later work, the handling is still tight and refined, and the intimate glimpse of nature in his mature landscapes is lacking; in the Metropolitan's *Evening at Medfield, Massachusetts* and *Spring Blossoms,* for instance, the breadth and scope of forms are drastically simplified and light is more subtly implied, more glowing and evanescent. But *Peace and Plenty* is still an effective paen to the serene America the artist hoped for after the end of the Civil War. The sense of autumnal fruitfulness and the fertile, well-kept land sustain the

125   1?

poetry of the title. The picture was painted in New Jersey from studies made near Medfield, where the painter lived until 1864.

CHURCH, Frederick Edwin

• **127. Heart of the Andes.** (1859)   This classic of the gargantuan aspect of the Hudson River School blends photographic realism with the romantic lure of far places. Its sweeping vista ranges from snow-topped peaks to tropical fauna. The brownish tonality is varied by the misty notes of the stream, trees and plants near the center. In 1853 and 1857, Church journeyed to Ecuador, inspired by Alexander von Humboldt's "Kosmos," the famous explorer's rhapsody to the landscape of South America. Church entranced the New York public by exhibiting this work in a darkened room, illuminated by gas jets and flanked by dried Ecuadorian foliage. The picture also created a stir in England.

BIERSTADT, Albert

• **128. The Rocky Mountains.** (1863)   The idylls of the Hudson River School gave way at about the time of this painting to detailed and vast landscape panoramas. The new style delighted the public with romantic glimpses of the still unexplored West and with the always-popular enjoyment of viewing a work of patience and skill. In addition, such paintings were deemed ideal for the mammoth new mansions of the period. In 1858, after touring in Europe, Bierstadt joined General Frederick Lander's expedition to survey the wilderness from the Mississippi to Southern Oregon. This painting, based on sketches made during the trip, most likely shows Mount Lander, now called Fremont Pass, in Wyoming's Windy River mountain range. The Indians are Shoshones. The grandeur of nature is depicted with minute surface detail, softness of atmosphere and spaciousness. The focal points of waterfall and lake provide luminous contrasts to the dark trees, grass and mountains.

WHISTLER, James Abbott McNeill

• **129. Portrait of Théodore Duret: Arrangement in Flesh Color and Black.** (1883)   For Whistler, a portrait was primarily an arrangement. (His celebrated portrayal of his mother, for instance, he called *Arrangement in Grey and Black*.) A portrait, Whistler maintained, should catch "an aroma of the personality . . . and, with all that, it should be a picture, a pattern, an arrangement, a harmony, such as only a painter could conceive." Here, the artist

128

adapts the more robust and luminous approaches of Velázquez
and Manet to his own idiom of delicate texture and fastidious
color. Forms are flattened into a simplified silhouette. Color notes
add subtle refinement: the dark grey suit, for instance, sets off the
pastel pink cape; the vermillion note of the fan echoes the ruddy
flesh; the white of the shirt and glove contributes an appealing
interval between face, fan and cape. Behind the figure, the light
grey wall and darker grey floor complete the elegant harmony.
The portrait seems almost effortless, but it was scraped and repainted some ten times. It resulted from a discussion in which
Whistler, who along with Duret and some friends had seen an
exhibition of portraits of red-robed dignitaries, contended that
modern man must be painted in contemporary clothes. Whistler
asked Duret to pose for this portrait to prove that an artist could
make modern evening clothes part of a fine composition. Thédore
Duret was a famous art-critic and a friend of Whistler. In his
1904 biography of the artist, he recalled this painting: "He made
me stand before a hanging of pinkish grey. He had used the
domino [cape] also to determine the character which the picture
was to have, a gentleman entering a ballroom. And further, it had
permitted him to escape from the stiff parallelism of the two sides
of the body and to diversify the contours." The Museum purchased the painting from Duret in 1913.

HOMER, Winslow
• **130. Northeaster.** (1895)   This lean, taut marine masterpiece
is rendered with eloquent simplicity. A massive thrust of rock
forms a strong diagonal base and, cut off abruptly at both ends,
creates a dynamic close-up effect. Towering cascades of spray
silhouette its slant and solidity, while flecks of brown-red relate
to the marble-like veining of the emerald green water. The restless movement is set off by an overcast grey-violet sky. Homer,
who loved storm-tossed seas, painted this and other seascapes at
Prouts Neck, near Portland, Maine. On a promontory overlook-

129

ing the Atlantic, he built a studio and set up a portable shelter on runners (with a plate glass window and a stove) in which he could be close to spray and surf and capture the effects of time and tide. Shown at the Pennsylvania Academy of Fine Arts in 1895, *Northeaster* won Homer his first award.

• **131. The Gulf Stream.** (1899)   Homer's most famous oil is a magnificent piece of illustration, vividly colored and handled with striking facility. Its finest passages occur in the surge of the waves, the alternating bands of sunlight and shade on the water and the gliding movements of the waiting sharks. But its story-telling so dominates the painting that it fails to rank with Homer's finest masterpieces. *The Gulf Stream* evolved from a watercolor of sharks swarming about a deserted sailboat which Homer made on his first trip to Bermuda—about 1885. (The sketch is now in the Cooper Union Museum.) Homer priced this final version at $4,000, his highest demand up to that time, and was chagrined when it remained unsold. One museum almost bought it, but two women on the board of trustees felt it was "unpleasant." It may have been these ladies who, in 1902, angered Homer by asking his dealer what the painting was meant to show. The artist replied: "I regret very much I have painted a picture that requires any description. The subject of this picture is comprised of its title. . . . The boat and sharks are outside matters of very little consequence. They have been blown out to sea by a hurricane. You can tell these ladies that the unfortunate Negro who is now so dazed and parboiled, will be rescued [,] returned to his friends and home and ever after lived happily." In 1906 Homer sent *The Gulf Stream* to a National Academy Exhibition, marked with the definitely higher price of $5,000. The jury immediately recommended the painting to the Metropolitan, which acquired it three days later for $4,500.

• **132. Searchlight: Harbor Entrance, Santiago de Cuba.** (1901) A crucial event in the Spanish-American War of 1898 was the blockading of Admiral Cervera's fleet at Santiago de Cuba by Commodore Schley. On July 3, when Cervera tried to escape to the open sea, the Americans sank four of his cruisers and three destroyers. On July 17 Santiago surrendered, and on July 26 the Spanish government sued for peace. In painting the defeat of the Spaniards (suggested by obsolete cannons, an old watchtower and

132

the ominous searchlights), Homer expresses drama through austere arrangement, rather than by story-telling. The understatement results in a picture of grandeur and suspense. The design is based on two potent pictorial factors: silhouetted masses and variations on horizontal lines. Tower, parapet and cannon fuse into a single mass. The stone base, cannon, parapet, dim horizon and sky make up the horizontal motif, while the diagonal inward slant of the stone step, the looming tower and the illumination from the searchlight provide eloquent contrasts. Against the dominant blues and blacks, Homers intrudes only a few color oppositions—the brownish terrace and the white on the parapet. The small half-moon and the sky seen through the arch suggest far space. Homer had sketched the old cannons on the ramparts of the Spanish fort at Santiago several years before the war—in 1885. The searchlight idea came to him in 1898, when he read news reports of Schley's blockade. When a critic remarked of this painting that something in it "repels [us so] that we cannot say that it is beautiful," Homer retorted it "was not intended to be *beautiful*."

EAKINS, Thomas Cowperthwait

• **133. Max Schmitt in a Single Scull.** (1871) Sober, dispassionate realism blends with high craftsmanship in this remarkable painting. The work of a young man of twenty-two just back from four years of study in Europe, the picture is astonishing in its appreciation of the local scene, untinged by European picturesqueness or mannerisms. Eakins shows Max Schmitt, a boyhood friend and well-known rower, seated in his shell "Josie." Eakins himself appears in the second scull, on the stern of which are his signature and the date. The place is the Schuylkill River, not far from the present Philadelphia Museum of Art. The picture captures with crystal clarity the crisp, warm atmosphere and languid mood of an autumn day. The unrippled expanse of water is delicately varied by the diagonal of the racing shell, while the back-

133

ground sculls play key roles in the composition's striking space effect. The severe regularity of the bridges is countered by the floating clouds. The paint surface is smooth and dry, but vigorous. "A boat is the hardest thing I know of to put into perspective," Eakins once said. "It is so much like the human figure, there is something alive about it." Appropriately he began this picture with precise scale drawings of the boats, oars and bridges.

CASSATT, Mary

• **134. Lady at the Tea Table.** (1883-85)   Simplicity and incisive characterization mark this restrained but striking portrait—a personal synthesis of the light and crispness of Manet and Degas and the flattened masses of Japanese prints. The dark blue dress, its curved silhouette set off by the soft blue wall, is balanced by the glossy hair and the chinaware. The gold ornamentation of the tea-set relates to the picture frame which forms a straight line behind the curves of hair and cape. The sense of the sitter's aloofness and details such as the hand reveal Miss Cassatt's expressive drawing and grasp of personality. The mood is informal and vivid, yet dignified. The sitter was Mrs. Robert Moore Riddle, a first cousin of Miss Cassatt's mother. The portrait was painted in return for Mrs. Riddle's hospitality to the Cassatts in London and for a gift of china—perhaps the set shown in the picture. Apparently the Riddles—"not very artistic in their likes and dislikes of pictures," according to the artist's mother—rejected the portrait, and it was put away. But in 1914, as Mrs. Henry O. Havemeyer has recalled, "Miss Cassatt showed me the *Lady at the Tea Table* and said, 'Tell me, what do you think of that?' I looked and answered, 'Very fine. Why have you never shown it before?' 'The family did not like it, and I was so disappointed. . . .' 'Well, I care for it,' I said hotly, 'and so will others,' and I insisted that it be shown. It was the sensation of the exhibition in the Rue Lafayette in 1914 [and] both the Luxembourg and the Petit Palais were anxious to have it." In 1923, the artist gave the portrait to the Metropolitan.

RYDER, Albert Pinkham

• **135. Toilers of the Sea.** (Date undetermined)   In this small panel, Ryder condenses the immensity, motion and mystery of the nocturnal sea. The haunting vision is organized simply on horizontals of sky and water, broken by the diagonal direction of the boat. The small craft seems to leap toward the moon, its form outlined by spray. The horizontal light at the edge of the sea gives immensity to space; the clouds echo the swirl of spray. Fused with the broad masses are color notes of blue-blacks and dark blues. Ryder probably borrowed the name for this picture from the title of Victor Hugo's novel about fishermen. When Ryder exhibited the painting in 1884, he wrote this verse for his catalog: "With the shifting skies/ over the billowing foam/ the hardy fisher flies/ to his island home." Ryder paintings like this recall Marsden Hartley's apt words: "Ryder is, I think, the special messenger of the sea's beauty, the confidant of its majesties."

• **136. Moonlight Marine.** (About 1880-90) In the force of its stark design and the inventiveness of its forms, this Ryder reaches a peak of hypnotic power. The sea is subordinate to the drama of the magnificent sky, in which dark, almost abstract silhouettes set off moonlit areas of phosphorescent ivory and emerald green. The darker mass of the boat links the patterns of the sky with the sea, while the perspective suggests infinite space. Broad, almost two-dimensional color masses are somehow invested with depth and solidity. Moonlit skies obsessed the painter, who loved to sit at midnight in Manhattan's Battery Park or stand on the deck of a ship and lose himself in what he described as "the eternal firmament with its ever-changing panorama of mystery and beauty." This picture's breathtaking simplicity of form and color exemplify his concentration on emotion rather than appearance. "The artist should fear to become the slave of detail," he said. "He should strive to express his thought and not the surface of it. What avails a storm cloud accurate in form and color if the storm is not therein?"

SARGENT, John Singer

• **137. Madame X. (Mme. Gautreau)** (1884) Sargent's most famous portrait, painted when he was only twenty-eight, depicts a chic Parisian beauty and arbiter of fashion. The artful simplicity of the pose and the quiet background set off the lithe figure in gleaming black satin. The stunning rendering of flesh (which recalls Manet) achieves a luminous translucence, while the restrained indication of folds in the dress adds subdued animation to the figure. The graceful curves of the hem and the table base complete an arresting composition in which what was later to become an addiction to bravura flourishes is sharply controlled. The woman's distinctly individual features—the sharp profile, slender neck, reddish hair, black eyebrows and even the pink luster of the ear—suggest a keen eye for characterization. Madame X was born Virginia Avengo, the daughter of a Louisiana

135

Confederate officer who was killed at the Battle of Shiloh. Her widowed mother brought her to Paris, where some twenty years later Miss Avengo married a banker named Gautreau and became a prominent figure in Parisian society. When Sargent was introduced to the lady, he wrote a friend, "I have a great desire to paint her portrait . . . and have reason to think she would allow it and is waiting for someone to propose this homage to her. [You] might tell her that I am a man of prodigious talent." The lady consented, but Sargent soon lamented "struggling with the unpaintable beauty and hopeless laziness of Miss Gautreau." Her flesh color was "a uniform lavender of blotting-paper color all over [but] she has most beautiful lines." Sargent finished the portrait after some thirty sittings and sent it to the Salon of 1884, where its mysterious title fooled few. The painting was ridiculed scathingly in the press. One critic jeered at the daring gown: "One more struggle and the lady will be free. . . ." The skin color was called "at once cadaverous and clownlike." Mme. Gautreau's mother accused Sargent of making her daughter the laughing stock of Paris and pleaded with him to remove the painting from exhibition. Sargent refused. Within a few years, however, the painting was widely praised, and the now world-famous artist, realizing that his youthful portrait was among his finest achievements, refused to sell it. It remained in his studio until 1905, when he sent it to the Pan-American Exposition in St. Louis and wrote the Metropolitan: "My portrait of Madame Gautreau is now in America. I rather feel inclined to let it stay there if a museum should want it. I suppose it is the best thing I have done. I would let the Metropolitan Museum have it for 1,000 pounds." The offer was accepted.

• **138. Mr. and Mrs. Isaac Newton Phelps Stokes.** (1897)   This jaunty double portrait demonstrates anew Sargent's skill with dazzling surface effects, especially in the handling of the starched skirt, perky jacket, belt and yellow straw hat. But despite the

138

bravura emphasis on her costume, it is the woman's face that retains dominion over the portrait. The tall man in the loosely worn suit serves largely to repeat the grace of her slender figure. Sargent's apparent spontaneity is in fact the result of patient work and many changes. Mrs. Stokes posed some twenty-eight times, and her head was repainted nine times. The painting was begun as a portrait of only Mrs. Stokes, arrayed in an evening dress, but when she came to one sitting in boating costume, Sargent decided to alter the picture. He had also originally included a Great Dane, but substituted the straw hat for the dog. He later added Mr. Stokes to complete the composition. Isaac Stokes, an architect, was the son of a banker, merchant and real estate tycoon who helped found the Metropolitan Museum.

DAVIES, Arthur Bowen

• **139. Unicorns.** (1906)   On the eve of explosive changes in American painting, Davies, one of the most modern-minded of American artists, chose to paint this romantic picture on an outmoded theme. But if *Unicorns* seems at first to belong to a bygone age, the quality of its design, its poetic feeling and its avoidance of sentimentality make it truly timeless. Asymmetrically arranged within a slow-paced horizontal sequence, the mountains, horizon, shoreline, figures and unicorns take on a stately processional aspect. The land projecting into the water intensifies the fresh disposition of masses and the carefully calculated balance. Melodic blues and browns unify the picture, while hints of Florentine painting, Medieval tapestry and Persian prints run through its charmed surface. The year before this picture, Davies had visited the West Coast, and the water and mountains he depicts here may be based on California landscape. In Medieval lore unicorns signified chastity, love and Christ.

MARIN, John

The Metropolitan owns superb examples of John Marin's work. The following are among the finest:

• **140. London Omnibus.** (1908)   Bands of color trace structure and activity, while the brevity and swing of the lines create a rhythmic beat. The bands above the vehicle anticipate the abstract

139

frames Marin later painted around his main forms. In fact, this early work, made during his only trip to Europe, is the first indication of Marin's personal style.

• **141. Rock and Scrub Pine, Small Point, Maine.** (1916) Large areas of white paper set off fluid colors handled with great economy.

142. Lower Manhattan from the River, No. 1. (1921) Recorded with compressed energy, the big masses of buildings, the churning water and the impact of sky are contained within a warm frame of tone and color. "When I got what I wanted," explained Marin, "I nailed the stuff down in those frames."

• **143. Mark Island and Light from Deer Island, Maine.** (1922) Terseness, bold authority of color and near-abstraction mark this watercolor. A dynamic sky of grey-blue and crimson arches over the blue-green trees, the island and the water.

• **144. Phippsburg, Maine.** (1932) Translucent washes of blue symbolize sky. Dynamic formations of earth and grass add vitality to the landscape. The grey wash of the frame stabilizes tossing lines and planes.

143

144

HARTLEY, Marsden

• **145. Portrait of a German Officer.** (1914) Shortly before
World War I, Hartley abandoned his dark, Ryder-like landscapes
and painted brilliantly colored abstractions influenced by his contact with Kandinsky, Klee and Franz Marc. These paintings are
among the boldest of American pioneer abstractions, and this
"portrait" is perhaps the finest of the series. Blaring, simplified
forms emerge from a flat background in a harmony of vivid contrasts. Bright colors and passages of black and white, circles and
curves, triangles and rectangles, are placed in symmetrical order.
The painting is not a complete abstraction, but a medley of military insignia and paraphernalia including pennants, epaulettes,
regimental banners, the Iron Cross, a lance and spurs. Hartley
was living in Germany in 1914, and this painting is a memorial
to a friend, a German officer killed early in the war. The officer's
initials, K v. F, appear at lower left.

HOPPER, Edward

• **146. From Williamsburg Bridge.** (1928) With simplicity and
seeming casualness, Hopper creates a vivid glimpse of a passing
scene. To increase the impromptu effect, the bridge railing and
the buildings are abruptly cropped. A downward slant suggests
swift movement, while the horizontal mass of the tenements restores stability to the design. In catching the character of the
buildings and the hard light on their worn walls, Hopper creates
depth and substance by contrasting their solidity against fleecy
clouds. Amidst the blank windows, a single person appears,
heightening a typical Hopper mood—loneliness in a big city.
Williamsburg Bridge, built in 1903, spans the East River from
Manhattan to northern Brooklyn.

DEMUTH, Charles

• **147. I Saw the Figure 5 in Gold.** (1928) This is the finest and
most famous of Demuth's series of symbolic compositions called

145

poster portraits. Its odd and seemingly-unrelated forms—like the triple repetition of "5" which floats and recedes against the background—appear merely decorative, but are actually an homage to the artist's friend, the poet William Carlos Williams, and to a Williams poem which has the same name as this painting. Williams' first name—"Bill"—appears at top right, and his initials— "WCW"—are painted in at bottom center; "Carlos" appears in electric lights on a skyscraper. The poem which Demuth celebrates reads, "Among the rain/ and lights/ I saw the figure 5/ in gold/ on a red/ firetruck/ moving/ tense/ unheeded/ to gong clangs/ siren howls/ and wheels rumbling/ through the dark city." (From the *Complete Collected Poems* of William Carlos Williams, New Directions. 1938.) Recalling the poet's vivid, fragmentary visions and broken lines, Demuth's images are ordered into a syncopated formation, terse in tempo and fastidious.

SHEELER, Charles

148. Golden Gate. (1955)   Sheeler combines visual fact, imaginative vision and near-abstract design in a taut composition of powerful impact. High-keyed colors evoke both solidity and airiness. With a limited palette, streamlined design and an exciting angle of vision, the painting depicts a soaring contemporary "cathedral." The artist was seventy-two when he painted this subject; he referred to it as "a gateway, a beckoning into the new."

O'KEEFFE, Georgia

• **149. Cow's Skull; Red, White and Blue.** (1931)   A cross-like symbol of life and death, the mystic skull dominates a novel formal design. A thin line down the center of the skull relates it to the heavy black vertical behind it. White is contrasted against black and blue. The simplicity of the setting gives full play to the delicate complexity of the skull's inner structure. Dark and light blues suggest sky and space. An abstract border of thick bars frames the elegant but emotion-charged image. As in her famous flower paintings, like the Metropolitan's *Black Iris,* Miss O'Keeffe's

close-up effect (derived in part from modern photography) gives starkness to the object and allows the eye to explore new-found beauty in the structure of familiar objects. This is one of a series of animal skulls and bones painted against the skies of New Mexico.

DICKINSON, Edwin

• **150. Ruin at Daphne.** (1943-53) This haunting image of transformed bits of architecture evolved slowly over a period of ten years; even after the painting entered the Museum collection, the artist was reluctant to call it fully resolved. With fastidious control, Dickinson conjures up an archeological maze in which eerie visions create a dramatic mood of desolation. Black, silver, violet-grey, blue and the surprising note of vermillion deepen the ghostly feeling. The fluted column is a focus of the rhythmic movement, while deep space is projected by the triple arch and a web of winding lines. Sculpture fragments, the flight of birds and the mirror of the pool cast lyric and cryptic overtones. The picture may be an allegory on art, fate or the remembrance of things past. Among the sources of inspiration, according to the artist, were Roman ruins at Arles and in Syria.

KUNIYOSHI, Yasuo

• **151. Exit.** (1948-49) Kuniyoshi's later paintings, with their tissue-thin glazes of fragile color, often comment on the state of the world. *Exit,* mingling images derived from Japanese masks, kites and other imaginative objects, celebrates the inglorious departure of war-makers. Its vivid hues adhere to the artist's philosophy of color: "In a world of festive dead-pan, the grimness of reality is heightened by the colors of unreality." The sweeping curves of the hat, man and horse relieve the vertical rigidity of the composition. The over-dressed rider and toy-like horse suggest a pompous pretender, an effect underscored by an over-sized Napoleonic hat. The gesture of the hands in the background signifies expulsion from Paradise.

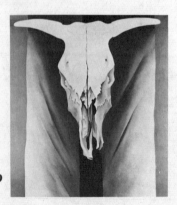

149

GORKY, Arshile

• **152. Water of the Flowery Mill.** (1944) In this composition, Gorky fuses reality with imagination. Resplendent and lyric, it turns natural forms into masses of sumptuous color cascading across the canvas. The vague suggestions of water, trees, flowers and the summer heat have overtones of voluptuousness and sensuality. The shapes sweep about so freely that the effect is of running movement. The handling is deft and rollicking.

POLLOCK, Jackson

• **153. Autumn Rhythm.** (1950) Serpentine patterns intertwine in a sprawling sweep of graceful rhythms. By restricting color chiefly to black and Indian red, Pollock gives maximum emphasis to the oscillating lines. They flow in an insistent surge, without beginning or end.

BLUME, Peter

154. South of Scranton. (1931) When this painting was awarded first prize in the Carnegie International of 1934, the artist explained that it presented an imaginative combination of sights he saw on an auto trip from Scranton, Pennsylvania, to Charleston, South Carolina: "The mountains of waste coal around Scranton, the deep quarries like bottomless chasms . . . the coal breakers that sprawled over the landscape like huge, prehistoric monsters, the miniature locomotive that puffed with busy agility around them . . . to these industrial details I next added the old streets with false front houses. [From] Charleston I took the broad, flat waters of its harbor and the German cruiser Emden which came into port one day, with its bristling, fighting masts and its German sailors whom I watched doing complicated calisthentic exercises on its enormous deck—all making a curious contrast with the atmosphere of the old town—as I tried to weld my

152

153

impressions into the picture, they lost all their logical connection." The jarring variety of forms is actually combined into a coherent order. The gun turret with its light and dark color is balanced by the yellow walls, the coal pile and the quarry. The jumping men lead to the street. The curve at the top of the deck matches the winding path of the quarry. Sky and water bind the forms together, even as they set them off so sharply.

WYETH, Andrew

• **155. A Crow Flew By.** (1949-50)   Overtones of loneliness and age are artfully implied through an arrangement of a figure against a large wall surface varied by the patterns of wrinkled garments. The contrasts of light and shade seem to symbolize life and death. In an article in Art News, the painter Elaine de Kooning recalled that Wyeth, out driving one September day, noticed Ben Loper, a Negro whom he had known all his life, standing in front of his shack. A few days later, the artist walked inside and found the man hunched over in the dim room, "a beam of sunlight settling for a moment in a blazing yellow triangle around one eye." The artist never again saw that light on his sitter's face, but in it he had found the spiritual focus of his theme. It took Wyeth about a month to persuade Loper to pose. According to Wyeth, "the clothes on the wall are symbols of a man's whole life lined up." The odd title came to Wyeth when a slow-witted boy kept opening and closing the door to the room in which he was painting. When Wyeth asked what he was looking for, the boy answered cryptically, "A crow flew by."

Some notable sculpture in the museum:

Assyrian. *Winged Bull* (from the Palace of Assurnasirpal at Nimrud), 825-20 B.C., stone relief.

Aztec. *Standard-Bearer,* from Vera Cruz, Mexico. About 1480-91, laminated limestone.

Bourdelle, Antoine, 1861-1929. *Hercules,* 1909, bronze.

Chinese. Kuan Yin, 618-906, painted wood.

Cyprus. *Procession of Two Chariots with Advance Guard*, about 560-40 B.C., sarcophagus, limestone.

Degas, Edgar, 1834-1917. *Girl Dancer at Fourteen*, 1880, bronze and fabric. Also, all but about two of the 73 bronzes cast from Degas' original works in wax.

Egyptian. *Sphinx of Queen Hatshepsut*, about 1496-80 B.C., red granite.

Two statues of *King Amun-Hotep III*, about 1397-60 B.C., porphyritic diorite.

Flannagan, John B., 1898-1942. *Figure of Dignity—Irish Mountain Goat*, date undetermined, stone.

Gothic. *The Virgin and Child*, 1200, painted wood.

St. James the Less, 1265-80 (German), painted wood.

Two Holy Women, 15th Century (Flemish), painted and gilded wood.

Greek (and Hellenistic). *Horse*, 8th Century B.C., bronze.

● *Statue of a Youth* (Kouros), about 600 B.C., marble.

Horse, about 480-70 B.C., bronze.

Horseman, 400 B.C., Roman copy of a Greek relief, marble.

Mourning Woman, about 400 B.C., marble.

Aphrodite, Roman copy of a lost Greek work of about 300 B.C.

Old Market Woman, 200 B.C., marble.

Eros, 250-150 B.C., bronze.

Houdon, Jean Antoine, 1741-1828. *The Bather*, 1782, marble.

Indian. *Vishnu*, by Dasoja of Balligrame, Mysore, about 1200, bronze.

Parvati, about 900, bronze.

Iranian. *Head of a Ruler*, about 200 B.C., patinated cast.

Bull's Head, about 500 B.C., bituminous limestone.

Incense Burner in the Shape of a Feline, 1181-82, bronze.

Lippold, Richard, born 1915. *Variation Within a Sphere, No. 10, The Sun*, 1953-56, gold wire.

Maillol, Aristide, 1861-1944. *Chained Action*, 1906?, bronze.

Female Torso, 1929, bronze.

Michel, Claude (called Clodion), 1738-1814. *Satyr and Bacchante*, about 1775, terra cotta.

Noguchi, Isamu, born 1904. *Kouros*, 1944-45, marble.

Powers, Hiram, 1805-73. *General Andrew Jackson*, about 1835, marble.

De Rivera, José, born 1904. *Homage to the Art of Minkowski*, 1955, stainless steel, forged rod.

Della Robbia, Andrea, 1435-1525. *The Archangel Michael*, about 1475, enameled terra cotta.

Rodin, Auguste, 1840-1917. *Age of Bronze*, 1876, bronze.

Walking Man, 1877-78, bronze.

Adam, 1880, bronze.

Eve, 1881, bronze.

The Thinker, 1870-1900, plaster.

Portrait of Puvis de Chavannes, 1891, bronze.

Beside the Sea, 1905, marble.

Roman. *Dionysus, The Four Seasons, Satyrs and Maenads,* about 270, marble, sarcophagus.

Saint-Gaudens, Augustus, 1848-1907. *Diana,* date uncertain, gilded bronze.

Sansovino, Jacob, 1486-1570. *Pluto and Cerberus,* date uncertain, bronze.

Sumerian. *Head of Gudea, Governor of Lagash,* about 2150 B.C., diorite.

Statue of Gudea, about 2150 B.C., diorite.

Thailand. *Buddha Explaining the Law,* 800-900, bronze.

Vischer, Peter, about 1455-1529. *Self-Portrait,* date uncertain, bronze.

Zorach, William, born 1887. *Mother and Child,* 1927-30, marble.

THE MUSEUM OF MODERN ART

53rd Street between Fifth & Sixth Avenues.
CI 5-8900

Hours: Mondays through Saturdays 11-6 (Thursdays 11-9); Sundays 12-6. Closed Christmas Day. Admission: adults $1; children under sixteen 25¢; group rates 50¢ (inquire at Secretary's office).
Transportation: All Fifth Avenue Buses to 52nd Street; Sixth Avenue Bus to 53rd Street. Eighth Avenue IND "E" Train or Sixth Avenue IND "F" Train to Fifth Avenue station.
Talks: Gallery talks Thursdays at 6, Fridays and Saturdays at 3:30. Frequent lectures and symposia in auditorium.
Films: Daily in auditorium.
Reference Library: Fourth floor.
Sales and Loans: Art and book shop; main entrance. Pictures and small sculptures from galleries available to Museum members for monthly rental or purchase; sixth floor.
Restaurants: Garden Cafeteria (Mondays through Saturdays, lunch 11:30-2:30, tea 2:30-5:45; Sundays, lunch 12-2:30, tea 2:30-5:45; Thursdays, dinner 6-8). Penthouse Cafeteria, for Museum members and their guests only (every day, lunch and tea 11-5:30; Thursdays, dinner 6-8).

The Museum of Modern Art is the only museum in the world with a permanent collection drawn from *all* the contemporary visual arts—not only painting, sculpture, drawings and prints, but photography, architecture, industrial and commercial design, films and posters.

Founded in 1929 by five forward-looking collectors—Miss Lillie P. Bliss, Mrs. John D. Rockefeller, Jr., Mrs. Cornelius J. Sullivan, A. Conger Goodyear and Frank Crowninshield—the Museum opened its doors at a time when the American public had little immediate contact with modern art. Its first director was twenty-seven-year-old Alfred H. Barr, Jr., who is today Director of Museum Collections.

In 1939, after a succession of rented locations, the Museum moved into its present building, designed by Philip Goodwin and Edward D. Stone and erected on the site of the former Rockefeller mansion. The first show in the new building was a three-floor survey of Picasso.

The Museum's collection has grown to some 20,000 items, including 1,800 paintings, 700 drawings and 7,000 prints. The Museum has mounted over 600 loan exhibitions—many of them landmark presentations of ideas, movements and masters of modern art—and has circulated traveling shows to thousands of institutions in the United States and nearly fifty foreign countries.

Choosing the best work from a period crowded with conflicting concepts has led Director Barr to comment: "Of course, artistic values change, and today's masterpiece is sometimes tomorrow's bore. The Museum is aware that it may often guess wrong in its acquisitions. When it acquires a dozen recent paintings, it will be lucky if in ten years three will still seem worth looking at, if in twenty years only one should survive. For the future, the important problem is to acquire this *one;* the nine will be forgiven and forgotten. But meanwhile we live in the present and for the present these other nine will seem just as necessary and useful."

Impressionists and Postimpressionists

CEZANNE, Paul

• **156. Le Château Noir.** (1904-06) In this typical late Cézanne, the elements of a landscape are abridged into broad planes of color, with each stroke an integral part of the majestic composition. The scheme is simple: a mountain-like diagonal of trees, running from upper left to lower right, is played against the horizontals of the chateau. In the sky, planes of color echo the rhythms of the trees, while the hill recalls the blue notes of both the trees and the ground below. The splendor of color surpasses Impressionism and attains the richness of Venetian painting. Depth is compressed to conform to the surface of the canvas,

and space appears simultaneously deep and almost abstractly
flattened. Cézanne rented a room in the Chateau Noir, near his
home in Aix, for a second studio. This painting of the chateau
once belonged to Monet.

SEURAT, Georges

• **157. Evening, Honfleur.** (1886) A sequence of horizontals
begins with the slanting shoreline and piers, glides on to the
dreamy but stable horizon (which is enhanced by the emphatic
zone of the light on the water at right) and ends in the clouds.
The uprights of the pier and the distant tint of smoke are secondary units which provide gentle vertical contrast. Despite the
atmospheric haze, forms are well defined. Seurat's systematically
juxtaposed color dots—cool notes opposed to warm—create a
firmness which contrasts with the more diffuse, impromptu forms
of the Impressionists, yet maintains their sense of outdoor light.
Seurat sometimes painted his frames to prevent a picture from
encountering the frame too abruptly and to extend the picture's
spatial effect. Here the frame also complements the composition
—purples, reds, blue, pale greens and orange, intense at top and
lighter at bottom, in interplay with the picture itself.

TOULOUSE-LAUTREC, Henri de

• **158. La Goulue at the Moulin Rouge.** (1891-92) Recalling
a masterly page in Flaubert, de Maupassant or Zola, Lautrec
achieves maximum characterization with a minimum of means.
La Goulue ("The Greedy One") was the nickname of Louise
Weber, the one-time laundress who became, at seventeen, a leading cancan dancer at the famous Moulin Rouge. In this probing,
unflattering portrayal, Lautrec effectively communicates the swagger of her gliding walk, the twist of her eyebrow, her half-sneer,
hawklike nose and pale, night-tinted flesh tinged with green. The
effect is sharpened by contrasting her absorbing face with the
conventionally pretty one of her intimate friend, a dancer called
La Mome Fromage. (The left-hand figure is probably La Goulue's
sister.) Viewed head-on and close up, as if the artist has responded
to a passing moment, La Goulue advances toward the right, turning her arrogant head to the left. Her sharply-contoured dress is
framed against the dark background and the dresses of her com-

157

panions. The supple curves of the right-hand girl's hat, profile, cupid's-bow lips, neckline, mutton-chop sleeves and wasp waist play against La Goulue's more angular forms. The abrupt cropping at both sides strengthens the sense of a scene caught rapidly, as though with a candid camera. Colors are rendered almost as flatly as in Lautrec's posters, yet as the three women advance toward the spectator depth is indicated by the shift in scale to the small figure of the man behind them and by the perspective of the lights reflected in the mirror. To Lautrec's friend and biographer Gustave Coquiot, La Goulue was a "haughty and impertinent [woman with] the dull, torpid eyes of some great bird of prey . . . the most alert and the most languid . . . the most cruel and the most candid, the youngest and the oldest face in the world." In the 1880's La Goulue was an idol of Paris night life. By 1895 she was merely a performer at street carnivals. (The two curtains which Lautrec gallantly painted for her booth—one showing her in her glory at the Moulin Rouge—are now in the Museum of Impressionism in Paris.) Eventually, she drifted to performing in a cage of tame lions at fairs on the outskirts of Paris. About 1900, a young American illustrator who had heard that she was once "the incarnation of all that was reckless and extravagant," found her by her gypsy wagon. He wrote: "La Goulue unearthed for me from the bottom of a trunk some of her past glory: a set of photographs . . . a framed certificate of a first prize for dancing bearing the date 1889 . . . a contract to dance for 3,700 francs a week. . . . 'There are those who have said hard things of me even in the old days,' said La Goulue, 'but they lied. I am a good girl with a good heart,' she cried looking me straight in the eye; 'it was the life that was bad, not I, Monsieur.' " La Goulue's grave is inscribed: "Muse of Lautrec."

VAN GOGH, Vincent

• **159. The Starry Night.** (1889) In this powerfully rhythmic composition, van Gogh transforms a landscape into a mystic in-

158

cantation to night. The dark cypress sweeps upward, its restless
spirit repeated in the rolling mountains. The Milky Way careens
amid a galaxy of exploding stars. The moon whirls in dazzling
yellows. Only the village, with its balancing horizontals, appears
stable and serene. Van Gogh's tattoo of brushstrokes speeds up
the drifting movements of the Impressionists into terse stripes and
crackling dabs. Mountains are defined with thick, firm strokes,
rooftops with short, sharp ones, trees with brisk, curling movements. Van Gogh wrote his brother Théo that when he had "a
terrible need of—shall I say the word—of religion, then I go out
at night to paint the stars." He wished to express "hope by a
star, the eagerness of the soul by a sunset radiance. Certainly
there is nothing in that of . . . realism, but is it not something that
exists?" Van Gogh made this painting while an inmate in the
gloomy asylum at Saint-Rémy, near Arles in southern France.
Even his sympathetic brother found the work too imaginative:
"I find that you are at your best when you do realistic things,"
he wrote. "I think these stylized researches weaken the feeling
of reality." But to Alfred Barr, Jr., *The Starry Night* marks a
turning point in van Gogh and in modern art: "The conflict between fact and feeling, between prose and poetry, realism and
imaginative vision." Like the Metropolitan Museum's *Cypresses,*
executed in the same month, *The Starry Night* goes far beyond
Impressionism's outward view and points the way toward a main
direction of 20th Century painting—Expressionism, with its stress
on inner emotion. Acquired only in 1941, this painting became
the first van Gogh oil to be purchased by a New York museum.

MONET, Claude

• **160. Water Lilies.** (Central panel of a triptych painted about
1920.)   Diffused in the pale light of dawn or of evening, the soft
shapes of this canvas resemble imaginative variations of free-form
abstraction, even as they retain the pleasure of the recognizable.
A shimmering panorama seems to embrace the spectator in a lull-
ing world of water. The hint of a horizon is deceptive; no actual
sky or land appear, only water and reflections. A few flowers help
establish the ripple of water, and mirrored clouds illumine the

160

misty surface. The fabric of color is fragile, but handled with breadth and firmness; cool violets, whites, blues and greens are accentuated by yellows and flecks of red. This panel is from the extraordinary cycle of water lily paintings which dominated Monet's last years. As in his *Rouen Cathedral* series, Monet sought to fix the fleeting appearances of one scene at different hours, but the water lilies are so epic, so unusual in concept and composition, that they are unsurpassed in the artist's long career. The cycle was painted at Giverny, Normandy, where Monet lived from 1883 until his death. The artist had deflected a stream across his garden into an oriental water lily pond fringed by willows. "I painted my water lilies for fun," he wrote later, "when all of a sudden I saw, like a revelation, that my pond had become enchanted. I seized my palette [and] since then I have had no other model." "I have begun the impossible; water with grass swaying on the bottom. It is striking to see, but madness to attempt." Later he added: "I was tempted to use the theme . . . for the decoration of a salon; carried along the walls, its unity enfolding all the panels, it was to produce the illusion of an endless whole, a wave without horizon and without shore; nerves strained by work would relax in its presence, following the reposing example of its stagnant waters, and for him who would live in it, this room would offer an asylum of peaceful meditation in the midst of a flowering aquarium." When Monet despaired before his immense ambition, his spirits were revived by his old friend, Premier Georges Clemenceau. On Armistice Day, 1918, Monet wrote Clemenceau offering two large panels to commemorate the peace. Clemenceau asked for an entire group, and in 1923 the artist offered the State eight water lily compositions. After Monet's death in 1926, Clemenceau supervised their installation in the Orangerie in Paris. Subsequently, with successive explosions of new styles, Impressionism receded from favor, and Monet's water lilies were largely ignored as a last whimper of a once-great movement. In 1955, however, the Museum of Modern Art startled many by acquiring a water lily panel over eighteen feet long. To the Museum, the late Monets had not only anticipated a future course of art but had achieved a superb synthesis of abstraction with reality. The avant-garde quality of the Museum's panel—not to mention its beauty—brought a consequent revival of interest in Monet. Unfortunately, the 1955 purchase was completely burned in a Museum fire in 1958. The present panels were acquired to restore the loss. The finest examples outside of the Orangerie, they had remained in Monet's studio at Giverny until the mid-1950's. Damaged during a World War II bombardment, they were painstakingly strengthened and restored by the Museum.

PRENDERGAST, Maurice Brazil

• **161. Acadia.** (1922)   In Prendergast's last important oil, thick, vibrant color-spots create a surface like a glowing tapestry. The drawing is boldly simplified to fuse with the striking handling of color. The larger masses are placed in an informal, rhythmic array, so that the figures move in stately sequence. Faces, parasols and bouquets provide accents to vary the large color-units of the dresses. Space is flattened, enhancing the effect of a tableau. Acadia is the old French name for Nova Scotia, the province south of Prendergast's native Newfoundland.

BONNARD, Pierre
• **162. The Breakfast Room.** (About 1930-31) This fusion of semi-abstraction with Impressionism's record of the fleeting moment recalls Bonnard's creed: "Our God is light." The cluster of objects and the striped table lead inward to a tall window flanked by flowered wallpaper. A burst of colors seen through the window is sustained in a luminous still life which is highlighted by a basket of bread, the orange circles of the saucer's rim, the rectangle of wine in a glass and the green side of a box. At both sides of the canvas, orange paneling frames ground, bushes and trees varied by the tracery of their branches.

Fauvism and Matisse

DERAIN, André
• **163. Blackfriars Bridge, London.** (1906) Misty London becomes as colorful as the Riviera. Condensed perspective strengthens the zest of the portrayal as the bridge sweeps dynamically to the far shore, buttressed by firm lines and massive arches. People and busses are dashes of color, almost in anticipation of abstraction. Typically audacious Fauve color is seen in the blue-against-pink of the center arch; in the dabs of yellow, blue and pink in the emerald-green water; in the blue buildings; and in the orange-pink sky. As a creative artist, Derain was painting not London as such, but his own sense of what is meaningful. This is one of a 1906 series of London paintings. The view is across the Thames

161   162

toward St. Paul's Cathedral. The name of the bridge refers to the habits worn by Dominican friars, whose ancient priory had been nearby.

MATISSE, Henri

• **164. The Dance.** (1909)   Matisse startles the eye with his zestful handling, rigorous simplicity and the impact he achieves through only a few flat but vivid colors. Expressive drawing and emphatic lines reinforce a composition electric with movement and rhythm. The main grouping is built on a diagonal running from the figure at lower left to the arm of the dancer at right. This line is joined by a sweeping diagonal in the linked arms of the other dancers. Matisse's novel approach to space, balance and form is evident in the intervals of blue between the figures and the joined arms and in the undulating line of the ground. In keeping with the directness of the color, the lines emphasize movement, form and design, as in the sweeping curve at left. The dark notes of the hair accent the shimmering blue, soft green and bright flesh. This is the first large version in oil for one of Matisse's most famous paintings, *The Dance*, a mural commissioned by the brilliant collector Sergei L. Schukin for his Moscow mansion. (Schukin's collection was nationalized and is now in the Hermitage Museum in Leningrad.) This version, which once belonged to Walter Chrysler, Jr., was presented to the Museum by Governor Nelson Rockefeller. Matisse's 1909 *Bather,* also in the Museum collection is a prelude to the verve of *The Dance.*

• **165. Red Studio.** (1911)   At the first glance, Matisse's painting of his studio at Issy-les-Moulineaux seems a random spotting of sketchy objects against a postery red. In reality, it is a carefully calculated composition in which the eye is guided continuously through an exhilarating harmony of line, form and color. The initial impact is the red. Then emerge the objects and pictures set against walls and floor like sparkling gems in a brilliant setting. At left, a table leads upward and inward. The pattern in the plate and the arabesque of the plant are related to the winding lines about the nude figure in the painting above. The slant of this picture leads the eye to the top nude painting. The frame and paintings on the floor form a counterbalance and a link with the face of the clock—the pivot of the entire composition. A band

163   1

of patterned cloth on the wall continues the movement toward the right. Above it, the paintings of the boy in blue, the bouquet (with petals echoing the face of the clock) and the nudes (by the chest of drawers) achieve a balance. The large green and blue painting at upper right and the two nudes facing left close off the composition. The white pattern of the upper right painting flows into the white sculpture profile, which, in turn, is contrasted with the bronze statuette. At bottom right, the curved yellow chair returns the spectator into the picture. Matisse often reverses orthodox color relationships to revitalize harmony. The vine leaf unit at lower left, for example, defies conventional color ideas by projecting cool green against vivid red; the luscious pink of the painting opposite the leaves creates a counter-harmony, while the empty, light green canvas at left provides bold opposition. Foreground and background melt into a continuous, flattened area. The emptiness of the floor balances the lively scattering of paintings and furniture. Modeling is minimized. Luminosity, space and depth are suggested by color surfaces which keep the frank character of decorative composition. Within the picture are well-known Matisse oils and sculptures and a ceramic plate of 1908.

• **166. Piano Lesson.** (1916)   Compared with the dash and the rhythm of the *Red Studio,* this painting of the artist's son Pierre (now a noted art dealer) is austere and compact. The stress is on vertical forms and rectangular geometric balance, reflecting a slight, temporary Cubist influence. The simple composition is based on the two vertical zones represented by green and gray at left and blue, orange and gray at right. These are subdivided and supported by the horizontals of the window grill, the Pleyel piano and the music rack. A diagonal of green cuts through to join the piano top, which is the pivotal point in the picture's asymmetrical balance. The metronome is a miniature repetition of the wedge of green. The piano's lush pink coloring and severe simplicity are contrasted with the black of the scrolled music rack. The grill of the casement window continues the line of the

166

music rack. At bottom left, a statuette maintains the base established by the piano. In the background appear grass and a gravel walk. The boy's face is integrated into the flattened space. The startling wedge of his shadowed eye provides the picture's deepest plane; it also acts in mild opposition to the slant of the nearby orange band and echoes in miniature the large green area. Above the boy, verticality is further emphasized by the tall figure, which Matisse borrowed from his earlier oil, *Woman on a High Stool*.

Expressionism

KOKOSCHKA, Oskar

• **167. Hans Tietze and Erica Tietze-Conrat.** (1909)   In this unorthodox double-portrait, the figures of the eminent art scholar and his wife emerge dramatically from a resonant background, their flesh made almost incandescent by the contrast of areas of bare canvas against patches of color. The remarkable hands form an arc that implies communion; the doctor's hands glow like a flame, their animated gesture revealing deep emotion. The double-portrait was meant, the artist wrote many years later, "as a symbol of the married life of the two sitters" in which he strove to "render the vision of people being alive due to the effect of inner light, resulting technically from layers of thinly painted colors." Dr. Hans Tietze served until 1926 as Director of Austrian State Museums. Erica Tietze-Conrat, the daughter of a poet whose work was given musical settings by Brahms *(Zigeunerlieder)*, was also a notable art historian. When the couple came to the United States in 1938 as refugees from the Nazis, Dr. Tietze became visiting professor of art history at Columbia. He sold this painting to the Museum shortly afterward.

WEBER, Max

• **168. The Geranium.** (1911)   "Two crouching figures of women dwelling and brooding in a nether unworldly realm," wrote

167

Weber of this painting, "were chosen as a means for the expression and revealment of the spiritual meaning of silence and suspense." This early example of American modernism combines emphasis on form and design with a brooding, meditative spirit. The figures seem hewn out; their rhythmic quality recalls El Greco, Cézanne and, more obviously, the Cubists. Against the angles and the blue, the flower pot with a geranium glows like some mystic sign. Elemental green forms and the dynamic tree expand and elaborate the massive rhythms and solemn spirit. When Weber was given an exhibition in Stieglitz' iconoclastic "291" gallery in 1911, one critic wrote: "No one is going to believe that nature alone ever made anybody so bad an artist as all this. Such grotesqueness can only be acquired by long and perverse practice."

ROUAULT, Georges
• **169. Three Judges.** (1913)   In its powerful handling and spirit of indignation, this famous painting ranks as Rouault's masterpiece on a favorite theme—courts and injustice. Finesse and refinement are almost totally rejected in a distillation of fierce moral anger. The frontal grouping of the three massive figures almost overflows the confines of the picture. The central figure is emphasized by the dark area of his hat and the verticality subtly extended by the smudge of white paper at his hand. His monstrous mass is exaggerated by his short, thin hands. The judge on the right seems withdrawn and indifferent, while his colleague at left is given a bestial face with coarse planes of color and thick lines. There are no hints of specific locale: the trio emerges from a timeless, universal background. Smouldering reds, smoky blues, dusky blacks and subdued greens underline the Dostoevskian mood and grand design.

School of Paris

MODIGLIANI, Amedeo
• **170. Reclining Nude.** (About 1919)   The basic scheme involves three horizontals defined by an elongated figure placed frontally between the sloping mass of the couch and the red background. To stress the length of the undulating torso, Modigliani exaggerates the rounded thighs and the circular unit of arms,

170

cushion and head. From thigh to arm the artist's masterly line describes one continuous contour, accenting the curve of the elbow (which forms a link with the edge of the cushion), suggesting gently modeled breasts and stomach and emphasizing the swelling thigh. Rich color and texture add to the sensuality. The painting almost recalls the color of Titian's nudes and the grace and delicacy of Botticelli.

Picasso: Cubists and Postcubists

PICASSO, Pablo

• **171. Les Demoiselles d'Avignon.** (1906-07) Few paintings have had such momentous impact as this composition of five distorted nude figures. The first essay into Cubism, *Les Demoiselles* heralded the future course of modern art, beginning the conscious transformation of shapes into pure abstractions. The odd title has no intrinsic significance; it was apparently coined by a writer around 1920 and may refer to a brothel on Avignon Street in Barcelona. The work could as well have been called "Angular Theme and Variation on Five Figures," for in reality it is the relationships of forms and space that give the picture its meaning. In a canvas bursting with energy, the nudes are reshaped into conformity with the diagonals of the main masses. The figure on the left, reminiscent of Picasso's earlier Rose Period, is modeled by triangular contrasts of pinks and tans. The second figure, the tip of her upraised elbow leading to a steeply sloping shoulder and a sharp-edged side, accelerates the dynamic movement. The raised elbow of the third figure injects a more drastic rhythm. A still life—melon, grapes, pears and tablecloth—links these three figures with the two on the right. The crackling of blue—perhaps the folds of a background curtain—introduces something very near abstraction, but the giant step toward Cubism occurs chiefly in the two figures at right. The standing woman's mask-like face is modeled from non-representational green stripes, and her body is a design of planes and angles. The squatting figure's savagely forceful features are shown full-face while the nose is sideways—a liberty which will lead to even more extraordinary angles of vision as Cubism develops. The inconsistency in the degree of distortion from left to right indicates that the picture's evolution was one of struggle and searching. In fact, some twenty preparatory drawings, watercolors and gouaches chart its course. It was originally planned as a wistful comment on wine, women and song; among the nudes appeared a sailor with a bottle, while another youth, holding a skull, stood watching the festive scene. Eventually, the romantic theme was discarded. Among the artist's sources in this work were Cézanne, who modified and distorted figures to make them conform to the architecture of his compositions; the forms of African Negro sculpture, and the dynamic volumes of El Greco, who was then only recently emerging from obscurity. It is not improbable, as Alfred Barr has suggested, that Picasso's angular nudes were at least in part the painter's challenge to Matisse's leadership of modern art. In the year in which *Les Demoiselles* was completed, Matisse's *The Joy of Life* appeared in the Salon of Independants; a masterpiece in which Arcadian nudes are drawn with sweeping curves, and colors are chosen not for realism but for compositional effect, it was greeted as the most advanced work of the time. Reaction to Picasso's painting, however, was one of shock. In an article called "The Wild Men of Paris," one journalist described its "monstrous, monolithic women, like Alaska totem poles, hacked out of solid, brutal colors, frightful, appalling." *Les Demoiselles* exerted its revolutionary influence not through exhibitions or reproductions, but from the quiet of Picasso's studio. In 1919, the painting was acquired by the collector and dress designer Jacques Doucet. After his death it was purchased by George Salles, Director of the Louvre, but it was not exhibited publicly in Paris until 1937, long after the hey-day of Cubism. The Museum of Modern Art acquired it in 1939 for $28,000; the price seems unbelievably low today, but in order to meet it the young institution had to raise $18,000 by selling a Degas and borrow the rest.

• **173. Ma Jolie (Woman with a Guitar).** (1911-12) This painting and the Braque *Man With a Guitar* which adjoins it belong to Cubism's most audacious phase, Analytical Cubism (roughly 1910-13.) The "subjects" of a composition have now become the arrangement itself and the visual drama created by transforming objects into an independent harmony of color, space and geometric forms. Physical matter is dissolved, then reassembled. Weight and solidity give way to X-ray transparencies of overlapping planes, cubes and angles. A figure exists as the raw material for a conceptual interplay expressing structural order.

71

173

Amid the abstract forms there are, to be sure, faint elements of
so-called reality—often a scattering of musical staves and words
which introduce echoes of the recognizable or the poetic. In *Ma
Jolie,* a face and figure emerge indistinctly from within the advancing and receding shapes. A face takes form from the planes
and angles at top center, a frontal view bisected by a line defining
light zones and dark. At right, the line of a slanting shoulder
swerves downward. At center are the sound hole of a guitar or
zither and elements, perhaps, of fingers. Planes and volumes
shimmer within the harmony of browns, grays and tans. Picasso
painted the words "Ma Jolie" (My Pretty One)—a phrase from
the chorus of a popular song—into some nine Cubist pictures of
this period. They refer to Marcelle Humbert, who succeeded
Fernande Olivier in the artist's affections in 1912. Picasso called
her Eva. "I love her very much and shall write it on my paintings," the artist told his dealer and friend, Kahnweiler; on two
of his pictures he actually lettered in the message "J'aime Eva."

BRAQUE, Georges
• **174. Man with a Guitar.** (1911)   In this second prime example
of Analytical Cubism, Braque compresses the form of a mah into
a compact pyramid. At right, the figure is defined and contained
by the long line running from bottom to top in a gentle, tilting
thrust; at left, another line indicates a shoulder, a bent arm and
the straight left edge of the torso. Above the shoulder, the back
of a chair provides a stable motif amid the complex network of
lines and planes. At bottom on both sides are the spiral volutes
of the chair and vague forms of a table-top. The guitar's sound
hole is compressed within the figure; its neck emerges at a slant
to the right and its cord hangs at left. Background and figure fuse
into overlapping planes to create a continuous, interrelated mass;
the guitar, for instance, is first assimilated into the figure, then
advances outward. The overall pattern, held together by emphatic
lines, suggests deep space within a flattened portrayal. *Man with*

174

1

a Guitar and Picasso's *Ma Jolie* are usually hung next to each other to show their unity, as well as their subtle differences. Some museum visitors regard their similarity as a weakness, but in point of fact the two artists worked so closely together in exploring and expanding Cubism that they deliberately achieved similar results. This sort of cooperative endeavor also existed among some Italian painters and among the Impressionists. In such cases, only devotees can tell the work of certain artists in certain phases from that of others.

GRIS, Juan

• **175. Guitar and Flowers.** (1912)   The picture's architecture is based on a continuous vertical bisecting the canvas from top to bottom. The triangular shape of the tablecloth's main fold extends through the guitar and the blossoms and proceeds into the brown vase at top center. Against this axis, Gris balances two opposing diagonals—one ascending to the edge of the curtain at upper right, the other formed by the slanting neck of the guitar at left. Within these subdivisions occur carefully calculated intervals, shapes and movements. The inverted triangle between the neck of the guitar and the shoulder of the brown vase, for example, is actually a magnification of the center fold of the tablecloth at bottom center. The series of alternating light and dark horizontals is opposed by the vertical at right (echoed in miniature in the neck of the guitar). The composition is varied and enriched by circles, triangles and diamonds. Cool blues and greens contrast with zones of subdued reddish tints. The fresh, delicate color gives a measure of freedom to the disciplined organization and heightens the faceted effect created by the shafts of light which define the composition's volume.

• **176. Breakfast.** (1913)   In a collage of pasted paper, crayon and oil, the artist assembles a table with cups, glasses, a bottle, a coffee pot, egg cups, a package tied with ribbon and a newspaper clipping in which the word "GRIS" serves whimsically as

a signature. Real and unreal are mingled with virtuosity. At top center is actual wallpaper. The folds and ribbon of the package are painted, but the stamp is real. The coffee pot and bottle are drawn on wallpaper. On the table are two kinds of wallpaper— one painted, the other real. Vertical space is stressed. The objects ascend in conformity with the flat surface of the canvas, rather than in the illusionistic depth of normal perspective. Tilting, opposing movements give vitality to the precise organization. Stabilizing forces are introduced in the center by the tobacco package, by the line of the center of the tablecloth and by the table-legs.

LA FRESNAYE, Roger de

● **177. Conquest of the Air.** (1913)   In La Fresnaye's masterpiece, Cubism achieves an equilibrium between semi-abstraction and representationalism. The two angularized men and the table are creative adaptations of Cézanne's compact geometric forms. A proud La Fresnaye image, the French flag, functions as a colorful pattern of curves and straight lines. Roofs link the base of the picture with spherical clouds in the sky, while shifting rectangles convey movement and depth. Each form is rendered with clarity and integrated into an ensemble of resplendent color. The two figures, symbols of Man as thinker and challenger, hover monumentally above the landscape. The head of the man at right is noble and classical, its curved back contrasting with a severely rectangular shoulder. Against this line is the graceful curve of his upper arm, while his forearm parallels the line of his leg. Under the arm, space continues the forward movement of the leg and the line from kneecap to tabletop. This pioneer homage to the Air Age was painted while France was a world leader in aeronautics. La Fresnaye portrays flight by the balloon visible at upper left, perhaps referring to man's first air ascent, which took place in Paris in 1783.

PICASSO, Pablo

● **178. Three Musicians.** (1921)   Among the greatest 20th Century paintings in the Museum collection, the *Three Musicians* has been described by Alfred Barr as "perhaps the culminating

178   1

work of Cubism, the most important movement in the art of the first quarter of our century." Three masquerade figures, each an imaginative repertoire of Cubist forms and colors, are seated before a table: Pierrot (left) plays a recorder; Harlequin (center) holds a guitar; the third figure, in a domino (a monk's costume worn at masquerades), holds a music score on his lap. On top of the table appears a still life including a pipe and a newspaper. Under the table lies a dog. The tight-knit, geometric composition is almost hypnotic in its tilting angles and in its juxtaposition of somber and bright colors, which suggest receding and advancing space. Despite the festive costumes, an enigmatically austere sensation is evoked by the majestic scale, the stately rhythms and the shadowy blacks and muted browns. As Pierrot's flattened form leans to the right, the blue of his costume (a counterpoint to his black arm) joins with that of Harlequin and becomes the latter's mask. The patterns of Harlequin's clothes contrast with the black-and-white cross-hatching of his collar, while the emphatic curves of his guitar vary the dominant motif of straight lines and angular edges. The neck of the guitar continues the eye toward the third musician, whose bearded mask, severe outline and dark color set off the gay costume of Harlequin. Two devices break the stark massiveness of this final figure's costume—the blue, which began with Pierrot, and the music score, which also functions to balance Pierrot's white mass. The three figures form verticals which are bisected by the linked horizontals of table and music score. The dog and floor line repeat the horizontal balance. The uptilted table, so typical of Cubist space rendering, pulls to the right, while Pierrot's thigh reverses the movement. A resourceful compression of space appears in the dog's shadowlike head (which looms up vertically in unity with Pierrot) and in its front legs (the first paw of which is much thicker than the second, abridging the perspective.) This is one of two paintings on the three musician theme painted by Picasso in 1921. (The other, now in the Philadelphia Museum of Art, is considerably brighter in color.) A year earlier, Picasso had designed costumes and scenery for *Pulcinella,* a ballet derived from an old *commedia dell'arte* pantomime; the ballet probably served as a stimulus for both paintings.

LEGER, Fernand

• **179. Three Women (Le Grand Déjeuner).** (1921) This Léger masterpiece aptly illustrates his feeling that "the human body has no more importance than keys or bicycles. . . . They are all for me objects of plastic value to be used as I wish." Léger ignores the conventionally romantic or erotic treatment of nudes in an interior scene. He celebrates instead a precise "mechanical ballet" curiously imbued with the impersonality, immobility and impassivity of classicism. Figures, furnishings and even the cat conform to the artist's conception of a modern epoch which can, if it chooses, create beauty and poetic vitality through its precision technology. The nudes may seem incongruous, but they function dramatically in an intricately engineered harmony; the picture's power rests in an organization outside the usual associative references of the subject matter. Léger devises an intricate arrangement of lines, poster-like colors and massive, staccato forms. Faces, hair, breasts, thighs, kneecaps and legs seem stamped out of metal. Colors clang and vibrate; bright, flat zones of greens, blues, citron yellows and shining blacks are organized into an abstract architecture. Each shape, color and contour is indispensible, as all the elements glide into one another with inflexible exactitude. The nude at right is emphasized over the others through her mass and color. Her pose is an insistent vertical, reinforced by the long glossy hair, the line of the body, the book in her lap and the placement of her legs. Balancing her are the two softer, whitish figures at left. (The right-hand nude's flesh tone also provides a foreground plane which places the other two into receding space.) Drapery, pictures, furniture and floor contribute to the tempo. Brushstrokes are minimized in keeping with Léger's aim of bright, smooth surfaces and to avoid the impetuous emotion of the Expressionists. The impassive faces intensify the air called for in a monumental composition. *Three Women* was painted in the same year as Picasso's *The Three Musicians*.

DOVE, Arthur

• **180. Grandmother.** (1925) This portrait without face or figure is possibly the most famous collage by an American. In a subtle ensemble, a thick needlepoint fabric forms a dramatic rectangle, while the title page torn from a Concordance of the Bible is a smaller, more fragile rectangle. Subdividing the background is a horizontal of worn wood, its delicate gray contrasting with the mellow color of the needlepoint. In each detail, Dove evokes undertones of mood and associative meaning. Rural calm, spirituality, time, place and person are conjured up more concretely than in many representational portraits.

FEININGER, Lyonel

• **181. The Steamer "Odin," II.** (1927) In a nocturne which

180

1

gleams like a precious stone, romantic mood is fused with the
structural discipline of Feininger's personal version of Cubism.
The composition divides into three horizontals—shore, sea and
sky—countered by the verticals of the ship and the three persons
(one almost dissolved by the brilliant light). Planes subdivided
by delicate lines give rhythm, depth and movement. Color chords
—like the iridescent green and the gray-blues of the steamer and
dark sky—add a brooding spaciousness. "The mystic quality in
the object has always kept me spellbound," said Feininger. Ships,
along with trains and Gothic churches, fascinated the artist. His
summers spent on the Baltic may have inspired this and similar
paintings.

BRAQUE, Georges
• **182. The Table.** (1928)   In the 1920's, Cubism underwent a
change: curvilinear, winding lines replaced angular, geometric
schemes as the style grew into a synthesis of semiabstraction and
decorative representation. The floor, table, wall and still life in
this painting are compressed within the narrow, carefully-plotted
space of a vertical panel. Emphasis is provided by a line which
subdivides the picture, ascending from floor to table and reap-
pearing in the still life and the panels of the blue-and-black
screen. Conforming to the space, the table-top rises in a steep
vertical. At left, a guitar is rendered through curvilinear planes
of light and dark, balanced by a cord which links its curves into
a unit with the tablecloth. At right, below a fruit dish, appears a
glimpse of the newspaper "Le Journal"; on it are two apples,
again subdivided by planes. The canvas's plaster-like surface adds
an appealing non-representational texture.

PICASSO, Pablo
• **183. Girl before a Mirror.** (1932)   Sinuous, linear design,
sensuous color and the lure of a cryptic theme characterize this
resplendent Picasso. Glittering with an almost stained-glass radi-

183

ance, its exotic hues suggest the bright-patterned odalisques of Matisse, but it has an emotional impact peculiarly its own. At left, in front of bright wallpaper, a girl stands gazing into a mirror. A halo-like white frames her blond hair and projects her head against the competing diamond and circle pattern of the background. Her face is shown as a classic profile in soft pink and as a three-quarter view in bright yellow, both within a single oval. In contrast, her firm neck is a sharp triangle subdivided into light and dark. Horizontal dark bands in her figure (perhaps suggesting a bathing suit) allow her to dominate and counterbalance the insistent background. Far more intense than the almost placid face at the left, her reflected image is encircled with bands of exceptionally vivid colors flowing like electric current to enhance the shadows and highlights. The girl's torso follows the curve of the mirror. Intriguing interpretations have been made of this sensual rhapsody. One scholar sees the girl's body as simultaneously clothed, nude and X-rayed, her true face as a moon (a female symbol) and her reflected face as a sun (a masculine symbol). Perhaps Picasso employs the mirror as a magical device, and the enigmatic painting treats the age-old theme of shadow and substance, reality and reflection, with some added psychological overtones. During 1932, Picasso's companion Madame Thérèse Walter was the inspiration for a group of oil paintings (including this one) and sculpture which featured her classic face and voluptuous figure.

BRAQUE, Georges

• **184. Woman with a Mandolin.** (1937) A thin, shadowy woman, mandolin in lap, sits meditatively facing a music stand. The enigmatic canvas is filled with decorative charm and elegance, yet its attractive color, texture, pattern and mellow indoor light are dominated by the mysterious, haunting quality of the woman's elongated silhouette. Thin, white lines, reminiscent of classical vase-painting, give a suggestion of volume to the wom-

184

an's two-dimensional figure, while the long vertical line down the center of the canvas acts as a foil to her restrained curves. A slender music rack echoes and balances her verticality. The light green of the wallpaper lends intensity and the illusion of depth to her figure. The violet design catches something of the restless contours of the chair.

PICASSO, Pablo

• **185. Guernica.** (1937) *Guernica* is Picasso's most famous painting and possibly his masterpiece. Its theme: mass destruction in war. Its form: a summation of Post-Cubism, Expressionism, Classicism and Symbolism. Its color: austere, expressive of mourning and death. By sheer visual power, Picasso plunges the onlooker into a stark drama stripped of sensual allure and superfluous detail. This great mural was commissioned for the Spanish Republican Pavillion at the 1937 Paris World's Fair. It memorializes history's first deliberate air attack on civilians. On April 26, 1937, the town of Guernica, ancient shrine of Basque independence, had been methodically destroyed by German bombers allied with the Spanish Insurgents. The town's normal population was swollen by refugees to 10,000, and the day chosen for the attack was a Monday—market day. Beneath the seeming chaos of figures, clashing darks and lights, and frenzied movement, the picture is built on a tight-knit version of the ancient pyramid design. The line from the arm of the running woman at right to the lamp held aloft describes one half of a triangle; the horse forms its apex and center; the other half is the line slanting down, beneath the bird, to the outstretched warrior's hand at bottom left. Two relatively vertical units formed by the bull and woman at one end and the burning building at the other frame the central action. At right, a woman falls from a burning building. A classic head swoops out of a window; the startled woman holds a lamp, signifying light cast on the tragedy. The sun-and-moon shape may symbolize the witnessing eye of Truth, while the electric light gives the ancient pictorial symbol a contemporary immediacy. The only suggestion of death from the air is the spear which wounds the horse. Agony and defiance are graphically evoked by the horse's mouth, its tongue rigid in outcry and

185

the dripping paint left near its teeth. The pattern on the horse's
body suggests, in its similarity with Picasso's collages, newsprint.
Between the collapsing front legs of the horse, the eye is directed
to a small flower and a broken sword held in a death-like grip;
the sword expresses a fight fought to the last, while the flower
poignantly evokes commemoration and a new blossoming. The
bull symbolizes brutality and darkness. Between horse and bull
appears a bird with its head lifted to the sky. Below the bull's
blank, stolid stare, a woman, her head raised in an agonized cry,
holds a lifeless child. Nearby, in the form of a classical cast, lies
the head of a fallen warrior. The outcry against slaughter is unmistakable. In transforming the bombing from mere documenta-
tion to classical symbolism, Picasso makes *Guernica* as urgently
relevant to today's fear of atomic war as it is to the destruction
of a Spanish town in the 1930's. The painting is owned by the
artist. It has been on loan to the Museum since 1939.

● **186. Night Fishing at Antibes.** (1939)   In theme, mood and
size, this is an unusual Picasso, combining whimsy with the romantic colors of a nocturne. Two men are spearfishing on a
moonlit Riviera night. They and their boat form a circular unit
which is balanced by two roughly vertical groupings—at right, by
two girls standing on a sea-wall; at left, by jagged brownish rocks
and the purple rooftops and towers of Antibes. At top center, a
burst of yellow moon is emphasized by spiralling rays—possibly
flares used to illuminate water and lure fish to the surface. The
girls wear snoods. One eats a double-scoop ice cream cone, her
tongue blue like the night. The second points to the yellow burst,
her arm tapering off and blurring into the dark sky. The sea-wall,
seen from above, reflects the green luminosity of the water, while
the wavering lines on its stones suggest the lapping of calm
waves. The large man at center seeks to impale the sole beneath
his lantern. His arm is amusing in its oversized strength and
power, but at the same time its scale is necessary in order to fill
the crucial interval between fishermen and girls. The smaller man
seems almost about to fall over the boat. The eye glides steeply
over his back (shadowed with moonlight) and his brown hair,
to the dislocation of the mouth and nostrils and to the edge of
his odd nose—one of the drollest faces in modern art. The panoramic composition is enlivened by large color areas whose direction and pattern contribute to a novel rhythm of undulating
movement.

186

LEGER, Fernand

• **187. The Divers, II.** (1942)   Léger's immobile geometric figures have been replaced in this joyous composition by an elaborate sequence of curving lines and forms. Figures intertwine in a revolving complex of faces, hair, shoulders, arms and legs. Emphatic lights and darks give the massive swimmers weight and volume and create insistently alternating patterns. Purely abstract forms, undulating around the divers to make an imaginative border of vivid colors, bring to mind water, sky, sun and green fields. They also convey receding and advancing space through their overlapping contrasts; the red at left, for instance, advances over the black, green and yellow, and the blue at right appears in front of vivid green. *The Divers, II* is one of a series of variations painted in the United States, though based on drawings made in Marseilles in 1940. In America, Léger said he found "a new energy . . . an increased movement within the composition. . . . I tried to translate the character of the human body evolving in space without any point of contact with the ground. I achieved it by studying the movement of swimmers diving into the water from very high."

Futurism

BOCCIONI, Umberto

• **188. The City Rises.** (1910-11)   This transitional masterwork of early Futurism celebrates the energy of labor. Boccioni, who declared that he was "nauseated by old walls and old palaces, old motives," was inspired by the building boom in Milan, Italy's industrial center, to make many sketches and studies of new construction projects. These culminated in *The City Rises,* which he described as "a great synthesis of work, light and movement." The horses evoke the idea of gargantuan power. The direction of the horses and the straining men underlies the forward surge of the composition. Other workers, sweeping in rhythmic rela-

188

tionship from the man at right to the figure pushing the wheelbarrow at left, continue the dynamic momentum. The head and neck of the red horse are countered by the vivid blue of its work collar—a shape exaggerated to expand into the teeming background. The diagonal panorama of wall, smokestacks, locomotive and bridge crowded with people chronicles the stir of the city. Radiant colors and light flood the scene with warmth and disintegrate solid shapes. Boccioni's style at this stage still depends on the broken brushstrokes of the Impressionists, but his dabs and spots are altered into a throbbing force. The left-hand third of the painting, badly damaged in a fire at the Museum in 1958, has been extensively restored.

CARRA, Carlo

• **189. Funeral of the Anarchist Galli.** (1910-11) During a general strike in 1904, the anarchist Galli was killed in a clash in Milan. His funeral, which young Carrà witnessed, developed into a battle between police and mourners. "Without wishing to," Carrà wrote later, "I found myself in the center of the struggle. I saw the bier covered with the red flag careening on the shoulders of the pallbearers. I saw the horses rear skittishly, canes and lances clashing, so that it seemed to me that the coffin would fall at any moment. . . ." Seven years later, fired by Futurism, Carrà painted his recollection in a picture which captures the tensions of Europe before World War I and seems to foretell the stormy decades which followed. Forms, movements and colors mingle in the confusion. The contenders, like the man with a straw hat at left and the mounted policeman, are enmeshed in a maelstrom. A succession of lines conveys the flailing movement of canes and the violent thrust of a lance. The coffin links the main masses at right and left. Above the melee on both sides are the black banners of the anarchists. According to a Futurist manifesto Carrà helped write, the spectator "must in the future be placed in the center of the picture. . . . If we paint the phases of a riot, [then] the crowd bustling with uplifted fists and the noisy onslaught of cavalry are translated upon the canvas in sheaves of lines corresponding with all the conflicting forces, following the general law of violence of the picture. These force-lines encircle and involve the spectator so that he will in a manner be forced to struggle himself with the persons in the picture."

189

SEVERINI, Gino

• **190. Dynamic Hieroglyphic of the Bal Tabarin.** (1912) This kaleidoscope of patterns, inspired by a famous nightclub near Place Pigalle, is based on simultaneous glimpses of figures, café tables and decorations. Hectic gaiety animates every area. Luminous violet and yellow, glowing blues, pinks, greens, shimmering whites and sudden accents of black flash across the canvas. From the giddy maze emerge the figures of two giant dancers. The pink hat of the first appears to the right of the word "Bowling". Her brown, curly hair and pink-and-blue face define sequences of movement. Her frothy skirt is adorned with real sequins, ribbons fly about her shoulders, her hem swirls about pink petticoats and her high-heeled shoes fly. The second dancer is to her right, wearing a yellow hat edged with blue and a dress adorned with more sequins. (This novel use of collage may have been in advance of even the Cubists.) The words "Polka" and "Valse" bring associations of music and dance. The dislocation of shapes, the dissolution of solids and the sharp-edged geometric units indicate the influence of Cubism, but Severini adapts the idiom to his own lyric flair for shimmering color and witty portrayals and his Futurist preoccupation with fluid, dynamic movement.

Fantasy and Surrealism

ENSOR, James

• **191. Tribulations of St. Anthony.** (1887) Ensor was a remarkable innovator. His color is much freer than that of the Impressionists, who were his contemporaries, and his shapes almost foretell the irregular forms of early Expressionism. His sense of fantasy, inventive and wry, is closer to Klee and Miró than to the 19th Century. Yet a prime Ensor like this one is a rarity in American museums. The Saint is shown distracted from his reading of the Scriptures by demons, fantastic musicians and a nude woman. Above, balloons disgorge more impish creatures, while a giant masked head peers out from the water. At right, a doctor stands holding a hypodermic needle and a red mass forms a huge entrance to Hell. The irregular bluish diagonal which drifts across the two brown-red areas forms the major subdivisions of the composition. A slithering monster establishes the base, while hurtling forms at top direct the eye downward into the main area. Shimmering colors reach a climax in the fluid opalescence of sea and sky and in the flamelike mass at upper right. St. Anthony, son of a rich Egyptian Christian, gave away his inheritance and devoted his life to self-denial. Living alone for twenty years in ruins near the Nile, he experienced the temptations of demons. He wears a monk's habit in this picture because he is the founder of monastic orders. This painting was removed by the Nazis from the Wallraf-Richartz Museum in Cologne and sold for less than $1000.

CHIRICO, Giorgio de

● **192. Nostalgia of the Infinite.** (1913-14) "Who can deny
the troubling connection that exists between perspective and meta-
physics," wrote de Chirico; "the perspectives of buildings rise full
of mystery and misgivings [and] corners conceal secrets." In the
haunting paintings he did shortly after his arrival in Paris, the
youthful de Chirico endowed vistas of city squares with a sense
of apprehension. Through a few flat colors, exaggerated perspective and contrast of light and shadow, he achieved a sense of
brooding loneliness. In this example, a strange tower, its front
shadowed and its side bright, looms against green sky. A flutter
of pennants provides the only animation in the quiet square. A
dark portico creates the illusion of distance and a thin line of sky
suggests far-off space. The orange ground becomes a bridge
between portico and tower and, with the white wall, suggests
bright sunlight. The shadows of the two thin, dwarfed figures
underline the sense of vast space. Even the narrow dimensions
of the panel enhance the dreamlike sensation.

● **193. The Sacred Fish.** (1919) A disquieting mood is projected through imaginative juxtapositions of forms and objects
and by magnifying a steeply receding perspective. The strange
setting, and the fish arranged almost like a cross, suggest some
religious significance. Toylike triangular shapes recall the artist's
comment that "The triangle is considered a mystic· and magic
symbol, and beyond question it arouses in the beholder, even
when he is ignorant of its significance, a feeling of apprehension,
perhaps even of fear." The vertical of the candle flanks the platform like a sentinel. A sliver of distant horizon completes a solemn
design. James Thrall Soby, the foremost de Chirico scholar, writes
of this painting, "One of the principal works of de Chirico's entire
career . . . it remains one of the most idiosyncratic and memorable
of all his works. . . . For here, presented in terms of extreme
realism, is a pictorial counter-logic based on subconsious sources

191

of inspiration soon to be explored by the Surrealists. The brilliant smoked fish are placed on a platform at the front of a stage and become the protagonists of a strange drama of the inanimate. They are accompanied by unreasonable objects—a toy-like form and a candlestick with a starfish impaled on its wick—the known and the impossible combined to create a believable entity . . ."

CHAGALL, Marc

• 194. I and the Village. (1911)   Chagall's audacious painting exemplifies the Hassidic notions that "in everything there are worlds, souls and divinities, an exalted union between the outer and inner world," and that "through ecstacy man could cross the zone between the known and the unknown." In his most famous painting, the artist blithely tosses about dreamlike images to conjure up a pastoral idyll, dislocating natural relationships to enhance imaginative power. The enormous heads of a youth and a calf form converging diagonals, bound by a large circle. The bouquet of spring flowers the youth offers forms a firm base, while the vividly-colored houses and green sky fill the complementary interval at top. The rough-textured reds, blues and greens have a Slavic earthiness. In the sharp diagonals, Chagall adopted the tools of Cubism to his own purposes. The symbols evoke a beguiling pattern of ideas. The youth's face, for instance, is in green, a color which in Chagall's work often implies the artist or creativity. (The green also serves to enliven the painting through its unexpected juxtaposition against the pink.) A thin thread of white binds the eye of the youth with the clock in the eye of the calf—memory leaping across space. Between the two profiles is a hill covered with fairy-tale snow, its white reflected in the youth's eye. The miniature cow and the upside-down figures and houses underscore the playful mood, while the cow also interrupts the flat planes of blue and white. The bucolic nature of the symbolism recalls Chagall's statement, "The fact that I made use of cows, milkmaids, roosters and provincial Russian architecture [is] be-

194

cause they are part of the environment from which I spring. . . .
Every painter is born somewhere; and even though he may later
return to the influence of other atmospheres, a certain essence—a
certain 'aroma'—of his birthplace clings to his work."

• **195. Calvary.** (1912)   Chagall's imaginative vision makes even
a theme as frequently depicted as the Crucifixion pulse with the
shock of strange emotion. Planes and movements are disposed
with dynamic power. Two key colors—vivid green and burning
vermillion—achieve a poignant forcefulness. A childlike Christ
and two figures are placed at far left. Countering their asymmetry
are the orange-red at lower right, the river, and the line of the
ladder reaching to the green planes. The great halo-like circle
above Christ, perhaps a symbol of the Earth, is echoed by the
circular shapes on the ground. The blue and white planes on
Christ's figure scintillate with jewel-like radiance. The style combines the splendid color, flat space and stylized form of Russian
Byzantine art with Chagall's highly individual adaptation of
Cubist planes and angles. Years after this painting, Chagall declared, "The symbolic figure of Christ was always very near me,
and I was determined to draw it out of my young heart. . . . When
I painted Christ's parents I was thinking of my own parents. My
mother was about half the size of my father. . . . The bearded
man is the child's Father. He is my father and everybody's father."
The Judas figure seemed too frightening and grotesque, so Chagall
gave him a ladder "to bring him down to a more familiar level."
The onlooker in the sailboat suggests "an element of tranquility
in contrast to tragedy. . . . The river, which is the river of my
native town, flows very peacefully." The mother is sprinkled with
stars; one breast is bared, as in many paintings of the Madonna,
as a token of motherhood.

KLEE, Paul
• **196. Around the Fish.** (1926)   "Symbols," wrote Klee, "reassure the spirit that it need not depend exclusively on terrestial
experience. . . . Art should give humanity a vision of God to
rejoice in the sacred vigils when the soul sits down to supper."
Hence this intriguing still life, in which mystic and religious
symbols revolve—literally and figuratively—"around the fish."

195

Two fish, ancient symbols of life and fertility adopted by the early Christians to represent Christ, float in a sea-blue void, surrounded by objects set in a black infinity. Above the fish are images of the moon. At right, rising from a gray, cylindrical shape, is an anemone, the red spots on its petals perhaps symbolizing the blood of Christ, the triple leaf representing the Trinity and the single red dot referring to the Godhead; beneath the image is a cross. At left, Klee introduces his famous personal device, the directional arrow, here emphasized by an exclamation mark. The arrow points to a masklike head on a stem, its neck repeating the Trinity symbol. Beneath the head is the flag of the Church Triumphant. The design at bottom left suggests pomegranate seeds, symbols of fertility and resurrection. The recurrent sprigs of evergreen also imply immortality. The die at bottom center recalls the Roman soldiers who tossed dice for Christ's garment at the Crucifixion, while the graceful shape beneath the die may represent a spear—or a *fleur-de-lys,* another symbol of the Trinity—or even Neptune's trident. Completing the circle is an image of plant life repeating the Trinity symbol once again. Klee's concern, however, is not merely with a chart of Christian iconography. Emotional overtones, elements of magic and the associative drama of images are also inherent in the masterly ensemble.

MIRO, Joan

• **197. Dutch Interior.** (1928)   In the year of this painting, Miró visited Holland and became intrigued with the lively, helter-skelter interiors depicted by 16th Century Dutch masters. He paid homage to them in a series of take-offs, exchanging the Dutch pictorial language for his own more imaginative idiom. In this instance, Miró transformed *The Lute Players* by Hendrick Sorgh (c. 1611-1670). Bright, flat colors confront each other abruptly, as sharp, curvilinear forms mingle with the stable, straight lines which subdivide the picture. A man with an enormous face is

198

singing. His eyes resemble birds' heads. A mustache appears curiously under his chin. His tiny hands pluck a mandolin with strings
geometrically askew. His legs are crossed. At left, lines flow from
his ears through the window. At top right is a bird encased by
horizontal lines that suggest a bar of music. At right center, a
table flows across the room; on it are a jug, a music score and a
rectangular shape probably representing the painter's palette. A
Miró-like painting hangs on the wall. Through the window are
a canal, a bridge, houses, trees and another bird. A dustpan lies
on the floor. The dog gnawing a bone at lower left is surely one
of the wittiest ever painted. The linoleum squares and white dot
again suggest musical symbols. A contented cat and a footprint
complete the bizarre domestic idyll.

DALI, Salvador

• **198. The Persistence of Memory.** (1931)   This startling vision
of limp watches in a bizarre landscape is the best known Surrealist
painting and one of the most familiar works of all modern art.
Examined individually the forms are smoothly naturalistic, but
encountered in juxtaposition they produce the jarring sense of
the monstrous which gives the best Surrealist work its enthralling
power. The literal and meticulous colors, somewhat dull from the
standpoint of "pure" painting, heighten the gripping fantasy. A
successful Surrealist painting is not a story or an illustration, but
a disquieting mood or spirit captured on canvas. The content is,
in a sense, the associations awakened in the mind of the beholder.
Dali once remarked that the melting watches in this picture signify relativity "and the artist's control over reality through art
by bending even time to his will." Certainly the key idea which
emerges from this painting is that time is malleable. The fly is a
Dali image of time's mobility, since it can disappear and reappear
elsewhere so rapidly. The strange amoeba-like form cast up on
the shore and "saddled" by time suggests a sea symbol relating
to the origins of life, yet it can also assume the contours of a
human profile. The eroded rock formation, a recurrent Dali theme
recalled from childhood, may also portray the face of time. In a
television interview in 1957, Dali called this painting a "complete
prophecy of new physics of disintegration." A watch, he added,
"is one true image you see very clearly before sleep [and is] one
classical image of depression." In the 1950's the artist painted a
second, quiet different version of this subject called *Disintegration of the Persistence of Memory*.

• **199. Portrait of Gala.** (1935)   As if transfixed, the sitter—
Dali's wife Gala—magically confronts herself across a room. Or
does she confront her husband? The larger scale and darker color
of the foreground figure lend odd mystery to the confrontation.
The painting's smoothness, mellow light and gradual deepening
of space suggest Dali's deep admiration for Vermeer; the un-

orthodox back view specifically recalls the Dutch's master celebrated *Artist and Model,* commonly believed to portray Vermeer
himself and a model who may represent fame—thus suggesting
an allegory on inspiration and immortality. Hanging behind Gala
is a Dali version of one of Millet's most famous paintings, *The
Angelus;* Gala is seated on a wheelbarrow-like form similar to
the one in the small picture. Though Millet's painting is custom-
arily viewed as a religious work, Dali sees it as a subconscious
image of passionate love in which, "like the praying mantis whom
the female eats during copulation [the] picture represents the
spectral attitude of two beings before copulation." Gala's costume
reflects Dali's admiration for the Renaissance, the period "when
women looked most beautiful." Gala Dali, the Russian-born
Elena Diaranoff, has been called the "Queen of the Surrealist
movement" and the "Surrealist muse." The former wife of the
poet Paul Eluard, who once described her as having "the look
that pierces walls," she met Dali when he invited Paris Surrealists
to visit him in Spain. According to the artist, they fell in love the
next day; they were married in the mid-1930's. Dali has often
painted Gala and acclaims her as his inspiration. The artist signed
this painting "Gala Dali."

BECKMANN, Max

• **200. Departure.** (1932-33)   This masterpiece of later German
Expressionism is the first and probably the most famous of Beckmann's nine allegorical triptychs. Its three panels are loosely
linked in a broad compositional scheme. The side sections are
related by their generally dark tones, their figures crowded into
congested space and their macabre activity. In the center panel,
however, all is calm and stately: the main rhythms are curvilinear,
as in the King's cloak and the fishing net; the figures are tall and
monumental; the horizon is high and far; colors are luminous.
Apparently an allegory on Man's fate, *Departure's* meaning is
not explicit. Many see it as a comment on the Nazi regime which
Beckmann loathed, the side panels representing torture and deg-

200

radation and the center showing the artist's—or Man's—departure from a ravaged homeland. Yet Beckmann himself has written, "This picture speaks to me of truths impossible for me to put into words and which, indeed, I did not even know before. . . . Departure, yes, departure from the illusion of life towards the essential realities that lie hidden." The right-hand panel is dominated by the figures of a man and woman tied together—"a symbol of a dark part of ourselves which we cannot escape." The figure in the blindfold—a bellhop or messenger—may signify Man's inability or unwillingness to see what is before him; he carries a decaying fish, which often represents death, corruption or decadent sex. The child, an Eros, is stunted. The mocking drummer in the foreground (whom the artist has described as Life playing a drum), the columns, the theatre boxes and the costumes suggest an enactment of the drama of Everyman. In the panel at left, a bound woman bends over a globe (a Renaissance symbol of worldly vanities); beneath the globe is a newspaper with the word *zeit* (time). One man is imprisoned in a garbage can, another is shown with truncated arms. A gangster-like executioner swings an axe—again bearing a decaying fish. Meanwhile, nature's bounty—represented by the fruit—and a mummer's hat seem totally ignored, an ironic comment on Man's failure to achieve life's potential. The center panel breathes freedom. Fish appear once again, but in this context possibly as symbols of fertility, creativity or plenty. A crowned man cloaked in royal red holds his hand in a gesture of teaching or benediction: the child is a symbol of freedom and a new beginning on what may be a momentous voyage to a better world. But is the strange figure whose features are covered by an odd helmet the boatman Charon, ready to take the party across the River Styx? The triptych, painted in Germany, was later shipped by Beckmann to America in a crate labeled "Scenes from Shakespeare's Tempest" —an appropriate reference to another work in which meanings are far from self-evident.

BLUME, Peter
• **201. The Eternal City.** (1934-37) On a January afternoon in 1933, the artist, traveling as a Guggenheim Fellow, was struck

201

by a strange light cast on ruins in the Roman Forum. Back in the United States, he pondered over the experience, made some detailed preparatory drawings (some in the Museum's collection) and, after three years' work, completed this painting. In his allegorical indictment of Mussolini's Rome, Blume combines bitter fantasy with polished naturalism to create one of the outstanding political critiques in paint. A dark diagonal subdivides the canvas, separating the area of shattered sculpture in the left foreground from the luminous triangle of plaza, mountains and sky. At the ends of the diagonal are opposing balancing units: the grotesque head of Mussolini and the illuminated figure of Christ surrounded by symbols of wealth, war and greed. The two figures before the grotto represent insincere worshippers. The beggar-woman is a personification of poverty. The fragments of sculpture would, if reconstructed, form two lovers. In the Forum, soldiers hesitate to attack as brave women throw themselves under the officers' horses. Priests run in panic. A woman tourist enjoys the unexpected spectacle. The mountains, as Blume has pointed out, are not the Apennines, but the Rockies, suggesting that such things as these can happen anywhere. The giant head of Mussolini is based on a *papier-mache* mask which dominated an exhibition commemorating the tenth anniversary of the Fascist March on Rome. Blume explained to art scholar James Thrall Soby, "I made the red lips clash with the green of the head, the color of the head strident and like nothing else in the picture; antithesis, dissonance; it hurt me to paint the head, but no compromise was possible. I felt that in doing this picture the question of harmony was superseded by other considerations." The jack-in-the-box motif suggests a hollow Caesar. Beneath the head are a Capitalist and a Blackshirt, supporters of the dictator.

TCHELITCHEW, Pavel
• **202. Hide-and-Seek.** (1940-42) Tantalizing symbols and skillful execution have made *Hide and Seek* one of the most popular paintings in the Museum. Translucent colors float over a host of fluid double images which are rendered as if transparent. The canvas seems infinitely divisible, yet integrated. A dark tree is encircled by heads, arms and figures. The eye moves into the vortex through the hands and toes at the bottom, the girl in the center and finally the figures falling between the finger-branches. The trunk of the massive tree is like the rib cage of a torso; the roots appear as a huge foot; the branches become an enormous hand. At left, the tree's contour forms a bearded head with tangled hair. About the center rotates a series of heads painted not as flesh and blood, but recognizable through the definition established by the sides of the tree. The galaxies of images within each head are nebulous compositions of air, water, flowers and other elements. The head at top left is April—greenish and fluid. Beneath is a small head of Summer. The large third head is Spring.

At right appear the head and shoulder of Autumn, with hair of red and orange leaves which also represent fire; Autumn is deftly transformed into a Winter theme, showing children playing and fighting. At top center, fruit hurtling down from the tree takes the form of children. Examination of a single area illustrates Tchelitchew's teeming vision: in the head of Summer, the eyebrow is a caterpillar, the nose a nude child, the ear another child and the hair singing birds. In addition, symbols of fertility are projected, as in the phallic mushrooms. The transformation and multiplication of images suggest many themes—time, space, birth, sex, inner and outer matter, the mysterious world of childhood, cellular structure and concepts of earth, air, fire and water. According to the artist, *Hide and Seek* "consists of three different subjects happening in three separate moments of time and seen from three points of view which must correspond to the three levels of perspective: above, straight-on and below."

MIRO, Joan

• **203. Large Mural Painting.** (1950-51) This semiabstract fantasy offers a repertoire of some of Miró's later images, forms and color concepts. Across a long, horizontal setting of cool colors and resonant browns range whimsically transformed figures, birds and stars. Soft colors and crisp lines oppose sharply-accented blacks and reds, as in the crescent of the bull's horns. The composition is a unique blend of lilting movement, lively patterns and sequences of shapes and color. In Miró's inventive vision, people, animals and landscape become fused. This painting was originally intended for a restaurant at Harvard University; when it was decided to replace the oil with a ceramic mural of similar size, Miró used this composition as a starting point for the final version.

TANGUY, Yves

204. Multiplication of the Arcs. (1954) Tanguy's last major painting presents a bizarre panorama of rocklike shapes intersected by jagged diagonals and slab-like forms with the appearance of eyes. The composition is based on the horizontal subdivision of two zones. The cryptic forms are united by areas of pink and yellow at right, blue at left. In contrast to the swarm of shapes is the hazy expanse of sky, which seems like a curtain about to close off the entire scene, yet also gives the appearance of being far behind the sharp, dark horizon. James Thrall Soby

writes: "I saw Tanguy several times in Woodbury when the *Multiplication* was in progress. He worked on the picture like one possessed, hurrying back to his studio after a brief lunch. . . . Clearly he sensed that the *Multiplication* was to be the summary of lifelong aims and preoccupations; he would arrive at the house at the end of the day, exhausted by the long hours of unrelenting concentration. . . ."

Realists and Romantics

MARIN, John Rutherford
- **205. Lower Manhattan.** (1920) Perhaps Marin's most famous watercolor, *Lower Manhattan* vibrates with the momentum of the sweeping washes and dashing lines which condense and frame the sweep of the city. The pace is sustained by the triangular enclosing lines that burst about the tower of the Woolworth Building and the lower zigzag border of brown and blue bands, an echo of the blues which compress the design at top and sides. The thin, dark line at extreme right and the curved form at lower right break the all-but-irresistible motion of the Third Avenue Elevated. The orange-pink around the Woolworth Building, compressed within a steep, tilting triangle, bursts like dazzling light.

HOPPER, Edward
- **206. House by the Railroad.** (1925) This view of an 1880's house with Mansard roof, cornices and bow windows combines a nostalgic glimpse of Americana with a mood of deep-felt loneliness. With simplicity and understatement, Hopper depicts a cold, sunlit sky and the base of a rusting railroad track. The scheme of a simple vertical against a horizontal is made arresting by the starkness and subtlety of spirit with which Hopper endows the forms and light. In the year of this picture, Hopper was at last able to give up commercial art to concentrate on his painting. This is the first painting given to the Museum of Modern Art.

OROZCO, José Clemente
- **207. Zapatistas.** (1931) *Zapatistas* has the rhythm of a drumbeat and an irresistible forward movement. The figures are marshalled in a powerful array, enhanced by a persistent staccato

5

206

emphasis of high-keyed colors. The leftward surge of the marchers and horsemen is accentuated by the ledge of ground, the curve of the mountain and the direction of the clouds. Bayonets lead to the right in pointed diagonals. Even the brims of the sombreros participate in the general militance. Sharply contrasted colors are applied with blunt vigor. The women are almost as monumental as figures in a Giotto fresco. Emiliano Zapata is a name idolized in Mexican history. During the revolution of 1910-20, he commanded an agrarian guerrilla army fighting under the slogan "Land, Liberty and Education." Orozco shows him riding to battle, with farmer-soldiers marching alongside, peasants helping to clear the road and stoic women following their men. A Diego Rivera painting of Zapata is also in the Museum's collection.

LEVINE, Jack

• **208. The Feast of Pure Reason.** (1937)   One of Levine's best-known paintings, this satire is the precocious achievement of a twenty-two-year-old. From its ironic title to its unsparing characterizations, the painting is a comment on civic corruption as timely today as it was in 1937. The artist has written in a Museum catalogue: "That part of my work which is satirical is based on observations gathered in countless hours [watching] crooked contractors, ward heelers, racketeers, minions of the law and the like. It is my privilege as an artist to put these gentlemen on trial . . . in my own terms. . . . If my frosty old gentleman in evening clothes beams with his right eye and has a cold, fishy stare in his left, that is not an accident. If a policeman reposefully examines a hangnail, that is to point out that he, too, has his cares and woes." The figures are organized within a compact pyramid. The thickly encrusted color at right suggests something of Rouault or Soutine. Juicy, jewel-like flickers give the entire surface a striking effect. This painting was among those made for the Federal Art Project program of the WPA.

HARTLEY, Marsden

• **209. Evening Storm, Schoodic, Maine.** (1942)   Hartley distills the grandeur and force of sea pounding against immobile rocks in a painting stripped of all but the most telling elements.

207

2

The basic scheme is a series of horizontals, with the massive red-brown rock as its foundation. A mountain of silvery spray sharply outlines the rock's jagged contour. Behind the breaker loom on-coming waves, the dark, far edge of the water and a faint horizon. Two dark clouds sustain the basic horizontality. Though the painting suggests Winslow Homer's austere sea, it is executed with the lean spareness of prose by Thoreau.

SHAHN, Ben

• **210. Portrait of Myself When Young.** (1943)   A straightforward recollection of the artist's boyhood in Brooklyn, this painting is nevertheless poignantly nostalgic. The illusion of distance and the small scale of the listening boy are eloquent compositional and emotional devices. Despite his size and location, the isolated youth remains the pivot of interest, holding the mass of musicians and the vivid red of the wall in magnetic balance. The space between the boy and the players heightens the feeling of isolation. As in Degas, each figure is portrayed with regard for individual character, and incidental data like the folds of the suits, the typography of the music score and the individual quality about the building strengthen the feeling of a particular experience in time and space. The palette is tellingly limited to a few key colors: the red of the building (artfully confined to the background by the sharply-defined contours of the musicians), the black of the suits, the gray of pavement and windows (blank as in a closed factory) and the gold of the instruments.

WYETH, Andrew

• **211. Christina's World.** (1948)   The mood of Wyeth's most famous picture derives largely from its striking disposition of space. The expanse of brown grass surrounding the girl surges like a sea, an effect heightened by the high, slanted horizon. In this memorable image of loneliness, Wyeth retains an elemental simplicity, despite his attention to detail. "When you lose simplicity, you lose drama," the artist has said, "and drama is what interests me." Wyeth portrays a Maine neighbor, Christina Olson, on her farm. As he told Time magazine, "Christina is a close friend of mine and crippled. Every other day she drags herself across the field from her house to visit the graves of her family. People might call that a gloomy thing to paint, but I don't look

210

at it that way. The field in Christina's world is not really that
large, but I felt it that way. Ever since I was a small kid I felt it
was big." Wyeth viewed the painting as a challenge "to do justice
to her extraordinary conquest of a life which most people would
consider hopeless. . . . Christina's world is outwardly limited—
but in this painting I tried to convey how unlimited it really is."

Abstraction

DELAUNAY, Robert
• **212. Sun Disks.** (1913)   While the shapes in this work are
abstract, they convey associations with clouds, sky, planetary
spheres and sun. The rotating disks at right multiply in blue space.
Opposing contrasts of luminous color are juxtaposed against
whites. Color itself becomes form and dominates the circular
composition. Continuous motion, soaring forms and whirling
rhythms fill the eye. In paintings like this, Delaunay bypassed the
geometry and muted colors of contemporary Cubists, accelerating
the shift toward pure abstraction.

KANDINSKY, Wassily
• **213. Composition (3)** and • **214. Composition (4).** (1914)
"The observer must learn to look for sensations, not objects,"
said Kandinsky of his abstractions; "of the calculation nothing
appears, only the feeling." By 1914 Kandinsky's paintings had become almost completely abstract. They still reflect elements of
visual reality, but not in the form of recognizable water, clouds,
mountains, fields, houses, sunlight or rainbows. The spirit of those
things is present throughout these panels, but transformed into
color, line, form, rhythm, texture and space. In the narrower
panel, a crescent of deep blue-violet establishes a floating base for
the composition. At right, a yellow movement gives the violet
theme sharpness. At both ends of the crescent, momentum is arrested by smaller, explosive shapes. Beneath the crescent, curved
yellow shapes echo its strong movement and direction. A red and
yellow form floats upward in an undulating movement, dissected

211

by lines and zones of color parrying its leftward thrust. In the second panel, a crescendo of more massive forms—resonant, tumultuous and intricate—is grouped at the top of the composition. A slender line of red leads diagonally down to the left; a variety of shapes and movements provides balance at the right. Two undulating verticals sway in echoing rhythms. These paintings, listed only as "two modernistic panels," were sold at an auction of household effects in Ridgefield, Connecticut, in 1953 for less than $50. The buyer, an antique dealer, learned that they were by Kandinsky and sold them to the Museum. Puzzled by the mystery of major, unknown Kandinskys turning up at a country auction, the Museum began an investigation into their history and discovered they were part of a set of four panels commissioned by Edwin R. Campbell, a Canadian industrialist, for the circular foyer of his Park Avenue apartment. The other two Campbell had disposed of in Florida, and a dealer had sold them to the Guggenheim Museum in 1941. Kenneth Lindsay, the leading Kandinsky scholar, was the first to link the Guggenheim panels with those in the Museum of Modern Art and suggest a possible theme—the Four Seasons.

MONDRIAN, Piet

• **215. Broadway Boogie Woogie.** (1942-43)   The culminating achievement of Mondrian's geometric abstraction, his last completed painting is an homage to jazz and the neon glitter of New York. The artist made this picture after his arrival in Manhattan. An old man, his spirits undiminished, he followed two of his old loves, dancing and jazz, visiting Harlem and Greenwich Village to participate, look and listen. In place of literal representation, Mondrian uses color and rhythm to conjure up the tempo of the city. Visual power is distilled from variations of the simplest elements: small and large rectangles; color restricted to red, yellow, blue, gray and white; oppositions of horizontals and verticals; and empty, negative areas juxtaposed against active color units. The

3   214

asymmetrical composition pulsates with movement. Too vivid and lively to be mere design, the painting possesses an insistent, staccato rhythm. No two elements or combinations are quite alike. All shading is rigidly eliminated from the smooth, flat surface, yet space effects are created through the relationships of color to color and to the flatness of the canvas itself. At upper left, for instance, the gray emerges from its red rectangular frame, while the horizontal and vertical yellow units below it recede. The red underneath advances, but the blue and yellow squares to the right are still more dominant in their projection from the plane. Mondrian once said, "True Boogie Woogie I conceive as homogeneous in intention with mine in painting; destruction of melody which is the equivalent of destruction of natural appearance; and construction through the continuous opposition of pure means—dynamic rhythm."

POLLOCK, Jackson
• **216. Number 1.** (1948) Pollock's unorthodox method of pouring or dripping paint on canvas aided him to accelerate his whirls, achieve a rapid vortex and to expand his impetuous vision. The unpredictable is, in part, precisely what he sought, but he also had a general idea of what he wanted and could coax it to life on canvas. In this creation, a maze of shape, color and line explodes across the surface. Vehemence is modified by the seductive luster of the gleaming color, the grace of the lines and the rhythmic alternation of light and dark. What may seem chaos reveals an irregular but apparent order. Shapes and colors compose a harmony independent of associative meaning, complete and alive within itself. Bursts of violet, silver and black play a counterpoint to the momentum of lines. Rhythms sustain themselves in a design without beginning or end. Shapes recede and advance from the surge, relaxing momentarily in the whirl of gentle, winding white at the top. Here, prints of the artist's hands emerge from within the nonobjective forms, maintaining the mood of spontaneous, impassioned sensation and evoking a haunting "real" image. About a year before this picture, Pollock wrote, "I prefer to tack the unstretched canvas to the hard wall or floor.

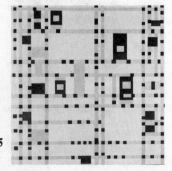

215

I need the resistance of a hard surface. On the floor I am more at ease. I feel nearer, more a part of the painting, since this way I can walk around it, work from the four sides and literally be *in* the painting. This is akin to the method of the Indian sand painters of the West."

TOBEY, Mark

• **217. Edge of August.** (1953)   Tobey told poet and art scholar Selden Rodman that *Edge of August* "is trying to express the thing that lies between two conditions of nature, summer and fall. It's trying to capture that transition and make it tangible. Make it sing. You might say that it's bringing the intangible into the tangible. In that sense, it's the opposite of an abstraction, though the means may appear abstract." Evanescent casein color and delicate form cascade across a violet-pink and green setting. A network of lines weaves across the shimmering background. Golden light helps to unify the elaborate forms. The effect is of a lyric reverie on the change of seasons.

Some Post-War Paintings

KOONING, Willem de

• **218. Woman 1.** (1952)   This is the first of a famous series in which the leading abstract expressionist replies scathingly to the concept of grinning calendar girls. Part representational, part abstract, the picture projects a massive, earthy form, instinct with energy, exploding on the vision with startling power. The grimacing face, huge breasts, lap composed of streaks and feet of dripping flesh-color seem an apotheosis of ugliness, yet the colors that enmesh the bizarre figure are rich, fluid and gleaming. Greens and soft pinks, flashing in animation, set off the stolid pose. The yellows and blues of the breasts and the brown-reds of the skirt vibrate against the lyrical background. The light vertical at right —probably a porch column—and the steps faintly indicated at

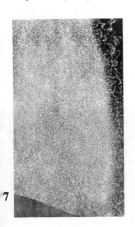

7

218

bottom give stability and counteract the vivid motion of the strokes. As the figure becomes defined, the background functions as a frame of melting color.

DUBUFFET, Jean

• **219. Business Prospers.** (1961) Elaborate textures, a shimmering mosaic of color and childlike placement and perspective are combined here with madcap humor. Dubuffet's dissection of piled-up buildings, interiors, streets, signs, buses, cars and people creates an extravagant cross-section of city activity. Amid an ironic tableau of typists, drinkers, street girls and strollers, a host of business signs are transformed into satirical jests that mock their outward messages.

Naives and Primitives

ROUSSEAU, Henri

• **220. The Sleeping Gypsy.** (1897) This enthralling painting seems simultaneously real and unreal, tense and calm, active and hushed. A massive lion stands silhouetted against the sky, his tail related to the undulating horizon. The sharp diagonal which traces his mane opposes the downward slant of the sleeping figure but parallels the line of the sleeper's shoulders. The contours of the Gypsy's robe flow like the edge of the sand. The curved shadows at her feet sweep back toward her head and mandolin. Alternating bands of color begin with the stripes of the pillow, continue with her headdress and culminate in the delightful reds, yellows, blues and greens of her costume. Her dark skin accents the delicate charm of the robe. A faint spotting of stars, linking the moon to the lion's light-tipped tail, suggests infinite space. Rousseau considered this one of his masterworks. In a letter to his native town of Laval, he wrote: "I have the honor of sending you these few lines as a compatriot of yours who has become a self-taught artist and is desirous that his native city possess one of his works, proposing that you purchase from me a genre painting called 'The Sleeping Gypsy.' [It depicts a] wandering Negress, playing the mandolin, with her jar beside her (vase containing drinking water), asleep, worn out with fatigue. A lion wanders by, detects her and doesn't devour her. There is an effect of moonlight, very poetic. The scene takes place in a completely

219

arid desert. The Gypsy is dressed in Oriental fashion. I will let it go for 1,800 to 2,000 francs because I would be happy that the city of Laval possesses a remembrance of one of its children." The letter was ignored.

- **221. The Dream.** (1910)   In his last year, Rousseau summed up a passion for exotic vistas in this epic panorama. Unlike the starkly simple *The Sleeping Gypsy,* this painting is as densely intertwined as an elaborate tapestry. The array of figures and objects is enriched by deep greens, delicate blues and violets, the soft grays of the elephant and the orange of the snake. The multitude of elements is harmonized with clarity and order, from the base of grass and leaves at bottom to the foliage outlined at top by the silver moon. Nude and couch form the pivotal unit. The couch outlines the emphatic definition of the girl's body and is in turn framed by huge orchid-like flowers. Lions, a curving snake and the striped cloth worn by the serenader define the midway point in the elaborate spatial design. When a critic asked for an explanation of the seemingly implausible combination of themes, the artist replied: "This woman asleep on the couch dreams that she has been transported into the forest, listening to the sounds of the enchanter's instrument." In 1953 Governor Nelson Rockefeller, a Museum trustee, bought and presented *The Dream* to the Museum on its twenty-fifth anniversary.

PICKETT, Joseph
- **222. Manchester Valley.** (1914-18?)   This is the finest of the three paintings by Pickett known to exist. Encircled within the undulating hillside and the fence, the New Hope (Pennsylvania) High School's enormous size makes the other structures seem toy-like. The trees swaying against pale sky, the railroad tracks and the smoke of the train continue the curvilinear motif, while the straight buildings and the line of the waterfall provide contrast. Sand mixed with the paint suggests solidity and substance. Appealing surface elaborations appear in the thick relief of smoke, the colorful train, the earth along the fence and the incisions on the bricks. Pickett was introduced to the art public in the first important exhibition of folk art, held at the Whitney and Newark Museums in 1930. Pickett's *Corryel's Ferry* is now in the Whitney, his *Washington Under the Council Tree* in Newark.

222

KANE, John

• 223. Self Portrait. (1929) Kane portrays himself with unflinching directness in a composition as rugged as an early Italian
primitive. A dark background outlines his spare, muscular body.
His hands join in a firm, almost mystic gesture, and his face looks
out with forthright intensity. Passionate vigor and icon-like rigidity summarize a man strong, proud and down-to-earth. Kane
painted himself at the age of sixty-nine, two years after he received his first recognition in the Carnegie International. A deeply
religious man, Kane quit a job in a steel mill during the days of
the seven-day week because it meant missing church on Sunday.
Years of hard labor show in a still-athletic body.

22

Some notable sculpture in the museum:

Archipenko, Alexander, 1887-1964. *Woman Combing Her Hair,*
1915, bronze.
Arp, Jean (Hans), born 1888. *Floral Nude,* 1957, marble.
Barlach, Ernst, 1870-1938. *Singing Man,* 1928, bronze.
Boccioni, Umberto, 1882-1916. *Unique Forms of Continuity in
Space,* 1913, bronze.
Brancusi, Constantin, 1876-1957. *Maïastra,* 1912, marble.
    Mlle. Pogany, 1913, bronze.
    Bird in Space, 1919, bronze.
    Fish, 1930, marble.
    Blonde Negress, 1933, bronze.
Butler, Reg, born 1913. *Oracle,* date uncertain, forged and cast
bronze.
Calder, Alexander, born 1898. *Lobster Trap and Fish Tail*
(mobile), 1939, steel wire, sheet aluminum.

Despiau, Charles, 1874-1946. *Assia,* 1938, bronze.

Duchamp-Villon, Raymond, 1876-1918. *The Lovers,* 1913, original plaster.
The Horse, 1914, bronze.

Epstein, Jacob, 1880-1959. *The Rock Drill,* 1912-13, bronze.
Mother and Child, 1913, marble.

Ernst, Max, born 1891. *The King Playing with the Queen,* 1944, bronze.

Flannagan, John B., 1898-1942. *Triumph of the Egg, I,* 1937, granite.

Gabo, Naum, born 1890. *Head of a Woman,* about 1917-20, celluloid and metal.
Spiral Theme, 1941, plastic.

Giacometti, Alberto, born 1901. *Man Pointing,* 1947, bronze.
City Square, 1948, bronze.
Chariot, 1950, bronze.
Dog, 1956, bronze.

Gonzales, Julio, 1876-1942. *Head,* 1935?, wrought iron.
Woman Combing Her Hair, 1936, wrought iron.
Torso, 1936?, hammered and welded iron.

Gross, Chaim, born 1904. *Handlebar Riders,* 1935, wood.

Harkavy, Minna R., born 1895. *American Miner's Family,* 1931, bronze.

Hepworth, Barbara, born 1903. *Hollow Form (Penwith),* 1955-56, wood.

Ipoustegy, Jean, born 1920. *David and Goliath,* date uncertain, bronze.

Kolbe, Georg, 1877-1947. *Grief,* 1921, bronze.

Lachaise, Gaston, 1882-1935. *Floating Figure,* 1927, bronze.
Standing Woman, 1932, bronze.

Lehmbruck, Wilhelm, 1881-1919.
  ● *Kneeling Woman,* 1911, cast stone.
Standing Youth, 1913, cast stone.

Lipchitz, Jacques, born 1891. *Man with a Guitar,* 1915, stone.
Figure, 1926-30, bronze.
Mother and Child, II, 1941-45, bronze.

Lippold, Richard, born 1915. *Variation Number 7; Full Moon,* 1949-50, brass rods, nickel-chromium, stainless steel wire.

Maillol, Aristide, 1861-1944. *The Mediterranean,* 1901?, bronze.
Desire, 1904?, plaster relief.
The River, 1939-43, lead.

Manzù, Giacomo, born 1908. *Portrait of a Lady,* 1946, bronze.

Marini, Marino, born 1901. *Curt Valentin,* 1954, bronze.
Miracle, 1953-54, bronze.

Marisol (Escobar), born 1930. *The Family,* 1962, painted wood and other materials.

Matisse, Henri, 1869-1954. *The Slave,* 1900-03, bronze.
Reclining Nude, 1, 1907, bronze.

Four Reliefs; The Back, 1909, 1914?, 1914?, 1929?, bronze.
Five Portraits, Jeannette, 1910-11, bronze.

Modigliani, Amedeo, 1884-1920. *Caryatid,* 1914?, limestone.
Head, 1915?, stone.

Moore, Henry, born 1898. *Two Forms,* 1934, pynkado wood.
Family Group, 1945-49, bronze.
Reclining Figure II, 1960, bronze.

Nadelman, Elie, 1882-1946. *Man in the Open Air,* 1915?, bronze.
Woman at the Piano, 1917?, wood, stained and painted.

Nevelson, Louise, born 1900. *Sky Cathedral,* 1958, painted wood.

Noguchi, Isamu, born 1904. *Even the Centipede,* 1952, kasama
ware, wood.

Pevsner, Antoine, 1886-1962. *Torso,* 1924-26, plastic and copper.
Developable Column, 1942, brass and oxidized bronze.

Picasso, Pablo, born 1881. *Woman's Head,* 1909, bronze.
Glass of Absinthe, 1914, painted bronze with silver spoon.
Pregnant Woman, 1950, bronze.
Baboon and Young, 1951, bronze.
Goat Skull and Bottle, 1951-52, painted bronze.
She-Goat, 1950, bronze.

Renoir, Auguste, 1841-1919. *The Washerwoman,* 1917, bronze.

Richier, Germaine, 1904-1959. *The Devil with Claws,* 1952,
bronze.

Rodin, Auguste, 1840-1917. *St. John the Baptist Preaching,* 1878,
bronze.
Monument to Balzac, 1898, bronze.

Rosso, Medardo, 1858-1928. *The Concierge,* 1883, wax over
plaster.
The Bookmaker, 1894, wax over plaster.

Roszak, Theodore J., born 1907. *The Spectre of Kitty Hawk,*
1946-47, welded, hammered steel, bronze, brass.

Smith, David, born 1906. *History of Leroy Borton,* 1956, steel.

THE FRICK COLLECTION

Fifth Avenue at 70th Street.   BU 8-0700

Hours: Tuesdays through Saturdays 10-5; Sundays and holidays 1-5. Closed Mondays, major holidays and during August. Free (children under sixteen must be accompanied by adults; those under ten not admitted).

Transportation: Fifth Avenue Buses except 5 and 15 to 69th Street; Madison Avenue Bus to 69th Street. Lexington Avenue IRT local to 68th Street.

Talks: Illustrated art lectures Wednesdays through Saturdays at 3, October through May.

Concerts: Chamber music Sunday afternoons; frequent organ recitals.

Reference library: Books, photographs and other reference material.

The Frick Collection, one of the greatest in America, was bequeathed to the public in its original palatial home. It includes paintings, sculpture, drawings, period interiors, painted enamels, antique furniture, rare porcelains and Renaissance bronzes.

Henry Clay Frick (1849-1919) was born in Westmoreland County, Pennsylvania. After working as farm hand and bookkeeper for his grandfather, the distiller Abraham Overholt, he began a spectacular financial career in 1871 by forming a company to operate coke ovens. He was a millionaire at thirty. In later years he directed such huge enterprises as U.S. Steel and the

151

Pennsylvania Railroad. An ardent anti-unionist, he defeated a historic 1892 strike at Homestead, Pennsylvania, in which ten men were killed and sixty wounded. In the bitterness caused by that struggle, Alexander Berkman, an anarchist, walked into Frick's office and shot and stabbed him. Frick recovered; Berkman was sentenced to 21 years in prison.

Frick's interest in art began when few Americans possessed important collections. He started with names that have since dimmed—Bouguereau, Lhermitte, Alma-Tadema and Ziem—but his taste deepened greatly. Eventually he acquired outstanding paintings by masters like Bellini, Titian, Rembrandt, Vermeer, El Greco, Velázquez and Goya.

Frick's will provided that, after the death of his wife, his mansion, a collection of 139 paintings and a fund of $15,000,000 be devoted to the study and enjoyment of art by the public. (The mansion, in Louis XVI style, was designed by Thomas Hastings and built between 1913 and 1914; Sir Charles Allom created special interior arrangements for favorite paintings.) Mrs. Frick died in 1931, and in 1935 the house was opened, after extensive remodeling, as a museum. While most of the paintings now on view were chosen by Frick himself, some, including masterpieces by Duccio, Chardin, Ingres and van Eyck, were acquired after his death.

Note: A floor plan of the Museum and its displays is available for 5¢ at the admissions desk.

Italian Painting

DUCCIO DI BUONINSEGNA

● **224. Temptation of Christ.** (1308-1311)   On June 9, 1311, the completed altarpiece of which this panel forms a part was borne in triumph from Duccio's studio to the Cathedral of Siena. An old narrative gives a glimpse of the role art played then in community life: "The shops were shut [and] one after another the worthiest, with lighted candles in their hands, took places near the picture . . . all the bells ringing joyously out of reverence for so noble a picture as this." The panel shows Satan offering Christ all the kingdoms of the world if He would fall down and worship him, an event tradition says took place on a hill near the road from Jerusalem to Jericho. In this rare work, Medieval concepts drawn from Byzantine symbolism are invigorated by the beginnings of dramatic realism. The encounter is depicted partly as symbol, partly as actuality: the gold background, for instance, is a traditional rendering of the idea of pure light, the dwelling place of God, but against this abstraction Duccio opposes the everyday familiarity of Sienese buildings and walls. Oppositions of dark

and light, warmth and coolness, heighten the tension of the confrontation. Jesus is resplendent in sinuous robes of blue and crimson, his gesture commanding and majestic. Satan's eerie form is
made darker still by silhouetting his wings and torso against the
gold sky. A semi-circle formed by the base swings the eye between Satan and Christ and his angels. Colorful buildings provide
geometric contrast to the predominant circular motif. Duccio's
Siena altarpiece, called the Maestà, depicts scenes from the lives
of Christ and of Mary, patroness of the city. It is his masterpiece.

PIERO DELLA FRANCESCA
• **225. St. John the Evangelist** (?). (1454-1469)   Power and stability are expressed in the Saint's rock-like stance and sharp contours, framed by the pale wall and sky. The head is austere. The
body is rooted to the earth, immovable and monumental. Resonant red is modulated in the geometric folds which Piero conveys
with vitality and rhythm. This panel belonged to an altarpiece
painted for the Church of St. Agostino at Borgo San Sepolcro.

BELLINI, Giovanni
• **226. St. Francis in Ecstasy.** (About 1480)   In this fervently
spiritual painting, one of the finest Italian pictures in America
and among the first great renderings of landscape, Bellini portrays
the climactic event in the life of St. Francis—his receiving of the
stigmata. A youthful profligate who gave up his idle existence to
"marry poverty," the founder of the Franciscan order had in 1224
retired to a rocky peak near Assisi for forty days of fast and
meditation. On or about September 14, an awesome vision appeared to him: a seraph bearing the image of the body of Christ
Crucified. The Saint felt great pain and subsequently found on his
own body marks of the five wounds of the Savior. These were
said to have remained with him until his death, two years later.
So deep is the spirituality of this painting that however dazzling
it is as visual description, the spectator senses it is no mere in-

24

225

ventory of land and sky. Everything seems isolated in a golden
moment of fervent intensity. The landscape glorifies man's harmony with nature—a fit setting for the patron Saint of animals.
Color and light heighten the mystic mood. A blue sky enhances
walls turned golden in late afternoon sun, while their warmth
sets off the strong forms and sweeping rhythms of the blue-grey
rocks. Slender, graceful plants not only relieve the rugged stone
mass but suggest a close-up, frontal space plane, intensifying the
effect of a vista. Each shape is painted with meticulous detail,
yet the Saint remains the commanding focus of the panorama,
balanced by trees at the right and upper left. The diagonal line
of grass framing the rocky slope is countered by a second diagonal, then by the horizontal line of the castle (or monastery) and
finally echoed in the distance. Behind the Saint, the lectern anticipates the diagonal thrust of the rocks. Though line and precise
contour are dominant and softness of atmosphere is only partially
conveyed, the use of glowing color to describe light and mould
form makes this painting a major prelude to later Venetian art.

TITIAN

• **227. Pietro Aretino.** (About 1548)   Friendly but unflattering,
Titian portrays his close companion, Aretino, the kitchen servant
who rose to international fame on the strength of his scurrilous
pen. Massive proportions give Aretino dignity. While the breadth
and scale of the figure almost dwarf the head, it is still the face—
sensual, keen, visionary and domineering—which holds the eye.
Fabrics shimmer with luminous color, as in the subdued glow of
the copper red sleeves against the quiet background. Aretino's
bawdy plays, erotic verse and, ironically, an imaginary "Biography of the Virgin Mary" were best sellers. His widely circulated
letters and poems functioned so effectively as literary blackmail
that many potential targets offered costly gifts to buy off his darts.
Aretino boasted that in eighteen years, "the Alchemy of my pen
has drawn over 25,000 gold crowns from the entrails of various

226

2

Princes." In 1527, to escape the wrath of Pope Clement VII, whom he had libeled in a satire, Aretino settled in Venice, where he and Titian began their long friendship.

VERONESE

• **228. The Choice of Hercules.** (About 1576)   Veronese retells a legend in which Hercules, in choosing between Virtue and Vice, symbolizes man's difficult path toward integrity. Oddly depicted as a mild and refined Venetian nobleman, Hercules seeks to escape the grasping fingers of Vice and enter the welcoming arms of Virtue. Virtue, dignified and serene, is crowned with laurels; Vice, wearing a cyclamen wreath (an ancient symbol of sensuality and death), holds a deck of cards and a love potion. Diametrical lines form the base of the composition and heighten its grandeur. The first runs from the curving mass of the arm and back of the left-hand figure, through the center figure, on to the woman at the right, and finally to the tree behind her. The other follows the direction of the clouds and runs downward to the angle of the edge of the green dress. The textures are lustrous, opulent and seductive.

• **229. Wisdom (or Virtue) and Strength.** (About 1576)   This companion piece to *The Choice of Hercules* lacks some of the power and splendor that give the first its vitality. Hercules appears here as a superman in lion's skin. Wisdom is a fashionably-gowned matron. They stand above earthly love (Cupid) and worldly wealth (the globe, crown and jewels). The sun, an attribute of Wisdom, appears above her head. Outstanding elements include the shimmering sky and foliage (a forerunner of the atmospheric effects in Rubens), the sparkle of the gown, and the resonance of the flesh coloring. An intriguing rhythm occurs in the swaying pose of Hercules and the opposing movement of the folds of Wisdom's gown. These two Veronese paintings, it is believed, were once in the palace of Emperor

8

229

Rudolf II in Prague. When the city was captured by the Swedes in 1648, the pictures passed into the collection of Queen Christina. Purchased long afterward for the French Government, they were later dispersed by the Revolution to England.

Flemish Painting

VAN EYCK, Jan (and PETRUS CHRISTUS?)
• **230. Virgin and Child with Saints and a Donor.** (1441-1443?) This jewel-like painting is one of the few in America attributed to the foremost master of Flemish art. The immediate impact of the panel is that of its superlative craftsmanship and minutely rendered detail. But once these qualities have asserted themselves, the dazzling host of objects coalesces into a compact and solemn composition. The arrangement centers on Virgin and Child, isolated within a frame-like canopy. The canopy and the red at left and lower right comprise handsome color notes against the generally cool tonality. The columns of the arches and the figures function as vertical motifs against the base of the floor and the horizon. Between the arches, a calm sky gives relief to the intense liveliness of canopy, figures, folds, landscape and tiles. The eye scans the world from near to far off. At left is St. Barbara, holding the palm leaf symbol of martyrdom and standing by the tower in which her father isolated her from suitors. When a Christian disguised as a physician visited the girl and converted her to Christianity, her furious father struck her head off himself. To the right stands St. Elizabeth, daughter of a King of Hungary and wife of a nobleman who died in the Crusades. Her short life was one of self-sacrifice on behalf of the sick and the poor; her triple crown indicates royal birth, high marriage and glorification in Heaven. The kneeling figure is probably Jan Vos, a Carthusian prior who may have commissioned the painting. It was Vos, in any event, who placed the panel above the altar of the monastery church at Nieuwhicht,

230

2

near Utrecht, in 1450. In the 16th Century the church was destroyed, and the painting disappeared until about 1850, when it entered the collection of Baron James de Rothschild of Paris. In 1954, the Frick Collection acquired it from the Rothschild family for a rumored price of about $750,000. Since van Eyck could not have completed the entire painting in the few months between its commission and his death, some scholars ascribe only the Virgin to him—perhaps because the figure of the donor is rather harsh and St. Elizabeth's crown seems inferior to the jeweled border on the Virgin's cloak—and the rest to his associate, Petrus Christus. Other authorities consider it a complete, but early, van Eyck.

VAN DYKE, Anthony

• **231. Frans Snyders.** (About 1625) Snyders (1579-1657), a painter specializing in animals and still life, was, like van Dyke, one of the ablest assistants of Rubens. Van Dyke painted him several times and in this version produced one of his most sensitive portraits. The swirling movement perfected by Rubens is adapted here in a graceful, elegant composition enhanced by rich, subdued colors. The curtain and glimpse of sky, echoing the pose of the figure, lend calm grandeur. The companion portrait of Snyders' wife Margareta—a sister of the still life painter Paul de Vos and of Cornelius de Vos, another able Rubens assistant—lacks fluency and élan and is weakened by an overemphasis of ornament on the stomacher. These two portraits were sold separately in London in 1792 and were reunited in the Frick Collection in 1909.

Spanish Painting

EL GRECO

• **232. Saint Jerome**. (About 1586-94) The Saint's elongated head, rising from the powerful pyramid of the flame-like mantle, holds the eye like a magnet. The worn, craggy face, the brooding

233

eyes piercing out from pallid flesh, and the scraggly gray-white beard contribute to a masterly characterization of intense spiritual power. The stark color contrasts heighten the drama. The signed original of several versions of St. Jerome by El Greco, this painting was bought secretly from the Cathedral of Valladolid in 1904. Although the Louvre tried to acquire it, it was sold to Frick in 1905. St. Jerome (347?-419), a father of the Western Church, translated the Bible from Greek into the Latin version still used in Roman Catholic services.

• **233. Expulsion from the Temple.** (About 1604-1613)   St. John relates that when Jesus found merchants and money changers in the temple at Jerusalem, he "made a scourge of small cords . . . drove them all out of the temple . . . and poured out the changers' money, and overthrew the tables; and said unto them that sold doves, 'Take these things hence; make not my Father's house a house of merchandise!' " This small but tempestuous composition attains epic impact. A sinuous pyramid centers on Christ, whose figure is repeatedly emphasized by placement, by the carmine and blue of His robes, by the arch above His head and by the space at His feet formed by the overturned table and the leg of the kneeling man. The picture vibrates with a counterpoint of movement and clang of color. One group of figures is linked by the angle formed by the table, the back of the man stooping to clutch a money chest and the back of the figure in green. As these move the eye diagonally left, an opposing action starts with the stooping man and continues past the figure raising his arm in protection. In the resulting V-shaped interval, an outflung hand extends an intricate space design that flows upward from the table, past Christ, through the arch and on to the buildings and sky. On the right, meanwhile, the curve of the kneeling man's back acts as a foil to the lines of his head and arm. Those lines are echoed in the hem of the skirt of the girl walking into the now purified temple, her rhythmic grace in harmony with the arches above her head. To Christ's right, meditative men, perhaps Apostles, ponder his action; at left are the merchants and money changers. On the temple wall appear the expulsion of Adam and Eve from Paradise (above the sinners) and the sacrifice of Isaac by Abraham, who, at the Lord's behest, was willing to give up his son—a sacrifice foretelling Christ's.

VELAZQUEZ, Diego
• **234. Philip IV of Spain.** (1644)   Velázquez objectively portrays his patron, the haughty King who ruled during the period of Spain's decline. The handling is quiet, but strong. Face and figure emerge gradually but vividly from the background. Colors that seem sumptuous are actually a sparse palette of red, silver, brown, black and flesh. Form bathed in light is projected with

ease, simplicity and dignity. Velázquez uses paint with such directness that his magic brushwork, which concentrates only on telling essentials and acts as much by suggestion as through detail, conveys a persuasive image of reality. His virtuosity is readily apparent in the silvery sleeve, stiff but flexible; in the silver trimmings on the cloak; in the darting strokes on the hilt of the sword, and in the lightly brushed flesh of the hands. The right hand, the black felt hat and the baton function as a base for the gentle pyramid scheme. Philip IV (1605-1665) ascended the throne in 1621. Velázquez, who became court painter two years later, portrayed him some 34 times, but this version, called the Fraga portrait, is unique among them—and practically unique among all old masters—in that an exact record of its progress has survived to this day. In April, 1644, the King journeyed to the Catalan town of Fraga to celebrate a victory against the French. During his stay, he ordered a portrait done, and the Royal Quartermaster dutifully recorded the following expenses: "Paid to the said carpenter . . . 6 reales for making an easel which he made so that Diego Velázquez might make a portrait of his Majesty." "On the first of June, at Fraga, his Majesty commanded the closet [chamber] for the taking of his portrait to be set in order, since it was very ill-appointed, and without any floor, and the walls were falling; for the whole place was but a chimney-flue. Total cost, shoring, wood frames and plaster, and opening a window, 24 reales." "The portrait took in the making three days at different times, each day was bought a load of rushes for the floor, cost of each load 4 reales." Then on August 16: "The King . . . sent to the Queen or Lady a portrait of himself as he is in the campaign; very, very life-like, and dressed in red and silver, carrying a baton." "The Catalans begged the King to lend it to them for this day [the day of the royal entry] which favor he granted with pleasure and grace. The canvas was hung in the church under a canopy embroidered in gold; where much people congregated to see it." In 1911, the

235

art dealer Joseph Duveen, who all but monopolized the sale
of old masters and was striving for Frick's exclusive patronage,
was shown a photograph of this painting and dismissed it as a
copy of the presumed original, which hung in Dulwich Castle,
England. A rival dealer, however, realized that the newly discovered work was in fact a lost Velázquez. Duveen, learning of
his mistake, tried to buy the oil, but his rival scored a great coup
by selling it to Frick for a reported $400,000. The Dulwich
painting is now considered a copy by Mazo, Velázquez's son-in-
law.

GOYA, Francisco

• 235. The Forge. (About 1818-1819) One of the greatest
Goyas in America, *The Forge* challenges the two dominant styles
of its time: Neoclassicism, with its lofty themes, precise outlines
and sober color; and Romanticism, with its love of the erotic and
flamboyant. In fact, *The Forge* foreshadows the realism of
Daumier, Courbet and Manet, and, through its emotional force,
anticipates aspects of modern Expressionism. The painting glows
with energy and motion achieved with economy of means. The
vigor of the composition is based largely on two opposing
diagonals: the line leading down from the upraised hammer,
past the anvil to the foreshortened foot of the opposite figure;
and a shorter line from the arm holding the hot iron toward the
outthrust foot of the man in the shirt. The greyish-greens, browns
and blacks are enlivened by the anvil—a burst of red which
binds all the figures together and, by its key role in the center,
intensifies the effect of the deep space in the background. *The
Forge* may have been painted when the artist was past seventy.
It is believed to have been bought by King Louis Philippe of
France from the artist's son. The King exhibited it in 1836 in
the so-called Spanish Museum in the Louvre; when he was
overthrown in 1848 and fled to England, he took with him many
of his Spanish paintings, including *The Forge*. It was later sold
at auction.

236

Dutch Painting

REMBRANDT

- **236. Nicolas Ruts.** (1631) Though the merchant Nicolas Ruts was probably one of the first subjects to pose for the twenty-five-year-old Rembrandt after his arrival in Amsterdam, the master's ability to paint physical facts is already evident—notably in the fur, flesh and chair. The young Rembrandt employs a rather common portraiture scheme—a figure posed against a gray background—but the color is subtle and rich and the man's attitude is at once informal and dignified. While Rembrandt's probing of character would go far beyond the emphasis on rendering evident in this painting, the handling of space does hint at his more dramatic later approach. The hand on the chair is used as a close-up frontal device, while the hand with the paper recedes at an angle. The right sleeve slopes back past the collar to the hat, where the soft flow of dark colors creates a gradual background depth. An interesting comparison may be made between the relationship of hands, face and background in this work and in the nearby, later *Self Portrait*. Owners of this painting have included two Dutch monarchs—Queen Frederica and William II—and J. P. Morgan. This oil is the earliest authentic Rembrandt in a New York museum.

- **237. The Polish Rider.** (About 1654) The warrior-on-horseback theme, usually rendered with military pomp and swagger, finds a fresh interpretation in this painting. Rembrandt creates a romantic picture in which tangibles are distilled into a mysterious vision, palpable yet hauntingly suggestive. Horse and rider are held within the frame of the rocky background. The turn of the rider's head creates a counter-rhythm to the movement of the horse. The irregular horizon, culminating in a domed fortress, provides a second counterbalance, functioning as a parallel mass to horse and rider. The background looms close; the sky behind it suggests infinite space, tinged by a strange dusk or sunset. Mountain and land fuse simply with water. What appears to be a watchfire becomes the key to a series of jewel-like notes in the reds of the hat and legs and the bursts of golden color on the face, elbow, saddle and boot. Firm planes of sculpturesque solidity mould the head of the horse and maintain the weight of its foreleg. This is one of only two known Rembrandt equestrian portraits. The young rider remains unidentified. The painting is first recorded as belonging to Stanislaus II, the last King of Poland. Frick acquired it in 1910.

- **238. Portrait of Himself.** (1658) This superlative autobiography is an epic image of the human spirit, embodied in a proud and indomitable emperor of the realm of art. The composition is superficially traditional: a pyramid formed by a figure in a chair, with lap and hands forming the base and sloping arms leading the eye to the head. The hand holding the silver-topped stick—a hand of massive structural planes—advances forward and is linked to the right hand by the sash. The smock and cloak lead gradually to the luminous climax of the intent face, with its piercing glance. Shadowed forehead and velvet hat flow into mysterious dark regions. The dazzling surface of golden light and velvety shadow employs only a few color tones and hues. They scoop out lights, recede into darkness and fuse with and overflow mass and line. Fluent brushstrokes mold structure, as in the facial features, neck, chin and left hand. This self-portrait was painted during the decline of Rembrandt's commercial popularity, though certainly not of his artistic power. In the same year, his house (now the Rembrandt Museum) was sold, and he technically worked as a consultant for an art firm organized by his mistress, Hendrickje Stoffels, and his son Titus—a device hit upon to prevent creditors from seizing the proceeds from his paintings.

VERMEER, Jan
• **239. Officer and Laughing Girl.** (About 1657)   This luminous painting exploits contrasting light values and the drama of scale, notably in the striking perspective of the window and the placement of the officer's looming silhouette against the smaller figure of the girl. The wall surface is a subtle composition of space intervals and counterbalances. A yellow-toned introductory unit, composed of the space between the edge of the window, the lion-headed chair, and the curving shoulder and hat brim, complements the inverted triangle of the portion of the wall between the map, the girl's shoulder and the back of her chair. The map's horizontal edge provides a stately line stabilizing the slant of the window. Restrained blue tones lend excitement to the vivid red of the uniform and the glisten of the gold-yellow dress. As late as 1866, this painting bore the forged signature of de Hooch, whose works brought higher prices.

238

• **240. Mistress and Maid.** (About 1670)   In this unspectacular but memorable composition, a quiet moment of everyday life is transformed into a subtle drama of mood and gesture. Every detail is co-ordinated: the slant of the maid's note relates to the position of the quill; the pearls in the mistress' hair define her head and complement the pattern of the fur; the delicate shadow slanting across her lap guides the eye past the table back to the maid's hand. This painting was once attributed to Terborch, a lesser master whose more obviously illustrational work hangs nearby. Joseph Duveen acquired the painting in 1919 and in the same year sold it to Frick. It was Frick's last acquisition.

German Painting

HOLBEIN, Hans, the Younger

• **241. Sir Thomas More.** (1527)   Here is an uncompromising essay in literal appearance, even to the stubble on the chin. While Holbein lingers upon (and perhaps overemphasizes) such surface details as the folds and highlights on the sleeve and the green curtain, his objective recording of visual fact vividly characterizes More's determination and forthrightness. Sir Thomas More, a leading humanist scholar, statesman and diplomat, was Henry VIII's Lord Chancellor. A staunch Roman Catholic, he refused to take the Oath of Allegiance acknowledging the King, not the Pope, as the chief authority of the English Church. Tried for high treason and beheaded in 1535, More was beatified in 1886 and canonized in 1935. More was a friend of Erasmus, the philosopher and satirist, who was in turn a friend of Holbein; on his first visit to England in 1526, Holbein lived at More's house.

241

French Painting

LA TOUR, Georges de
• **242. Education of the Virgin.** (About 1640)   The dramatic
use of light from a single candle or torch—which in painting
often symbolizes the presence of the spirit of Christ—is typical
of de la Tour. It not only unifies his compositions but greatly
heightens their spiritual mood. While de la Tour, unlike Rembrandt and Vermeer, sometimes stressed his light effects at the
sacrifice of other elements, they are employed here in a highly
personal and striking manner. The artist achieves an indefinably
solemn relationship between the figures of the young Virgin and
St. Anne and the forms of the candle, book and workbasket.
Simultaneously, he explores the blending of form and outline,
as in the Virgin's hair.

FRAGONARD, Jean Honoré
• **243. The Pursuit;** • **244. Storming the Citadel;** • **245. Love
Letters** • **246. The Lover Crowned.** (1771-1773)   These famous
panels were commissioned by Mme. du Barry, successor to Mme.

242

244

de Pompadour as mistress of Louis XV, for the dining room of her new country pavilion at Louveciennes. Known as *The Progress of Love* or the *Romance of Young Love*, they are the quintessence of Fragonard's art, abounding in charm, delicate and decorative color and crisp, featherlight handling. Wistful gaiety and light-hearted sentiment hover over Fragonard's light-opera world of aristocrats playing at rustic lovers. Yet there is dignity in the sensitive composition—in the upward flow of space, the rhythmic sway of dark, plume-like foliage, and the landscapes which convey an eternal summer mood. Fabrics rustle and shimmer, and the artist's touch is deft. In *The Pursuit,* a lover proffers a rose to a maiden who pretends to flee his romantic intrusion. In *Storming the Citadel,* a maiden, beneath a statute of Venus and Cupid, warns her lover, who climbs to her from a ladder on the parapet. In *Love Letters,* the girl shares with her beau the pleasure of his missives. In *The Lover Crowned,* the lady wreathes her paramour with roses while a rapt artist sketches the romantic tableau. Mme. du Barry eventually rejected Fragonard's panels in favor of the more up-to-date minor Neoclassicist Joseph-Marie Vien, teacher of David. In 1790 Fragonard took them to his home in Grasse, where they remained almost unknown for a century. They were purchased by J. P. Morgan for $310,000, and in 1915 Frick acquired them from Morgan's estate for a reported $1,250,000.

CHARDIN, Jean Baptiste
• **247. Lady with a Bird-Organ.** (1751)   Rich colors bathe each surface with texture and luminosity. Chardin "draws" as much with soft tones and hues as with masses and outlines. The flow of colors and the drift of light and dark carry the eye from the window, to the stand and bird cage, to the figure in the gleaming dress (believed to be Chardin's second wife) and finally to the background. Every unit is firmly but unobtrusively releated. Atmosphere becomes almost palpable. A bird-organ was a device

247

used in teaching canaries to sing. This painting was owned by
King Louis XV, the Marquis Marigny (a Director of Fine Arts
to the King) and D. V. Denon (famed Director of the Louvre
under Napoleon.)

INGRES, Jean Auguste Dominique
• **248. Comtesse D'Haussonville.** (1842-45)   Ingres is admired
today more for his portraits than for his elaborate and sometimes pretentious classical paintings. This oil of a lovely lady
posed in her salon ranks with his best. The artist made many
drawings for this picture, and the patient Comtesse, whose first
child was born between the painting's start and completion,
recorded that "for the last nine days Ingres has been painting
on one of the hands." "To paint a portrait like this," declared her
friend the statesman Thiers, "[Ingres] must have been in love
with the model." Every placement plays a meticulous role in the
precise ensemble. The Comtesse's figure inclines to the right, while
the mantel provides a diagonal balance toward the left. The
mantel affords a charming interlude between the figure and the
mirrored reflection. Depth is developed by the reflection, the
shawl at lower right, the mantelpiece (which also links the
two sides of the composition), the woodwork extending the movement of the mantelpiece, the Sèvres vases and the placement of
flowers, visiting cards and opera glasses. The finesse of the drawing and the enamel-smooth surface embody Ingres' belief that
"the touch is simply an abuse in execution." His color, usually
subordinate to contour and line, achieves high quality here, especially in the marvellously painted dress, the wood, the red of
the hair ribbon and the flowers. Louise de Broglie d'Haussonville
was the granddaughter of the famous writer Mme. de Staël,
daughter of the President of the National Council, and wife of
a member of the Academy. She wrote a life of Byron, a book on
the Irish nationalist martyr Robert Emmet and a life of the 16th
Century beauty and wit, Margaret of Valois. She also painted,

248

acted and produced amateur theatricals. Notable artists and writers—including the two giant opponents, Delacroix and Ingres —were guests in her salon.

ROUSSEAU, Théodore

● **249. Village of Becquigny.** (1857-1864)   Rosseau worked on this famous painting for years. "To finish a picture," wrote a close friend, "was the misery of his life." Another Rousseau enthusiast lamented that "for this poor hamlet in Picardy, Rousseau painted a firmament in which Buddha would have chosen his throne of light." The quiet composition is based on an unspectacular but appealing use of devices adopted from Dutch landscape painters: the horizontals of the fields, rooftops and sky and the verticals of trees. Flecks of color in the sky, the rough surface of the grass and the thatched rooftops add the interest of texture and rhythm to a sober scene. Light suffuses the fields. The road, rider, diminishing houses and trees outlined against the sky add a delightful sense of vista. The artist promised this canvas to his most devoted patron, Frederick Hartman. As years passed and the picture remained incomplete, Hartman pleaded for possession before he became too old to enjoy it. The collector seized the painting from the studio the day before Rousseau died—probably to bypass the cumbersome legal process of proving ownership of an item from the estate.

COROT, Jean Baptiste Camille

⊃ **250. The Boatman of Mortefontaine.** (About 1865)   With consumate charm, Corot captures morning mist, cool light and the tranquility of water fusing with sky. A few subdued tones play over the painting with great resourcefulness. The greyish-violet reflections of the house and trees merge into a continuous mass, its straight edges providing a graceful foil to the curve of a slender birch. Everything is feathery, yet substantial. The mood is fresh and happy as morning, a blend of blithe romanticism and reality in which Corot's highly personal vision of nature serves as a prelude to Impressionism.

251

RENOIR, Pierre Auguste

• **251. Mother and Children.** (About 1874)   Grouped as if the artist had merely glanced at them for a moment, the figures are actually artfully moulded into a pyramid. Even the dark color of the doll's jacket adds its accent to an arrangement which centers on the mother's figure, with its sloping shoulders and skirt flaring at the bottom. The edge of the garden path recedes in a contrasting direction to that of the main group, assisting the gentle sequence of frontality from children, to mother, to the cluster of figures and finally to the trees. Atmosphere bathes all. Characteristic of this period in Renoir's career are the porcelain delicacy of surface and the emphatic pattern of light and dark. The canvas gleams with bouquet-like sparkle and delicate color. The airy grace and charm recall Renoir's fondness for 18th Century French art. Acquired in 1918, the year before the death of both the artist and the collector, this painting joins a Degas oil as probably the only major works chosen by Frick while their artists were still alive.

British Painting

HOGARTH, William

• **252. Miss Mary Edwards.** (1742)   Too realistic to idealize his sitters, Hogarth received relatively few portrait commissions. Even in this one, while the composition does reflect the elaborate poses and settings favored by English followers of van Dyke, the face is conceived with a shrewd and terse directness. The curtain serves as a counterpoint to the warm flesh. The white fabric, rendered with detailed, lively folds, acts to frame the face and prevent its features from being overwhelmed by the large red areas and the contrasting cool, dim background. The unconventional Mary Edwards, whose father was a patron of Hogarth, inherited vast land holdings throughout England. The year before this portrait she had replied to critics of her unorthodox clothes

252

by commissioning Hogarth to paint a scathing satire, *Taste in High Life*. She married Lord Hamilton secretly but eventually disclaimed the marriage to safeguard her holdings.

GAINSBOROUGH, Thomas
• **253. The Honorable Frances Duncombe.** (1777-1778) The English full-length portrait, evolving from van Dyke and too often oversweetened, here achieves a genuine charm. Without diluting quality, Gainsborough conjures up a scintillating, silky surface, filled with lightness, freshness and sheen. The luminous landscape with its sway of delicate trees adds rhythmic contrast to the figure, and the typical portrait props of the period function as well-organized units of high quality. Frances Duncombe was the daughter of Lord Laversham, Baron of Downtown Wilts.

CONSTABLE, John
• **254. The White Horse (A Scene on the River Stour).** (About 1819) Nearly all the ingredients of a conventionally pretty landscape appear in this brilliant painting of the Suffolk countryside near the artist's birthplace. Form and mass are united in a relaxed but firmly woven composition. The white horse at left guides the eye past the water and the thatched roof to the central trees, the clouds, the curve of the road and finally to the smaller tree. The foreground is underlined by handsomely painted rushes linked to the dark reflection of the tree, to the tree itself and again to earth and sky. The painting is suffused with light and enriched by glowing color. Clouds pulse with windy motion, water glistens and the rushes sway rhythmically. The artist described this picture as "one of my happiest efforts on a large scale, being a placid representation of a serene morning of summer." Archdeacon Fisher of Salisbury Cathedral, an intimate friend, paid Constable one hundred pounds for it, but the artist later bought it back and kept it the rest of his life. After the triumphant reception of his *Haywain* in Paris, he was invited to exhibit in Lille, chose this painting and was awarded the gold medal. *The White Horse* was acquired by Frick from the J. P. Morgan Collection.

American Painting

WHISTLER, James Abbott McNeill
• **255. Mrs. Leyland (Symphony in Flesh Color and Pink).** (1872-1873) Whistler combines the representation of a figure with a fastidious arrangement of low-keyed tones, balanced space divisions, novel rhythmic patterns and subtle, almost flat decorative surfaces. The woman emerges delicately from within the setting. Face, chiffon gown, wall and floor compose a delicate harmony as graceful and fragile as the spray of almond blossoms which defines the edges of the painting. The artist spent much time selecting a dress to fit the scheme and made so many erasures

and fresh starts that he eventually called in a model when working on the gown. Mrs. Frederick R. Leyland was the wife of a
Liverpool shipping tycoon and art collector who, incidentally, is
credited with suggesting that Whistler call his night pictures
"nocturnes." Whistler was engaged for a brief period to Mrs.
Leyland's younger sister, but in 1877 his friendship with the family ended with a bitter dispute. The magnate had bought a mansion in London and had hung Whistler's *Arrangement in Rose
and Silver; the Princess from the Land of Porcelain* in the dining
room. An eminent interior decorator, however, had covered the
room's walls with richly painted old Cordova leather, which
Whistler considered a highly unsuitable setting. The Leylands,
about to go on a trip, gave the artist permission to make some
changes. Whistler painted blue and gold peacocks over the
leather, then held receptions and gave press interviews in the
room, which he now called "Harmony in Blue and Gold." When
the Leylands returned, they were astounded, but decided to accept the affront in good grace. Unfortunately, Whistler shortly
afterwards referred to Leyland with the gibe, "Well, what can
you expect from a *parvenu*?" Mrs. Leyland overheard him and
ordered him out of their house. The house was sold in 1892.
Collector Charles Freer bought the room and the *Arrangement
in Rose and Silver*. Both, along with a Whistler portrait of
Frederick Leyland, are in the Freer Gallery in Washington.

254

Some notable sculpture in the museum:

Barbet, Jehan de Lyon (active 1475-1514).
● *Angel,* 1475, bronze.
Houdon, Jean Antoine, 1742-1828. *Diana,* 1778?, terra cotta.
Laurana, Francesco da, 1420-1500. *Bust of a Lady,* 1470?, marble.
Attributed to Pollaiuolo, Antonio, 1433?-1498. *David,* date uncertain, bronze.
Vecchietta, Lorenzo di Pietro, 1412?-1480. *Resurrection of Christ,* 1472, bronze.

THE SOLOMON R. GUGGENHEIM
MUSEUM

Fifth Avenue between 88th & 89th Streets.
EN 9-5110

Hours: Tuesdays through Saturdays 10-6, except Thursdays 10-9; Sundays and holidays 12-6. Closed Mondays (except Labor Day), July Fourth and Christmas. Admission: 50¢; children under six free.

Transportation: Fifth Avenue Buses 2, 3 or 4 to 89th Street; 86th Street Crosstown Bus to Fifth Avenue. Lexington Avenue IRT to 86th Street.

Talks: Illustrated art lectures periodically, in auditorium.

The Guggenheim exhibits some of the most controversial modern art in the most controversial museum building in the world—Frank Lloyd Wright's mammoth concrete spiral overlooking Central Park.

The Guggenheim Museum, like the Whitney, was conceived and financed by a wealthy patron with a crusading zeal to bring new art to a wider public. Solomon R. Guggenheim (1861-1949) was the fourth of seven sons of Meyer Guggenheim, a Swiss emigrant who founded a vast mining and financial empire. He began collecting old masters in the 1890's, but by the 1920's he had become absorbed with contemporary art—especially with its most daring aspect, abstraction. Guided by Baroness Hilla Rebay, a painter and collector, Guggenheim eventually assembled the world's largest collection of abstract art, together with work by artists like Seurat, Bonnard, Modigliani, Chagall and Klee.

At first the collection was seen only by visitors to Guggenheim's suite at the Plaza Hotel. But in 1937 the collector incorporated the Solomon R. Guggenheim Foundation to provide "for the promotion of art and to develop understanding and appreciation of art by the public." His Museum of Non-Objective Painting opened subsequently at 24 East 54th Street.

In 1943 Guggenheim commissioned Wright to design a new building that would be as anti-traditional as the collection itself. Before his death six years later, the collector approved plans for the novel structure and bequeathed his entire collection—plus $8,000,000—to his Foundation; $2,000,000 was earmarked for the erection of the building.

Construction on New York City's only building by America's most famous architect began in 1957. Wright described the project as "organic architecture" in an "atmosphere of the quiet unbroken wave." "Here for the first time," he declared, "architecture appears plastic, one floor flowing into another (more like sculpture) instead of the usual superimposition of stratified layers cutting and butting into each other by way of post and beam construction."

In October, 1959, the new Museum opened. Reaction was sharply divided: some praised it as "the most beautiful building in the world," while others denounced it as an example of Wright's ego playing down art to glorify his own architecture.

The collection, enlarged and broadened since Guggenheim's death, contains nearly 3000 works of art. Though it is still thin in a few areas, it is exceptionally rich in others: Guggenheim had, for instance, amassed the largest Kandinsky collection in the world, and Klee, Chagal, Franz Marc, Delaunay and Brancusi are also well represented. Furthermore, the gift of the Justin K. Thannhauser collection, a group of about seventy-five Impressionist, Post-Impressionist and 20th Century masterpieces to open to the public in a permanent, separate gallery, closes important gaps.

The Late Nineteenth Century

CEZANNE, Paul

• **256. The Clock Maker** or **Man with Folded Arms.** (About 1895-1900)   An informal pose and a seemingly-simple pyramid construction acquire monumental strength in this painting. The portrait seems hewn from some massive substance. The strong face—like the rest of the painting—is expressed as a structure of planes that mould form with pigment. Background strokes and shapes add dynamic echoes to the main movement. The relationship between the tilt of the body and the angle of the floor accelerates the sensation of motion within an outer appearance of stability. The subsidiary design of the palette and picture at lower left indicates receding planes in space. Rich, deep color explores infinite variations in a series of contrasts of cool and dark notes against the warm flesh and light shirt. This painting was chosen the public's favorite in a poll in 1960.

ROUSSEAU, Henri

• **257. Artillerymen.** (About 1895) The rigid placement of the soldiers, shown as if posing for a daguerreotype (from which the composition may indeed have been derived), is one of the chief charms of this unselfconscious painting. A pervasive slanting from left to right gives movement to an otherwise quiet picture. The line of the soldiers is repeated in the cannon, the trees, the dark grass outlining the edges of the pantaloons and bases of the dark blue jackets. The group surrounding the cannon-wheel forms a mild pyramid about its green spokes. At right, an officer in white alters the insistent pattern. The soft trees and grass and sky provide a serene setting which heightens the air of nostalgia.

• **258. A Game of Football.** (1908) With disarming directness and bland simplicity, Rousseau turns his gentle gaze on an athletic scene in which men move like stylized dancers in slow motion. The dark foreground, smooth as a floor, converges with the sharp lines of the white fence and the symmetrical trees of the background. On either side, trees recede in a stately colonnade. The detailed rendering of the autumn leaves sustains the bright notes of the striped costumes. This painting was shown in the Salon of Independants in 1908, the year Picasso gave Rousseau a now-legendary banquet, attended, among others, by Gertrude and Leo Stein, Marie Laurencin, Braque, Vlaminck and Apollinaire. The picture is one of the Museum's major recent acquisitions.

256

BONNARD, Pierre

• **259. Dining Room on the Garden.** (Before 1933) The delicate fabric of color seems illuminated from within. Objects are transposed into motifs in a brilliant play of light infiltrating every inch of the composition. Few paintings of the 20th Century give light such all-powerful dominion. The picture is divided into two main, asymmetrical elements: the table, which seems to move gently to the left, and the window, set off-center to the right. Further balance is given by the placement of the woman (her ruddy features almost matching the color of the wall), who is linked to the magnificently-rendered flowers and the orange-red vertical stripe on the table. The window's vivid blue and green play exquisitely with the pink and violet of the table.

MODIGLIANI, Amedeo

• **260. Nude.** (1917) Supple flesh is enriched by a resonant background. Thick paint textures, which add to the sensuality, create a highly appealing surface. Lest shadows and modeling disturb the simplicity of the long figure, its face, breasts and torso are treated with a restraint which barely suggests swelling forms, yet implies solidity. Sensitive, flowing line defines the long nose, the weight of the breasts, the supple contours. The straight line of the necklace subtly relieves the play of curves, while the abrupt cropping of the knees conveys the informality and frontality of a Degas figure arrangement. The artist further stresses the girl's tapering slenderness by extending her body diagonally from the line of the pillow to the thighs, a device combining movement with repose.

• **261. Yellow Sweater (Mme. Hébuterne).** (About 1919) The girl is Jeanne Hébuterne, Modigliani's last love, shown about two years after they met. In this year of this portrait, she gave birth to a daughter, Jeanne (author of a recent book about her father); a year later Modigliani died of tuberculosis, and Jeanne, expecting another child, committed suicide. From hair to hips,

8

259

contours flow in one sinuous movement. The undulating figure
contrasts with the gently-slanted chest of drawers and the blurred
line of the wall at left. The sensitivity and calculation of the pose
are shown in the way the curve of the bottom of the sweater
joins with the floor line. The typical Modigliani head—elongated,
oval, almond-eyed, set on a swan-like neck—simultaneously suggests stylized early Italian Madonnas, primitive African sculptures
and the concise simplifications of the artist's friend Brancusi.
In contrast to the thick texture of the 1917 nude, this painting
features a delicate, fresco-like surface. Another fine Modigliani
in the Guggenheim is *Boy in Blue Jacket*.

Cubism

PICASSO, Pablo

● **262. Accordionist (Pierrot).** (1911)   In this prime example of
Cubism's most abstract phase—Analytical Cubism—representational images all but disappear. Through an intricate web of in-
tersecting planes and alternating patterns, a pyramid shape becomes apparent: at right, an arm and fragments of an accordion;
below, a triangular elbow and the spiral volutes of a chair. The
head is a tilting rectangle placed against the conical point of the
hat. Behind, dimly visible, are stone buildings, steps and trees.
But complete identification is neither possible nor relevant. The
hints and traces of "real" forms are not meant to present the

260

2

262

2

onlooked with a baffling picture-puzzle. They function as the framework and core of a pure harmony—a new vision of intricate geometric design, subdued light and dark, and sensitive play of brush and texture. The result is an extraordinary transformation from figure into a hitherto unexplored world of near-abstraction. This painting was made in Céret, the southern French town where Picasso and Braque spent the summer of 1911. Céret is sometimes called "the Barbizon of Cubism."

• **263. Mandolin and Guitar.** (1924)   In the early 1920's Picasso composed still lifes of sumptuous color, rounded forms and relatively natural appearance. *Mandolin and Guitar* is one of the largest and most colorful examples of what is sometimes called Curvelinear Cubism. The artist revels in ingenious variations on familiar forms. The tall bottle at the center, for instance, boasts a circle within a rectangle for its mouth, a swaying dark form, a violet label and a red circle motif for its bottom. Beneath, another charming design occurs in the interlacing black-and-white lines of apples. The guitar's white front is framed and set off by the brown, black and red variations of its extended sides. The undulating lines and patterns of the tablecloth compliment the heavier units on the table.

BRAQUE, GEORGES

• **264. Violin and Palette** and   • **265. Piano and Lute.** (Both 1910)   In these two still lifes, among the most lyric of Braque's Analytical Cubist compositions, complex harmonies are confined within narrow physical boundaries that dictate upward vertical movement. Objects are re-designed into myriad angular planes. Surfaces gleam iridescently within restrained tonal ensembles. In *Violin and Palette,* the violin, given a massive structure, is tilted as if seen from above. A sheet of music continues the upward direction as it veers toward the right. At top, the painter's palette hangs from a nail of naturalistic depth, in contrast to the dominant Cubist flattening-out. *Piano and Lute* is even richer in com-

4

265

plexity and rhythmic organization. The piano is seen from a
drastic elevation. The keyboard at the base of the composition is
a prelude to its veering, tilting forms. Curves at the sides link
with the lute's more angular contours. The candle at left functions as a projection of space.

GLEIZES, Albert

● **266. Brooklyn Bridge.** (1915)   A taut play of arcs and diagonals marks one of the most audacious near-abstractions of its
time. Dramatic tension is based on shapes derived from arches,
girders and cables, redesigned in terms of momentum. Within
the careful equilibrium, the curve which catapults across the
canvas is sustained by the sweep of a massive vertical. Simple,
powerful forms are underscored by the general austerity of the
dominantly black color scheme. The Guggenheim also owns a
1917 Gleizes oil of the Brooklyn Bridge.

DELAUNAY, Robert

● **267. St. Séverin.** (1909)   Delaunay's first truly individual paintings were of the interior of St. Séverin, the famed Gothic church
in Paris's Latin Quarter. Typically, nave, pillars, pavement and
vaults sway beneath the rhythmic movement of arches and
valuting. Whites, greens, greys and blues help reflect the spirit of
the dark interior. This painting, once in the Mannheim Museum,
was one of hundreds purged by the Nazis.

● **268. Eiffel Tower.** (1910)   Pliant in movement and rhythm,
the Eiffel Tower looms above swaying buildings. Light blurs some
of its contours; shade accentuates others. The buildings zig-zag in
rhythmic counterpoint to the tower. Above the tower, spherical
clouds anticipate the circular rhythms of Delaunay's total abstractions, such as the Guggenheim's *Circular Forms* of 1912.
This work was among the Delaunay oils in the 1911 Salon of
Independants, now famous as the first meeting between the
public and Cubism. The 1000-foot Eiffel Tower, erected in 1889,

266

has appealed to painters from Seurat to Chagall, but to none more than Delaunay. In 1909, when Delaunay began to paint the tower, it was saved from demolition because the French Army placed an experimental wireless at the top. In 1911, Delaunay painted *The City*, in which the tower is viewed through the checkerboard pattern of curtains; this work also hangs in the Guggenheim.

MARC, Franz
• **269. Stables, Sindelsdorf, Upper Bavaria.** (1913-14)   Horses and stalls are organized into a tightly-linked frieze. Rhythm is established by the successive arcs and the curves of the manes, flanks and tails, framed by the stall partitions. Exciting staccato patterns of color, each note a link to another, guide the eye from area to area: the form of the first horse at right, for example, is subdivided into planes of brown, blue, green, yellow and red; the same blue and green appear in the rendering of the stall and the yellow and blue are reflected in the horse in the second stall. Fire-like reds and radiant greens help project the sense of powerful animals. It was in the village of Sindelsdorf, where Marc lived, that he met Kandinsky in 1910.

• **270. Unfortunate Land of Tyrol.** (1913)   Most of Marc's paintings are exultant visions which the artist believed reflected the rapturous feelings of animals. This bleak and brooding mountain scene, inspired by the Austrian frontier village of Scharnitz, is a notable exception. Binding the angular, sprawling areas are emphatic lines and masses. Two scrawny horses and the curve of the central hill link the two sides of the composition. The rainbow above the eagle and the lines of the cemetery hill and mountainsides reflect the influence of Kandinsky. The painting is not quite completed.

LEGER, Fernand
• **271. The Smokers.** (1911)   Léger's interpretation of Cubism stressed solid volumes, contrasting forms and stylized drawings

269

270

68

with strong contours. *The Smokers* is a fine example. Three men are seated outdoors, smoking. One face appears at lower right, a second immediately to the left of the first. Higher up, at extreme left, the third man is seated at a table which projects toward the foreground. On the table is a fruit dish. Dense, rounded shapes, based on ascending smoke formations, contribute vertical movement. Above the smokers appear roofs, trees and fields, with flattened space transformed into an upward recession above the landscape. Relaxation was a favorite Léger theme.

● **272. The Great Parade.** (1954)   Léger's last major painting is a vivid circus tableau unified by broad bands of color, simplified outlines and poster-like planes of shallow space. The composition contains clowns, acrobats, a banjo player, a horse with a yellow side-saddle, a platform and an array of poles, bars, dumbbells and ropes. The letter "C" towards the center stands for the circus motif. A colossal swath of blue carries the eye from left to right, where a red circle concludes its momentum. Another circle provides contrast to the rectangular brown forms. Finally, the red disc is repeated and modified in the green circle at lower left. Yellow shapes help bind the large canvas. Placed in juxtaposition, the colliding colors imply depth and recession. The few touches of shading vary the effect, suggesting solidity. The strong outlines recall the bluntness of folk art, yet exhibit the originality of a highly sophisticated artist. The monumental figures sway with rhythmic animation. *The Great Parade* is the finale to some sixty studies and finished works on the theme of acrobats and musicians dating back to the 1930's.

Futurism

SEVERINI, Gino
● **273. Red Cross Train.** (1914)   Landscape and train fuse to project the dynamic, irresistible motion exalted by the Futurists.

271

Horizontal and tilting diagonals increase the momentum of the speeding train, which is dissected by the line of the bridge and houses. Fragments of lettering—a device adapted, like the emphasis on diagonals, from Cubism—probably depict words chalked on the side of the train. Severini lived near a railroad station outside Paris, where he saw army trains leaving for the front.

Abstraction

KANDINSKY, Wassily

274. Study for Composition 11. (1910) Exuberant colors, complex masses and energetic rhythms recall Matisse, but go beyond the French master in surge and intensity. Forms emerge slowly from the glittering medley. Toward the center, blue and white horses leap in opposing directions. In the left foreground, figures in robes stand watching; a figure in green reclines at the center, two others at right. To the right of the horses, below a bridge and weeping willow, children play and women wash at a stream. In the center appears the peculiar tower-like treetrunk Kandinsky often employed; behind it are towers, mountains, hills, trees and clouds. The curvilinear shapes converge in a succession of restless staccato movements. The setting may have been inspired by the artist's earlier visit to Tunisia.

• **275. Little Pleasures.** (1913) Transfused with cosmic rhythm and exploding with the splendor of a great bouquet, this golden, mystic picture is the quintessence of Eastern exuberance. The

3

5

276

mountain at center, encircled by waves, dominates the composition. A boat appears at right and trees rise just above the water.
In the right foreground, two tall, swaying forms join the pervasive
curving movement. A domed church sits on a mountain-top;
behind it rises a second mountain, its line and momentum continued in the blue of a dark cloud. The curved lines at top left
summarize the famous Kandinsky galloping horses; another such
simplification appears in the two parallel S-lines below these
horses and to the left of the first mountain. At top left appears
the sun.

• **276. Picture with White Edge.** (1913)   Kandinsky wrote of
this painting: "At the lower left, an abyss. A white wave rising
from it, which falls suddenly and then encloses the right side
of the painting in a lazily winding form, traces a lake at the
upper right and disappears at the upper left corner in order to
emerge one last time and definitively as a white zigzag. Since this
white border was the solution of the problem, I named the whole
painting after it." From a central vortex, zones of blues, greens
and reds undulate in parallels. A whiplash of white extends into
space at upper right. At left, small, curving shapes create a lively
tempo. The three lines which project from above—perhaps
Kandinsky's symbol of a troika—counter the coiled leap of the
main line that moves off at far right. Almost in the center is a
sun-disc, from which projecting rays flow above a shape suggesting mountain tops. The essence of the picture is the motion
and drama that project life into an abstraction.

• **277. Autumn** and • **278. Winter.** (1914)   Prime examples
of the breakthrough from Expressionist representation to the
new abstraction, these two paintings project upheaval and restless
emotion. *Autumn*, a turbulent, whirling abstraction, has hints of
mountain, sky and water, sombre in ochres, browns and dark
blues. In contrast, *Winter* is a sparkling scherzo, dashing and

277

restless. *Autumn* and *Winter* are two of four panels Kandinsky painted for a Park Avenue apartment. Details of the unique commission appear in the section on the Museum of Modern Art.

• **279. One Center.** (1924) In the early 1920's Kandinsky's surging masses gave way to more precise forms, partly due to his contact with Russian geometric painters and to the influence of Germany's new Bauhaus school. In *One Center,* Kandinsky marshals contrasting forms and rhythms into a novel arrangement. A black central circle is the dramatic pivot for expanding circles, the thrust of rock-like forms and the more relaxed lower shapes. The upper background is dark, the lower radiant; bars of lighter color behind the circles soften the contrasts, as does the whiplash line which forms a counter-balance to the thrusting movements. From the mysterious core, the geometric shapes establish momentum and drama. Evolved from earlier Kandinsky motifs are the jagged rain cloud at top left, the geometric pattern of fields, the small spot patterns, the large curved forms with seed-like elements, and the curving lines which simultaneously depict force and wave. Even under this geometric discipline, Kandinsky sustains mystic spirit and emotion. The painting is not merely form and color, but a lyric image of the universe.

• **280. Several Circles.** (1926) In a letter to a friend, Kandinsky wrote: "Why does the circle fascinate me? It is (1) the most modest form, but asserts itself unconditionally; (2) a precise but inexhaustable variable; (3) simultaneously stable and unstable; (4) simultaneously loud and soft; (5) a single tension that carries countless tensions with it. The circle is the synthesis of the greatest opposites. It combines the concentric and the eccentric in a single form, and in balance. . . . Of the three primary forms [triangle, square and circle] it points most clearly to the fourth dimension." Like a cosmic vision, a galaxy of spheres floats against an infinity of space. A black circle is the

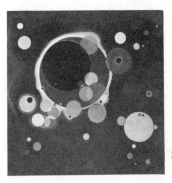

9   280

center of the drama; the blue circle expands forms and movement. The whitest area forms an incandescent halo between the intensity of the spheres and the endless blackness. The Nazis purged *Several Circles* from Dresden's National Gallery as "degenerate art."

• **281. Accompanied Contrast.** (1935) After his austerity of the 1920's, Kandinsky's Paris compositions are affirmations of lyric joy. The work of an aged, self-exiled painter in a world on the brink of war, *Accompanied Contrast* is nevertheless serene and radiant. Handsome forms float against an ethereal background. They are linked by horizontal and vertical bars, the dynamic form at bottom and the rectangle which overlaps the blue and showers "stardust" or seed forms on the opposing crimson shape. Large and sumptuous, the forms recall the colors of Russia and the East, while the background brings to mind the luminous air of Paris. The pink glow at the edge of the cool rectangle at upper right is intensified in the crimson of the large form and the red half-circle of a sun motif. At left, a thread of yellow makes the blue contours intense, and a faint blue opposes the pink of the thickly textured rectangle. The painting suggests heraldic symbols of water, sun, earth, air and space.

CHAGALL, Marc
• **282. The Soldier Drinks.** (1912-13) With lush colors and irresistible rhythm, Chagall paints a frolicsome idyll of his native land. The composition disregards conventional design, space and scale. The sharp thrust of the table-edge bisects it, leading the eye to the window and the colorful peasant house. On either side are balancing forms—the samovar and the soldier, who leans into the picture with almost the force of the table line. Chagall adroitly adopts the Cubist idiom of cross-cutting lines and emphatic planes in the soldier's face, hands and uniform. The surprise of the flying cap is climaxed by the Lilliputian dancers on the table. Are they in the soldier's dreams, or do they

281

actually carouse somewhere else in the room? In either case, they add immensely to the blithe spirit and at the same time effectively fill in the open foreground.

• **283. Paris Through the Window.** (1913) A poetic mood is set by exhilarating colors and audacious fancy. A sweeping angular movement—adapted from Cubism—gives both vitality and cohesion to the wide-spread areas of the composition. Radiant, triangular color formations increase the sensation of spacious boulevards and sky. Chagall again stirs the imagination. Does the blue-and-yellow Janus head signify night and day— or sadness and gayety? What of the heart offered in the palm of the hand? Is the cat (whose head resembles the young Chagall) a synthesis of all the cats who sit blinking at windows? Do the "strollers" who are irresistibly propelled towards each other, as if by some magnet, signify the common horde—or lovers? The upside-down train at left probably derives from reflections of trains crossing bridges. A balloonist—from the June Fair that used to be held near the Eiffel Tower—floats down slowly past the Fair's Ferris Wheel.

FEININGER, Lyonel
• **284. Gelmeroda IV.** (1915) Fascinated by the soaring archi- tecture and mystic spirit of Gothic churches, Feininger painted them many times. Among the earliest and most brilliant versions, *Gelmeroda IV* is a synthesis of Expressionism and the artist's personal approach to Cubism. Swaying angles and planes evoke strange rhythms of light and space. Enclosed by the slanting roofs of the buildings in the foreground, a steeple ascends obliquely into the flood of sky. Shafts of light all but annihilate the solidity of forms. The rectangle of the emerald window glows intensely, balanced and contrasted by a similar violet form.

KLEE, Paul
• **285. Open Book.** (1930) This arresting essay in geometric composition seems to reflect Klee's intensive reading of Greek,

83   284

Chinese and Indian poetry at the time of its execution or his trip to Egypt two years earlier. The book appears charged with cryptic significance. Its blank pages open out to reveal a black center—a core within a core. Does the triangular device at bottom signify a pyramid? Can the pages be seen as slab-like doors of a tomb structure, luring the imagination to pierce its ancient secrets? And what of the textural treatment of the surface? Like mottled stone or ivory, it doubles the interest of the haunting space in which rectangles float asymmetrically, horizontal balanced against vertical.

• **286. Severing of the Snake.** (1938)   At the time of this painting, Klee was very ill. A year earlier, the Nazis had confiscated over one hundred of his works, some of which they included in their infamous exhibition of "degenerate" art. Nevertheless, back in his native Switzerland, Klee's outlook began to seem brighter: his pictures were being shown in Paris and New York galleries and in a Museum of Modern Art exhibit commemorating the Bauhaus, which the Nazis had also closed. Perhaps these events are reflected in the theme of the snake which, though severed, still lives. A macabre drama is enacted against a pattern of appealing pastels. The rectangles—the colors of which may denote earth and summer—function as a decorative geometric setting for the arabesque of the snake. The bizarre mood is heightened by the snake's red eyes and the drop of blood suspended from the knife. Klee "drew" snake and knife by leaving clear the burlap on which the background is thickly painted, then lightly tinting the exposed forms.

285   2

Some notable sculpture in the museum:

Archipenko, Alexander, 1887-1964. *Médrano,* 1915, painted tin, wood, glass, oilcloth.

Arp, Jean (Hans), born 1887. *Growth,* 1938, marble.

Brancusi, Constantin, 1876-1957. *Portrait of George,* 1911?, marble.
  Muse, 1912, marble.
  Sorceress, 1916, wood.
  Adam and Eve, 1921, wood.
  King of Kings, date uncertain, wood.
  Miracle (White Seal), 1936, marble.
  Flying Turtle, after 1943, marble.

Calder, Alexander, born 1898. *Mobile,* 1936?, wood, metal.

DuChamp-Villon, Raymond, 1876-1918. *Head of Maggy,* 1911, bronze.

Gabo, Naum, born 1890.
  ● *Column,* 1923, plastic, wood, metal.
  Linear Construction, 1942, plastic.

Giacometti, Alberto, born 1901. *Standing Woman,* 1926-27, bronze.

Maillol, Aristide, 1861-1944. *Pomona with Lowered Arms,* 1937, bronze.

Miró, Joan, born 1893. *Portico,* ceramic. (In collaboration with ceramicist J. L. Artigas)

Modigliani, Amedeo, 1884-1920. *Head,* 1912?, limestone.

Moore, Henry, born 1898. *Standing Figure,* 1956, elm wood.

Paolozzi, Eduardo, born 1924. *St. Sebastian, No. 2,* 1957, bronze.

Pevsner, Antoine, 1886-1962. *Twinned Column,* 1947, bronze.

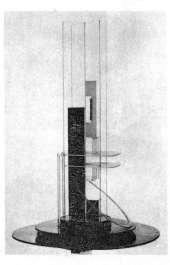

WHITNEY MUSEUM OF AMERICAN ART

54th Street between Fifth & Sixth Avenues.
PL 7-2277

(Moves in Spring of 1966 to Madison Avenue
at 75th Street.) Model.

Hours: Every day 1-5. Closed major holidays. Free.
Transportation: Same as to Museum of Modern Art.
Talks: Saturdays and Sundays at 2.
Sales desk: Main entrance.
Restaurant: Museum of Modern Art Garden Cafeteria available to Whitney Museum visitors.

The Whitney Museum—unique in its sole dedication to 20th Century American Art—was established by two remarkable women, Gertrude Vanderbilt Whitney and Juliana Force. It climaxed their long efforts to help American artists overcome the ultra-conservatism which dominated art circles at the turn of the century.

Gertrude Vanderbilt Whitney (1877-1942), granddaughter of railroad magnate Cornelius Vanderbilt, was herself a prominent sculptor; her work includes the *Titanic Monument* in Washington, the *Peter Stuyvesant Memorial* in New York and the *Columbus Monument* in Palos, Spain. Juliana Force (1876-1948), a school teacher turned private secretary, joined Mrs. Whitney in 1914 and for over thirty years played a role second only to hers in establishing the Museum.

The Museum originated haphazardly. In about 1907, Mrs. Whitney settled in a studio at 19 MacDougal Alley in Greenwich Village. Guided by artists like Arthur Davies and Robert Henri, she soon became aware of the poverty and struggle facing the younger and less traditional artists in her new neighborhood. She began helping them by exhibiting their work in her studio, then opened a gallery at 8 West 8th Street "to help the artist to help himself." Meanwhile, she was buying many works which would in time become the core of the yet-unborn Museum.

In 1923 the Whitney Studio Club moved to larger quarters at 10 West 8th Street. By 1928, some 400 artists were members of the exhibiting association, with hundreds more on the waiting list. The club's collection of American art had now become the largest in existence, including some 600 paintings. By this time, creative American artists were gaining recognition, and Mrs. Whitney decided to close the club and offer the entire collection to The Metropolitan Museum, along with a wing to house it. When the offer was turned down, she, Mrs. Force and Forbes Watson decided to establish a new museum. It opened in November, 1931, with an exhibition of its own collection. In 1954 the Whitney moved to 54th Street, and very shortly it will move again to new quarters, designed by Marcel Breuer, at Madison Avenue and 75th Street.

The Whitney's permanent collection now contains over 800 paintings, more than 200 pieces of sculpture and some 500 watercolors and drawings. (Unfortunately, the entire collection is rarely on view due to space limitations.) The Museum, maintained by an endowment left by Mrs. Whitney, holds varied exhibitions each year, including one-man shows of living artists and loan surveys of particular movements.

GLACKENS, William Joseph

• **287. Hammerstein's Roof Garden.** (About 1901)   Glackens' eye for the essentials of a situation and his fluent brush record this glimpse of a tightrope walker in a leading vaudeville theatre of the turn of the century. The novel composition plays off the verticals of the doorways, the boxes and the three performers against the horizontals of the ropes, the ornamental walls and the seated figures in the foreground. The rhythmic motions of the three girls at right direct the eye to the master of ceremonies, then to the ladder, parasols and tightrope walker. The color, somewhat reminiscent of Manet, sparkles within an ochre-gray setting, punctuated by the performer's blue costume.

LUKS, George

• **288. Armistice Night.** (1918)   Luks' eyewitness painting exudes the jubilant excitement of the end of the First World War. Darts and strokes of color help to evoke the sweep and swagger of the scene. As the figures flow to the right, billowing flags and street lamps sweep irresistibly back again toward the center. The misty tonality of the upper portion emphasizes the surging crowds.' Flags and lights act as a transition to buildings which give scale to the setting; the people appear as a compact host of tiny figures.

• **289. Mrs. Gamely.** (1930)   With breezy works like this, Luks thumbed his nose at the fashionable portraits of the conservative artists he scorned as "the pink and white idiots of the Academy." His characterization is vivid and unsparing, even to the raw flesh color. What would be a garish red in another context, here works in harmony with the whitish hair, the blouse, and the skirt with its bronze-red folds. The ungainly woman is given a monumental aspect, imbued with strength and dignity. The white rooster becomes a focal point, its sweeping form a clean-cut relief to the less defined contours, its crest a vivid note against the green blouse. The blue-black stove and purplish surfaces give the room strong depth.

287

SLOAN, John

• **290. Backyards, Greenwich Village.** (1914) An informal
winter moment, replete with the tang of snow and wind, comes
alive in a canvas full of fluent rendering and incisive observation.
The diagonals of the fence create sweeping space, and the placement of the two cats and the boys accentuates an exhilarating
movement from the foreground across to the right. The blowing
clothesline quickens the breezy motion. Sloan's colors suggest less
black-and-white tonality than in his previous oils—possibly as a
result of the Impressionist and Post-Impressionist paintings he
saw at the Armory Show or of his summer of outdoor painting
in Gloucester. This picture "was painted from memory after careful observation," Sloan wrote; "the winter atmosphere and color
well rendered, the cats unforgettable."

• **291. Sixth Avenue Elevated at Third Street.** (1928) Sloan's
beguiling views of New York continued until the 1930's. This one,
facing uptown toward 12th Street, is one of his finest later interpretations. Contrasted against a violet and blue sky and the silhouettes of buildings and lamp-posts, the onrushing trains imbue
the canvas with drama and a romantic aura. The receding perspective of the girders intensifies the feeling of space suggested
by the perspective of the train. The city-scape is given scale by
the lively girls who undulate across the painting in a frolicsome
S-curve. At left is a famed Greenwich Village landmark, the Jefferson Market Court House; designed in 1876 by Frederick C.
Withers and Calvert Vaux, who helped design the present Metropolitan Museum, it is now a public library. The "L" was removed
between 1928 and 1939.

BELLOWS, George

• **292. Floating Ice** (1910) A breezy panorama is filled with
light, space and the vigor of winter air. The horizontal expanse,
interrupted only by the slender tree trunk, is emphasized by the

290

sky, the snow-covered Palisades, and the alternating bands of green and gray on the water. Figures contribute to the grand scale of the vista.

● **293. Dempsey and Firpo.** (1924) A star athlete himself, Bellows used the prize ring as a source of significant art material. In this, his last painting on the theme, he builds a composition of vivid, if somewhat formal, action. The two contenders, their bodies integrated in a dynamic relationship of arms and legs, form a firm central pyramid, while the dark space between the standing Firpo and the referee creates a complementary triangle. A long continuous line flows from Dempsey's shoe through his arm at lower right. In earlier, and greater, prizefight paintings— *Stag at Sharkey's* (1907, Cleveland Museum of Art) and *Both Members of This Club* (1909, National Gallery, Washington)— Bellows' flair for vigorous action is rendered with far more verve; the fighters' torsos are strong and flexible, the brushstrokes zestful and slashing. In *Dempsey and Firpo,* however, Bellows plotted the composition through theories of color and dynamic symmetry, and the result shows rigidity and constraint. *Dempsey and Firpo* catches one of the most electrifying moments in boxing. On September 14, 1923, the world heavyweight champion Jack Dempsey met Louis Angel Firpo, champion of South America, at the New York Polo Grounds. In a fight which lasted less than four minutes, Dempsey floored Firpo seven times in the first round, but Firpo suddenly knocked the champion clear out of the ring—the moment depicted here. When Dempsey's count reached nine, reporters actually pushed him back into the ring, and he won by a knockout in the second round. Bellows, who appears at the far left, was at the ringside as an artist for the New York Journal. He made sketches on the spot and later worked them into two lithographs and this painting.

DU BOIS, Guy Pène
● **294. Jeanne Eagels in "Rain."** (1922) Du Bois' gift for stylization and his sense of personality helped project this vibrant image tinged with the make-believe of the stage. The deep greenish background provides a striking setting for the three-dimensional figure in ornate dress and pink shawl. A jaunty plume and sash help relate the light colored figure to the dark setting without

291

obtaining a cut-out effect, a traditional challenge in portraiture. Jeanne Eagels became an overnight sensation in 1922 as the prostitute in "Rain," a play based on Somerset Maugham's short story "Sadie Thompson." Her director commissioned Du Bois to paint this portrait, but her producer refused to purchase it.

HOPPER, Edward
• **295. Early Sunday Morning, Seventh Avenue, New York, New York.** (1930) Hopper's way of seeing things makes the commonplace uncommon. As he himself remarked, "Just to paint a representation or a design is not hard, but to express a thought in painting is." Bleak buildings washed with harsh early-morning light are charged with some brooding inner quality. The arrangement is daringly simple: long horizontals of sky, buildings and pavement, placed parallel with the canvas itself. Identical storefronts are varied only by the barberpole, the glimpse of higher wall at the right, the signs and their slanting shadows, a hydrant and the white-and-blue awning. Everything is placed unerringly within the scheme, but the bright note of the off-center pole is particularly effective in moving the eye across the composition.

MARSH, Reginald
• **296. Why Not Use the "L"?** (1930) In a genre picture brimming with the feel of grimy elevated trains, the riders, carefully observed as both types and individuals, are grouped in a casual but artful manner. A sprawling sleeper links the two girls, his lapels and the contours of the cap continuing the curves of the

294

295

standing girl and leading the eye to the weary girl who stares blankly into the aisle. Even the spotting of newspapers sustains the rhythmic relationship of the passengers. Marsh's color often merely fills in expressively drawn figures; here, however, it is used more resourcefully, notably in the orange placards binding the central portion, to form a pattern.

WEBER, Max

• **297. Chinese Restaurant.** (1915)   This is probably the most daring semiabstraction in American painting up to 1915. The artist has fondly recalled the excitement of its creation: "On entering a Chinese restaurant from the darkness of the night outside, a maze and blaze of light seemed to split into fragments the interior and its contents, the human and inanimate. For the time being, the static became transient and fugitive—oblique planes and contours took vertical and horizontal positions, and the horizontal and vertical became oblique, the light so piercing and so luminous, the color so liquid and the life and movement so enchanting. Therefore, the glow, the charm, the poetry of geometry was stressed." Solid forms become transparent as they overlap. Flatly-painted, highly-patterned areas and thrusting, angular lines recall Cubism, while a sequence of faces in continuous motion reflects the Futurist synthesis of forms. The entire composition seems to rock and tilt with dynamic movement—lines thrusting out in the center, the zigzag tug of the white-and-pink border on the floor, the intersection of the blue border of the carpet, the flash of faces, the slant of a wall border and the pyramidal door and stair-like theme at upper right.

• **298. Adoration of the Moon.** (1944)   At once majestic and warmly humorous, this painting is an affectionate interpretation of Jewish patriarchs celebrating the ancient ceremony of Rosh Hodesh, the beginning of the new month. On the Sabbath before Rosh Hodesh, special prayers ask for a time of blessing for all Israel. Between the third and fourteenth day of the new month

297

occurs the ceremony of sanctification of the moon, when prayers are offered outdoors. In the 1940's Weber's style was characterized by dashing drawing, swift, agile lines and soft, lyric color. This is among its best examples. Four figures, placed in graceful vertical procession, fill most of the canvas. Skimming lines define crisp contours. The curves of hats and clothing and the twist of a beard find echoes in the wispy clouds. Glazes of red, orange and blue and tints of yellow convey an ethereal mood.

STELLA, Joseph

• **299. The Brooklyn Bridge: Variation on an Old Theme.** (1939) "Many nights," wrote Stella, "I stood on the bridge—and in the middle alone—lost—crushed by the mountainous black impenetrability of the skyscrapers—here and there lights resembling suspended falls of astral bodies—I felt deeply moved, as if on the threshold of a new religion or in the presence of a new divinity . . . The massive towers dominated the surrounding tumult of the surging skyscrapers with their Gothic majesty sealed in the purity of their arches. The cables like divine messages from above . . . It impressed me as the shrine containing all the efforts of the new civilization in America." Two arches loom majestically as blue and gray-white cables frame water, buildings and sky. Lights add accent and rhythm; translucent harmony is intensified by the diamond-like luster of the blues, crimsons and greens. Below, as in a panel on an altarpiece, are stars, a span of the bridge, silhouetted skyscrapers and a decorative scroll suggesting lights and the endless motion of wheels. The Brooklyn Bridge—which has inspired many other painters, including John Marin and Albert Gleizes—was conceived in 1867 by John A. Roebling "as a great work of art, and as a successful specimen of advanced bridge engineering." Roebling died before construction began, and his son took over; he too was injured, but continued to supervise construction from a window in Brooklyn Heights. The bridge was opened in 1883 and in 1964 was declared a National Monument.

300

DICKINSON, Edward

• **300. The Fossil Hunters.** (1926-28)   Dickinson's one clue to
the theme of this painting, to which he devoted almost two hundred sessions, is that it was inspired by some fossils he had found.
Apparently, it represents a fusion of past, present and future: as
fossils were once living things, so will living things eventually lie
in some underground prison awaiting future discovery. An elegaic
mood hovers over the cryptic tableau. Three-dimensional rendering of everyday figures and drapery gradually ceases to reassure
the onlooker. Bodies and objects seem almost tossed about in
deathlike sleep; the harmony of pale and dark greens begins to
suggest dim light filtered through water. The edge of the twisting
curtain at upper right forms an emphatic angle with the girl's
figure while it follows the line of the man's back. The man's outflung arm, in turn, coordinates with the girl's position. The
shroudlike drapery beneath him repeats his pose in its folds, but
its outer contour forms an angle to the girl at lower right. The
vertical wall and drapery balance the diagonals and the steep perspective. In November, 1928, the Carnegie International provided
newspapers with gleeful stories by inadvertently hanging *The Fossil Hunters* upside down for several weeks. The press had still
more fun when the National Academy of Design hung it sideways
and awarded it the second Altman Prize of $500. (In neither in-
stance was the artist present.)

DEMUTH, Charles

• **301. My Egypt.** (1927)   One of Demuth's most famous paintings, *My Egypt* is a testament to the proud beauty some artists
see in utilitarian architecture. In depicting the massive forms of
a grain elevator in his native Lancaster, Pennsylvania, the artist
somehow communicates the grandeur of an ancient Egyptian
monument. The two main cylindrical structures are crisscrossed
by prismatic rays of light which clothe them with a poetic quality.
The predominant whites, grays and blues are countered by the

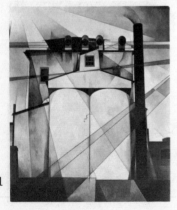

301

dark note of the smokestack and the vivid red of the building, echoed at left by the chimney. The refined, geometric style represents an approach sometimes called Immaculate or Precisionist.

DOVE, Arthur

• **302. Ferry Boat Wreck.** (1931)   This semiabstract oil reflects Dove's desire to condense in his work "the part that goes to make the spirit of painting and leave out all that just makes tons and tons of art." Dove imaginatively exploits the dark brown timbers of a wrecked boat and the undulating green and gray-blue water. A calm mood is heightened by the slow, rhythmic curve of the waves and the related massive curves of rotted wood and rusty iron. The round orange form is a symbolic flower motif. While retaining Dove's typical delicacy, the composition possesses forthright ruggedness.

KUNIYOSHI, Yasuo

• **303. I'm Tired.** (1938)   This is one of a series in which Kuniyoshi invented his provocative female type. "I like to paint women," he wrote, "but I don't paint just one woman, I put in what I know and sense about all women. I think this is in the Eastern tradition but the way I paint is in the Western tradition." A sense of solidity is evoked with fragile means. The rendering of the girl's pale, golden-toned flesh is as thin as the newspaper she holds, yet it possesses a quality of substantiality, dramatized by hair, scarf and cool green background. The mottled wall surface adds textural interest and depth as it gently leads the eye to the upper right, in a path contrasting with the main direction of the girl. Against areas of soft color, a delicate, animated line reinforces the picture's sensuousness.

BLOOM, Hyman

• **304. The Anatomist.** (1953)   John I. H. Bauer, Associate Director of the Whitney Museum, has written that "the putrescent corpses which long obsessed Hyman Bloom may seem im-

304

ages of pure horror, but they are part of a quest for an understanding of suffering and death. Bloom's corpses turn oddly into
bouquets of brilliant color suggesting an unsuspected beauty in
decay, a transformation rather than a loss." Bloom, like Rembrandt, faces the theme of autopsy unflinchingly. The violated
corpse, viewed from above, is given a rich, raw color. Magenta
and orange notes glow against the pale blue-green of the arm on
the right. The basin of orange, the doctor's violet hands and the
white sleeves add to the searing impact. Tilted upward, the table
provides a counterpoint to the writhing aspects of body and or-
gans. Anguish is evoked in the head, the exposed brain and the
outflung arm, with its delicate tracery of blood vessels.

GORKY, Arshile

• **305. The Artist and His Mother.** (About 1926-36)   Gorky's
last and most important representational oil, based on an old
family photograph, is a nostalgic recollection of his mother and
himself as a youngster. Two vertical figures—the youth placed
slightly higher, the woman larger and flush with the lower edge
of the canvas—are given graceful coordination by their sinuous
contours. The handling is broad and flat, the colors soft and
highly individual. The mother's firm oval face is framed and
emphasized by the shawl. Her expression is stoic and monumental, her hands—possibly left unfinished—at once soft and strong.
The boy's sharply defined hair and dark lapels are balanced by
the shading at the right of his coat, the dark legs and the curved
edge of the slippers. Soft, free shapes, as in the orange above
the bouquet and the soft pastels of the sleeve, foreshadow Gorky's
later abstract forms. There are hints of Ingres and Picasso in
the mother's face and in the finesse of the handling, but the total
effect is highly original in its style and in its haunting lyricism.

• **306. The Betrothal, II.** (1947)   Dreamlike shadows skim the
edge of associative meaning. Exotic colors burst against a golden
ochre background. Restless shapes flow within agile linear bound-

305

aries. Gorky's oil is at once so blithe, so tense and so typically cryptic. Ethel Schwabacher, student, friend and patron of the artist, points out that at the time of this painting he was intrigued by large photographs of Paolo Uccello's *Battle of San Romano*. From it, he adapted the horse and rider, the echoes of a plumed helmet and the spear perceivable in the key unit of this composition. If the horse and spear can be said to symbolize love and death, *The Betrothal* probably relates to Gorky's major theme, *"Liebestod"* (Love-Death). The picture illustrates Gorky's remark, "I do not like to put a face on an image."

TANGUY, Yves

• **307. Fear.** (1949)   Despite its finesse and deceptively charming colors, Tanguy's enigmatic fantasy arouses vague, ominous emotions. Bristling, jagged forms suggesting bones and stones are in reality complete abstractions. White shapes thrust sharp points inward, as if poised against a target. The dark ground fuses with a mild sky, leading the eye to the wispy clouds and the final flash of pink. Tanguy visited Arizona in 1940; perhaps some of the color and strangeness of *Fear* reflect the Southwest landscape interpreted through his typical abstract forms.

DAVIS, Stuart

• **308. OWH! in San Paõ.** (1951)   The title and the lush colors relate to the painter's visit to São Paolo, where Brazil's new museum included Davis' work in its first International Biennial exhibition. Davis plays flat, sharply defined forms of exotic hues against flowing caligraphy and even polka dots. All vibrate with a brassy gaiety. The artist has described his works as "as simple as a tabloid headline. Anyone with enough coordination to decipher a traffic beacon, granted they accept the premise of its function, can handle their communicative potential with ease. The title of this painting is reasonable in the same way as the image itself. It has been scientifically established that the acoustics of

308

idealism give off the humanistic sounds of snoring, whereas
reality always says 'Ouch!' Clearly, then, when the realism has
San Paõ as its locale, a proper regard for the protocol of allitera-
tion changes it to, 'Owh!' "

● **309. The Paris Bit.** (1959) A parade of crisp designs and
bracing colors expresses memories of Paris in a composition as
lively as a passage of fine jazz. Firmly controlled, and sustained
by imaginative variations, their impact is reinforced by a background of billboard flatness. While the general effect is of abstraction, "real" objects abound—as in the facades, the beer mug
and the siphon bottle—and signs, words and numbers play a
major role. Compared to Davis' *Place Pasdeloup* of 1928, also in
the Whitney, lettering has become a primary element, both for
its variety of forms and its associative meaning. "Pad," for example, is "beat" slang for a living place. "Belle France" and "28"
refer to Davis' year in Paris. Every word and word-fragment contributes similar illusions in the jaunty arrangement.

SHAHN, Ben
● **310. The Passion of Sacco and Vanzetti.** (1931-32) A scathing denunciation is made more eloquent by quiet understatement.
The grim forms of the coffins frame the pallid faces of the dead.
The three formally clad figures with silk hats, a mortar board
and drooping lilies provide sudden contrast. The Grecian court-
house, with its refined facade and steps, repeats the severe rhythm
and horizontality of the coffins. This large panel, part of a mural
in three sections, was exhibited soon after its completion in a
show of mural projects at the Museum of Modern Art. Shahn's
indictment of prominent persons caused a furor. Someone had
even offered to buy the picture for $2,000 to prevent its exhibi-
tion. "I realized," Shahn recalled, "that I was being offered
graft [and] I kept saying over and over to myself, 'There's power
in the brush—there's power in the brush.' " Nicola Sacco and

309

Bartolomeo Vanzetti, two Italian-born anarchists and minor labor leaders, were arrested for the killing of a paymaster and a guard in a factory payroll robbery at South Braintree, Massachusetts, in 1920. With most of the country in the grip of a Red scare, they were convicted on slight evidence. Millions protested the sentences, and a series of legal proceedings postponed execution until 1927, when the Lowell Committee, which had been appointed to review the trial, upheld the decision. Standing over the coffins are the members of that committee: Lawrence Lowell, president of Harvard; Samuel W. Stratton, president of the Massachusetts Institute of Technology, and Judge Robert Grant. The portrait in the background is of Webster Thayer, presiding judge at the trial, and the building is the Dedham County Court. Before this painting, the young Shahn had exhibited twenty-three gouaches on the Sacco-Vanzetti theme which brought him his first significant recognition.

• **311. Cherubs and Children.** (1944) In a haunting idyll balancing realism with poetic imagination, the artist expresses an image of war's homelessness, destruction of present and past and victimization of the young. Huddled, sleeping children form a diagonal across the grass, their bodies and slender legs set off in a sequence of lights and darks. The diagonal is repeated in the wall, the tilt of an elaborate lamp and the bridge. The line of the grass, the trees and the pedestals of the cherubs establishes a stable base. These solid masses are deployed against the linear network of the bridge. Shahn's *Reconstruction,* also in the Whitney, belongs to the same series as this painting.

LEVINE, Jack

• **312. Gangster Funeral.** (1952-53) This is one of the most ambitious and successful of Levine's narrative essays on ironies and corruption in modern life. The composition is dominated and unified by throbbing dark-golden tones. A fragmented pattern of highlights on flesh, shirts, boutonnieres, coffin and chapel window helps fuse the twelve figures and their setting into a whole. The steep, downward perspective of the coffin and the mourning woman in the foreground dramatize space without

1

312

sacrificing a compact "close-up" grouping. The mourners are
caught with a keen eye for characterization and a relish for details. While executing this oil, the artist discussed it at a Museum
of Modern Art symposium. "I should like to paint a narrative," he
said, "because it is possible for adolescents to buy marijuana and
cocaine on our streets with the connivance and the complacency
of the powers-that-be. Consequently, I am at work on a painting
of a gangster funeral . . . The chief of police has come to pay his
last respects—a face at once porcine and acute—under no cir-
cumstances off to one side as a watcher . . . filing past to view
for the last time the earthly remains of his old associate. . . . If
the chief's function is thus made clear, then it becomes possible
to add a patrolman in a watchful capacity. I must now look for
ways of establishing the identities of the mayor, the governor, et
alia. It may be said that the idea is more fit for a novel or a film
but as far as a novel is concerned, a picture is still worth a thousand words; as far as film is concerned, the Hays Code requires
it to show that crime does not pay, which is not my thesis either."

SOYER, Raphael

• **313. The Brown Sweater.** (1952)   Soyer's artful casualness
recalls the compositional innovations of Degas, while his color has
a rich quality reminiscent of the glowing surfaces of Corot. The
introspective young woman—a typical Soyer type—is placed
against a Lower East Side tenement facade; her large figure, with
its gentle, relaxed curves, fuses with the verticals and horizontals
of storefront, doorway and stoop. Further interest is added by
the varied forms and delicate colors of the sculpture and steps
and the fading paint of an iron baluster. The suggestion of depth
created by the steps and the dark rectangle of the door contrast
with the frontal pose of the young woman, while her meditative
mood is offset by the livelier action of mother and son in the
background.

313

Some notable sculpture in the museum:

Archipenko, Alexander, 1887-1964. *Torso in Space,* 1936, metallized terra cotta.

Baizerman, Saul, 1889-1957. *Slumber,* 1948, hammered copper.

Baskin, Leonard, born 1922.
● *Hephaestus,* 1963, bronze.

Calder, Alexander, born 1898. *Big Red,* 1959, sheet metal and steel wire.
The Cock's Comb, 1960, sheet iron.

De Creeft, José, born 1884. *Himalaya,* 1942, beaten lead.

Davidson, Jo, 1883-1952. *Gertrude Stein,* 1920, bronze.

Ferber, Herbert, born 1906. *Sun Wheel,* 1956, brass, copper and silver solder.

Flannagan, John B., 1898-1942. *Chimpanzee,* 1928, granite.

Gabo, Naum, born 1890. *Linear Construction in Space, Number 4,* 1958, plastic and stainless steel.

Gross, Chaim, born 1904. *Sisters,* 1946, Italian pink marble.

Lachaise, Gaston, 1892-1935. *Standing Woman,* 1912-27, bronze.

Lipchitz, Jacques, born 1891. *Sacrifice, II,* 1948-52, bronze.

Lipton, Seymour, born 1903. *Sorcerer,* 1957, nickel-silver on monel metal.

Marisol (Escobar), born 1930. *Woman and Dog,* 1964, wood and mixed media.

Nakian, Reuben, born 1897. *Olympia,* bronze.

Noguchi, Isamu, born 1904. *Integral,* marble.

De Rivera, José, born 1904. *Construction 67,* 1959, forged bronze.

Roszak, Theodore, born 1907. *Night Flight,* 1958-62, steel.

Smith, David, born 1906. *Lectern Sentinel,* 1961, stainless steel.

Stankiewicz, Richard, born 1922. *Kabuki Dancer,* 1956, steel and cast iron.

Zorach, William, born 1887. *The Future Generation,* 1942-47, Botticini marble.

THE GALLERY OF MODERN ART
(Huntington Hartford Collection)

Columbus Circle at Broadway.   LT 1-2311

Hours: Tuesdays through Saturdays 11-7; Sundays and holidays 12-6. Closed Mondays. Admission: adults $1; children 25¢.
Transportation: Seventh Avenue IRT or IND "A," "B," "C" or "D" Trains to Columbus Circle.
Films: Special showings. (Inquire at desk.)
Sales desk: Catalogues and reproductions; main floor.
Restaurants: Gallery Lounge, cocktails and light refreshment (regular museum hours), eighth floor. Gauguin Room, luncheon and dinner, ninth floor.

The Gallery of Modern Art, including the Huntington Hartford Collection, was opened in March, 1964. Sponsored and financed by George Huntington Hartford, Jr., grandson and heir of the founder of the Atlantic & Pacific Tea Co., the museum is dedicated to a special point of view: "That there is a valid alternative to the present dominance of abstract art. At the same time, it offers an alternative view of the recent past—a view relatively inaccessible to the public—as well as giving attention to artists and movements not considered of major significance currently, but who, in fact, deserve closer attention." Accordingly, in spite of its name, visitors will find no Picassos, Mirós or Mondrians on exhibit.

The museum's original collection consists of roughly seventy paintings and some sculpture and drawings by artists ranging from Courbet, Monet, Pissarro, Vuillard and Dali to names in lesser esteem today, such as the Victorian favorite Sir Edward Landseer. Among the sculpture is work by Rodin, Renoir and Jacob Epstein.

The museum's unusual building, rather Byzantine in inspiration, was designed by Edward Durell Stone, co-architect, in the 1930's, of The Museum of Modern Art. Only ninety-seven feet wide at its greatest dimension, it looms white and slender on a narrow, irregular island of land, its curved facade supported by an arcade. The luxurious interior presents a subtle solution to the problem of exhibition galleries in condensed space. Four floors are devoted to selections from the permanent collection and frequent loan exhibitions, two floors to offices and storage, and two floors to restaurants. The basement houses an auditorium equipped for films and lectures.

Note: A checklist of the paintings on display is available at the admissions desk.

MONET, Claude
• **314. The Jetty at Le Havre.** (1868)   Monet knew Le Havre since childhood, and this vigorous example of early Impressionism is alive with his lifelong response to its sea, wind, foam and waves. The diagonal thrust of the jetty emphasizes space and movement between the horizontal subdivisions of sea and sky. The rows of stones, the small, dark figures and the lamposts—preludes to the climax of the lighthouse—form sharp verticals against the relatively soft-toned expanse of space. In the year of this painting, Monet was practically penniless, in spite of having won a silver medal in an international maritime exhibition at Le Havre. Many of his paintings were seized by creditors until his patron Gaudibert came to the rescue by buying them for some eighty francs each.

MOREAU, Gustave
• **315. Salome Dancing Before Herod.** (1870-76)   When Herodias divorced her husband to marry his brother, Herod Antipas, John the Baptist condemned her. Herodias wanted to have him killed, "but she could not, for Herod feared John." When her daughter Salome danced for the King, however, she so inflamed

him that he offered her any wish up to half his kingdom. The
girl's mother replied for her: "The head of John the Baptist."
Moreau shows Salome holding a lotus, symbol of voluptuousness.
Beside Herod stands an executioner. The strongest appeal of the
painting is in the lure of its color, which lends splendor and
iridescence to a theatrical setting; golden yellows, red and rich
blues are artfully relieved by muted tones. The effect of great
space is reinforced by the height above the figures and the succession of receding arches. Moreau captures something of Delacroix's exotic spirit and exuberant color and adapts with sensitivity
Rembrandt's thick surfaces, but excessive ornamentation, as in
the overemphasis of the dancer's dress, dilutes the drama into a
minor spectacle.

PUVIS DE CHAVANNES, Pierre

• **316. Saint Geneviève.** (1879)   This is a typical Chavannes
fusion of classical forms, early Italian decorative flatness and
sensitive handling of line and mass. The figures, in dignified,
frieze-like unity, undulate in a slow, rhythmic massing across the
three panels. Placement, gestures, folds and the spotting of color
lead the eye to the little girl and the two Bishops. The vertical
accents of the trees echo the figures, while distant mountains continue the horizontal scheme. The color is delicate and luminous,
the drawing simple and expressive. St. Geneviève, patroness of
Paris, was an obscure nun who rallied the city in 451 against half
a million Huns under Attila. Years later, she saved the city again
during a siege by the Franks and helped convert the enemy
leader, Clovis, to Christianity. In 1874, Chavannes was commissioned to paint two murals for the Panthéon on the Saint's childhood. These panels, final studies for one of the murals, depict
a legend in which Sts. Germanus and Louis, enroute to England
to fight heresy, stopped in Nanterre, scene of Geneviève's childhood. Among the welcoming throng was the young girl. In her
face St. Germanus saw the sign of God, and he prophesied her

314

316

high destiny. In subordinate action, boatmen prepare a skiff for the voyage to England, a sick man is brought to receive blessing and the child's parents listen to the prophecy in awe before the kneeling townsfolk.

BURNE-JONES, Sir Edward Coley

• **317. Perseus and the Graiae.** (Between 1877-93) • **318. The Doom Fulfilled.** (1884-88) • **319. The Death of the Medusa.** (1884-88) These three paintings, part of a series of eight commissioned by Arthur James Balfour several years before he became Prime Minister, are among the most interesting examples of the Gallery of Modern Art's sponsorship of rarely seen and relatively unfashionable paintings. Burne-Jones based the series on the poem "The Doom of Acrisius," a retelling of the Perseus legend by the artist's great friend, the writer, designer and pioneer Socialist William Morris. King Acrisius of Argos, fearful of a prophecy concerning his grandson Perseus, set the child and his mother adrift. Found and raised by King Polycrates of Seriphus, Perseus was tricked into setting off on what the King hoped would be a fatal mission: to cut off the head of the Medusa, the sight of whose face turned men to stone. The goddess Athena, however, gave Perseus a highly reflective shield which enabled him to slay the monster without looking at her. The eerie spirit and stark composition of *Perseus and the Graiae* make it one of the most effective of the series. An almost hypnotic sensation is created by the rhythmic gestures of the arms, the folds of the robes, the curves of rocks and mountains and the icy green tonality. The graceful, almost effeminate form of Perseus, emphasized by his gleaming armor, climaxes the theatrical sequence of figures. The Graiae, sisters of the Medusa, had only one eye and one tooth among them; Perseus stole them and refused to restore them until the three crones told him where to find winged shoes, a magic wallet and a helmet which made its wearer invisible. The artist shows the Graiae groping blindly for the stolen eye. *The Death of the Medusa,* an unfinished chalk-and-gouache, contrasts with the languor of most of the Perseus series, but its attempts at

318

drama through violent movement seem only superficial echoes of Tintoretto and Michelangelo. Among its more subtle effects is the classic pose given the decapitated figure—a curving form continued and varied by the line of the shore. The Medusa, the only one of the three Gorgons who was mortal, had been ravished by Poseidon in the temple of Athena. The angry goddess transformed her into a monster. Perseus surprised the Gorgons and succeeded in cutting off the Medusa's head, accomplishing the goal of his adventure. After slaying the Medusa, Perseus flew over Ethiopia and saw, chained to a rock, the maiden Andromeda, with whom he immediately fell in love. The girl's mother, Queen Cassiopeia, had boasted that her daughter's beauty surpassed even that of the sea-dwelling Nereids. Poseidon, in revenge, sent a monster to ravage the country; the curse would cease only if the guiltless girl were chained to a rock to be devoured. Perseus rescued the maiden and married her. In *The Doom Fulfilled,* the coils of the monster and the struggling form of Perseus create a novel composition, with the two antagonists merged by the light and dark modelling of the glistening serpent and the reflections on the youth's armor. Their seething movement contrasts with the quiet grace of Andromeda, but the effect is marred by the girl's Victorian prettiness and waxen flesh. Some scholars believe the Perseus and Andromeda legend inspired that of St. George and the dragon.

MARSH, Reginald

• **320. Wonderland Circus Sideshow, Coney Island.** (1930)   In this lively vignette of a seething summer-evening crowd, Marsh revels in characterization, the play of glittering lights and continuity of movement and gesture. The fun seekers are intertwined into a frontal frieze which provides a base for the pyramidal group on the platform. The edge of the sideshow entrance, accentuated by a row of lightbulbs, forms a striking contrast to the deep space effect of the dark violet sky. Notes of vivid color—green against red, blues opposing yellows, a sharp line of black—add sparkle and vivacity to the animated drawing.

319

DALI, Salvador

• **321. The Discovery of America by Christopher Columbus.**
(1959) The gallery in which this picture hangs was especially
designed for it and its companion piece, *The Battle of Tetuán*.
Such foresight has been rewarded: Dali's controversial reputation
and the lure of a familiar theme treated with both photographic
realism and tantalizing symbolism have made this huge work one
of the museum's chief attractions. The painting presents a dream
in which Columbus, depicted as a youth, is mystically identified
with Jesus—what Dali calls "two double, invisible images of
Christ." Eyes closed in rapture, Columbus places on the New
World the banner of the Immaculate Conception, patroness of
Spain (posed for by the artist's wife Gala) as testimony that "all
the history of Spain develops in the idea of empire towards God."
Columbus brings with him, according to Dali, "all the religious
belief and metaphysical knowledge of the Middle Ages." The
enormous sea urchin symbolizes the fundamentals of America's
outstanding scientific achievement—the development of atomic
science; its pear shape resembles that of the earth as discovered
by the American satellite Explorer II. Columbus is greeted by St.
Narcissus, patron of the Spanish province of Gerona. (Dali believes it was from Gerona, not Genoa, that Columbus came.) The
Saint's figure consists partly of crosses and flies, relating to the
legend that a French cavalry attack in 1808 was defeated by
swarms of flies emanating from his grave. Moreover, to Dali flies
suggest particles of nuclear matter. At center, an image of the
Holy Grail appears on the topsail of the Santa Maria. In the sky,
beneath Christ and the Madonna, are Queen Isabella and King
Ferdinand. At right, amid dots and stripes (again suggesting nuclear matter), appears the Crucifixion. Youths hold banners of
the provinces of Spain. The monk at bottom right center is depicted with Dali's face. The basic composition consists of a symmetrical balance of the vertical units at right and left, with the
ship as their center. The sharply defined line of the base heightens

1   322

the sense of misty space conveyed by the pearly blue of the surface. The egg-shaped light at the top balances the spherical sea urchin at bottom. The red and yellow notes of the banners are carried through in the crosses on the sails and in the Madonna's halo. The painting sums up recent trends in the artist's work: a tendency toward the grandiose (the picture is fourteen feet high), an emphasis on themes of Christianity and an interest in the dissolution of forms, relating to new concepts of the structure of matter.

• **322. The Battle of Tetuán.** (1962) In his second striking tour-de-force, Dali again combines photographic accuracy with flights of Surrealism. The horse at upper left and the arm and sword at right frame the onrush of warriors. Some figures fade; others fuse mysteriously into numbers. At center, on a galloping horse, appears the artist's wife Gala; beside her is Dali. The group of horsemen in the sky is handled in the style of Mariano Fortuny (1838-1874), whose unfinished painting of Spaniards fighting Moroccan Berbers inspired this work. The horse at upper left recalls Velázquez. The long equine thigh and leg in the sky are a dream image Dali used in his *The Ghost of Vermeer of Delft, Which Can Be Used as a Table* (1934). To some extent this painting, so opposed in style and subject to contemporary abstraction, is Dali's own battle against much of modern art. At the same time, it recalls the 19th Century "salon machines"—spectacular, naturalistic canvases meant to attract attention at official Paris exhibitions.

Some notable sculpture in the museum:

Bourdelle, Antoine, 1881-1929. *Portrait,* 1910-12, bronze.
Davidson, Jo, 1883-1952. *John D. Rockefeller,* 1929, bronze.
    Portrait of Gandhi, 1931, bronze.
Epstein, Jacob, 1880-1959. *George Bernard Shaw,* 1934, bronze.
    Helen Keller, 1945, bronze.
Renoir, Auguste, 1841-1919. *Bust of Madame Renoir,* 1910, bronze.
Rodin, Auguste, 1840-1917. *The Kiss,* 1880-82?, bronze.
    The Thinker, 1880, bronze.

THE BROOKLYN MUSEUM

Eastern Parkway & Washington Avenue, Brooklyn. NE 8-5000

Hours: Mondays through Saturdays 10-5; Sundays and holidays 1-5. Free.
Transportation: Seventh Avenue IRT to Brooklyn Museum station.
Sales desk: Main floor.
Talks: Regular gallery talks and lectures.
Concerts: Periodically throughout the year.
Restaurant: First floor cafeteria (Mondays through Saturdays 10-4:30; Sundays and holidays 1-4:30).

The Brooklyn Museum—almost unknown territory to most Manhattanites, let alone out-of-towners—possesses an exceptional collection of American oils and watercolors, fine European paintings, a remarkable group of primitive sculpture and fabrics and some of the best Egyptian art in the country.

The Museum, along with its important art school, is an adjunct of the Brooklyn Institute of Arts and Sciences, which also includes the Brooklyn Children's Museum, the famous Brooklyn Botanic Garden (adjoining the Brooklyn Museum) and the

Brooklyn Academy of Music. The Institute was established in 1843, partly by the wealthy local distiller Augustus Graham. In 1884 a committee was organized to establish a museum of the arts and sciences, and in 1890 the city allocated funds for the building on the present site. The West Wing, designed by McKim, Mead and White, was opened in 1897; sections were added in 1905, 1907 and 1925.

The Museum's greatest paintings are 18th and 19th Century American. Its collection of primitive arts—aboriginal American, Oceanic and African Negro—is handsomely and effectively displayed. The Museum also exhibits a costume collection which is a central source for designers; European and American sculpture; American period rooms; Japanese, Persian and Chinese art; Jewish ceremonial objects; colonial Mexican interiors; and special loan shows.

One of the Museum's most appealing features is its unusual Gallery Shop, which sells original contemporary folk art from Alaska, Mexico, South America, Europe and Asia at surprisingly moderate prices.

Note: A floor plan of the Museum is available at the sales desk.

Spanish Painting

RIBERA, José de

● **323. Saint Joseph.** (About 1635)   The face and figure of the solidly painted Saint gain vitality from the picture's deep space and stark pyramid design. Placed as a diagonal leading the eye from left to right, the tense figure is further emphasized by the position of the flowering rod and by the dynamic countermovement of the cloak's broad folds. The sober, dramatic mood is in-

323

tensified by the use of only a few contrasting colors. When this painting was given to the Museum in 1911, it was so obscured by dirt, overpainting and varnish that the gift seemed almost inconsequential. In the 1930's, however, staff members established that it was an early Ribera, and cleaning and restoration revealed the flowers on the rod, which had been overpainted. The painting had previously been thought to depict Aaron, whose barren rod bore flowers when he placed it in the Ark of the Covenant; now it is believed that the flowers relate to the old legend that during St. Joseph's courtship, the barren rod he held blossomed with flowers and almonds—a token of God's choice of him as Mary's husband.

Dutch Painting

HALS, Frans
• **324. The Fisher Girl.** (Date uncertain)   Hal's impetuous style challenged the tradition of formal poses and muted studio light. His agile brush eliminates detail and compresses and simplifies drawing. In this captivating example of the spontaneity which blows like a fresh wind in his paintings, colors almost crackle through the crisp strokes, and the lively reds make the blue sky appear cooler and breezier. The seashore is bathed in a brisk outdoor light. The artist's initial "H" appears on the barrel.

HOBBEMA, Meindert
• **325. Hamlet in the Wood.** (Date uncertain)   Soft, airy sky serves as balance and contrast to the dark massing of trees to the left and, through its reflection in the stream, to link background and foreground. The level ground is varied by a receding road, while a peasant in red adds a tiny focal point of color and indicates the scale of houses and trees. This landscape once belonged to Jan Six, Burgomaster of Amsterdam in 1691, a collector and close friend of Rembrandt.

326

French Painting

GERICAULT, Théodore

● **326. The Wounded Cuirassier.** (1812-14)   This painting demonstrates the glorification of war and physical heroism stimulated during the Napoleonic epoch. The use of contemporary
material—a battle, a stormy sky, a spirited horse, the intense
officer—combined with the bold handling of color and brushstrokes, mark the budding romantic revolt against the classicism
of David. The graceful curves of the horse, the plumes of the
helmet, the cloak and the contours of the arm holding the bridle
all intensify a supple, dynamic arrangement, a scheme repeated
in the lines of the slope and the mass of shadow. These flowing
movements are countered by the turn of the officer's head in the
opposite direction, by his halting walk and by the left arm supported on the sheath of the sword. The picture is a study for
Géricault's *The Wounded Cuirassier* in the Louvre.

DELACROIX, Eugène

● **327. The Disciples at Emmaus.** (About 1853)   Delacroix depicts St. Luke's story of the two disciples who met Jesus after the
Resurrection and did not at first recognize Him. The eye is immediately led toward Christ by the focus of light, by His being
the only standing figure and by an artful distribution of lines and
masses. In the mystic act of breaking bread, Christ's pose sum-
marizes the tension of the shifting diagonals structured into the
composition. Silver, browns, reds and deep greens vibrate with
luminous splendor. The forms are strong and massive. Delacroix,
one of the few artists of his period to appreciate Rembrandt's
profundity, may have been inspired to paint this theme by a
Rembrandt masterpiece in the Louvre (also a small painting).
When this painting was shown in the Salon of 1853, a critic
wrote: "It is a serious fault to sanction through his [Delacroix's]
examples the endeavors of materialistic art and to lower the gran-

327

deur of a story from the Gospel to the level of an incident in a
Flemish inn." Another critic, however, felt: "This small canvas is
a true miracle. It contains nobility, truth, power, harmony, grace
and refinement. Christ is Divine."

COROT, Jean Baptiste Camille
● **328. Ville d'Avray.** (Date uncertain)   This gemlike landscape,
painted near Corot's home outside Paris, is exceptionally luminous and clear in tonality. Its forms are broadly treated, as in the
house at right and the row of trees at left. Although fresh and
spontaneous in its deft sketchiness, the handling conveys volume
and substance. Particularly effective are the soft gray-green, the
crystal-clear pond, the ivory-gold of the house at left and the
clear, soft sky. Small figures are grouped in a loose pyramid. Such
paintings by Corot foretell Pissarro's early work and early Impressionism.

● **329. Young Girls of Sparta.** (1868-70)   A reclining girl dressed
in an odd studio assortment of Greek and Italianate costuming is
painted firmly, with clean and limpid color. A strong setting for
her figure is provided by the red cushion, which also helps establish a base for the dark green trees in the background. Behind the
three dancers, the sky throbs. While the canvas employs conventional pseudo-romantic trappings, Corot's artful simplicity, dis-
interest in prettiness and, above all, his magnificent handling of
pigment, tone and color result in a truly lyrical picture. As with
Henri Rousseau, what at first seems naive and superficial exoti-
cism becomes, through earnest feeling and genius, oddly touching
and profound.

MONTICELLI, Adolphe
● **330. Fête Champêtre.** (Date uncertain)   Ribbons of color
mould the figures as they emerge from the background, animated
by the sparkle of artificial light. The sky, fresh and free, is enlivened by violet, tan and orange. The figures are grouped in
rhythmic masses, punctuated by notes of sonorous red. The juicy
surface delights the eye. Typical of Monticelli's festive scenes,
action and costumes are subordinated to the painter's broader
interest in color, texture and movement.

331

PISSARRO, Camille

● **331. The Climbing Path.** (1875)   This well-knit early Impressionist landscape done at Pontoise explores a novel composition—the placing of a climbing path directly in the foreground and to the far right. The arrangement intensifies the effect of overlooking the landscape from a high vantage point. Winding across fields, the path's graceful curve forms an eye-pleasing movement between the slender trees. White houses with pink and purple roofs are disposed in geometric order amid irregular masses of foliage. The landscape is steeped in fresh, cool atmosphere and dappled by light and shade. Large portions are handled with a palette knife, lending solidity and enhancing the texture and luminosity of the color.

MONET, Claude

● **332. The Ducal Palace at Venice.** (1908)   Despondent over dimming eyesight and waning health, Monet accepted in 1908 an invitation from a friend of John Singer Sargent to visit Venice for the first time. He painted about thirty compositions of the city, completing many after his return to France, and exhibited the entire series in 1912. In this painting, the Ducal Palace looms suddenly against a soft sky, as if seen from a gondola. Its pink and pearl facade glows above the dazzle of reflections which make up a mosaic of vibrating gold, green and violet, set off at both sides by areas of green water. Only the violet wall at left and the wall of the far, low building vary the dramatic frontal presentation. Under the impact of light, the palace dissolves into a delicate, insubstantial structure, its surface enlivened by quick brush strokes which create intriguing textural effects. The vibrating expanse of the Grand Canal may have stimulated Monet's later *Water Lilies.*

SISLEY, Alfred

● **333. Landscape.** (Date uncertain)   In this captivating glimpse of a vibrant early spring morning, deft touches of glistening color envelop the gleaming stream, the translucent river and the vivid notes of red roofs above the white house. With its slender, swaying trees and its wispy, animated sky (a special love of Sisley's), the landscape sparkles and snaps, exhibiting the full charm of the artist's vision of nature.

332

CEZANNE, Paul

• **334. Village of Gardanne.** (1885-86) This unfinished oil, showing the hillside village in Provence where Cézanne lived during 1885-86, offers an insight into the artist's search for a basic solidity of structure, undissolved by light and atmosphere as in the work of his Impressionist colleagues. Houses are defined and disposed in a way which emphasizes a geometric design of interlocking shapes. The massed trees repeat, in vertical areas of cool color, the angularity of the horizontal, warm-colored notes on the houses. As the buildings begin an ascending movement, space is flattened and shifted to suggest vertical emphasis. A church forms the apex of a pyramid which has its base in the foreground.

DEGAS, Edgar

• **335. Mademoiselle Fiocre in the Ballet La Source.** (1866-68) This historic Degas is the first of his many portrayals of ballet themes. A transitional painting, its dark tonality suggests the influence of Courbet, while the smooth handling reflects Degas' love of Ingres' polished style. In the blue dress and passages like the pink ballet slippers (the only indication that this is a ballet scene on a stage), precise, sensitive drawing reveals Degas' own characteristics. Also typical is the grasp of informal action, as in the turning to the right of the girl with the lute and the pose of the seated attendant at right. The horse also foretells the many Degas drawings, paintings and sculptures on that theme. *La Source,* an opera by Délibes, was first performed in 1866, the year this painting was begun. Ballerina Eugenie Fiocre danced the leading role of Nouredda, fiancée of the Khan.

• **336. Portrait of a Man.** (1866) Meticulous draftsmanship, like that of Ingres, is combined with the free, casual pose of a Manet. The tilt of the red chair and of the man himself add forceful motion. Degas makes effective use of the white in the tablecloth and of the white curtain framing the figure's silhouette. The

4   335

face recalls an aim of Degas: "One should make people's portraits in everyday, typical attitudes. Beauty should mean no more than a certain type of face."

TOULOUSE-LAUTREC, Henri de

• **337. Woman Smoking a Cigarette.** (1890)   Lautrec poses his subject informally off-center, facing far right with her body half-turned in that direction. The back of a chair, the basin and the towel help restore balance and hold the observer's eye within the picture. The slashing, vividly expressive drawing presents a shrewd characterization, as Lautrec catches the pout of the lips, the pull of the sleeves, a twist of the wrist and the loosely held cigarette. Dashes of gold and blue create striking and decorative textural effects.

FANTIN-LATOUR, Henri

• **338. Portrait of Mme. Léon Mâitre.** (1882)   A brown wall and the rich red sofa and cushions set off the dark dress, the blue fan and the froth of white material around the bosom. In these accessories and in his exquisite feeling for fabrics and soft lights and darks, Fantin-Latour goes beyond mere facility to achieve a portrait of high quality—distinctive, if conservative; informal, yet dignified. Externally dry and precise, the painting reveals inner sensitivity and refinement and the eye of a keen realist. Léon Mâitre and his wife were among the artist's closest friends.

MORISOT, Berthe

• **339. Mme. Boursier and Her Daughter.** (Date uncertain) Sparkling color is handled with directness and enlivened by buoyant contrasts of vivid blues, violets, warm flesh tones and the gleam of the red bow in the sitter's bonnet. Morisot's drawing is both firm and, as in the child's oval face, delicate. The influence of Manet's luminosity and suave but rigorous handling is strong. Mme. Boursier was the painter's cousin.

336

3:

BONNARD, Pierre

• **340. The Breakfast Room.** (Date uncertain)   This novel arrangement of figures, furniture and shimmering color achieves Bonnard's characteristic synthesis of radiant light glorifying a moment of everyday life. Lively patterns heighten the appeal. The silken white of the table is accentuated by the softly flecked, glowing still life, which relates to the yellow dress and brown hair of the girl in the foreground. Her warm tonalities, in turn, are linked with the red in the sideboard and the green and pink of the still life. The smaller girl, opening a drawer, provides a rich green against the dark cabinet. The table's horizontal creates the dominant direction. The girl with the cup follows the steep inward movement of the table-edge. Her gently curving shoulder leads to the right side of the standing child, whose simple gesture is transformed into an exquisite design. Modeling is suppressed in favor of a compact sense of space and simplification of form.

American Painting

WILLIAMS, William

• **341. Deborah Hall.** (1766)   Deborah Hall, here depicted at fourteen, four years before her death, was the daughter of David Hall, Benjamin Franklin's partner in the printing business. Her stiff pose (emulating the genteel European tradition) and the setting of the formal garden give the painting a stately charm, but one which is oddly contradicted by the unsophisticated handling of flesh, fabric and foliage. Extensive restorations are intentionally indicated by a faint, groovelike grain separating the original paint from the restored areas.

8

0

339

COPLEY, John Singleton

● **342. Elizabeth Goldthwaite (Mrs. John Bacon).** (1769-70) Strong, unpretentious and sensitive, Copley's rendering is realistic without sacrificing a dramatic sense of personality. The conventional design of a bust against a background is made forceful by space effects. Copley's facility with fabrics and textures, notably in the sheen of the sleeves and treatment of the lace, does not detract from the features but leads the eye back to the severely simplified face with its ivory yellow tonality. Elizabeth Goldthwaite, at the time of the portrait, was the wife of the Rev. John Bacon of Old South Church, Boston.

PEALE, Charles Wilson

● **343. George Washington.** (1776) Most of Peale's paintings are more important as historical mementos than as works of art. This is one of the most historic—the first portrayal of Washington as an American. Despite the pose and weak drawing of the arms, the painting possesses a robust and rude vigor. The face is delineated with broad, strong planes and striking flesh tones. Against a dark sky and low horizon, Washington looms on a majestic scale. The blue ribbon represents the insignia of Commander in Chief. The second of seven portraits Peale made of Washington from life, this version was done for John Hancock, then President of the First Continental Congress. For more than eighty years it hung in the Hancock mansion in Boston. When the building was demolished in 1863, the painting was sold at auction.

STUART, Gilbert

● **344. George Washington ("The Landsdowne Type").** (1796) Though he places Washington in surroundings which recall Rubens and van Dyck, Stuart lacks the grandeur of the Flemish masters. The arrangement seems somewhat pompous and pretentious; the color is thin and without distinction. Washington is rendered with little substance or characterization. But his face,

341

3

when seen in isolation from the ornate curtains and columns,
does have firmness and sensitivity. One of two portraits of Washington which Stuart made in Philadelphia in 1796, this version
was painted for William Constable, an aide to Lafayette. In its
size and pose it forms a companion to one the artist painted for
the Marquis of Landsdowne (hence, the identifying phrase
"Landsdowne type"). Constable bequeathed it to his son, from
whom it passed on to a brother-in-law, H. B. Pierrepont. When
Lafayette saw the painting in Pierrepont's Brooklyn mansion in
1824, he exclaimed, "That is my old friend, indeed."

GUY, Francis

• **345. Winter Scene in Brooklyn.** (1817-20)   An 1867 history
of Brooklyn testifies to the authenticity of this view taken from
a second-story window of the artist's residence at 11 Front Street:
"Mr. Thomas W. Birdsall [one of several well-known Brooklynites
depicted], who appears on the canvas not far from his dwelling
and store, related that Guy, as he painted, would sometimes call
out of the window to his subjects as he caught sight of them on
their customary ground, to stand still while he put in the characteristic strokes." Through finesse of forms and appealing contrasts
of pattern and color, light and shade, the panorama is endowed
with both breadth and sharply-observed detail. The expanse of
sky helps emphasize the clean-cut, slanting roofs, the design of
the buildings and the figures set off by snow. Severely burned in

344

346

1881, the painting was extensively restored several years later. Another Guy version of this theme is in the New York Historical Society.

HICKS, Edward

• **346. The Peaceable Kingdom.** (About 1833) The Biblical prophecy of the Peaceable Kingdom occurs in the eleventh chapter of Isaiah: "The wolf also shall dwell with the lamb, and the leopard shall lie down with the kid; and the calf and the young lion and the fatling together; and a little child shall lead them." About one hundred Hicks paintings on the *Peaceable Kingdom* theme are known, dating from about 1825 to the day before Hicks died, when he completed a final *Peaceable Kingdom* for his daughter. He sold some for about $30 and gave others to friends. Hicks delights in the crouch of a lion, the curving horn of an ox, the spotting of a leopard. Grouped compactly and strongly outlined, the tranquil animals are opposed in this version by a group borrowed from Benjamin West's famous painting *Penn's Treaty with the Indians* (1771, Pennsylvania Academy of the Fine Arts, Philadelphia). Hicks also wrote a poem on *The Peaceable Kingdom* which concludes thus: "The illustrious Penn this heavenly kingdom felt/ then with Columbia's native sons he dealt/ without an oath a lasting treaty made/ in Christian faith beneath the elm tree's shade."

COLE, Thomas

• **347. A View of the Two Lakes and Mountain House, Catskill Mountains, Morning.** (1844) Like other significant Cole works, this painting interprets his idea that "to walk with nature as a poet is the necessary condition of the perfect artist." "In looking over the uncultivated scene, the mind may travel far into Futurity. Where the wolf roams, the plow shall glisten; on the gray crags shall rise temple and tower." Cole transforms the Catskills into a Byronic vision of solitude and grandeur. Mingling the Dutch landscape motifs of Ruisdael, the spaciousness of Claude Lorrain and the Arcadian visions of early 19th Century poets and painters, Cole represents the poet-artist's spirit imbuing a wilderness with Romantic vision. The artist himself stands at the left.

INNESS, George

• **348. June.** (1882) In its recording of a summer mood, this green lyric is one of Inness' finest landscapes. The basic arrange-

347

ment—as in a fine Corot—seems casual: an amplitude of green,
rich in nuance, is complemented by the light blue sky and stream;
the horizontal mass of the ground balances the vertical thrust of
trees; long thin streaks of light green re-emphasize the horizontality and deeply recessed space. The water gleams like transparent silk as it reflects trees, sky and drifting white clouds. Its
winding movement gives drama to the flat ground and quietly
corresponds to the slight swell at right, where one tiny figure suggests a drowsy stillness in the early-summer haze. Throughout,
detail is subdued to emphasize overall effect; the handling is firm,
yet gentle.

EAKINS, Thomas

• **349. Home Scene.** (About 1870-71) In this interior scene
depicting the artist's sisters Caroline and Margaret, Eakins savors
the sober beauty of light and shade, fabric and wood, subtle
movement and deep, enclosed space. Light is used rhythmically
on flesh, fabric, the piano keyboard and the music score. Key
colors, as in the child's striped red dress, and light accents like
those on her face are echoed in the piano player's costume, in the
carpet and in the relationship of the dress to the carpet's patterns.
Movement is a primary element, but the tempo is slow, as in the
child's motion to the left, the slant of the older girl's figure, the
right-ward thrust of the music score and the upward direction of
the carpet.

• **350. Mrs. Letitia Wilson Jordan Bacon.** (1888) Restrained,
yet relaxed, the meditative subject is shown in a pose expressing
both intimacy and dignity. Against the deep brownish-red setting,
the warm complexion of the face and the silvery flesh of the arms
emerge softly but strongly. Blue scarf and yellow gloves provide
muted but resonant accents within the quiet tonality. The sitter
was a sister of a pupil of Eakins, David Wilson Jordan.

• **351. William Rush Carving His Allegorical Figure of the
Schuylkill River.** (1908) Eakins painted three versions of this

350

theme, probably alluding to his battle against Victorian prudery in Philadelphia. After scandalizing that city by using undraped nudes in his coeducational classes at the Pennsylvania Academy of the Fine Arts, Eakins resigned his post and set up his own classes, where he taught without accepting payment. In this painting, he depicts an earlier art scandal which had erupted in the same city when William Rush (1756-1833), the first important native-born American sculptor, used a nude model for *Water Nymph and Bittern* (now in the Philadelphia Museum of Art). To make matters worse for Rush, the girl who posed for him (while a chaperone sat by knitting) was the daughter of a rich merchant. In the name of decency, Rush, like Eakins, was slanderously attacked. In this earnest painting, a quiet spatial drama emerges in the emphatic contrast between the color and light of the nude and the grayish tonality of the rest of the picture. Although the color is generally thin, it possesses an inherent somber richness. The carefully-modeled nude stands out forcefully from the setting, between the seated chaperone and the sculptor's dim yet firm figure. A charming contrast occurs between the sketchily-rendered carvings, tools and table and the careful details of the model. The girl's figure is deliberately kept from resembling the more fashionable voluptuous or nymph-like nude. Eakins' vision is prose, not poetry; it is subtly alive with character.

HOMER, Winslow

• **352. In the Mountains.** (1877) This majestic composition holds the eye through its mass of dark green mountains slanting steeply between foreground and sky. A vigorous outdoor atmosphere is communicated by cool color and dashing brushstrokes. The girls—in lively, broad notes of blue and red—provide a pivot and an equilibrium for the mountains, while their figures suggest the scale of the setting. The branch and the small plant act as boundaries in the foreground, while the sky, touched with irregular cloud contours, frames the terse, powerful movement of the mountains. The spatial effect is bold and simple, deriving from a series of diagonals. The Brooklyn Museum also owns an exceptional group of watercolors by Homer, of which twelve were acquired in 1912 from the artist's brother, Charles Homer, Jr.

351

SARGENT, John Singer

• **353. Paul Hellieu Sketching with His Wife.** (1889.)   Sargent, a friend and admirer of Monet, sometimes employed an Impressionist approach in his own work. Here, he captures Impressionist surface effects with verve and zest. The composition is brisk and informal, with its placement of the man and woman toward the right. Sargent depicts the artist, tense and absorbed in the act of painting, in subtle opposition to the relaxed attitude of his wife. Particularly effective against the predominantly cool colors are the two yellow notes of the hats, which form a pivot for the composition. Even the touch of yellow on the pole of the easel functions to centralize the warm notes. Paul Hellieu (1859-1927), painter and etcher, was a friend of Sargent from their student days. This painting was made when he and his wife visited Sargent in England. Hellieu sold it to the Brooklyn Museum in 1920.

RYDER, Albert Pinkham

• **354. The Grazing Horse.** (1880's)   The thick textures of this enchanting little pastorale gleam out richly. A simplified mass of reddish-brown earth and trees is set off by the handsome silvery-blue of the sky—an area which echoes the light-colored horse. Gentle contours of foliage are designed to correspond with the curve of the horse's back. The appealing interval established by the counter-slant of the tree trunk at right against the neck of the horse lends an opposing direction to the more placid movements of the composition.

• **355 The Waste of Waters is Their Field.** (Date uncertain)   An irresistible sense of movement is achieved primarily by the toss of the boat and the dramatic slant of the sail. Additional drama is provided by the compression of shapes into broad, majestic silhouettes. The imaginative cloud forms are painted as tossing, animated ribbons of color. There are four other Ryder paintings in the Brooklyn Museum's collection (*The Old Red Cow, Autumn's Golden Pathway, The Sheepfold* and *Shepherdess: Evening Glow*) but they are marred by deterioration.

354

BLAKELOCK, William

● **356. Moonlight.** (Date uncertain) The staple subject matter of calendar art—moonlight, campfire, Indian sentinel, canoe, rippling stream—is here transformed by an authentic romanticist into a hauntingly eloquent reverie. Space, projected by chiaroscuro and by the majestic height of the tree silhouetted against a misty sky, is deepened by the distant trees and hills, the relationship of the foreground stream to the horizon, the small scale of the immobile horsemen under the trees, and the contrast of firelight with moon. Bathed in dark russet and shimmering gold, the elements are integrated into a composition that touches the heart with its sense of a faraway world—half dream, half reality.

GLACKENS, William

● **357. Park on the River** (1905) and   ● **358. Nude with Apple** (1910)   Only five years apart, these two paintings illustrate key phases in Glackens' art. *Park on the River* represents the zestful, jaunty portrayals of big-city life which Glackens shared with John Sloan, George Luks and Robert Henri. His brush captures the tang of a grayish, windswept day with colors that recall the dark tonalities of Manet. The picture seems impulsively jotted down on the spur of the moment, an effect reinforced by terse, expressive drawing. In *Nude with Apple,* the palette has grown richer, more varied and luminous—closer to Renoir. The subject is a studio theme which, in spite of seeming informality, is carefully plotted and organized, focusing on the silken, glowing warmth of supple flesh. The young girl is placed as a gentle diagonal from upper left to lower right, her contours emphasized

355

357

by the curves and sumptuous red of the couch. Silken whites
intrude to set off the notes of hat and shoes. Glackens' sense of
character makes the girl not merely a model but a specific individual—a little awkward, yet graceful; relaxed, yet somewhat
rigid. The large hats of the period provide a wryly amusing note
of elaborate costume.

BELLOWS, George
• **359. A Morning Snow—Hudson River.** (About 1910)   The
view is from the New York bank facing the New Jersey Palisades.
Crisp and energetic, full of the sense of a raw, windy moment, the
picture is steeped with the tingling stir of winter sunlight. The
artfully organized expanse of white is varied by the blue of the
river. Especially charming are the blurred strokes defining figures
and the brisk handling of the structure at right.

PASCIN, Jules
• **360. Three Girls.** (About 1927)   The trio is rendered with
silken delicacy of color, exquisitely expressive line and rhythmic
alternation of dark and light. The figures form a linked mass
which slopes diagonally to lower right, but the table softly pulls
the eye back to upper right. The central figure, with dark hair,
dark dress and bouquet, is the focal point. Color which almost
seems to be breathed on gives an overall unity reminiscent of
Renoir. A line suddenly defines a leg or a bonnet; a wash of color
forms a delicate flower.

FEININGER, Lyonel
• **361. Zirchow.** (1916)   Feininger painted this German church
in the Baltic island town of Zirchow a number of times. In an
absorbing reinterpretation of Cubism, the artist compresses tower,
gable, roofs, buildings, tree and sky into a design as compact as
a diamond. The forms, which lean toward the right to create a
dynamic movement, are dominated by the dark mass of church
and steeple. At left, an almost abstract tree further impels the eye
toward the church, while the small buildings below provide a base
and give scale to the church's height. A broad blue plane serves
as a luminous backdrop, then shifts left to create equilibrium.
Feininger's harmony roams sharply but subtly, from the dark
chords of greens and browns to the singing colors of the sky.

360

The light is almost as spiritual, in its way, as that in an El Greco. The planes heighten the sense of thrust that flows through the entire painting.

SHEELER, Charles

• **362. Incantation.** (1946)   Based on the continuous-flow unit of an oil plant, *Incantation* bears out Sheeler's comment that "the great realist offers a final enhancement, a plus. We get the vision of the facts as well as the facts." The fervent complex of lines, bands and contrasting colors presents actual industrial forms yet retains the appealing sequence of patterns that gives excitement to semiabstraction. Rendered flat and smooth, the colors are placed in a brilliant unity amid a multiplicity of shapes. The key forms—verticals framed by sky and varying in scale and color— are countered by horizontal pipes and a rhythmic parade of three diagonals at bottom and a heavier red one at top. Shadows round a few forms (as at right) within a composition that stresses clear flatness.

361

Some notable sculpture in the museum:

African. *Power-Figure,* Lower Congo River Style, wood.
    Woman Seated on Animal Stool, Lower Congo River Style, wood.
    Mother and Child, Lower Congo River Style, wood.
    Nimba Mask, Baga Tribe, French Guinea, wood.
    Guardian Figure, Fang Tribe, Gabon, French Equatorial Africa, wood.
    Flute Player, Benin, Nigeria, bronze.
    Firespitter Mask, Ivory Coast, wood.

Archipenko, Alexander, 1887-1964. *Reclining Torso,* 1929?, ceramic.

Armitage, Kenneth, born 1916. *The Sentinels,* 1955, bronze.

Assyrian. *Figures,* reliefs from Palace of King Assurnasirpal, Nimrud, about 880 B.C., alabaster.

Barye, Antoine-Louis, 1796-1875. *Theseus Slaying the Centaur,* 1850, bronze.

Butler, Reg, born 1913. *Girl in Shift,* 1953-54, bronze.

Chinese. *Horse* (Head and Body), Han Dynasty, 206-00 B.C.— 220 A.D., unglazed grey pottery.

De Creeft, José, born 1884. *Semitic Head,* 1937, lead.

Egyptian. *Metheny as a Young Man,* about 2420 B.C., painted wood.

Metheny as an Aging Man, about 2420 B.C., painted wood.

Head of a Queen, about 1900 B.C., basalt.

Colossal Royal Head, about 1410 B.C., stone.

Portrait of an Egyptian Official, about 60 B.C., stone.

Etruscan. *Head of a Goddess,* about 100 B.C., terra cotta.

Gross, Chaim, born 1904. *Ballerina,* 1938?, wood.

Kolbe, Georg, 1877-1947. *Sea Nymph,* 1921, bronze.

Lachaise, Gaston, 1882-1935. *Standing Woman,* 1932, bronze.

Lipton, Seymour, born 1903.

   ● *Earth Forge II,* 1955, nickel-silver on steel.

Medieval: *Madonna and Child,* (Spanish?) 1490?, polychrome marble.

St. John on the Isle of Patmos, (German) about 1490, wood.

The Birth of the Virgin, (German) about 1490.

Mestrovic, Ivan, 1883-1962. *Archangel Gabriel,* 1919, marble.

Meunier, Constantin, 1831-1905. *Dock Laborer,* 1884, bronze.

The Quarry Man, 1900, bronze.

Nevelson, Louise, born 1904. *First Personage,* 1955?, wood.

Oceania. *Ancestral Figure,* Melanesia, New Ireland, painted wood.

Ritual Figure, Nicobar Islands, carved wood shells.

Ancestral Figure, Easter Islands, Polynesia.

Smith, David, born 1906. *The Hero,* 1952, stone.

Sumatra. *Effigy Dye Vessel,* iron.

Weinberg, Elbert, born 1928. *Temptation of Eve, No. 1,* 1960, bronze.

Zorach, William, born 1887. *The Embrace,* 1933, bronze.

OTHER NEW YORK CITY
MUSEUMS AND INSTITUTIONS

OTHER NEW YORK CITY
MUSEUMS AND INSTITUTIONS

THE PIERPONT MORGAN LIBRARY
36th Street and Madison Avenue.   MU 5-0008

Hours: Mondays through Saturdays 9:30-5. Closed Sundays, holidays, Saturdays from May 30 to Labor Day, and all of August. Free.

Transportation: Madison Avenue Bus to 37th Street; Fifth Avenue Buses 2, 3 and 4 to 37th Street. Lexington Avenue IRT to 33rd Street.

The Morgan Library is world-famous for its collection of drawings, manuscripts and books. It houses the oldest and rarest of all printed books, the Constance Missal (about 1450), now believed to predate even the Gutenberg Bible and is probably the work of the same master.

John Pierpont Morgan (1837-1913), the financier who in 1901 formed the world's first billion-dollar corporation—U.S. Steel—was a lordly art collector. Only a few of his paintings remain in the Morgan Library, however; many, like the Raphael *Collona Madonna* in the Metropolitan, were given to other museums, while others, including the Fragonard panels now in the Frick Collection, were sold.

Morgan's Renaissance-styled palace, designed by McKim, Mead and White, was built in 1905. Originally the financier's private library, it was incorporated as a public museum in 1924.

The paintings are in Morgan's former study, the West Room. The following are the most important: MEMLING, Hans: *An Elderly Woman* and *A Young Man Kneeling with Patron Saints*, two wings of a triptych; *Portrait of a Man with a Pink*. CRANACH, Lucas, The Elder: *Martin Luther and His Wife, Catherine*. PERUGINO, Pietro: *Virgin and Two Saints Adoring the Child*. TINTORETTO, Jacopo Robusti: *Portrait of a Moor*.

THE NEW YORK HISTORICAL SOCIETY
Central Park West at 77th Street.   TR 3-3400

Hours: Tuesdays through Fridays 1-5; Saturdays 10-5; Sundays 1-5. Closed Mondays, major holidays and during August. Free.
Transportation: Eighth Avenue and Central Park West Buses to 79th Street; 79th Street Crosstown Bus to Central Park West. Eighth Avenue IND to 81st Street (American Museum of Natural History exit).
Group tours: Available after 2:30 Tuesdays through Thursdays; reservations in advance.

Concerned with material relating to United States history, particularly that of New York State, the privately-endowed society was organized in 1804 and is the second oldest historical society in the country. As such, it has fallen heir to important treasures, including the entire collection of the New York Gallery of Fine Arts, important Egyptian art (transferred in 1936 to the Brooklyn Museum) and the Thomas J. Bryan collection of European paintings.

It is noteworthy that the Society began to collect and exhibit folk art in about 1911, before it was widely valued as an art form. Also of special note is its collection of 460 of the 500 original watercolors done by John James Audubon (1785-1851) for his *Birds of America* (about 1827-38).

The society's original home was in New York City's Federal Hall, where Washington was inaugurated as first President. The present building, begun in 1908, was designed by York and Sawyer. Two wings were added in 1938 from plans by Walker and Gillette. In addition to paintings, the collection includes rare period rooms and furniture, early fire-fighting equipment, early advertising and trade cards, maps, prints, the Beekman family coach, Washington's camp cot, the tool chest of Duncan Phyfe, the original articles of surrender of General Burgoyne, a nautical gallery, the remains of a statue of George III which was pulled down in New York City by soldiers during the Revolution, and genre sculptures by John Rogers.

Among the notable American paintings are these: Unknown artist: *The De Peyster Boy.* SMIBERT, John (born Scotland): *Captain and Mrs. Johannes Schyler.* WEST, Benjamin: *Charles Wilson Peale.* PEALE, Charles Wilson: *The Peale Family.* EARL, Ralph: *Mrs. James Duane.* DUNLAP, William: *The Artist Showing a Picture from Hamlet to His Parents.* DURAND, John: *The Rapalje Children.* GUY, Francis (born England): *Tontine Coffee House.* VANDERLYN, John: *Aaron Burr; Theodosia Burr.* MORSE, Samuel Finley Breese: *Allegorical Landscape Showing New York University.* DURAND, Asher Brown:

Sunday Morning; The Old Oak. COLE, Thomas (born England):
The Course of Empire, five paintings depicting a nation's begin-
ning, progress, greatness, destruction and final extinction; the en-
tire drama occurs around the same landscape of rock and lake.
MOUNT, William Sidney: *Bargaining for a Horse.* HEADE,
Martin: *Study of an Orchid.* KENSETT, John Frederick: *White
Mountain.* JOHNSON, Eastman: *Hackensack Meadows, Sunset.*
CHURCH, Frederick Edwin: *Cayambe.*

Notable European paintings include these: Flemish school:
Rest on the Flight into Egypt. Attributed to MANTEGNA, An-
drea: *Virgin and Child with Saints; The Crucifixion.* CRANACH,
Lucas, The Elder: *Venus and Cupid.* BROUWER, Adrian: *Rob-
ber Examining Coin by Candlelight.* TENIERS, David, The
Younger: *A Lady Playing with a Dog.* OSTADE, Adrian van:
five paintings entitled *Taste; Sight; Hearing; Smell; Touch.*
CUYP, Aelbert: *Farmyard Scene.*

SPANISH MUSEUM
(HISPANIC SOCIETY OF AMERICA)

Broadway between 155th & 156th Streets.
WA 6-2234

Hours: Tuesdays through Saturdays 10-4:30; Sundays 2-5. Closed
Mondays, July Fourth, Thanksgiving and Christmas. Free.
Transportation: Fifth Avenue Buses 4 and 5 to 155th Street.
Seventh Avenue IRT Van Cortlandt Park Train to 157th Street;
Eighth Avenue IND Washington Heights local to 155th Street.

The Hispanic Society was founded in 1904 by Archer M. Huntington (1870-1955), son of railroad magnate Collis P. Huntington, to widen public interest in Iberian culture through a museum,
a library and publications. The first building of the so-called
Washington Heights (or Audubon) Group, the Museum was
erected on land once part of John James Audubon's estate. The
main building was opened in 1908, the north building in 1930.

Among the important exhibits are a number of Spanish paintings (both classic and modern); sculpture, carvings and pottery
(including pre-Roman and Moresque); superb ironwork; luster-
ware; furniture; textiles; manuscripts, charts, and prints.

The most distinguished paintings include: Castilian school:
The Presentation in the Temple. Catalan school: *Virgin and Child
Enthroned.* MORALES, Louis de: *Virgin with the Yarn Winder.*
EL GRECO: *Two Miniature Portraits; Pieta; Saint James the*

Great; Saint Luke or Saint Simon (?). RIBERA, José de: *Saint Paul; The Ecstasy of Saint Mary Magdalene.* ZURBARAN, Francisco: *Saint Rufina; A Saint of Seville; A Procurator of a Carthusian Monastery.* VELAZQUEZ, Diego Rodriguez: *Conde de Olivares; Cardinal Camillo Pamphili.* GOYA, Francisco: *The Duchess of Alba; Don Manuel Lapena, Marquis of Bondad Real; Sketch for Scenes of the Massacre of May Third.*

THE CLOISTERS

Fort Tryon Park.   WA 3-3700

Hours: Tuesdays through Saturdays 10-5; Sundays and holidays 1-5. Closed Mondays. Free.
Transportation: Fifth Avenue Bus 4 to Fort Tryon Park (Cloisters stop). Eighth Avenue IND "A" Train express to 190th Street (exit by elevator), then to No. 4 bus (or short walk).
Sales desk: Reproductions.

A branch of the Metropolitan Museum devoted exclusively to Medieval art, the Cloisters is one of the most beautiful museums in the country, with a superb view overlooking the Hudson River. The Cloisters evolved from the collection of the sculptor George Grey Barnard (1863-1938), who assembled many Medieval sculptures and architectural fragments. In 1925, assisted by funds from John D. Rockefeller, Jr., the Metropolitan purchased Barnard's entire collection. In 1930 Rockefeller gave the Fort Tryon property to New York City, and four-and-a-half acres were reserved for a museum site. The building, designed by the architect Charles Collens, incorporates four cloisters, an arcade, a chapel and various exhibition rooms; it was opened in 1938.

The chief glories of the Cloisters are its architectural units— most notable the 12th Century Spanish apse from San Martin at Fuentidueña; the Romanesque chapel; the Cuta Cloisters, and the Saint-Guilhem Cloisters. Outstanding among the exhibits are: tapestries, including the rare 14th Century *Nine Heroes* and the breathtaking *Unicorn* series of about 1545; carvings, including a 12th Century Spanish crucifix and a Burgundian Virgin; chalices, including the famous 5th Century Chalice of Antioch; stone sculptures and reliquaries.

Paintings are relatively few, but they include the celebrated *Merode Altarpiece* of about 1420, a Flemish gem attributed to Robert Campin (1380?-1420).

COOPER UNION MUSEUM
FOR THE ARTS OF DECORATION
7th Street between Third & Fourth Avenues.
AL 4-6300

Hours: Mondays through Saturdays 10-5. Closed Sundays, major holidays and on Saturdays from June 1 to October 1. Free.
Transportation: Third Avenue Bus to 7th Street. Lexington Avenue IRT local to Astor Place.

The Museum is a department of the Cooper Union for the Advancement of Science and Art, an institution opened in 1859 as a gift of Peter Cooper (1791-1883). Cooper, an inventor and industrialist who rose from an apprenticeship to build America's first practical locomotive—the Tom Thumb (1830)—was also an educational pioneer. He organized his new school as a free, co-educational institution, barring distinction of race and creed, and linking science with art.

The structure, which now houses both Museum and classrooms, was New York's first attempt at a fireproof building. Designed by Frederick A. Peterson, it is also an example of the use of wrought iron beams and includes the first elevator shaft—a circular one, still in use. Abraham Lincoln and twelve other Presidents have spoken in the building's auditorium.

The Museum was inaugurated in 1897 by two of Cooper's granddaughters. Its collection includes textiles spanning almost 3,500 years; thousands of architectural drawings dating from the 16th Century, and a large collection of wallpapers, furniture, ceramics, woodwork, metalwork and costumes. It also owns some drawings, small oils and watercolors by Winslow Homer, prints by Dürer and Rembrandt and works by others.

THE AMERICAN ACADEMY OF
ARTS AND LETTERS
Broadway between 155th & 156th Streets.
AU 6-1480

Hours: Open daily during exhibitions 2-5. Closed Mondays. Free.
Transportation: Same as to Spanish Museum.

Founded in 1904, the academy elects as members persons prominent in the arts. Exhibits include paintings and sculpture by members and a permanent exhibition of works by Childe Hassam.

MUSEUM OF THE CITY OF NEW YORK

Fifth Avenue between 103rd & 104th Streets.
LE 4-1672

Hours: Tuesdays through Saturdays 10-5; Sundays and holidays 1-5. Closed Mondays (when a holiday falls on Monday, the Museum is open Monday and closed Tuesday). Free.
Transportation: Fifth Avenue Buses 2, 3 or 4 to 103rd Street. Lexington Avenue IRT to 103rd Street.

Devoted exclusively to the city's history, the Museum boasts small scale-models of historic events and such memorabilia as a streetcar, a sleigh, fire-fighting equipment, furniture, silver and other items. Noteworthy paintings include works by Ralph Earl, Gilbert Stuart, Francis Guy, Thomas Birch, Samuel Lovett Waldo and early primitives by unknown artists. One surprise is a small oil by Ralph Blakelock, *Fifth Avenue at 89th Street,* revealing his style before he turned to moonlight scenes.

MUSEUM OF EARLY AMERICAN FOLK ARTS

53rd Street between Fifth & Sixth Avenues.
LT 1-2474

Hours: Tuesdays through Sundays 10:30-5:30. Closed Mondays. Admission: adults 35¢; children under fourteen 25¢.
Transportation: Same as to Museum of Modern Art.

Opened in 1962, the Museum is the only one devoted exclusively to American folk art—from tools to paintings. At its present, temporary address, the Museum's permanent collection is meager, and loan exhibitions are featured. Future plans include the creation of a central reference library of slides, films, books and other material.

THE JEWISH MUSEUM

Fifth Avenue at 92nd Street.   RI 9-3770

Hours: Mondays through Thursdays 12-5; Fridays 11-3; Sundays 11-6. Closed Saturdays. Hours subject to change.

Transportation: Fifth Avenue Buses 2, 3 and 4 to 92nd Street. Lexington Avenue IRT to 96th Street.
Talks: Gallery talks throughout the year, except July.
Sales desk: Original graphics.

By 1947 the collection of ceremonial objects at the Jewish Theological Seminary of America had grown sufficiently large to become a separate function of the Seminary—the Jewish Museum. They were moved into a mansion given by Mrs. Felix M. Warburg, and around their core the new Museum initiated a program of exhibitions of modern art. In 1963 the museum was enlarged through a gift of the adjacent Albert A. List Building, designed by Samuel Glaser.

The Museum contains the most comprehensive collection of Jewish ceremonial and art objects in existence, including a 17th Century Italian synagogue facade, the first book printed in Hebrew, Torah headpieces, crowns and breastplates, passover plates, lamps and textiles. Due to the widespread destruction of Jewish ceremonial art at many points in history, objects from before the year 1500 A.D. are rare.

The Museum also exhibits avant-garde painting and sculpture and the work of established artists of international importance. Its own collection of modern art is still small but includes Max Weber and Chaim Soutine, as well as young sculptors like Lee Bontecou. Loan exhibitions are frequent.

The Museum also houses The Tobe Pascher Workshop of Contemporary Jewish Ceremonial Objects—a division of the Seminary's school of fine arts.

NEW YORK CITY HALL

City Hall Park (Broadway at Park Row).

Hours: Mondays through Fridays 9-4. Closed Saturdays and Sundays. Free.
Transportation: Lexington Avenue IRT to Brooklyn Bridge Station; BMT to City Hall Station.

Based on a prize-winning design by the French architect Joseph F. Magnin, City Hall was completed in 1811. It reflects the style of the 18th Century Hotel de Ville in Paris.

City Hall contains historic furniture (including a mahogany writing table used by Washington during his first Presidency) and noteworthy American portraits by John Trumbull, Samuel F. B. Morse (*Lafayette,* 1824), John Vanderlyn, Henry Inman and Charles Loring Elliott.

RIVERSIDE MUSEUM
Riverside Drive at 103rd Street.   UN 4-1760

Hours: Tuesdays through Sundays 1-5. Closed Mondays, holidays
and during July and August. Free.
Transportation: Fifth Avenue Bus No. 5 to 103rd Street. Broadway IRT to 103rd Street.

Organized in 1938 by Mr. and Mrs. Louis Horch, the privately-endowed Museum presents changing exhibitions of contemporary art. A small permanent collection includes Tibetan paintings.

NEW YORK PUBLIC LIBRARY
Fifth Avenue at 42nd Street.   OX 5-4200

Hours: Mondays through Saturdays, 9 a.m.-10 p.m., Sundays and
holidays 1-10. Free.
Transportation: All Fifth Avenue Buses. IND "D" Train to
42nd Street, Lexington Avenue IRT to 42nd Street.

The main branch of the New York Public Library system
offers changing exhibitions of books, manuscripts, prints, maps
and stamps and a permanent picture collection hung chiefly in
the Berg Collection room. The most notable paintings include
examples by Copley and Stuart.

THE MUSEUM OF PRIMITIVE ART
54th Street between Fifth & Sixth Avenues.
CI 6-9493

Hours: Tuesdays through Saturdays 12-5, Sundays 1-5. Closed
Mondays. Admission: adults 50¢, students 25¢; reduced rates
for groups.
Transportation: Same as to Museum of Modern Art.

Opened in 1957, the Museum is devoted to the art of the
indigenous civilizations of the Americas, Africa and Oceania
and of pre-historic Europe and Asia. It exhibits works from its
own collection and special loan shows.

ASIA HOUSE GALLERY

64th Street between Park & Lexington Avenues.
PL 1-4210

Hours: Mondays through Fridays 10-5; Saturdays 11-5; Sundays and holidays 1-5. Free.
Transportation: Lexington Avenue IRT to 68th Street.

Asia house features several major loan exhibitions of Asian art each year. Warning: since the Gallery is closed for about one month between exhibitions, it is advisable to telephone ahead.

MUSEUM OF CONTEMPORARY CRAFTS

53rd Street between Fifth & Sixth Avenues.
CI 6-6840

Hours: Mondays through Saturday 12-6; Sundays 2-6. Admission: 25¢.
Transportation: Same as to Museum of Modern Art.

Sponsored by the American Craftsmen's Council, the Museum presents changing exhibitions of contemporary crafts from all over the world. The Museum cafeteria is open to the public.

JACQUES MARCHAIS CENTER OF TIBETAN ARTS

340 Lighthouse Avenue, Staten Island.   EL 1-3208

Hours: Tuesdays through Saturdays 2-5; second and fourth Sundays of each month 2-5. Closed October 31 to April 1.
Transportation: Staten Island Ferry to St. George, thence by Bus No. 113.

Situated on the grounds of the Marchais home, the Museum rises in the form of a Tibetan temple, complete with terraced gardens.

MUSEUM OF THE AMERICAN INDIAN
Broadway at 155th Street.   AU 3-2420

Hours: Tuesdays through Saturdays 1-5. Closed Mondays and holidays. Free.

Transportation: Fifth Avenue Buses 4 or 5 to 157th Street. Broadway IRT to 157th Street.

Founded by George G. Heye in 1916, the Museum is the largest institution devoted exclusively to the culture of the Indians of the Americas. The Museum shop sells a variety of Indian crafts.

NICHOLAS ROERICH MUSEUM
319 West 107th Street.   UN 4-7752

Hours: Mondays through Fridays 2-5. Closed Saturdays and during July and August. Free.

Transportation: Fifth Avenue Bus No. 5 to 110th Street. Broadway IRT to 110th Street.

The collection consists chiefly of art from India and Tibet and decorative paintings by Nicholas Roerich, Russian author, painter and explorer.

BIOGRAPHIES AND
EVALUATIONS OF
THE ARTISTS

BIOGRAPHIES AND
EVALUATIONS OF
THE ARTISTS

ALLSTON, Washington. Georgetown Co., S.C., 1779; Cambridgeport, Mass., 1843.

Brooklyn Museum; **Metropolitan Museum** 119.

America's first Romantic painter, Allston was widely regarded in his time as a man of enormous talent—a position with which he heartily agreed. Even Coleridge marveled "that such a man with such a heart and such genius [should be] an American." Today much of Allston's work seems strained, yet in his search for lyric beauty he remains an important figure in early American art. Allston grew up in Newport, R.I., was graduated from Harvard (where he was class poet) and studied in London under Benjamin West. During four years in Rome he began lifelong friendships with Coleridge and Washington Irving. In 1809 he moved to Boston, where he knew Emerson, Longfellow and Lowell. In 1811 he returned to England with his young pupil, Samuel F. B. Morse. There he began his colossal *Belshazzar's Feast* (Detroit Institute of Arts), which remained uncompleted at his death. His romantic novel "Mondaldi" was published in 1841.

BECKMANN (*bek*-mahn), **Max.** Leipzig, 1884; New York, 1950.

Museum of Modern Art 200.

Among the most important modern German painters, Beckmann is best known for his harsh, brooding views of man trapped in what he called "the heaven and hell which together form the world in which we live." Usually classified as an Expressionist because of the intense emotion which characterizes much of his work, he also composed monumental compositions of grave serenity. Beckmann studied in Paris and Florence and in 1905 joined the vanguard Secessionist movement in Berlin. By the late 1920's, his reputation was well established (he won second prize in the Carnegie International in 1929), but his paintings fell victims to the Nazi purges of the 1930's. In 1937 he fled to Amsterdam, and in 1947 he took a teaching post at Washington University in St. Louis. He also taught at the Brooklyn Museum Art School.

BELLINI (bell-*lee*-nee), **Giovanni.** Venice?, about 1430; Venice, 1516.

Frick Collection 226; **Metropolitan Museum** 6.

Much that is significant in Venetian art appears in embryo or maturity in the work of Bellini. He set new standards for landscape, religious painting and portraiture, and his use of color, which seems to virtually permeate the physical structure of his forms, was a crucial breakthrough in the depiction of substance through mass, rather than outline. Son of the important Venetian painter Jacopo Bellini (1400?-1464?), he belonged to an artistic dynasty which included his half-brother Gentile (1427?-1507?) and his brother-in-law Mantegna. Among his students were Giorgione and Titian. Giovanni Bellini began a set of triptychs for the Carità Church in Venice (now part of the Academy) in about 1460. In 1479 he completed a vast project (since destroyed by fire) which Gentile had begun in the Doge's Palace. In 1506 he met Dürer, who recorded that despite his great age he was still "the best of painters." His last major composition, *The Feast of the Gods* (completed by Titian), now hangs in the National Gallery in Washington.

BELLOWS, George Wesley. Columbus, O., 1882; New York, 1925.

Brooklyn Museum 359; Metropolitan Museum; **Whitney Museum** 292-293.

With his gifts for expressive drawing, dashing brushwork and racy realism, Bellows delighted in portraying the drama of everyday life. In addition to his famous sports scenes, his themes included sharp social criticism, romantic landscapes and probing portraiture. Bellows was a baseball and basketball star at Ohio State University and worked as cartoonist for a Columbus newspaper before coming to New York. He studied under Robert Henri and in 1908 won first prize in the Pennsylvania Academy Annual with *North River* (now in the Metropolitan). He taught at the New York Art Students League in the 1910's and married one of his students, Emma Louise Story. Beginning in 1916, he became America's most important lithographer. He died suddenly of a ruptured appendix.

BIERSTADT, Albert. Solingen, Germany, 1830; New York, 1902.

Brooklyn Museum; **Metropolitan Museum** 128; New York Historical Society.

Bierstadt blended realism and drama in grandiose landscapes which exhibit infinite patience and high technical skill. They appeal today chiefly as images of a romantic past, but they were so widely acclaimed in their time that they netted Bierstadt an estate of over $2,000,000. Bierstadt's family settled in New Bedford, Mass., when he was two. He studied in Düsseldorf, Rome and Switzerland.

BINGHAM, George Caleb. Augusta Co., Va., 1811; Kansas City, 1879.
Brooklyn Museum; **Metropolitan Museum** 124; New York Historical Society.

A rarity among painters, Bingham was also an active politician. His best paintings, the subjects of which he described as "our social and political characteristics," were highly popular glimpses of American frontier life. He composed them with an almost classical order. Bingham's family moved to Missouri when he was eight. He later worked as an apprentice cabinet maker and studied law and theology, but at thirty-four he set himself up as a portraitist and painter of genre scenes. He served in the Missouri State Legislature, then resumed art studies for three years at Düsseldorf. After a year in the Union Army, he served as Missouri State Treasurer and Adjutant General. He also taught art at the University of Missouri.

BLAKELOCK, Ralph Albert. New York, 1847; Elizabethtown, N.Y., 1919.
Brooklyn Museum 356; Gallery of Modern Art; Metropolitan Museum.

A strange and somewhat dim figure in American art, Blakelock shifted from relatively detailed early landscapes to dream-like nocturnes filled with ethereal light and hushed stillness. His aim was to achieve beauty through color "until it seems to flow upon the senses, as some melody." His thickly encrusted surfaces often take on a jewel-like luster. After exhibiting in the National Academy at twenty, Blakelock traveled to the Far West, Mexico, and Panama. Years of increasing poverty led to a mental attack in 1891; plagued by delusions of wealth, the artist was eventually committed to Middletown State Hospital in Connecticut. Subsequently, prices for his work began to soar; in 1912 one painting brought $13,900, long the highest price paid at auction for the work of a living American. In 1915 his eldest daughter, an artist whose paintings were often sold by others as Blakelock's, was also committed to an asylum.

BLOOM, Hyman (born Hyman Melamed). Brunoviski, Lithuania, 1913; lives in Boston.
Metropolitan Museum; Museum of Modern Art; **Whitney Museum** 304.

A mystic Expressionist, Bloom paints highly emotional pictures in which iridescent color is often combined with vigorous animated forms. He has described his art as "an attempt to cope with one's destiny and become master of it." Bloom's family moved to the United States when he was seven. He later shared a studio with

Jack Levine and during the Depression worked on the WPA's Federal Art Project. His themes have included synagogues, archeological treasure, childhood, death and, since 1951, anatomical dissection.

BLUME, Peter. Smorgon, Russia, 1906; lives in Sherman, Conn.
Metropolitan Museum 154; **Museum of Modern Art** 201; Whitney Museum.

Blume invigorates his remarkably polished illusionistic technique with paradox, fantasy and overtones of mystery. His best work offers complex allegorical judgements on man and his times: "When I first began painting," he has said, "I was satisfied with putting shapes and colors together on canvas. Now I have to put ideas together." Blume arrived in the United States in 1911. After working as a lithographer's assistant and a jewelry designer, he had his first one-man show in 1930 and was awarded Guggenheim Fellowships in 1932 and 1936. His work includes murals for the U.S. Treasury Building in Washington.

BOCCIONI (bought-*cho*-nee), **Umberto.** Reggio Calabria. 1882; Verona, 1916.
Museum of Modern Art 188.

Artist, theorist, writer and lecturer, Boccioni was the most gifted of the Futurists. His style developed from a virtuoso realism to a highly original synthesis of movement and energy in which line and color are used to express states of mind. His *Unique Forms of Continuity in Space* (1913, Museum of Modern Art) is one of the masterpieces of modern sculpture. His premature death robbed modern Italian art of one of its greatest lights. Boccioni studied under Balla and later settled in Milan, where he joined the Futurists. In 1911 he traveled to Paris, met Picasso and Braque and fell under the influence of Cubism. In 1915 he volunteered for the Army and in the following year died after falling from a horse during military exercises.

BONNARD (bone-*nar*), **Pierre.** Fontenaye-aux-Roses, 1867; Le Cannet, 1947.
Brooklyn Museum 340; **Guggenheim Museum** 259; **Museum of Modern Art** 162.

Like the work of his friend Matisse and his Impressionist precursors, Bonnard's paintings reveal an artist in love with ravishing color and enthralled by sunlight. He delighted in capturing serene moments in canvases of exquisite pattern. Bonnard shared a studio with Vuillard and, after meeting Lautrec and Redon, helped organize the Nabis (Hebrew for "prophet"), a movement of painters using flat color and bold pattern. Painting in the south of France, he became friendly with Renoir and Monet. In 1912 he and Vuillard both declined the Legion of Honor. He visited the United States as a juror for the Carnegie International of 1926. His wife and Vuillard both died in 1940.

BOSCH, Hieronymus (hee-*ron*-ee-mus boss) (real name Hieronymus van Aeken). 'S Hertogenbosch, Flanders, 1450?-1516.
Metropolitan Museum 31.

Master of fantasy and grotesque imagery, Bosch is most famous for his allegorical satires on man's vices and foibles. The dominant mood of pessimism in his work reflects the period in which he lived—a time of religious strife and sudden death from plague. The keys to some of his symbolism have been lost, but his compositions are invariably striking, alive with rhythmic patterns and expressive color and arrestingly organized. Among the little known about Bosch is the fact that he belonged to a local religious group's orchestra and apparently took part in some of their theatricals.

BOTTICELLI (bought-tee-*tchell*-ee), **Sandro** (real name Alessandro di Mariano del Filipepi). Florence 1444?-1510.
Metropolitan Museum 4.

Highly regarded in his own time, the painter of two of the world's most famous masterpieces—the *Primavera* (about 1478) and *The Birth of Venus* (about 1486)—lapsed into a long obscurity until the Victorians rediscovered him as a "primitive" genius. His paintings are exceptional for their refined melancholy; their intricate, sensitive and extraordinarily rhythmic line; their unusual organization of space and pattern; and their subtle distortion of form. His work falls sharply into two categories: that which glorifies the Medici world of pleasure, pageantry and classicism, and that which is dominated by a tense, mystic spirit inspired by the Florentine monk Savonarola. Botticelli (a nickname meaning "little barrel") was apprenticed to a goldsmith and later worked in the shop of Fra Filippo Lippi (1406?-1469) and possibly under Verrocchio (1436-88), the teacher of the young Leonardo. In 1472 he set up his own workshop with Filippino Lippi (1457?-1504), son of his former teacher, and painted for several of the Medici—including Piero, Lorenzo and Giuliano. In 1481 he painted three frescoes for the Sistine Chapel.

BRAQUE (brahk), **Georges,** Argenteuil-sur-Seine, 1882; Paris, 1963.
Guggenheim Museum 264-265; **Museum of Modern Art** 174, 182, 184.

The son of a house painter and decorator, Braque grew to become the most important Cubist after Picasso. He was a master of elegant, sensitive and serene compositions in which elaborate textural effects and sumptuous patterns and colors combine in highly original harmonies. "One should not imitate what one wishes to create," he felt. "I would much rather put myself in unison with nature than copy it." After working for his father, Braque moved to Paris and eventually joined the Fauves. In 1907 the poet Apollinaire took him to see *Les Demoiselles d'Avignon* at Picasso's studio, and he began contributing to the evolution of Cubism; he was a close friend of Picasso between 1909 and 1914. The name "Cubism" was invented when a critic viewing Braque's first one-man show at Kahnweiler's gallery wrote that he "mistreats form, reduces everything, sites, figures and houses, to geometric outlines, to cubes." In 1912 Braque initiated the modern collage—or "paste-up"—technique. He was wounded in World War I and after a long convalescence resumed painting in 1917. His work grew less abstract; by the 1920's classical figures began to appear, and in the 1930's his compositions were marked by curvilinear form and resonant, decorative color.

BREUGHEL (*broy*-gul), **Pieter,** The Elder. Brughel, Flanders, 1525?; Brussels, 1569.
Metropolitan Museum 33.

Breughel was widely acclaimed during his lifetime but afterward dismissed as coarse and vulgar; only within the last half century has he been restored to his rightful place. He perfected one of the most highly individual styles in art, blending everyday reality with almost abstract patterns and vibrant, mellow color. In addition to his celebrated landscapes, he painted unforgettable pictures of peasant life—panoramic compositions in which patterns are arranged in vivid new ways and movement is highly expressive. He was also a master of rollicking genre painting, of bitter commentary on Man's fate and of fresh insights into religious subjects. His *Hunters in the Snow* (Kunsthistorisches Museum, Vienna) has entered the Valhalla of paintings known to almost every art lover in the Western world. Breughel was the progenitor of a remarkable artistic dynasty: his two sons and three grandsons were painters; three daughters of one of his grandsons married artists; still another progeny had five sons who were painters. All but Breughel's two sons, however, were mediocre artists; one son, Jan, became an assistant to Rubens. Breughel was admitted to the Antwerp painters' guild in 1551 and the next year traveled to Italy. In 1563 he married a girl believed to be the daughter of his teacher and settled in Brussels. During Spain's occupation of the Flemish provinces, he lashed out against the injustices of the Inquisition in searing paintings thinly disguised as Biblical narratives.

BURNE-JONES, Sir Edward Coley. Birmingham, 1833; Fulham, 1898.
Gallery of Modern Art 317-319; Metropolitan Museum.

Burne-Jones was a leading member of the Pre-Raphaelite brotherhood, a group of British painters who sought to achieve a more sincere depiction of moral themes by using early Renaissance art for their inspiration. Burne-Jones himself specialized in romantic idealizations: "I mean by a picture," he wrote, "a beautiful, romantic dream of something that never was, never will be, in a light better than any light that ever shone, in a land no one can define or remember—only desire." His sensitive adaptation of Florentine linear effects and his languid moods occasionally resulted in appealing, if sometimes sentimental, compositions. Burne-Jones left for Oxford to prepare for the ministry but soon moved to London to study art under the poet-painter Dante Gabriel Rossetti. He traveled to Italy in 1859 and in 1861 began designing tapestries, tiles and stained glass for William Morris' company. He illustrated Morris' famous Kelmscott edition of Chaucer. In 1880 he completed his best known painting, *The Golden Stairs* (Tate Gallery, London). In 1894 Queen Victoria made him a Baron.

CARAVAGGIO (cah-rah-*vahd*-joh), **Michelangelo.** Caravaggio, 1573?- Porto Ercole, 1609.
Metropolitan Museum 18.

During his brief and stormy lifetime, Caravaggio profoundly affected the course of Italian painting. Breaking harshly with the idealized Renaissance approach—which had by then grown feeble and pretentious—he painted starkly realistic, earthy compositions that give fresh insight and new vitality to religious themes. He also revolutionized the use of *chiaroscuro*—strong contrasts of light and shade—and startled conservatives with his blend of naturalistic appearance and mystical light. Many contemporaries considered his works vulgar and brutal. After studying in Milan and Venice, Caravaggio moved to Rome, where in 1603 he was arrested in a libel suit. In 1606 his *Death of the Virgin* (Louvre) was refused as too coarse by the Chapter of Santa Maria della Scala, but on the advice of Rubens it was acquired by the Duke of Mantua. In the same year, Caravaggio killed a man and was himself seriously wounded in a brawl after a tennis match. He fled to Naples, then to Malta, where he painted the Grand Master of the Knights of Malta and received the society's Cross of the Order. He subsequently fought with a Knight and was imprisoned; he escaped to Sicily and later to Naples, where he was attacked and wounded by enemies. En route to Rome to seek a pardon, he was imprisoned at Porto Ercole; within days he was dead of malaria.

CARPACCIO (car-*pot*-choh), **Vittore.** Venice, 1455?-1526?.
Metropolitan Museum 8.

Carpaccio enlivened his religious paintings with the pageantry and bustle of his contemporary Venice. His work is remarkable for its rhythmic, highly patterned but uncrowded arrangements in which figures and architecture join in beautifully controlled space. His clear, limpid color anticipates the golden light of later Venetian painting. Carpaccio probably studied with Gentile Bellini. In 1488 he was commissioned to paint his celebrated series on the *Life of St. Ursala* (Academy, Venice). He later worked with Gentile on the *Miracle of the True Cross* (Academy, Venice) and painted a series for the Doge's Palace (destroyed by fire in 1577).

CARRA (cah-*rah*), **Carlo.** Quargnento, 1881; lives in Milan.
Museum of Modern Art, 189.

One of the most creative of the Futurists, Carrà later turned to enigmatic paintings in which silent and fantastic mannequins convey uncanny moods. In 1900 Carrà painted decorations for the International Exposition in Paris, along with Matisse. He joined the Futurists about 1909. He withdrew from them about 1915 and, together with Giorgio de Chirico, founded the Metaphysical School.

CASSATT (cuss-*at*), **Mary.** Allegheny City, Penn., 1845; Mesnil-Theribus, France, 1926.
Brooklyn Museum; Gallery of Modern Art; **Metropolitan Museum** 134.

Mary Cassatt was the only American artist actively associated with the French Impressionists and America's only major woman painter of the 19th Century. Her art evolved from naturalism to a style marked by broad handling, luminous color and novel arrangements. She worked closely with Mrs. H. O. Havemeyer, one of the greatest benefactresses of the Metropolitan Museum, who said of her, "without her aid, I should never have been able to make the collection. . . . [One] of her earliest bits of advice was 'never omit the modern note' and we collected Courbets, Manets, Degas and the Impressionists. Another time, she said, 'We must collect old moderns also,' and in our gallery were added Veroneses, Grecos, Goyas, etc." Daughter of a banker and mayor of Allegheny City, Miss Cassatt toured Europe as a child and later studied at the Pennsylvania Academy of Fine Arts. In Paris in the 1870's, she met Degas and was invited to exhibit with the Impressionists. She painted decorations for the Women's Pavilion of the 1893 World's Columbian Exhibition in Chicago and was awarded the Cross of the French Legion of Honor in 1904. She was nearly blind in her last years.

CEZANNE (say-*zahn*), **Paul.** Aix-en-Provence, 1839-1906.
Brooklyn Museum 334; **Guggenheim Museum** 256; **Metropolitan Museum** 110-111; **Museum of Modern Art** 156.

Generally scorned most of his life, Cézanne is today enshrined as *the* greatest master of modern art. Cézanne combined the architectonic grandeur of the old masters with the fresh color and new insights of the Impressionists. He could endow even an apple, a fold of drapery or a rock with true monumentality. Abandoning the "correct" anatomy of the conservatives, he distorted objects, figures and perspective at will—a great advance in the liberation of painting from literalism. He reinforced his forms by modeling with small brush strokes of light-steeped color. His color— aglow and rich—seems part of the object, not a skin superimposed on it. Avoiding the incidental, he abridged and clarified every form until he reached its essence. "To paint," he wrote, "is not to make a servile copy of the motif, but to grasp the harmony between a number of relations, transpose them in one's own scale and develop them according to a new, original logic." In 1861 Cézanne abandoned law studies to take up painting in Paris, where he joined his old school friend Emile Zola. He returned to Aix to work in his father's bank, but was soon back in Paris, where he met Monet, Renoir, Sisley and Manet. He painted with Pissarro at Pointoise in 1872 and exhibited with the Impressionists in 1874. He eventually retired to Aix, his father's death leaving him well off. The Director of Berlin's National Gallery acquired two Cézanne oils in 1900, but was prevented from exhibiting them in the museum. In 1903 ten Cézannes sold at an auction of Zola's effects aroused violent attacks in the press. Cézanne exhibitions in 1905, 1906 and 1907 helped initiate Cubism.

CHAGALL (shah-*gahl*), **Marc.** Vitebsk, Russia, 1887; lives in France.
Guggenheim Museum 282-283; **Museum of Modern Art** 194-195.

Chagall's fanciful compositions dress elements of folk lore, autobiography and personal philosophy in the trappings of symbolism and myth. Imbued with aggressive innocence and poetic imagination, his "pictorial arrangements of images which obsess me" use "color and line to underscore emotion." Chagall challenged what he considered the disregard of Cubism and Fauvism for "states of the soul." His concepts strongly influenced the Expressionists and Surrealists. Raised in the Vitebsk ghetto, Chagall studied at the Imperial Art Academy in St. Petersburg and in 1910 moved to Paris, where he met La Fresnaye, Delaunay, Léger, Modigliani and the poet Apollinaire. After his first one-man show—in Berlin in 1914—he returned to Vitebsk, married, was mobilized into the Russian Army and served during the Revolution as Minister of Arts for Vitebsk. He returned to Paris in 1923. During World War II he lived in the United States. In 1959-61 he executed his twelve famous stained glass windows for a synagogue at the Hadassah-Hebrew University Medical Center, near Jerusalem; exhibited at the Museum of Modern Art, they drew enormous crowds. In 1964 his stained glass memorial to Dag Hammarskjöld was installed at the United Nations headquarters in New York.

CHARDIN (shar-*dan*), **Jean Baptiste.** Paris, 1699-1779.
Frick Collection 247; **Metropolitan Museum** 80.

The finest French painter of his time, Chardin produced beguiling oils characterized by powerful structure and space arrangement, rich color, soft, glowing light and a remarkable sense of the tangible. He rejected the amorous themes fashionable among his colleagues, finding his inspiration in the quiet moments of middle-class home life which had delighted the masters of the Dutch tradition. His dignified compositions veil a passionate spirit: "You use colors," he said, "but you paint with your feelings." He was widely popular in his own day, but his fame suffered an eclipse after the French Revolution. The son of a cabinet maker who produced billiard tables for the King, Chardin first attracted attention at an annual open-air art exhibition. He was granted membership in the Royal Academy and later given an apartment-studio in the Louvre. His sight began to fade about 1777. Chardin's son, Pierre-Jean, was a minor painter who died by suicide.

CHIRICO (*kee*-ree-coh), **Giorgio de.** Volo, Greece, 1888; lives in Rome.
Museum of Modern Art 192-193.

In his early years, de Chirico painted lonely, enigmatic visions arresting in their originality and haunting in their evocations of foreboding; his use of everyday sights to project dreamlike moods had a profound influence on Surrealism. The paintings of his mature years, however, are merely skillful recollections of Renaissance and Baroque artists. Born in Greece of Italian parents, de Chirico studied art in Athens and Munich, spent two years in Italy, then moved to Paris, where he had his first one-man show and met Picasso and Apollinaire. He was called into the Army in 1915 and afterward joined the ex-Futurist Carrà in establishing the Metaphysical School of painting. His work was included in the first Surrealist exhibition, but with the later change in his style was attacked by the Surrealists as an art reactionary.

CHRISTUS (*cree*-stuss), **Petrus.** Baerle, Flanders, about 1410; Bruges, 1473.
Frick Collection 230; **Metropolitan Museum** 25.

Christus' style, which owes much to the van Eyck tradition, excells in delicacy, elegance, subtle color relationships, enamel-like surfaces and effective spatial designs. Christus may have actually worked with the van Eycks in Bruges, where he is recorded as having become a citizen in 1444. He was nominated dean of the painters' guild a year or two before his death.

CHURCH, Frederick Edwin. Hartford, 1826; New York, 1900.
Brooklyn Museum; Metropolitan Museum 127.

Church's vast compositions, inspired by travels to South America, Labrador, Europe and the Near East, form romantic travelogues in which photographic realism is applied to grand subjects. After studying with Cole in the Catskills, Church opened a studio in

New York. He was a prize winner at the Paris Exposition of 1867. Rheumatism eventually crippled both his hands.

CLAUDE LORRAIN (lor-*ran*) (real name Claude Gellée). Chamagne-sur-la-Moselle, 1600; Rome, 1682.
Frick Collection; **Metropolitan Museum** 77.

Claude pioneered in the portrayal of radiant outdoor light and in the emancipation of landscape as an independent theme in art. Even in religious and mythological scenes, his main interest was in exploring the pictorial aspects of atmosphere; detail is subordinated to epic panorama, and figures usually serve as minor props. Apprenticed as a pastry maker, the young Claude came to Rome to cook for the landscape painter Agostino Tassi, but his artistic talents soon prevailed over the culinary. He spent most of his life in and around the Italian capital; in 1623 he visited the Bay of Naples, a motif which appears often in his later paintings. He was a friend and neighbor of Poussin, and the two are believed to have sketched outdoors together.

COLE, Thomas. Bolton-le-Moors, Lancashire, 1801; Catskill, N.Y., 1848.
Brooklyn Museum 347; **Metropolitan Museum** 121; New York Historical Society.

The first major landscape painter in America, Cole had a profound effect on 19th Century American art. He and his followers favored romantic and lyric vistas of scenes along the Hudson River and in the Catskill Mountains—a taste which prompted a derisive newspaper critic to dub them the Hudson River School. Like his friend William Cullen Bryant, Cole saw American landscape as an image of unspoiled nature—"no ruined tower to tell of outrage, no gorgeous temple to speak of ostentation . . . only abodes of plenty, virtue and refinement." In his later years, Cole turned to grandiose compositions dealing with history and morality. After arriving in the United States at nineteen, Cole became a wandering portraitist. By 1825 his landscapes were beginning to arouse interest, and in 1829-32 a patron sent him to Europe, where he met Turner. In 1848 his exhibition of *The Course of Empire* (New York Historical Society) was visited by half a million people.

CONSTABLE, John. East Bergholt, Suffolk, 1776; London, 1837.
Frick Collection 254; Metropolitan Museum.

One of history's greatest landscapists, Constable sought to capture "light—dews—breezes—bloom—and freshness." He revitalized the Dutch tradition by replacing dark brown tonalities with vivid, light-filled color. His best works—strong, sketchy and simple—reveal a keen observation of nature. "The landscape painter must walk in the fields with an humble mind," he said. "No arrogant man was ever permitted to see nature in all her beauty." His lyrical work proved to be a prelude to Impressionism. Son of a well-to-do miller, Constable studied at the Royal Academy and was encouraged by Benjamin West. He married after inheriting a legacy and subsequently fathered seven children. In 1821 his masterpiece *The Hay Wain* (National Gallery, London) received a lukewarm reception at the Royal Academy; bought by a French dealer, it won a gold medal in the Salon of 1829.

COPLEY, John Singleton. Boston, 1731; London, 1815.
Brooklyn Museum 342; New York Historical Society; New York Public Library; **Metropolitan Museum** 117.

The finest of native-born Colonial American painters, Copley taught himself a direct, forceful approach to portraiture. His best work blends perceptive characterization with strong rendering of forms in space, a resourceful line, sober but luminous color and compact organization. In his later years, a straining for pomp and glitter adulterated his initial power. Helped by his step-father, an English-born painter, Copley set up as an engraver while in his early teens. In 1769 he married Susannah Clarke, the daughter of a rich Tory merchant to whom was consigned one of the shipments of tea which figured in the Boston Tea Party. In 1775 Copley settled in London, where he became a favorite painter of portraits and Biblical and historical themes. In 1783 he was named to the Royal Academy.

COROT (caw-*roh*), **Jean Baptiste Camille.** Paris, 1796; Ville D'Avray, 1875.
Brooklyn Museum 328-329; **Frick Collection** 250; **Metropolitan Museum** 85-86.

Corot was the master of the Barbizon School and the most important French landscape painter before Impressionism, a movement which he greatly influenced. In idyllic oils filled with clear golden light and subdued silver tonalities, he modified and suppressed detail for the sake of over-all harmony. His brushwork is forceful and spontaneous, yet his effects are delicate and graceful. Corot's parents, who ran a dress shop, gave him an annual stipend to pursue his painting. He produced early masterworks in Rome around 1825, later painted in Normandy and Brittany, and was a prize winner in the Salon of 1834. In 1843 his rejection by the Salon aroused loud protests from fellow artists, but in 1846 he received the Legion of Honor and the French government acquired several of his important paintings. In the 1850's growing demand for his work brought him a substantial income. He won high honors at the 1855 Paris World's Fair, and numerous forgeries testified to his public esteem. In 1874, when academicians awarded the Grand Medal of Honor to the painter Gérôme, outraged art progressives raised money for an award for Corot.

COSIMO, Piero di. See PIERO DI COSIMO.

COURBET (coor-*bay*), **Gustave.** Ornans, 1819; La Tour de Peilz, Switzerland, 1877.
Brooklyn Museum; Gallery of Modern Art; **Metropolitan Museum** 87-88.

Aggressive, boastful and an outspoken Leftist, Courbet fought—and won—an impassioned battle against the Classicists and Romantics. His emphasis on commonplace realism was one of the turning points in the course of modern art. "Show me a goddess," he exclaimed, "and I will paint one. I paint what I see, giving you real nature, crudities, violence and all." "It is better to paint railway stations or engine houses, mines and factories, for these are the saints and miracles of the 19th Century." In Courbet's rugged work, planes and masses are forceful, and firm, rich color is applied with thick strokes—often with a palette knife. After his early success with *After Dinner at Ornans,* Courbet became a friend of Corot, Daumier, Baudelaire and the Socialist philosopher Prud'hon. His sombre 1851 masterwork *The Burial at Ornans* (Louvre) created a furor. Acclaimed as a leading spokesman of Socialism in both painting and politics, he was elected Art Commisar in the short-lived Paris Commune, but when the conservative forces returned to power he was sentenced to six months in prison, accused of having incited the people to tear down the 143-foot-tall monument to Napoleon in the Place Vendôme. After his release, he was fined 323,000 francs; unable to meet this enormous burden, he escaped to Switzerland, where he died in exile. In 1948 Ornans opened a Courbet Museum.

CRANACH (*crah*-nahk), **Lucas,** the Elder (real name Lucas Sunder or Lucas Müller). Kronach, Bavaria, 1472; Weimar, 1553.
Metropolitan Museum 39; Morgan Library.

Cranach's expressive and decorative distortion has much in common with contemporary art, and the same can be said for his piquant whimsy and his disarming humor. Famous for both portraits and re-interpretations of mythological themes, Cranach was a master of flowing line, lively pattern and sharply contrasting colors. He painted the first nude Venuses in Northern European art. Cranach lived in Vienna from 1502 to 1505, when he took a position in Wittenberg as court painter to the Electors of Saxony. At Wittenberg, where he and Martin Luther were close friends, Cranach was twice elected mayor; he also owned a printing shop and an apothecary.

CRIVELLI (cree-*vell*-ee), **Carlo.** Venice?, 1430?-1493?
Brooklyn Museum; **Metropolitan Museum** 3.

Largely ignoring the realism, warm colors and new oil media of his contemporary Venetians, Crivelli executed lustrous temperas which display a striking command of line, pattern and archaic Gothic ornamentation. He filled his paintings—all of them religious in theme—with individual charm, aloof dignity and restrained emotion. Crivelli was recorded as a master painter in Venice in 1457 and afterwards at Ascoli, where he painted altarpieces for local churches. He was knighted by Prince Ferdinand of Capua. In 1486 he painted his masterpiece, *The Annunciation with St. Emidius* (National Gallery, London).

DALI (*dah*-lee), **Salvador.** Figueras, Catalonia, 1904; lives in the United States and Spain.
Metropolitan Museum; **Gallery of Modern Art** 321-322; **Museum of Modern Art** 198-199.

Dali's rich imagination, technical facility and flair for publicity have helped establish him in the public eye as the grand master of Surrealism. Drawing from such diverse sources as de Chirico and Ernst, da Vinci, Vermeer and Raphael, the Catalan architect Gaudi, Freud, and atomic physics, he produces meticulous, glossy paintings he has described as handmade photographs of dreams and hallucinations. His work is based, he says, on "the interpretive-critical association of delirious phenomena," and his aim is to "synthesize confusion and thus help discredit the world of reality." In recent years his themes have leaned heavily toward the religious: "The Holy Mother of God," he has written, "is more important than a fruit bowl and a knife." Suspended at twenty from the Madrid Academy of Fine Arts, Dali experimented in realism and Cubism and in 1927 began to develop fantastic themes. He joined the Surrealist movement in Paris in 1929. Dali moved to the United States in 1940 and had his first full-scale survey exhibition at the Museum of Modern Art the following year. In 1942 he published his autobiography, *The Secret Life of Salvador Dali.*

DAUMIER (dome-*yay*), **Honoré.** Marseilles, 1808; Velmendois, 1879.
Metropolitan Museum 90.

Known almost exclusively during his lifetime as a political and social cartoonist, Daumier is most admired today for his unique paintings and for the heads and busts with which he revitalized modern sculpture. His paintings are small in size, but their monumental impact has something of the force of Tintoretto and El Greco. His use of dark and light and his economic range of colors recall Rembrandt—one of his chief inspirations. His forms are organized with architectural compactness, and his expressive drawing ranks with that of the finest masters. Daumier learned the new process of lithography as a child and published his first examples as a teen-ager. He joined the staff of La Caricature, of which Balzac was an editor, in 1830, was imprisoned in 1832 for a cartoon critical of King Louis Philippe, and later plied his social criticism on the staff of Le Charivari. He numbered among his friends Courbet, Millet, Rousseau and Baudelaire, the last of whom published an essay on his cartoons in 1857. Around 1863 the French government bought his *Drunkenness of Silenus* (Calais). Plagued by poverty and increasing blindness, he had a one-man show sponsored by Victor Hugo shortly before his death; it attracted scant attention. His last days were spent in a house bought for him by Corot. He was buried at public expense.

DAVID (*dah*-veet), **Gerard.** Oudewater, Holland, 1460?; Bruges, 1523.
Metropolitan Museum 29-30.

David, whose austere portrayals bring to a close the Flemish tradition of impassioned realism, concentrated on isolated figures, solemn and spiritual. He was famous in his own time, but was almost forgotten until the end of the last century. David studied with Memling and married a miniature-painter. He established a large studio and became dean of the Bruges painters' guild in 1501. In 1502-08 he painted his masterwork, *The St. John the Baptist Triptych* (Musée Communale, Bruges).

DAVID (dah-*veed*), **Jacques Louis.** Paris, 1748; Brussels, 1825.
Metropolitan Museum 81.

"That icy star," was Baudelaire's apt description of David, the chief of Neoclassicism and the unofficial dictator of French taste —even to dress, furniture and styles of acting—during and after the Revolution. David and his followers sought to depict ideal beauty in compositions stressing themes of virtue, stoicism and lofty morality. Their formal, stately work subordinated color to classical drawing, clear outline and declamatory poses and action. A sharp reaction to the frivolity of the Rococo, Neoclassicism did instill new vigor into painting, but its strict doctrines subsequently held back the rising tide of Romanticism. David's applications of Neoclassicism included not only themes from antiquity but strong and realistic oils on contemporary events and a number of fine, sober portraits. Chief among the many artists he influenced was Ingres. David was encouraged in his youth by Boucher, a distant cousin. He won the Grand Prix de Rome in 1775, returned from the Italian capital in 1781 and married a daughter of an architect to Louis XVI. In 1782 the King commissioned his *Oath of the Horatii* (Louvre). Despite his royal patronage, he joined the Revolutionists and, after his election to the National Convention in 1772, voted for Louis' execution. In 1795, after the fall of his friend Robespierre, he was imprisoned for a short term. Napoleon later named him Artist to the Emperor; he painted his vast *Coronation of the Emperor Napoleon* (Louvre) in 1806-07, and when Napoleon escaped from Elba he was quick to rally to his support. In 1816 he was among the regicides sentenced to exile.

DAVIES, Arthur Bowen. Utica, N.Y., 1862; Florence, 1928.
Brooklyn Museum; **Metropolitan Museum** 139; Whitney Museum.

A member of The Eight—the group more popularly known as the Ashcan School—Davies painted romantic visions which suggested avant-garde compositional approaches. His description of El Greco's work reveals something of his own aims: "rhythmical co-ordination of line, color, form, light, all the elements involved in the making of an emotional design." Davies was among the most active organizers of the epochal New York Armory Show of 1913. Davies came to New York in his twenties and worked as a magazine illustrator. In 1893 he traveled in Europe, chiefly in Italy, on a subsidy from the collector Benjamin Altman. He exhibited with The Eight in 1908 and became president of the Association of American Painters and Sculptors.

DAVIS, Stuart. Philadelphia, 1894; New York, 1964.
Brooklyn Museum; Metropolitan Museum; Museum of Modern Art; **Whitney Museum** 308-309.

A pace-setter of American abstraction and semi-abstraction, Davis borrowed from Cubism's geometry and collage and from Léger's precise shapes and high-keyed, flat colors to evolve a brilliant personal idiom. His dynamic compositions are filled with imaginative shapes inspired by billboards, buildings and landscapes and the rhythms of jazz. His arrangements are characterized by energy and tension, crisp forms, lively harmonies and shifting planes of color. Davis's father was art director of a Philadelphia newspaper which employed Sloan, Glackens and Luks. Young Davis studied under Robert Henri and exhibited in the 1913 New York Armory Show. He taught at the Art Students League, worked on the WPA's Federal Art Project and was editor of Art Front magazine. Among his dynamic murals are those for the Radio City Music Hall, the New York broadcasting station WNYC, the Communications Building at the 1939 New York World's Fair and Drake University in Des Moines.

DE CHIRICO, Giorgio. See CHIRICO, Giorgio de.

DEGAS (duh-*gah*), **Edgar.** Paris, 1834-1917.
Brooklyn Museum 335-336; Frick Collection; Gallery of Modern Art; **Metropolitan Museum** 104-109; Museum of Modern Art.

Degas's fresh compositions reveal a genius for extracting the significant from the seemingly commonplace. His daring angles of vision challenged stereotyped arrangements and contributed greatly to a sense of spontaneity. Although often grouped with the Impressionists, he actually preferred evocations of character and mood to those of landscape and weather. He is a master of the supple, delicate line: "Above anything," he said, "I was born to draw." He was also one of the greatest sculptors of the 19th Century and an important art collector. Son of a banker, Degas abandoned law to study art. In the 1850's he traveled to Italy to copy the old masters and painted an early masterpiece—*The Belleli Family* (Museum of Impressionism, Paris). In the 1860's, he became a close friend of Manet and met Monet, Pissarro, Renoir, Cézanne, the photographer Nadar and Emile Zola. In 1873 he visited his uncle in New Orleans, and the following year he exhibited in the first group show of the Impressionists. He began a long friendship with Mary Cassatt in 1877 and in 1885 met Gauguin, of whom he was to become one of the first collectors. By 1907 he was approaching blindness. His last work includes pastels and sculptures.

DE HOOCH, Pieter. See HOOCH, Pieter de.

DE KOONING, Willem. See KOONING, Willem de.

DELACROIX (duh-lah-*cwah*), **Eugène.** Charenton, 1798; Paris, 1863.
Brooklyn Museum 327; Metropolitan Museum 84.
Inspired by such artists as Veronese, Rubens and Rembrandt, Delacroix battled for some forty years against the inflexible Ingres and his Neoclassical followers. He conceived of a picture as a color ensemble and explored the drama of contrasting complementary hues by interweaving fiery reds and gleaming blues. His figures surge with energy and emotion. But if he restored life blood to 19th Century French painting, he also shared the weaknesses of the Romanticists whom he led—a tendency toward the excessively flamboyant and a disregard of everyday material as fit subject matter. Nevertheless, Cézanne placed him in "the great line," saying, "he remains the finest palette in France; we all paint in him." Legend has it that Delacroix was the illegitimate son of Talleyrand, a leading statesman under Napoleon and Louis XVIII. His legal father, a French ambassador to Holland, left him an orphan at sixteen. He studied music with a friend of Mozart, then entered the studio of the painter Guérin. After meeting Géricault, who had a strong influence on him, Delacroix attracted wide attention in 1822 with his *Dante and Virgil Crossing The Styx* (Louvre). Two years later he became the leader of the fight against Neoclassicism with his *Massacre at Scio* (Louvre). He completed murals for the Luxembourg Palace and the Chamber of Deputies in 1847 and a ceiling for the Gallerie d'Apollon at the Louvre in 1851.

DE LA FRESNAYE, Roger. See LA FRESNAYE, Roger de.

DE LA TOUR, Georges. See LA TOUR, Georges de.

DELAUNAY (duh-loh-*nay*), **Robert.** Paris, 1885; Montpellier, 1941.
Guggenheim Museum 267-268; Museum of Modern Art 212.
Delaunay's painting evolved through Cubism into a near-abstract

style in which whirling disks and contrasting colors express the poetic rhythms the artist sensed in life. "Color," he proclaimed, "is both form and subject." Léger stated that "it was with Robert Delaunay that we fought the battle . . . for the liberation of color. Before us, green was tree, blue was the sky, and so on. After us, color has become an end in itself." Apollinaire called Delaunay's work Orphism, after Orpheus, the legendary Greek who could stir even inanimate objects with his wonderful music. Delaunay influenced Kandinsky, Klee and Léger. Delaunay began to paint under the influence of Gauguin, but by 1909 he had begun his highly original Eiffel Tower series. In 1910 he married the Russian-born painter Sonia Terk. He was included in the first public group show of Cubists, in 1911, and was invited by Kandinsky to exhibit with the Blue Riders in Berlin. He painted murals for the 1925 International Exhibition of Decorative Art in Paris and for the Palace of Air at the 1937 Paris World's Fair.

DEMUTH (*day*-mooth), **Charles.** Lancaster, Penn., 1883-1935.
Metropolitan Museum 147; Museum of Modern Art; **Whitney Museum** 301.

Demuth's art is exquisite and urbane, his technique precise and fastidious. In addition to subtle and often whimsical renderings of buildings and gem-like pictures of fruit and flowers, he painted vaudeville performers, café scenes, dancers and wry, brooding works inspired by Zola's "Nana" and Henry James' "The Turn of the Screw." One of America's masters of watercolor, he developed a delicate style worlds apart from the gruff, impetuous pictures of his friend John Marin. An early leg injury left Demuth permanently lame. He studied at the Pennsylvania Academy of Fine Arts and traveled to Paris, London and Berlin. In 1913 he published a play, "The Azure Adder," and in 1915 he had his first one-man exhibition. Shortly afterward he became a friend of Marcel Duchamp. In 1922 he entered a sanatorium for treatment of diabetes and was among the first to receive insulin.

DERAIN (duh-*ran*), **André.** Chatou, 1880; Garches, 1954.
Gallery of Modern Art; Metropolitan Museum; **Museum of Modern Art** 163.

A magnificent virtuoso, Derain was equally at ease with simplified, bold-hued landscapes and with serene, classical portraits rendered in delicate color. He made his greatest contribution to modern art in his early years as a leading Fauve artist; in those days, he recalled later, "we were always drunk with color, and the sun that gives life to color." Derain worked with Matisse, painted with Vlaminck and was among the first to assimilate elements of Negro sculpture into modern European painting. In 1912 he began to paint in a stylized Gothic manner. He fought in World War I. After the war he designed sets for the Ballet Russe. He won first prize in the Carnegie International of 1928.

DICKINSON, Edwin. Seneca Falls, N.Y., 1891; lives in New York City and Wellfleet, Mass.

Metropolitan Museum 150; Museum of Modern Art; **Whitney Museum** 300.

An aloof and highly individual painter, Dickinson uses misty tonal effects to produce mysterious sensations. His enigmatic paintings are characterized by deft handling, dramatic space and fresh vision. Dickinson served in the Navy during World War I, then painted in France, Italy and Spain. To avoid having to support himself through commercial art, he learned telegraphy. He has spent many years teaching in art schools and universities.

DOVE, Arthur Garfield. Canandaigua, N.Y., 1880; Center Port, L.I., 1946.

Metropolitan Museum; **Museum of Modern Art** 180; **Whitney Museum** 302.

Probably the first American to plunge into abstraction, Dove sought to find a mystic, underlying sense in nature. A statement of fact, he believed, has "no more to do with the art of painting than statistics with literature." After viewing the work of Cézanne during a trip to France in 1906-07, Dove ended his career as a successful magazine illustrator to concentrate on fine art. In 1910 he bought a farm in Connecticut and for six years he and his wife supported themselves by raising chickens and by lobster fishing. In 1920 he lived and worked on a houseboat off Long Island. In 1961 the Whitney Museum mounted a retrospective Dove exhibition.

DU BOIS, Guy Pène. Brooklyn, N.Y., 1889; Boston, 1958.

Museum of Modern Art; **Whitney Museum** 294.

A lively, sophisticated painter of genre, du Bois filled his compositions with simplified volumes and satirical insight. "Painters quite naturally become like surgeons," he wrote. "They operate in cold blood. They make few slips." Son of a music critic on the New York American, the artist was named after Guy de Maupassant, a friend of the family. He studied under William Merritt Chase and Robert Henri. After his father's death he became art critic on the American, the New York Herald Tribune and the New York Post; he was also editor of Arts and Decoration and a contributor to Vogue and Vanity Fair. He painted murals for post offices at Saratoga Springs, N.Y., and Rye, N.Y.

DUBUFFET (doo-boo-*fay*), **Jean.** Le Havre, 1901; lives at Vence.

Guggenheim Museum; **Museum of Modern Art** 219.

Dubuffet, who emerged as an important new talent only after World War II, has written: "My art is an attempt to bring all disparaged values into the limelight. . . . Personally, I believe very much in values of savagery. I mean instinct, passion, mood, violence, madness. . . ." Rejecting the idea of ugliness as the opposite of beauty, Dubuffet has introduced a whole new repertoire of technique. His pictures are often built up in thick layers of plaster and putty, and he has even used bark, leaves, tar and cement. He replaces accepted canons of beauty with unselfconscious and seemingly disordered images reminiscent of scribbles on walls or pictures from primitive cultures. Dubuffet studied painting in Paris after World War I, but gave it up for music, classical studies, paleography and ethnology and became interested in studies on psychotic art. In 1939, after a brief Army service, he left his wine business and devoted himself fully to painting. His first exhibition in Paris in 1944 aroused antagonism, but subsequent shows in New York, London and elsewhere have made him world-famous.

DUCCIO DI BUONINSEGNA (*doo*-chee-yo dee boo-on-een-*sane*-yah). Siena?, 1260?-1319.
Frick Collection 224.

The founder of the Sienese School, Duccio, like his younger and far greater contemporary Giotto, loosened the hold of stylized Byzantine conventions on art and prepared the way for the humanism of the dawning Renaissance. His paintings linger in the Medieval world of gold background and stiff forms, but they also advance toward dramatic narrative, more realistic observation and individuality of style. In 1298 Duccio served on a government advisory board, but the next year he was fined for refusing to take an oath of fidelity to the "captain of the people," a civic official. He was later fined again for insubordination, fined for refusing military service and fined for a vague activity which may have been related to sorcery. In 1308 he was commissioned to paint his masterwork, *The Enthroned Madonna and Child Altar.*

DURER (*doo*-rur), **Albrecht.** Nuremberg, 1471-1528.
Metropolitan Museum 38.

Dürer's lifetime straddled the twilight of the Middle Ages and the dawn of the new humanism inspired by the Italian Renaissance. Both are reflected in his art—a fusion of his native heritage of mystical fervor and precise delineation with the voluptuous forms and sensuous colors of the new Venetian manner. His paintings and drawings rank with the greatest, and in woodcuts and engravings he stands virtually supreme. His imaginative vision and restless mind are evident in the broad range of his work, which embraces unflinching portraits, technically flawless studies of plant life and religious themes which pulsate with the spiritual passion of the Reformation. His writings reveal that he, like his great contemporary da Vinci, was absorbed in a search for eternal verities. "What beauty is," he confessed, "I do not know, though it adheres to many things." "I believe that there is no man alive who might think out the maximum of beauty in the lowliest living creature, let alone in man. . . ." Dürer trained with his father, a goldsmith, then traveled about Germany and began publishing wood engravings. He married the daughter of a Nuremberg merchant in 1494 and the following year visited Venice. Fame came to him with his *Apocalypse* and *Great Passion* woodcut series. Declining the post of state painter in Venice, he was appointed court painter to the Holy Roman Emperor Maximilian I. In the years before his death, he published books on fortifications and human proportions.

DYCK, Sir Anthony van. See VAN DYCK, Sir Anthony.

EAKINS, Thomas Cowperthwait. Philadelphia, 1844-1916.
Brooklyn Museum 349-351; **Metropolitan Museum** 133.

America's greatest realist and portrait painter, Eakins produced sensitive pictures characterized by restraint, simplicity and an utter lack of affectation. In his best compositions, forms are rendered in space with masterful drama, and limited color is used with eloquent force and harmony. His uncompromising forthrightness seemed to many of his contemporaries brutal and inelegant, and his name did not even appear in a list of over twenty-five leading American painters published in the mid-1890's. In his entire lifetime it is estimated he made only about $15,000 from painting. Eakins studied drawing and anatomy in the United States and France. His 1875 masterpiece *The Gross Clinic* (Jefferson Medical College, Philadelphia) was placed in the medical, rather than the fine arts section of the Philadelphia Centennial Exposition, and even at that was criticized as degraded art. In 1876 he began teaching at the Pennsylvania Academy of Fine Arts, and in 1884 he married his talented pupil Susan Hannah Macdowell. Under the auspices of the University of Pennsylvania, he conducted experiments in the photography of movement in 1884. In 1887 he painted cowboys in the Dakotas and a portrait of Walt Whitman. His *Between Rounds* (1899, Philadelphia Museum of Art) was awarded a gold medal by the Pennsylvania Academy in 1904, but he scornfully cashed it in at the Mint for $75.

EL GRECO (real name Domenicos Theotocopoulos). Candia, Crete, 1541?; Toledo, Spain, 1614.
Frick Collection 232-233; Hispanic Museum; **Metropolitan Museum** 42-45.

El Greco was so highly regarded in his own day that when a price dispute arose over one of his works, an arbiter decided that "if it were to be assessed, taking into account all the qualities apparent in its manifold parts, one would have to value it so highly

that few, or none, could pay for it." Nevertheless, subsequent
centuries dismissed him as a talent ruined by what one critic
called "the distorted fancies of a morbid brain," and only over
the past hundred years has he been restored to the ranks of the
supreme. El Greco's restless line, glowing light, intense color and
intricate forms contribute to the profound mystic fervor generated by his paintings. In his leap beyond realism into the realm
of the spirit, he employs daring distortions which intensify mood
and design. As a youth, El Greco (whose nickname is Spanish
for "the Greek") left Crete, then a Venetian possession, for
Venice, where he may have studied with Titian. He went to Rome
in 1570 and in 1575 moved to Spain, where he settled in Toledo.
In 1578 he became father of a boy, Jorge Manuel, who later became his assistant; Jorge's mother (there is no record of a marriage between her and El Greco) apparently posed for the Madonna in many of El Greco's paintings. In 1586 he painted his
masterpiece, *The Burial of Count Orgaz* (Church of Santo Tomé,
Toledo). An inventory drawn up at his death lists scarcely any
furniture but mentions a library of books in Spanish, Greek,
Italian and Latin. The Metropolitan Museum and the National
Gallery in Washington own the finest groups of El Grecos outside the Prado in Madrid.

ENSOR, James. Ostend, Belgium, 1860-1949.
Museum of Modern Art 191.

Belgium's foremost painter of modern times, Ensor was a brilliant
master of what he called "adorable fantasy, the heavenly flower
of dew which inspires the creative artist," and a major forerunner
of Expressionism. His themes cover a wide range: rollicking
genre, genteel interiors, pearly still lifes, seascapes, unorthodox
portraits, religious subjects freshened by whimsy and macabre
visions. Many of his works blend burlesque and solemnity to
create unique worlds peopled by droll and disquieting puppets and
errie rogues. Ensor's English father and Belgian mother ran a
curio shop. After several years at Brussels Academy, Ensor returned to Ostend, where he remained the rest of his life. In 1882
he had his first showing at the Salon. In 1889 his huge masterwork, *Entry of Christ into Brussels* (on loan to Brussels Museum), was rejected by Brussels' avant-garde group Les XX,
which he had helped to organize. After 1900 his greatness began
to decline. In the 1920's, he was named a baron by King Albert I.

EYCK, Hubert and Jan van. See VAN EYCK, Hubert and Jan.

FANTIN-LATOUR (fahn-*tan*-lah-*toor*), **Henri.** Grenoble, 1836;
Buré, 1904.
Brooklyn Museum 338; Metropolitan Museum.

Fantin-Latour strolled a modest path through the art revolutions
initiated by his friends. He was a painter of exquisite studies of

flowers; brilliant group portraits of artists, poets, musicians and relatives; and romantic musical fantasies inspired by Berlioz and Wagner. Fantin-Latour studied with his father, copied in the Louvre for some twelve years and spent a brief period in Courbet's studio class. In 1863 he had three paintings accepted by the Salon, but he also exhibited with Whistler and Manet in the famous Salon of the Rejected. In 1867 his portrait of Manet created a Salon sensation. He married a painter of flowers.

FEININGER (*fine*-in-gur), **Lyonel.** New York, 1871-1956.
Brooklyn Museum 361; **Guggenheim Museum** 284; **Museum of Modern Art** 181.

One of the most individual artists to develop out of Cubism, Feininger painted romantic pictures characterized by movement and light and by the gossamer color he superimposed over a firm structure of lines and planes. His chief inspiration was his love for musical form: "Bach has been my master in painting," he wrote. "The architectonic side of Bach, whereby a germinal idea is developed into a huge polyphonic form, is the important thing." In 1887 Feininger left for Germany to study music, but he soon switched to art. (He was to remain in Germany until the triumph of Hitler.) He supported himself by doing comic strips—Kinder-kids and Wee Willie Winkie's World—for the Chicago Tribune, but by 1907 he was ready to devote his full time to painting. In 1911 he met Delaunay and other Cubists in Paris, and three years later he showed with Kandinsky and Marc. He was the first professor of painting at the Bauhaus. Around 1920 he composed organ fugues. His friendship with Paul Klee began around 1922. After his art was condemned by Nazis and the Bauhaus was closed, he settled in the United States. He painted murals for the 1939 New York World's Fair. His sons Andreas and Lux are a photographer and a painter, respectively.

FRAGONARD (frah-go-*nar*), **Jean Honoré.** Grasse, 1732; Paris, 1806.
Frick Collection 243-246; Metropolitan Museum.

Fragonard's nimble brush dashed off compositions of lively color and spontaneous movement. Master of delicate eroticism, he was also a virtuoso of sparkling scenes of everyday life, appealing portraits and lyrical, airy landscapes. Fragonard studied with Chardin and Boucher and in 1756 won the Prix de Rome. He toured Italy, and after his return to France he was named associate of the Royal Academy. In 1769 he married Marie-Anne Gerard, a painter of miniatures, and settled near Paris. He escaped to Grasse during the Revolution and returned to become a member of the Jury of Arts and an official of the committee to create the Louvre Museum. In 1806, however, he was deprived of his pension, evicted (after forty years) from his apartment-studio in the Louvre and died in poverty.

GAINSBOROUGH, Thomas. Sudbury, 1727; London, 1788.
Frick Collection 253; **Metropolitan Museum** 71.

Gainsborough, the painter of the celebrated *Blue Boy,* was a sensitive colorist, a master of cool harmonies and fluid brushwork and a far less stereotyped portraitist than his chief rival, Sir Joshua Reynolds. Despite his popularity as a painter of society figures, his heart was in idyllic (and generally unappreciated) landscapes. "I am sick of portraits," he lamented, "and wish very much to take my viol-da-gamba and walk off to some sweet village where I can paint landscapes and enjoy the fag end of life in quietness and ease." Philosophically, he added that an artist is sure to starve "if he does not conform to the common eye in choosing that branch which they will encourage and pay for." Apprenticed to a silversmith, Gainsborough set up a portrait studio about 1748 and in the following years became the most fashionable portraitist in England. He was a founding member of the Royal Academy and was named painter to George III in 1784.

GAUGUIN (go-*gan*), **Paul.** Paris, 1848; Fa-tu-iwa, Marquesas Islands, 1903.
Brooklyn Museum; **Metropolitan Museum** 112-113; Museum of Modern Art.

Gauguin was among the first to abandon Impressionism: "They keep the shackles of representation," he declared. "They look for what is near the eye, and not at the mysterious beauty of thought." The first painter to rejuvenate the European tradition by borrowing from primitive or forgotten cultures, he urged artists to "have always before you the Persians, the Cambodians and a little of the Egyptians." His highly personal style is characterized by broad, decorative areas of contrasting, non-naturalistic color, arabesque line, striking patterns, sharp contours and almost bizarre simplifications. The trail he blazed prepared the way for the Fauves, the Expressionists (particularly the Germans) and early abstractionists like Kandinsky. Gauguin was the son of a liberal Republican journalist who fled with his family to Peru when Louis Napoleon made himself emperor. (Gauguin's maternal grandmother was the famous South American radical Flora Tristan.) Young Gauguin lived in Lima until 1865, when he returned to France and enlisted in the Navy. He later became a successful stockbroker, but his interest in painting and sculpture steadily increased. In 1876 he exhibited in the Salon, and in 1882 he finally left his job, settled his family with relatives in Copenhagen and concentrated entirely on art. Extremely poor, he worked for a while as a bill poster. In 1887 he shipped for Panama, where he worked on construction of the Canal, and for Martinique. He returned to Brittany and joined van Gogh at Arles, but left for Paris when van Gogh had his breakdown. In 1891 he auctioned his paintings and sailed for Tahiti, where he settled with a native mistress. He returned to

France for an exhibition in 1893 and had his last meeting with his family in Copenhagen the following year. Back in Tahiti, he was plagued by ill health but continued work on his Tahitian journal, "Noa-Noa." In 1901 he moved to the Marquesas, where he was tried for the slander of a policeman and died while appealing a three months' prison sentence.

GERICAULT (zhay-ree-*coh*), **Théodore.** Rouen, 1791; Paris, 1824.
Brooklyn Museum 326; Gallery of Modern Art; Metropolitan Museum.

A moody, passionate soul, Géricault was the founder of Romanticism, the style his younger friend Delacroix would later perfect. His best oils are filled with tempestuous emotion and energetic action. Géricault studied in Paris with a pupil of David and was acclaimed at the Salon of 1812. During the Hundred Days, he joined the King's Musketeers against Napoleon. He traveled to Italy in 1816-19 and was influenced by Michelangelo. In 1819 he exhibited his masterwork, *The Raft of the Medusa* (Louvre), the painting which initiated a half-century of struggle between Neoclassicists and Romanticists. He later painted race horses in England, where he suffered a spinal injury in a fall from a horse. He was bedridden for some two years before his death.

GHIRLANDAIO (gear-lahnd-*ah*-yoh), **Domenico** (real name Domenico Bigordi). Florence, 1449-94.
Metropolitan Museum 5.

One of the most popular painters of Florence, Ghirlandaio produced graceful, rhythmic pictures which strike a pleasing balance between realism and decorative appeal. When Michelangelo was fourteen, he entered Ghirlandaio's studio as an apprentice; the master was so impressed with his student's genius that he sent him to Lorenzo de Medici. Ghirlandaio was the son of a goldsmith whose fanciful garlands *(ghirlande)* were highly esteemed. (The nickname Ghirlandaio means "garland maker.") In 1481 he assisted Botticelli on his frescoes in the Sistine Chapel, and he later organized his own art workshop in Florence. His most famous portrait is the *Portrait of an Old Man with his Grandson* (Louvre). A picture by his son Rudolfo, *The Nativity with Saints,* is also in the Metropolitan.

GLACKENS, William. Philadelphia, 1870; Westport, Conn., 1938.
Brooklyn Museum 357-358; **Whitney Museum** 287.

A master draftsman and magnificent technician, Glackens filled his early paintings with vivid drama taken from everyday situations and later enlarged his scope by adapting Impressionist color and Renoir's silky textures. Glackens was an illustrator on Philadelphia newspapers and shared a studio with Robert Henri before visiting Paris in 1895. Back in Philadelphia he shared a studio with Luks and became a leading magazine illustrator. He was sent by Hearst to sketch the Spanish-American War and was present at the Battle of San Juan Hill. In 1900 he settled in New York, and in 1904 he married the artist Edith Dimock. In 1908 he exhibited with The Eight (the Ashcan School). He later sailed to Paris to acquire the first French moderns for the vast collection of the Barnes Foundation in Merion, Penn. He was chairman of the committee for selection of American art for the 1913 New York Armory Show.

GLEIZES (glehz), **Albert.** Paris, 1881; Saint-Rémy de Provence, 1953.
Guggenheim Museum 266.

A leading theorist of Cubism during its pioneer period, Gleizes has been eclipsed by the more famous names of the movement. His work is distinguished by compact organization, inventive variation of forms and a poetic translation of religious themes into visual terms. Gleizes began as an Impressionist, became a Fauvist, and after meeting Apollinaire and Picasso shifted to Cubism. He was among the exhibitors in the first group show of Cubism in 1911, and, with the painter Jean Metzinger, he wrote the first major book in the Cubist movement. After serving in the French army, he settled in the United States, then returned to Europe and became interested in Medieval religious art. He wrote "Return to Christian Man" in 1932. In 1950 a Gleizes exhibition was held in the Vatican; in 1964 an exhibition was given by the Guggenheim.

GOGH, Vincent van. See VAN GOGH, Vincent.

GORKY, Arshile (real name Vosdanig Manoog Adoian). Khorkom Vari, Turkish Armenia, 1904; Sherman, Conn., 1948.
Metropolitan Museum 152; Museum of Modern Art; **Whitney Museum** 305-306.

Gorky blended abstraction with inventive and highly personal Surrealistic images. His early work was derivative, but in his last decade he poured out passionate pictures in which fantastic symbolic forms flow amid luxurious and sensuous colors. His balance of forms in space is exceptional. His color, ranging from opaque to thin wash, is often smouldering. His juxtapositions of odd shapes tease the eye with their freshness and their dramatic and erotic overtones. Gorky left Armenia at sixteen to join two sisters living in Boston. He worked in a factory, studied art briefly and moved to New York, where he changed his name. (Gorky means "bitter" and Arshile refers to Achilles.) He taught until 1931 and worked on the WPA's Federal Art Project in 1935-39. He painted murals for the Newark Airport and the Aviation Building of the 1939 New York World's Fair. In 1946 fire destroyed many paintings in his Connecticut studio. The same year he was operated on for cancer. In 1948 he was severely hurt in a car accident; he committed suicide by hanging.

GOYA (*go*-yah), **Francisco.** Fuente de Todos, 1746; Bordeaux, 1828.
Frick Collection 235; Hispanic Society; **Metropolitan Museum** 48-50.

The greatest Spanish painter after Velázquez, Goya was the last of the old masters and the first of the moderns. In his paintings, drawings and etchings can be found romanticism, realism, satiric fantasy, the seeds of Impressionism and elements that were to be developed by the Expressionists. His best work stresses abbreviated lines and vivid color and combines light, mass, space and drawing into an indivisible whole. His art is candid and often edged with social or political criticism: "The slumber of reason," he wrote on one typical picture, "produces monsters." His favorite targets were corrupt feudal society, repressive nobility, superstition, vanity and war. He was also a master at pageantry (most notably bullfights), portraiture and religious painting. The son of a gilder, Goya failed twice to get a scholarship to Madrid's Academy of San Fernando (which he was afterward to direct). He traveled in Italy about 1770, and in about 1775 was studying at Madrid with Francisco Bayeu, a prominent painter whose sister he married. (Only one of their five children survived past childhood.) He began designing for the Royal Tapestry Works and was soon appointed court painter to Charles III. During this period he conducted a liaison with the Duchess of Alba. He fell ill in 1792 and by 1794 was completely deaf. In 1799 he published his *Caprichos* etchings, grotesque social satires, but withdrew them under pressure from the Inquisition. In 1800 he painted *Charles IV and His Family* (Prado, Madrid). During the Napoleonic campaigns he welcomed French troops as liberators from feudalism, but he later supported uprisings against France, notably in such works as *The Execution of May 3, 1808* (about 1814, Prado). Between 1809 and 1918 he made his etchings *The Disasters of War* (not published in full until 1863). In 1819 he bought a villa outside Madrid—it came to be called the Deaf Man's House—and decorated its walls with eerie masterpieces (Prado). He also took up the new medium of lithography. He spent his last years in Bordeaux, in voluntary exile from the repressive measures of the Spanish throne.

GRECO, El. See EL GRECO.

GRIS (greess), **Juan** (real name José Victoriano González). Madrid, 1887; Boulogne-sur-Seine, 1927.
Guggenheim Museum; **Museum of Modern Art** 175-176.

The most single-minded of the Cubists, Gris was a master of precise, classical order who sought what he called "sensibility and sensuality in the form of flat, colored architecture." He explained that while most artists "have thought to produce poetic effect with beautiful models or beautiful objects, [we] on the other hand, produce it with beautiful elements, for those of the intellect are certainly the most beautiful." Gris evolved a highly personal approach to collage. After World War I, striving for a classical transformation of Cubism, he painted less abstractly. Gris quit engineering studies for art, went to Paris and became a friend of Picasso, Apollinaire and Kahnweiler (who was to become his dealer and author of his definitive biography). While painting in the Cubist style, he supported himself through magazine illustrations. Kahnweiler contracted to buy all Gris' work, but during the War he was forced as a German national to leave for Switzerland; Gris fell into poverty, but was aided by Gertrude Stein and Matisse. In the early 1920's Gris designed sets for the Ballet Russe. He delivered a major lecture at the Sorbonne, later published as "On the Possibilities of Painting."

GUARDI (*gwahr*-dee), **Francesco de'.** Venice, 1712-93.
Metropolitan Museum 20.

The last important painter of Venice, Guardi used his fluent brush to achieve effects of silvery light and atmosphere. Besides zestful views of Venice, he painted vistas of ruined buildings tinged with melancholy. Today his vividness and sense of airy spaciousness rank him as an important precursor of the 19th Century landscape tradition. Guardi was the son, the brother and the father of painters and the son-in-law of Tiepolo. He was admitted to the Venetian Academy only in 1784, when he was seventy-two.

GUY, Francis. Lorton, England, 1790?; Brooklyn, N.Y., 1820.
Brooklyn Museum 345; New York Historical Society; New York
    Public Library.

A silk dyer in London, Guy arrived in the United States about 1795 and lived in New York, Brooklyn, Philadelphia and Baltimore. He continued to work at silk dying but also painted views of towns.

HALS (hahlss), **Frans.** Antwerp, 1580?; Haarlem, 1666.
Brooklyn Museum 324; **Metropolitan Museum** 53-54.

The first major artist of Holland's golden century, Hals was a remarkable virtuoso who invigorated painting with his agile brushwork, informal poses and spontaneous gestures. A master of brusque economy, he abbreviated detail and annihilated unnecessary description. At its best, his art bursts with rollicking vitality, but when he is carried away by his own swagger he tends to render little more than surface effects. Before he was thirty, Hals had painted his large portrait group *The Banquet of the Officers of St. George* (Frans Hals Museum, Haarlem). Despite his many commissions, he frequently had to face law suits over debt. Nevertheless, he was several times elected president of the painters' guild. He applied for relief as a pauper in 1652 and ten years later entered the Haarlem poorhouse. In 1664 he painted his bleak masterpiece *The Lady Regents of the Haarlem Almshouse* (Frans Hals Museum). Of his twelve children, seven sons became painters, one son was committed to a mental institution and a daughter was charged with delinquency.

HARNETT, William Michael. Clonakilty, Ireland, 1848?; New York, 1892.
Brooklyn Museum; **Metropolitan Museum** 122.

America's leading master of *trompe l'oeil*—literally, "fool-the-eye" realism—Harnett was popular in his lifetime with the general public but scorned by art circles. In the late 1930's, however, he rose dramatically from obscurity to attain the rank of America's major still life artist. His work is cherished for its precise but subtle arrangement, its contrasts of space and textures and its almost mystic response to the spirit of commonplace objects. Harnett studied at the Pennsylvania Academy of Fine Arts, had his first picture exhibited in 1875 at New York's National Academy, and lived in France and Germany in 1880-85. He exhibited his largest painting, *After the Hunt,* in the Paris Salon of 1885; acquired for a celebrated saloon in the United States, it inspired many imitators.

HARTLEY, Marsden. Lewiston, Me., 1878; Ellsworth, Me., 1943.
Brooklyn Museum; **Metropolitan Museum** 145; **Museum of Modern Art** 209; Whitney Museum.

Hartley painted some of the strongest and simplest pictures of his generation. A pioneer in early abstraction, he attempted to see with what he defined as "the eye of the imagination, that mystical third somewhere in the mind which transposes all that is legitimate to expression." In his efforts to convey mood and emotion, he avoided Expressionist turbulence and retained a characteristic discipline. His final phase is forceful and direct, with an almost folk-art simplicity and freshness. Hartley's early landscapes were influenced by Ryder. His first exhibition was in 1909, at Stieglitz's Photo-Secession Gallery. He went to Paris in 1912 with the help of the painter Arthur B. Davies and was influenced by the Cubists and Fauves. He exhibited in Germany with Kandinsky's Blue Rider Group and in the 1913 New York Armory Show. In 1918 he went to Bermuda with Charles Demuth. He published his first volume of poetry in Paris in 1922.

HICKS, Edward. Bucks Co., Penn., 1780; Newtown, Penn., 1849.
Brooklyn Museum 346.

One of America's finest self-taught painters, Hicks was among the first primitives to be re-discovered. A Quaker preacher, he painted reluctantly, considering painting "one of those trifling, insignificant arts which has never been of substantial advantage to mankind" and "not in the real spirit of Christ [but] a companion of voluptuousness and pride." He concentrated on several pious and patriotic themes: *Penn's Treaty with the Indians, The Grave of William Penn* and, over and over, *The Peaceable Kingdom.* A descendant of the Pilgrims, Hicks was orphaned in childhood and adopted by Quakers. In his youth he painted ornament on coaches. After 1811 he became minister of the Newtown Friends meeting house, supporting himself largely by farming and painting tavern signs. He preached in New York, Ohio, Indiana and Canada.

HOBBEMA (*hob*-uh-mah), **Meindert.** Amsterdam? 1638-1709.
Brooklyn Museum 325; Frick Collection; **Metropolitan Museum** 57.

The long-neglected Hobbema, the last painter of Holland's great century of art, rose in esteem with the renewal of interest in landscape painting at the beginning of the last century. Hobbema found his own personal approach within the Dutch tradition, perfecting a typical motif of picturesque wooded glades, sunken roads and red-roofed cottages imbued with solidity and serenity. Hobbema studied with Ruisdael, married the cook to the Burgomaster of Amsterdam and was given the post of Assessor of Wine Measures. His *The Avenue, Middleharnis* (1689, National Gallery, London) belongs among the most celebrated Dutch landscapes.

HOGARTH, William. London, 1697-1764.
Frick Collection 252; Metropolitan Museum.

Significant British painting can be said to begin with the pugnacious Hogarth. Deriding the then-current vogue for minor Italians, whom he assailed as the "black masters," Hogarth pilloried the bawdy, brawling world of corrupt 18th Century English society in a series of story-telling pictures reminiscent of scenes in a novel or play. He circulated his satires through his skillful engravings, which he sold in large numbers by public subscription. After an apprenticeship to an engraver of silver and gold plate, Hogarth opened his own engraving shop in 1720. In 1729 he eloped with the daughter of the artist Sir James Thornhill. He painted his *A Harlot's Progress* series in 1731 (the originals survive only in his engravings) and his *The Rake's Progress* series in 1735 (Sir John Sloan's Museum, London). Angered by the pirating of his engravings, he was instrumental in having a copyright law passed. He painted the *Marriage à la Mode* cycle in 1743-45 (National Gallery, London) and wrote "The Analysis of Beauty" in 1753. He also left an autobiography in manuscript (British Museum, London).

HOLBEIN (*hall*-bine), **Hans,** the Younger. Augsburg, Germany, 1497?; London 1543.
Frick Collection 241; **Metropolitan Museum** 40-41.

Holbein's portraits record physical appearance with detached precision and technical perfection. He was a master of interesting relationships of objects, and the subtle, precise and expressive line studies he made for his paintings are among the world's finest drawings. His color, however, sometimes serves for little beyond pleasing surface embellishment. After an apprenticeship in the studio of his father, Holbein moved to Basel, where he worked for publishers and painted frescoes and portraits. About 1515 he met the great philosopher and satirist Erasmus (1466?-1536), whom he painted three times; he also illustrated Erasmus's satire "The Praise of Folly." Holbein's major woodcut series *The Dance of Death* (1523-24) was an amazing success for those days, selling ten editions in twelve years. In 1523 he made his first visit to England; nine years later he returned and became court painter to Henry VIII.

HOMER, Winslow. Boston, Mass., 1836; Prouts Neck, Me. 1910.
Brooklyn Museum 352; **Metropolitan Museum** 130-132.

Ranked with Eakins and Ryder as a major American painter, Homer was somewhat hampered by his concern for objective fact, but he nevertheless brought blood, muscle and bone to genre painting and explored novel designs and new methods of rendering light and atmosphere. His paintings are lean and rugged records of the virile outdoors. With characteristic brevity, he summed up his concepts by declaring, "When I have selected a thing carefully, I paint it exactly as it appears." After apprenticeship to a Boston lithographer, Homer moved to New York and became an illustrator for Harper's Weekly, for which he made drawings of the Union Army during the Civil War. He won fame with his 1866 *Prisoners From the Front* (Metropolitan Museum) and was represented in the 1867 Paris World's Fair. He lived in France for a year. In the 1870's he painted scenes of Virginia Negro life, like *The Carnival* in the Metropolitan. He settled in Maine in 1884, but he later visited the Bahamas, Bermuda, Cuba and Florida. He suffered a paralytic stroke in 1908.

HOOCH (hoke), **Pieter de.** Rotterdam, 1629?; Amsterdam?, 1684?
Metropolitan Museum 65.

Among the best of the Dutch "little masters" of serene interiors, Hooch was more literal and less poetic than Vermeer but had a fine sense of space, texture and pattern. His early training was with a landscape painter. In 1653 he was in Delft (possibly in contact with Vermeer) and joined the painters' guild. Around 1657 he moved to Amsterdam, where the charming idylls of his

Delft period gave way to less convincing portrayals of palatial interiors.

HOPPER, Edward. Nyack, N.Y., 1882; lives in New York City and Cape Cod.

Gallery of Modern Art; **Metropolitan Museum** 146; **Museum of Modern Art** 206; **Whitney Museum** 295.

The dean of American realists, Hopper has developed a direct and vivid style which communicates a discreet sense of drama. What may first seem banal literalness in his themes gradually reveals breadth and spirit. He has painted many striking New England landscapes alive with a windy exhilaration, but his dominant motif is city life—brooding glimpses of isolated lives and the dull monotony of brick buildings. Hopper studied under Robert Henri, visited Europe and settled in New York. He was included in the 1913 New York Armory Show, in which he sold his first and last painting until 1923. He concentrated on commercial art from 1915 to 1920, when he had his first one-man show at the Whitney Studio Club. In 1964 the Whitney Museum held a widely-acclaimed retrospective of his work.

INGRES (*an*-gruh), **Jean Auguste Dominique.** Montauban, 1780; Paris, 1867.

Frick Collection 248; **Metropolitan Museum** 82-83.

Ingres, the stern leader of the French conservatives, admired Raphael above all. He believed in exactitude and finish, but he also understood that details must not "compromise the aspect of the great masses." To Ingres, color was secondary and drawing was "three-and-a-half quarters of the content of painting." He sought to portray only what he considered truly beautiful. His sober themes, his thin, glossy color applied with satin-smooth brushstrokes and his emphasis on line (to say nothing of his self-assurance) made him anathema to the more avant-garde painters of his century, most notably to Delacroix. He not only evolved a creative new approach to Neoclassicism but achieved masterworks of portrait characterization. Ingres received his first art lessons from his father. As a youth he played second violin in the Toulouse theatre orchestra. In 1797 he entered David's studio in Paris, and within the next six years he won the Grand Prix de Rome, made his debut at the Salon and was commissioned by Napoleon to paint his portrait. He was in Rome from 1806 until 1824. On his return he was awarded the Legion of Honor and commissioned to paint his Louvre ceiling decoration *The Apotheosis of Homer*. He returned to Italy for seven more years. In 1855 he was given an entire gallery at the Paris Universal Exposition, and in 1862 he was appointed a Senator of the Empire. He bequeathed the paintings and drawings in his collection to the Montauban Museum, now called the Ingres Museum.

INNESS, George. Newburgh, N.Y., 1825; Bridge of Allan, Scotland, 1894.

Brooklyn Museum 348; Gallery of Modern Art; **Metropolitan Museum** 126.

Inness refreshed 19th Century American art with his shimmering, varied color, his free brushstrokes and his ability to weld details into simplified compositions. With the "mystery of nature" as his inspiration, he believed that "a work of art does not appeal to the intellect. It does not appeal to the moral sense. Its aim is not to instruct, not to edify, but to awaken an emotion." His style recalls the Barbizon School in its insistence on broad masses and large areas of color. He rejected Impressionism as "visual imbecility." Inness studied in New York, London and Rome. On a visit to France he met Corot, Rousseau and Millet. He returned to settle in Medford, Mass., where he recruited a volunteer company during the Civil War but was kept by illness from seeing active service himself. In 1876 he settled in Montclair, N.J. He died while traveling in Scotland.

JOHNSON, Eastman. Lovell, Me., 1824; New York, 1906.

Brooklyn Museum; **Metropolitan Museum** 125; New York Historical Society.

One of America's best portraitists, Johnson was a painter of everyday scenes which were often sentimental and often perceptive. Son of Maine's secretary of state, Johnson apprenticed in the Boston lithography shop which later employed Homer. He studied in Düsseldorf and shared a studio with Emanuel Leutz, the painter of *Washington Crossing the Delaware* (Metropolitan Museum). After four years in the Hague, he returned home in 1855 and opened a studio in New York. He traveled to the South and painted such scenes of Negro life as *My Old Kentucky Home* (New York Historical Society). He was an artist with the Union Army during the Civil War. Afterwards he concentrated on portraits, including among his sitters Daniel Webster, Longfellow, Emerson, Edwin Booth and Grover Cleveland. He was a founder and trustee of the Metropolitan.

KANDINSKY (can-*din*-skee), **Vassily.** Moscow, 1866; Neuilly-sur-Seine, 1944.

Guggenheim Museum 274-281; Metropolitan Museum; **Museum of Modern Art** 213-214.

Though he did not concentrate on painting until he was thirty, Kandinsky became one of the most significant 20th Century artists and the first pioneer in the brave new world of pure abstraction. By eliminating representation, Kandinsky sought to liberate painting from "the necessity of responding to the many purposes it had earlier been forced to serve." "The observer," he wrote, "must learn to look at the picture as a graphic representation of a mood and not as a representation of objects." Through abstraction, he felt the sensitive artist could release the inner essence of a composition, making it timeless, pure and free of irrelevant material associations. Feeling should be "the decisive factor," for abstraction is "the realism of the visionary." His innovations have affected modern art decisively, inspiring painters from Klee to Miró and Gorky. Kandinsky studied political economy and law, but in 1896 he declined a university professorship and went to Munich to study art. About the time of his first abstraction (1911-12), he began a lifelong friendship with Klee, he and Franz Marc founded the Blue Rider Group and he published his influential book on the concepts of abstraction, "Concerning the Spiritual in Art." The first Kandinsky shown in America—at the 1913 New York Armory Show—was *Improvisation 27;* it was bought by Alfred Stieglitz and is now in the Metropolitan. At the outbreak of war Kandinsky returned to Russia, where the Revolutionary government appointed him to the Department of Fine Arts of the Commissariat of Public Education. When Soviet hostility toward modern art became oppressive, he left for Germany, where he became a professor at the Bauhaus. In 1933, after the Nazis had closed the Bauhaus, he settled in Paris.

KANE, John. West Calder, Scotland, 1860; Pittsburgh, 1934.
Museum of Modern Art 223; Whitney Museum.

Possibly America's finest 20th Century primitive, Kane painted "because I like the puttin' on o' the color." He believed that "with art comes goodness and beauty," and that a painting "has a right to be as exact as a joist." He has been called the painter laureate of Pittsburgh for his many portrayals of that city. Kane began working in the coal mines of Scotland at the age of nine. He came to the United States in 1880 and worked in steel mills and on railroad and street paving gangs. In 1891 he lost a leg saving a cousin from a train accident. He subsequently painted freight cars and houses for income and painted pictures in his spare time. His recognition began with the Carnegie International of 1927. Secretary of Labor Frances Perkins exhibited fifteen of his pictures at the opening of a new Labor Department Building in Washington. An autobiography based on interviews by Marie McSwigan was published in 1938.

KLEE (clay), **Paul.** Münchenbuchsee, Switzerland, 1879; Muralto-Locarno, Switzerland, 1940.
Guggenheim Museum 285-286; **Museum of Modern Art** 196.

One of the most original and influential modern artists, Klee was a master of poetic enigma and bizarre invention. His audacious interpretations of emotion, mood, myth and symbol are among the most enchanting experiences in 20th Century painting, and his variety matches that of Picasso. Klee's art exalts inner vision. To achieve the power of mysterious meaning, he rejected the in-

fluence of the main-stream of Western art—the depiction of physical reality—and studied Far Eastern and primitive art, as well
as Cubism and abstraction. "Reality," he wrote, "is merely an
isolated phenomenon latently outnumbered by other realities. . . .
Things take on a broader and more varied meaning, often in
seeming contradiction to the rational experience of yesterday."
Son of a German music teacher and a Swiss pianist, Klee became
an adept violinist but decided to concentrate on art. After studies
in Munich and travels in Italy and France, he married a pianist
in 1906, and in 1911 he had his first one-man show, in Munich.
He met Franz Marc, Kandinsky, Picasso and Delaunay and joined
the pioneering Blue Rider Group in 1912. During World War I
he served behind the lines. He taught at the Bauhaus in 1920-29,
maintaining a close association with Kandinsky. In 1933 the Nazis
dismissed him from his post at the Düsseldorf Academy and he
returned to Bern. In 1937 his work was exhibited in the Nazi's
Munich exhibition of "degenerate art."

KOKOSCHKA (coh-*cosh*-kah), **Oskar.** Pöchlarn, Austria, 1886;
lives in Austria.
Guggenheim Museum; **Museum of Modern Art** 167.

One of the most important Expressionists, Kokoschka has painted
tense, deeply emotional compositions ranging from brooding med-
itations to works of anguish, scorn and satire and pictures of lyric
charm. His vigorous canvases tingle with slashing strokes and
sonorous color. "I never intended to entertain my contemporaries
with the tricks of a juggler," Kokoschka declared, "in the hope of
being recognized as an original. I simply want to create around
me a world of my own in which I could survive the progressive
disruption going on all over the world." In 1908 Kokoschka was
dismissed from art school for exhibiting what then seemed shock-
ing pictures; the production of two of his plays (later set to music
by Hindemith) further exasperated the conservatives. In 1910 he
joined the editorial staff of *Sturm,* the famous Berlin avant-garde
literary and art periodical. A love affair with the widow of Gustave Mahler inspired his most famous painting, *The Tempest*
(1914, Kunstmuseum, Basel). He was wounded on the Eastern
Front during the war. Afterward he became an art professor at
Dresden. When his work was included in the Nazi Munich exhibition of "degenerate art," he defiantly painted his *Self Portrait
of a Degenerate Artist* (private collection). He was in London
during the Blitz and became a British citizen.

KOONING, Willem de. Rotterdam, 1904; lives on Long Island.
Brooklyn Museum; Metropolitan Museum; **Museum of Modern
Art** 218; Whitney Museum.

De Kooning is one of the few American painters with a growing
international reputation. After a period of precise drawing and
calm harmonies, he evolved his striking impromptu style of mean-

dering wash and drip and dynamic surges of the brush. His best oils use forceful movement and colors which shift from subtle and sensuous to dry and highly textured. His space effects are based on interweaving planes, and his surfaces are varied and lively. Although he is famous for abstractions, some of his best recent paintings have been freely-rendered representational portrayals. De Kooning studied art in Brussels and Antwerp. Emigrating to the United States, he became a house painter and commercial artist. He began abstractions about 1928, sharing a studio with Gorky. He worked on the WPA's Federal Art Project and did murals for the French Lines pier in New York and for the Hall of Pharmacy at the 1939 New York World's Fair. He married the painter and art writer Elaine Fried in 1943, had his first one-man show in New York in 1948, and taught at Yale in 1950-51. In 1951 he was awarded first prize in the Chicago Art Institute Annual.

KUNIYOSHI (coon-ee-*yoh*-shee), **Yasuo.** Okayama, Japan, 1892; New York, 1953.

Brooklyn Museum; **Metropolitan Museum** 151; Museum of Modern Art; **Whitney Museum** 303.

Sensitive and delicate, witty and romantic, inventive yet close to tradition, Kuniyoshi's highly original style blends Oriental elegance and fantasy with the vitality of Western art. His themes range from rollicking depictions of children and wistful, sensuous images of women, to enigmatic social comment. Kuniyoshi arrived in California in 1906, worked at odd jobs while studying art at night, and in 1910 moved to New York, where he entered Robert Henri's school. The first of his three marriages was in 1914. In the 1930's he turned to photography for a livelihood, made several trips abroad and met Pascin. He was chairman of the Arts Council of Japanese-Americans for Democracy during World War II and broadcasted to Japan. In 1948 he was given the Whitney Museum's first retrospective of a living artist.

LA FRESNAYE (la fray-*nay*), **Roger de.** Le Mans, 1885; Grasse, 1925.

Museum of Modern Art 177.

In contrast to the austere and restless near-abstraction of Picasso and Braque, La Fresnaye's Cubism is almost representational. In his earlier years he adapted Cubism's visual power to subject matter reflecting the enthusiasm, patriotism and optimism of pre-war France. After World War I he moved towards delicate drawings and paintings depicting meditative classical figures. As a young artist, La Fresnaye was influenced by Cézanne and by Maurice Denis, who transmitted to his students the flattened surfaces and decorative forms he had derived from Gauguin. By 1911 he had joined the Cubist revolution and become a friend of Apollinaire, Gleizes, Léger and Jacques Villon. He served in the

Infantry for the duration of the war. In his late years, suffering
from tuberculosis, he drew and painted largely while confined
to bed.

LA TOUR (la *toor*), **Georges de.** Vis-sur-Seille, 1593; Lunéville,
1652.
Frick Collection 242; **Metropolitan Museum** 74.

La Tour's identity was lost for centuries—until 1914—and his
works, too impressive to be bypassed, were ascribed to artists as
varied as Zurbarán, Velázquez and Vermeer. Most of his pictures
are dominated by a mysterious quality emanating from contrasts
of light and dark. His forms are simplified, and his colors are
highly personal. At his best, he achieved hypnotic visions and,
in his earlier work, strong genre scenes. La Tour received a commission from Duke Charles IV of Lorraine early in his career and
by 1646 was painter to King Louis XIII. In 1648 he became a
founding member of the Royal Academy.

LAWRENCE, Sir Thomas. Bristol, 1769; London, 1830.
Frick Collection; **Metropolitan Museum** 72.

"Sir Thomas," in the astute words of an old biographical dic-
tionary of artists, "was the ideal of a fashionable portrait painter,
thanks to his facile use of color, the superficial elegance of his
style and his skill in the art of flattering the many distinguished
people whose portraits he did." Lawrence was selling pastel portraits at twelve. At seventeen he wrote his mother that, except for
Sir Joshua Reynolds, "for the painting of a head I would risk my
reputation with any painter in London." In 1792, after Reynolds'
death, he did in fact become chief portrait painter to George III.
He was knighted in 1815, and in 1820 he became President of
the Royal Academy.

LEGER (lay-*zhay*), **Fernand.** Argentan, 1881; Gif-sur-Yvette,
1955.
Guggenheim Museum 271-272; **Museum of Modern Art** 179,
187.

One of the most original artists to evolve from the Cubist revolution, Léger worked in almost strident color which contrasts with
the harmonies of Matisse, Picasso and Braque. Léger saw poetry
in the compact order of machines and in the precise shapes and
staccato rhythms of the 20th Century. "I have a horror of discreet
painting," he declared. He felt that "a painter should not try to
represent a beautiful thing [because] nowadays, a work of art
should bear comparison with any man-made object [and] the artistic picture is false and out of date." His best paintings, pulsating
and dynamic, are often unified by strong patterns and cylindrical
shapes. Among his key inspirations were Romanesque mosaics,
the forthrightness of Rousseau, movie close-ups and the bold

colors of posters, yet he also reinterpreted the calm and poise of David. Léger went to Paris in 1900 and worked as an architectural draftsman. He first studied painting with the aging Gérôme and by 1910 had completed his first major canvas, *Nudes in a Forest* (Rijksmuseum, Otterlo, the Netherlands). In 1911 he exhibited in the first public Cubist exhibition. During the war he was gassed near Verdun. In 1924 he collaborated on a film short called *Le Ballet Mécanique* and traveled to Greece with Le Corbusier. He later designed sets for Alexander Korda's film of H. G. Wells' *The Shape of Things to Come*. He spent World War II in the United States, where he painted murals for Nelson Rockefeller and taught at Yale University and Mills College. He later designed a mosaic for the facade of the church in Assy, France, and stained glass windows for the University of Caracas, Venezuela. After his death, a Léger Museum was established at Boit, on the Riviera.

LEVINE, Jack. Boston, 1915; lives in New York.
Brooklyn Museum; Metropolitan Museum; **Museum of Modern Art** 208; **Whitney Museum** 312.

Levine, who calls himself "a romantic humanitarian" and "an editorial artist," is one of the best among the relatively few contemporary artists who focus on the plight of Man in society. His paintings—ironic or compassionate, brooding, angry and satirical —are battles in his personal struggle for a better world. Able and eloquent, he seeks inspiration from such masters of the past as Rembrandt, Velázquez and El Greco to achieve an individual synthesis as up-to-date as today's paper. Levine studied art at the Boston Museum and in the 1930's worked on the WPA's Federal Art Project. He had his first one-man show in 1939, in New York. He served during the war in the Air Force, and in 1946 he married the painter Ruth Gikow. In 1950-51 he traveled in Italy on a Fulbright.

LORRAIN, Claude. See CLAUDE LORRAIN.

LUKS (lukes), **George.** Williamsport, Penn., 1867; New York, 1933.
Brooklyn Museum; Metropolitan Museum; **Whitney Museum** 288-289.

A champion of the down-to-earth, Luks slashed out brash, garish and exciting pictures. He was an uneven artist, but his best pictures, like his 1905 *The Wrestlers* (Boston Museum of Fine Arts), are as rousing as his philosophy of art: "Technique, did you say? My slats! Say, listen, you—it's in you or it isn't. Who taught Shakespeare technique? Guts, guts! Life! Life! That's my technique!" Luks' father was a doctor in a mining town and both his parents were amateur painters. Young Luks was a lightweight boxer. He studied painting at Pennsylvania Academy, traveled in

Cuba in 1895-96 as a war correspondent and illustrator and later
became an editorial and comic cartoonist.

MANET (mah-*nay*), **Edouard.** Paris. 1832-83.
Metropolitan Museum 91-95.

The first truly modern painter, Manet dealt a death blow to the
dark-toned tradition of the academicians. His daring juxtapositions of sparkling color bypassed half-tones to reveal rich new
possibilities; his incisive, zestful drawing discarded all but the
most essential details; his magic brushstrokes glide vivaciously.
In demonstrating the immense possibilities of pure painting—
painting independent of the story-telling favored by the Neoclassicists and Romantics—Manet chose his themes primarily for
their potential in terms of color, line, light and space, proving
that the first criterion is not in *what* is painted, but *how* it is
painted. Inspired by Velázquez, Hals, Goya and Courbet, Manet
in turn greatly influenced Whistler, Renoir, Degas, Cézanne, Gauguin and Matisse. Few artists were ever derided by the press as
unrelentingly as Manet, but his vindication has come with history.
Manet studied under the famed conservative Couture. In 1863 his
Déjeuner sur l'Herbe (Museum of Impressionism, Paris) was rejected by the Salon and aroused a furor at the Salon of the Rejected. Two years later, his *Olympia* met with similar abuse.
When Zola published praise of Manet he was forced to leave his
newspaper position. Refused exhibition at the 1867 World's Fair,
Manet defiantly built his own pavillion. In 1873, however, his *Le
Bon Bock* (Philadelphia Museum of Art) scored a success at the
Salon. The following year he painted with Monet at Argenteuil.
He died in 1882 after amputation of his left leg. In 1890 Monet
and Sargent organized a subscription to purchase *Olympia* for the
state; after great public opposition, the government reluctantly
accepted it for the Luxembourg. In 1907 Premier Georges Cle-
menceau placed *Olympia* in the Louvre, marking the official triumph of the "modernists." Through the bequest of Mrs. H. O.
Havemeyer, the Metropolitan Museum owns the finest group of
Manets outside of Paris.

MANTEGNA (mahn-*tay*-nyah), **Andrea.** Near Vicenza, 1431;
   Mantua, 1506.
Metropolitan Museum 7.

One of the finest North Italian artists of the early Renaissance,
Mantegna combined Gothic intensity and fondness for minute
detail with realism and the new passion for classical sculpture.
His arresting compositions are reinforced by masterful perspective and advanced depiction of anatomy and action. His modeling
is firm and his forms are bound together by sharply defined contours, but his color is rarely deep and structural. In his late teens,
Mantegna began six important frescoes in Padua (almost completely destroyed by bombing in World War II). In 1453 he

married a sister of the Venetian master Giovanni Bellini. He painted a major altarpiece for the Church of San Zeno in Verona and afterward worked chiefly for the Gonzagas of Mantua. His series of major frescoes in the Gonzaga palace includes the first illusionistic perspective in Renaissance ceiling painting.

MARC, Franz. Munich, 1880; Verdun, 1916.
Guggenheim Museum 269-270.

The aim of Marc's poetic and dynamic work was unique: to interpret the soul and mood of animals. "Is there any more mysterious idea for an artist," he asked, "than the conception of how nature is mirrored in the eyes of an animal? How does a horse see the world, or an eagle, or a doe, or a dog?" During World War I, writing to his wife from the horror of the Western Front, he added: "The impure men and women who surround me (in particular the men) did not arouse any of my real feelings, while the natural feeling for life possessed by animals set in vibration everything good in me." Marc studied theology and philosophy, then attended Munich Art Academy. He had an unhappy first marriage. In Paris in 1907 he was influenced by the works of van Gogh, Gauguin and Cézanne and began sculpture and animal themes. In 1910 he met Kandinsky and the two established the Blue Rider, a poetic Expressionist movement. In 1912 he met Delaunay and became interested in Cubism. When the war began he volunteered. He was killed at Verdun.

MARIN, John. Rutherford, N.J., 1870; Cape Split, Me., 1953.
Brooklyn Museum; **Metropolitan Museum** 140-144; **Museum of Modern Art** 205; Whitney Museum.

One of the major American pioneers of modern art, Marin developed a strikingly original style characterized by taut, condensed forms, free, sweeping brushstrokes and flowing washes of color. He was a sensitive lyricist in oils, but his greatest achievements were in watercolor compositions as tense as a coiled spring and alive with dynamic rhythm. Marin spent four early years in an architect's office but about 1888 began painting in watercolors. He studied at the Pennsylvania Academy of Fine Arts and the Art Students League and subsequently made two long trips to Europe. In 1906 the French government purchased one of his works from the Salon, and in 1909 the photographer Edward Steichen arranged an exhibition of his work at Stieglitz's Photo-Secession Gallery in New York. In 1936 he had a one-man exhibition at the Museum of Modern Art.

MARSH, Reginald. Paris, 1898; Dorset, Vt., 1954.
Brooklyn Museum; **Gallery of Modern Art** 320; Metropolitan Museum; Museum of Modern Art; **Whitney Museum** 296.

"Go out into the streets, stare at people, go into the subways, stare at people. Stare, stare, keep on staring." Such was Marsh's advice

to young artists. Practicing what he preached, he left a vast pictorial record of New York—its burlesque girls, down-and-outs,
Coney Island multitudes, opera dowagers and girls striding triumphantly in short, windblown skirts. The strength of his affectionate but unsentimental pictures lies most often in his vivid
drawing, his ability to fuse crowds into rhythmic groupings, his
gift for energetic movement and his sense of character. Both
Marsh's parents were artists. At Yale, he was art editor of the
Yale Record, and he afterwards illustrated for Vanity Fair, Harper's Bazaar, The New Yorker and the New York Daily News. His
first marriage ended in divorce. He began to paint about 1923
and had his first one-man show at the Whitney Studio Club in
1924. In the 1930's he married the painter Felicia Meyer. He
painted frescoes for the Post Office Department Building in Washington and did murals for the New York Customs House. In 1943
he was an artist-correspondent for Life magazine in Cuba, Brazil
and Trinidad. He published "Anatomy for Artists" in 1945.

MATISSE (mah-*teess*), **Henri.** Le Cateau-Cambrésis, 1869;
   Cimiez, 1954.
Brooklyn Museum; **Museum of Modern Art** 164-166.

Matisse, the leader of the Fauves, is often ranked with Picasso as
the most important painter of our time. A superb colorist, his
highly individual and seemingly inexhaustible harmonies are startling and brilliant—at times exotic, at times delicate and lyric.
He was also a pioneer of daring space arrangements, expressive
simplification, exceptionally free handling and masterfully varied
patterns. At the core of his sophisticated compositions are buoyant charm, exotic spirit and the joy of life. Matisse deliberately
avoided the inner depths explored by many old masters, but within his chosen range of expression he is a front-rank painter and
an important sculptor. His immediate sources were the Impressionists, but he also invigorated the Western tradition with ideas
inspired by Oriental art, Japanese prints, Persian miniatures and
Near Eastern rugs and fabrics. His daring concepts influenced
early abstractionists like Kandinsky, as well as a host of representational painters. Matisse studied under the arch-conservative
Bouguereau and under the inventive painter and teacher Gustave
Moreau. In 1899 he went to Paris, where he began to sculpt. In
1904 he had his first one-man show, at Vollard's. Two years later
he exhibited at the Salon d'Automne with Derain, Rouault and
others; a startled critic gave them the label Les Fauves—meaning
"the wild beasts"—to describe their brilliant color and dashing,
impromptu handling. In 1905-06 he painted his masterwork, *Joy
of Life* (Barnes Foundation, Merion, Penn.). Between 1907 and
1911 he traveled extensively in Europe and Africa. In the 1930's
he visited New York, San Francisco and Tahiti and painted murals for the Barnes Foundation. He designed furnishings, decora-

tions and stained glass windows for a Dominican chapel at Vence in 1947-51. His last work includes large gouache collages.

MEISSONIER (may-sown-*yay*), **Jean Louis Ernest.** Lyons, 1815; Paris, 1891.
Metropolitan Museum 116.

Meissonier's intensely photographic depictions, characterized by minute detail, were admired in his day as the peak in "modern" art. Though he is generally considered only a minor figure today, occasional work, such as his small *The Barricade* of 1849 (Louvre), still arouses interest through its striking sensitivity. He was particularly fond of genre and military scenes. Meissonier had his first Salon acceptance in 1834. He was elected to the French Institute in 1861 and was the only artist to become a three-time winner of the Grand Medal of Honor. He was a commander, in the same guard unit with Manet, during the Franco-Prussian War. In 1872 he used his influence as a leading juror to exclude Courbet from the Salons because of his activities during the Commune.

MEMLING (or Memlinc), **Hans.** Near Frankfurt, 1433?; Bruges, 1494.
Metropolitan Museum 26-28; Morgan Library.

Memling lacks the dramatically expressive approach of greater Flemish masters, but his mood is serene, graceful and refined and his work has more charm than his predecessors'. Memling may have studied with Roger van der Weyden in Brussels. By 1465 he was a citizen of Bruges, where he married, received many commissions and was given a studio by the community. Among his most famous paintings are the *Seven Joys of the Virgin* (1478-80, Alte Pinakothek, Munich) and his *Shrine of St. Ursula* series (1489, Hospital of St. John, Bruges).

MILLET (meel-*lay*), **Jean François.** Gruchy, Normandy, 1814; Barbizon, 1875.
Brooklyn Museum; **Metropolitan Museum** 89.

One of the most important members of the Barbizon group, Millet painted unadorned, brooding homages to the hard life of the peasant. Attacked as a dangerous revolutionary, he defended his themes staunchly: "They may call me a painter of ugliness, a detractor of my race, but let no one think they can force me to beautify peasant types. I would rather say nothing than express myself feebly. [These] peasant subjects suit my nature best, for I must confess, at the risk of your taking me to be a Socialist, that the human side is what touches me most in art." Today Millet is often dismissed as a sentimental illustrator, but at their best his drawing, forms and color are highly expressive and some of his landscape pastels presage Impressionism. His forthright style and passionate concern for the humble influenced Pissarro and van Gogh. Millet worked on his father's farm, studied art at Cherbourg and received a grant from that city's municipal council to study in Paris, where he made his Salon debut in 1840. Extremely poor, he painted saleable pictures in the style of Boucher. After the death of his first wife, he moved to Le Havre, remarried and raised nine children—always in desperate financial straits. He began peasant themes in 1847 and two years later moved to Barbizon, where he received financial help from Théodore Rousseau and American painters including William M. Hunt. Among his important works are *The Gleaners* (1856, Louvre), *The Angelus* (1859, Louvre) and *The Man with the Hoe* (1863, H. E. Huntington Library, San Marino, Calif.) The French government commissioned paintings for the Panthéon, but Millet died before he could begin them. His destitute widow was aided by Corot.

MIRO, Joan (hwahn mee-*row*). Near Barcelona, 1893; lives in Palma de Mallorca.
Guggenheim Museum; **Museum of Modern Art** 197, 203.

Miró's poetic whimsy, blithe technique and rich vocabulary of signs and symbols rank him among the modern masters of fantasy, while his gay and lyric color motifs know few contemporary equals. His best paintings, sometimes complex, sometimes terse, are distinguished by unhackneyed metaphors and robust zest. Miró's exhilarating style was inspired by Catalan frescoes, folk art, Kandinsky's abstraction and Hans Arp's free forms. "Music and poetry," he declared, "this has always been my goal, to transcend the purely plastic fact to reach other horizons." Miró set up his own studio in 1915, had his first one-man show in 1918 and in 1919 fell under the Cubist influence in Paris. In 1921 he returned to his family's farm, where he painted *The Farm,* one of his greatest works. (It was bought from the artist by Ernest Hemingway.) In the mid-1920's he returned to Paris, joined the Surrealists and, with Max Ernst, painted sets for the Ballet Russe. In 1937 he made a large mural for the Spanish Republican Pavilion at the Paris World's Fair, the same pavilion for which Picasso painted his famed *Guernica.* In 1947 he painted a mural for the Terrace Hilton Hotel in Cincinnati. In 1955-58, with the ceramicist Artigas, he made two large ceramic walls, *Night* and *Day,* for the UNESCO headquarters in Paris.

MODIGLIANI (mode-eel-*yah*-nee), **Amedeo.** Livorno, 1884; Paris, 1920.
Guggenheim Museum 260-261; Metropolitan Museum; **Museum of Modern Art** 170.

Modigliani's appealing and highly personal style and the romantic aura of his star-crossed Bohemian life have ranked him with van Gogh as a legendary figure in modern art. Set against his period of artistic revolution, Modigliani's work seems almost traditional, devoid of the startling techniques usually recognized as new ex-

pression. Yet he went far to freshen tradition through his sensuous approach embodying individual devices of high quality—
devices like elongated bodies, mask-like faces, glowing color, a
marvelously sensitive line, subtle placement of figures in space
and occasional echoes of Negro sculpture and Cubist-like planes
and angles. Son of estranged parents (his father was manager of
a broker's office), Modigliani knew poverty from childhood. (His
brother later became a Socialist member of Parliament.) He
studied in Rome, Florence and Venice, and in 1906 arrived in
Paris, where he shared a studio with Brancusi and became interested in sculpture. He was friendly with Soutine, Utrillo, Picasso
and Jacques Lipchitz and in 1914 met the Polish poet Leopold
Zborrowski, who undertook to help him financially and win him
recognition. Modigliani's first and only one-man show was held
in the Weill Gallery (scene of Picasso's first Paris show) in 1918;
it was closed by police, the pubic hair on his nudes being considered scandalous. The following year he contracted tuberculosis,
and in 1920 he died in a Paris hospital.

MONDRIAN (*mown*-dree-ahn), **Piet** (real name Pieter Cornelis
   Mondriaan). Amersfoort, Holland, 1872; New York, 1944.
Guggenheim Museum; **Museum of Modern Art** 215.

The master of pure geometric abstraction, Mondrian represents a
titanic effort "not to be dominated by the physical-natural." In
non-objective compositions of the utmost clarity and order, he
sought to express a new spirit and a new century. "The true content of all painting," he believed, "is the rhythm of life. . . ." His
work developed from early realism, to vivid, Fauve-like oils, to
sensitive personal adaptations of Analytic Cubism, and finally to
his severely simplified elaborations of the rectangle. "Abiding
equilibrium," he said, "is achieved through opposition and is expressed by the straight line (the limit of plastic means) in its
principal opposition, i.e., the right angle." Some scoffers still liken
his art to kitchen linoleum, but few artists have so concretely
affected everyday life by influencing the forms and colors of
architecture, furniture, advertising art and typography. Son of
an amateur painter and nephew of a landscapist, Mondrian taught
drawing during the early 1890's. An exhibition of his church
tower series in 1909 caused a wild uproar. (His uncle, Fritz Mondrian, hastened to inform the press that they were not his paintings.) In 1911 he went to Paris, where his style evolved from
Cubist semi-abstraction to pure abstraction. In Holland, with
Theo van Doesburg, he started the journal *De Stijl* in 1917,
writing important essays on abstraction. In 1940 he found a haven
in New York, and in 1942 he had his first one-man exhibition
in America. He died of pneumonia after completing *Broadway
Boogie Woogie* (Museum of Modern Art), leaving unfinished the
glowing *Victory Boogie Woogie* (private collection).

MONET (moh-*nay*), **Claude.** Paris, 1840; Giverny, 1926.
Brooklyn Museum 332; **Gallery of Modern Art** 314; **Metropolitan Museum** 96-99; **Museum of Modern Art** 160.

Monet's paintings offer an unrivaled panorama of Impressionism, evolving as they did from early figure compositions to vigorous, lyrical landscapes, to the grandeur of his final water lily themes. With a flashing brush and glowing color, he rendered evanescent effects of sunlight, fog and mist with both boldness and silken delicacy. Manet called Monet "the Raphael of water," and Cézanne declared, "He is nothing but an eye, but, God, what an eye! The sky is blue, isn't it? Well, it was Monet who found that out." As a youth in Le Havre, Monet made caricatures of local celebrities. The pioneer landscapist Eugène Boudin interested him in outdoor landscape subjects, and he came to Paris in 1859 to study painting. After military service in Algeria, he met Renoir, Sisley, Bazille, Courbet and Cézanne. A family quarrel over his career resulted in the discontinuance of his allowance. His portrait of Camille Donceaux, *The Woman in the Green Dress* (Kunsthalle, Bremen), was a success at the Salon of 1866, but he was rejected in the Salons of 1867 and 1869. He was in London during the Franco-Prussian War, and in 1879 he painted with Manet and Renoir at Argenteuil. The first Impressionist group show included Monet's *Sunrise* (1872, private collection, Paris). In 1888 he refused the Legion of Honor, and in 1897 he joined Zola, Clemenceau and Pissarro in the fight to secure justice for Alfred Dreyfus.

MONTICELLI (mon-tee-sell-*ee*), **Adolphe.** Marseilles, 1824-86.
Brooklyn Museum 330; Metropolitan Museum.

An intriguing minor painter, Monticelli filled his masquerades and portraits with thick ribbons of color which his admirers acclaimed as "painted music." His jewel-like oils are recollections of Veronese and Watteau. Van Gogh was fond of Monticelli's "juicy" color. Napoleon III bought Monticelli's work, but in the artist's later years his vogue waned and he lived in obscurity. Monticelli studied in Paris in 1846, returned to that city in 1863 and spent his last years in Marseilles.

MOREAU (moh-*roh*), **Gustave.** Paris, 1826-98.
Gallery of Modern Art 315; Metropolitan Museum.

An absorbing talent and an exceptional teacher whose students included Rouault (his favorite) and Matisse, Moreau painted mystic, fantastic compositions which contrast sharply with the Impressionists' searchings for visible reality and scientific truth. Sometimes theatrical and over-literary, Moreau nonetheless often achieved strong and imaginative drama. Among his myriad works are visions so bold that they approach the liberty of contemporary abstractions. Son of a government architect, Moreau studied with academic teachers and with the Romanticist Théodore Chasérieu. He visited Italy in 1857 and was awarded Salon medals in 1864 and 1865. In 1891 he became a teacher at the official Beaux Arts school. He bequeathed his paintings and studio to the people of Paris (Musée Gustave Moreau), stipulating that Rouault be its director. After long neglect, large exhibitions in 1961-62, including one at the Museum of Modern Art, renewed interest in his art.

MORISOT, Berthe (bert moh-ree-*zoh*). Bourges, 1841; Paris, 1895.
Brooklyn Museum 339.

But for Mary Cassatt, Berthe Morisot was the only woman among the Impressionists. She was also among the first to work outdoors and use luminous atmospheric effects. Her highly individual work is filled with zest, grace and charm. To Renoir, she was "the last truly feminine painter since Fragonard." Daughter of a prefect of Bourges, she studied under Corot. She was a lifelong friend of Manet; she posed for him, married his brother Eugène and helped organize a large retrospective of his work after his death. Shortly before her own death, the Luxembourg acquired her *Young Girl at the Ball* (1879-80, Museum of Impressionism, Paris).

MORSE, Samuel Finley Breese. Charlestown, Mass., 1791; New York, 1872.
Metropolitan Museum 120; New York Historical Society.

Before he invented the telegraph, Morse's burning ambition was, in his own words, to be "among those who shall revive the splendor of the 15th Century; to rival the genius of a Raphael, a Michelangelo or a Titian." His hopes proved unattainable, but his portraits, allegories and occasional landscapes are nevertheless among the best American work of his period. Son of the Rev. Jedediah Morse, the "Father of American Geography," young Morse studied at Yale, traveled with Allston in England in 1811-1815 and studied with Benjamin West. During his years of struggle and near poverty, he was commissioned by the city of Charleston, S.C., to paint President James Monroe (1819, City Hall, Charleston) and by New York City to paint Lafayette on his visit to the United States (1825, City Hall, New York). He studied in Europe in 1829-33 and on his return evolved the principles of transmission by electric telegraph. In 1835 he ran for mayor of New York on an anti-foreigner, anti-Catholic platform. About 1837 he gave up painting, and in 1838 he finally perfected the telegraph. In 1843 Congress voted $30,000 to build an experimental line from Washington to Baltimore; Morse's first message was transmitted the following year. In 1854 he was defeated in an election to Congress.

MOUNT, William Sidney. Setauket, N.Y., 1807-68.
Brooklyn Museum; **Metropolitan Museum** 123; New York Historical Society.

Mount was among the first Americans to reject so-called "history"
painting, preferring to paint beguiling scenes of life on his native
Long Island. (He was admonished by critics to paint pictures
showing a "higher grade in the social scale.") A cheerful man
who loved to play the fiddle, he explored his neighboring countryside in a studio on wheels equipped with a stove and a skylight.
Mount spent his youth as a farmhand and in 1826 entered the
National Academy of Design. Illness caused him to retire to
Setauket the following year. In 1833 a portrait of a bishop
brought him fame. About 1859 he shifted to depicting everyday
life, especially in its humorous moments.

O'KEEFFE, Georgia. Sun Prairie, Wisc., 1887; lives in New
Mexico.
Metropolitan Museum 149; Museum of Modern Art; Whitney
Museum.

Miss O'Keeffe's paintings are at once austere and delicate, fastidious and strong, objective and aloof. Both her early pioneer abstractions and later representational work are endowed with nuances of enigma and elusiveness. Her paint surfaces are as thin
and delicate as an egg shell. In her stark close-ups and vistas, the
viewer senses fresh insight into reality and imagination. Her pictures are unmistakably individual. Miss O'Keeffe studied in Chicago and New York and has taught at colleges in South Carolina,
Virginia and Texas. Her abstract drawings were included in a
group show by Alfred Stieglitz ("At last a woman on paper," he
exclaimed), and she became Stieglitz's second wife in 1925. She
moved to New Mexico in 1946. After Stieglitz's death, she dis-
tributed large portions of his collection to various museums.

OROZCO (oh-*roh*-scoh), **José Clemente.** Guzmán, 1883; Mexico
City, 1949.
Gallery of Modern Art; **Museum of Modern Art** 207.

In his many watercolors, lithographs, drawings, easel paintings
and frescoes, Orozco recorded a world of struggle and upheaval.
His subjects ranged from glimpses of peons and prostitutes to
titanic, symbol-packed compositions inspired by Greek mythol-
ogy, pre-Columbiana, the Mexican Revolution and by the Machine Age. "My theme is humanity, my drift is emotion, my
means the real and integral representation of bodies," he declared.
His fiery, forceful style borrows from the simplicity of folk art,
the monumentality of Giotto's frescoes and the dynamic agitation of El Greco. While he was a youth, an accidental powder
explosion caused Orozco the loss of fingers on his left hand and
impaired his sight and hearing. His first solo exhibition, in 1916,

consisted of watercolors on the sorrows of war. On a trip to California, customs officials destroyed half a hundred of his paintings as obscene. His important work includes frescoes for the National Preparatory School in Mexico City (1922-23), his *Races of Man* for the New School for Social Research in New York (1927), frescoes on the Prometheus theme for Pomona College, Claremont, Calif. (1930), some 3,000 feet of frescoes for Dartmouth College in Hanover, N.H. (1932-34), and frescoes in the Mexico City Palace of Fine Arts and in the University and Orphanage at Guadalajara (1936-39). In 1940 he painted *Dive Bomber and Tank,* a portable fresco of six panels, as a public demonstration in the Museum of Modern Art. His studio in Guadalajara is now an art workshop and Orozco museum.

PASCIN (pass-*can*), **Jules** (real name Julius Pincas). Widden, Bulgaria, 1885; Paris, 1930.

Brooklyn Museum 360; Metropolitan Museum; Museum of Modern Art.

A master of the sensuous, Pascin produced many passionate studies of nudes and semi-nudes. But he was equally gifted in capturing the look of a wistful child, a moment in a café, a street, a harbor scene, or a landscape. Something wry and ironic, yet sympathetic, hovers over his canvases—something occasionally lightened by a flash of humor. His color is, by turns, firm and delicate. He could control space relationships in a single figure as well as in a teeming mass, and he spoke brilliantly with line. Son of a Spanish-Jewish father and an Italian-Serbian mother, Pascin ran away from his Bulgarian home and at fifteen found himself in Munich, where he illustrated for the celebrated satirical journal *Simplicissimus.* He moved to the United States in 1914 and to Paris in 1920. In 1930 he committed suicide on the opening day of a major exhibition of his work.

PATINIR (pah-tin-*eer*) (or Patenier), **Joachim.** Bouvignes, Flanders, 1480?; Antwerp, 1524.

Metropolitan Museum 32.

Patinir was one of the earliest and most important artists to become absorbed with landscape motifs. In his religious paintings, stories tend to serve as pretexts for magnificent panoramas. Patinir was listed as a master painter of the Antwerp Guild of St. Luke. His friend Dürer was present at his wedding in 1421, and his collaborator Quentin Massys (1466-1530) was appointed guardian of his two young daughters when he died suddenly at forty-four.

PEALE, Charles Wilson. Kent County, Md., 1741; Philadelphia, 1827.

Brooklyn Museum 343; Metropolitan Museum; New York Historical Society.

The leading painter in America during the Revolution, Peale

favored vigorous and often unorthodox compositions. He was not only an artist, but a veteran of Valley Forge, a statesman, an inventor, founder of one of the first museums of natural history and an originator of the Pennsylvania Academy of Fine Arts. At twenty Peale married, established a saddle shop and began to paint. He went to London in 1766, studied with Benjamin West, met Franklin and exhibited at the Royal Academy. In 1772, at Mt. Vernon, he painted his first portrait of Washington. After the Revolution he served in the Pennsylvania Legislature. He assembled the first public art exhibition in the United States. In Philadelphia, during a yellow fever epidemic in 1802, he published suggestions on hygiene calling for free health centers. He also introduced the first nude models into American art classes, devised, with Jefferson, a machine for multiple writing, and invented porcelain false teeth. Two of his sons, Rembrandt and Raphael Peale, became painters of significance. (The Brooklyn Museum's mellow and delicate *Still Life with Cake* demonstrates Raphael's gifts.)

PICASSO (pee-*cah*-so), **Pablo.** Málaga, Spain, 1881; lives in France.
Guggenheim Museum 262-263; **Metropolitan Museum** 51-52; **Museum of Modern Art** 171, 173, 178, 183, 185-186.

For more than half a century, Picasso has been the most discussed, most influential, most stimulating and most imitated artist in the world. His modes of expression are of such extraordinary variety that he seems a dozen artists in one. "If the subjects I have wanted to express have suggested different ways of expression, I have never hesitated to adopt them," he explains. "Different motives inevitably require different methods of expression." In addition to his painting, he is a leading force in modern sculpture, the finest and most prolific of contemporary lithographers and etchers, a popular potter and a master book illustrator; his drawings, ranging from near-abstraction to precise realism, are without peer among his contemporaries. Son of an artist and art professor, Picasso established his first studio in 1896 and had his first one-man show the following year in Barcelona. He edited and illustrated an art review in Madrid in 1901, and in 1902 he settled in Paris, where Vollard held an exhibition of his work and he entered his Rose Period. At Gertrude Stein's he met Matisse in 1906. Around 1907 he began the development of Cubism, and in 1909 he made the first Cubist sculpture. The first Picassos shown in the United States appeared at Stieglitz's Photo-Secession Gallery in New York in 1911 and in the New York Armory Show of 1913. In Italy in 1917 he was influenced by Greco-Roman art. In 1918 he married the ballerina Olga Koklova. The 1920's saw the development of his neo-classic and "bone" periods and the influence of Surrealism. During the Spanish Civil War he was appointed by the Loyalist government to an honorary directorship of the Prado. During World War II he worked in Paris, where, after the Liberation, he joined the Communist party. In 1952 he gave his *War and Peace* murals for the Temple of Peace Chapel at Vallauris. In 1961 he married Jacqueline Roque.

PICKETT, Joseph. New Hope, Penn., 1848-1918.
Museum of Modern Art 222; Whitney Museum.

Pickett's panoramas of the countryside around New Hope reveal an exceptionally gifted primitive with a firm sense of composition, a poetic response to nature and an ingenious grasp of space, pattern, rhythm and texture. Pickett worked with his father building canal boats, followed carnivals as concessionaire and ran a shooting gallery, which he decorated with his own paintings (now lost). He married about 1893, opened a grocery store and began to paint. In 1918 he submitted a painting to the Pennsylvania Academy Annual; it was rejected.

PIERO DELLA FRANCESCA (pee-*yay*-roh *dell*-ah frahn-*chess*-cah) (real name Piero de Franceschi). San Sepolcro, Umbria, 1416?-1492.
Frick Collection 225.

As modern eyes have learned to see past the story-telling elements of a picture and to appreciate the abstract qualities which make up composition, Piero's rank has steadily risen. His grave and monumental figures are handled with stark simplification. His color is dramatic and highly individual, and his massing is skillfully balanced. His work combines passion with dignity and sober precision. Piero studied mathematics and art, served as a town councilman and about 1449 painted frescoes for the Ducal Palace at Urbino. For twelve years he worked on his cycle *The Story of the True Cross* (Church of San Francesco, Arezzo), one of the greatest achievements in Italian fresco. His frescoes in the Vatican were later whitewashed over to make place for Raphael. Piero wrote one of the first scientific treatises on the laws of optics and perspective. Beginning about 1480 he suffered from diminishing eyesight.

PIERO DI COSIMO (pee-*yay*-roh dee *coh*-zee-moh) (real name Piero di Lorenzo). Florence, 1462-1521?
Metropolitan Museum 9-10.

Vasari, the 16th Century chronicler, described Piero as an "odd and thoughtful" artist who "kept himself shut up, and would not permit anyone to see him at work, and lived the life of a wild beast, rather than that of a man." Absorbed in Greek and Roman lore, Piero portrayed classical themes with an eye for the imaginative and fantastic. Son of a goldsmith, Piero was trained by his godfather, Cosimo Rosselli, whose name he adopted. About 1480 he journeyed to Rome to help decorate the Sistine Chapel.

In addition to his many paintings, he designed carnival masquerades.

PISSARRO (*pee*-sahr-*roh*), **Camille.** St. Thomas, Danish West Indies, 1830; Paris, 1903.
Brooklyn Museum 331; Gallery of Modern Art; **Metropolitan Museum** 100.

One of the founders of Impressionism, Pissarro retained firm structure and vigorous modeling in his compositions despite the veils of atmosphere with which he covered them. His resonant and sensuous color and his brushwork often convey an almost tapestry-like effect. Less buoyant and dashing than Monet, Pissarro seems more rooted to the woods and earth of the peasant. He was enormously influential as a teacher: "He was so wonderful," said Mary Cassatt, "that he could have taught a stone to draw correctly." Cézanne, who spent two crucial years with him, wrote, "As for old Pissarro, he was a father to me. He was a man to be consulted, something like a God." Pissarro was the first painter of Jewish parentage to achieve international fame. A Socialist, he saw art in broad human terms; thus he wrote of Gauguin, "I criticize him for not applying his synthesis to our modern philosophy, which is absolutely social, anti-authoritarian, and anti-mystical." Son of a Frenchman and a Creole, Pissarro worked in his father's store at Saint Thomas, ran off to Caracas to paint, and in 1855 began to study art in Paris, where he met Corot, Courbet and Monet. In 1866 he settled in Pontoise, living a life of poverty. During the Franco-Prussian War, he moved to England; on his return he found his house looted and many of his paintings destroyed. He exhibited in the first Impressionist exhibition (1874), had a one-man exhibition at the important Durand-Ruel gallery and painted with Gauguin at Rouen and with Monet at Dieppe.

POLLOCK, Jackson. Cody, Wyo., 1912; East Hampton, L.I., 1956.
Guggenheim Museum; **Metropolitan Museum** 153; **Museum of Modern Art** 216; Whitney Museum.

The foremost figure in abstract art after World War II, Pollock is the most influential and controversial of recent American painters. His startling method opened a new road in art, combining the impetuous fervor of the Expressionists with abstract motifs. Though it proved a practical means of capturing spontaneous emotion, nothing but the very concept of abstraction itself has raised such an uproar. Pollock's swinging, zestful compositions are like vigorous dances or musical improvisations—like "jam sessions," with color instead of sound as the medium. Pollock was raised in Arizona and California, came to New York in 1929 and studied with the noted representational painter Thomas Hart Benton. In 1943 he had his first one-man exhibition—at Peggy

Guggenheim's Art of This Century Gallery. During the early 1940's he began his pure abstractions and married the artist Lee Krasner. When he died in an automobile crash, an exhibition which the Museum of Modern Art intended as a survey of his work in mid-career became a memorial show.

POUSSIN (poo-*san*), **Nicolas.** Villieres, Normandy, 1594; Rome, 1665.
Metropolitan Museum 75-76.

Poussin is the father of the so-called Grand Manner in painting, the tradition in which calmly posed figures illustrate lofty themes or re-enact mythological stories. The greatest French painter of the 17th Century, he produced works which are serenely disciplined, rhythmic, rich in color, masterful in architectural composition and philosophical in spirit. He combined the epic sense of mood and drama he found in Homer and Virgil with linear grace and refinement derived from Raphael and the throbbing color of Titian. "Colors in painting," Poussin wrote, "are as allurements for persuading the eyes, as the sweetness of meter is in poetry." Like Claude Lorrain, Poussin left his native France to spend most of his life in Rome. Around 1612 Poussin worked on decorations for the Luxembourg Palace in Paris. He settled in Rome in 1624, studied under Domenichino and married in 1635. Awarded an annual pension by King Louis XIII and requested to paint and direct decorations for the galleries of the Louvre, he left Rome reluctantly for Paris; he was unhappy with the project and harassed by the jealousy of rival French painters. In 1641 he was named first painter to the King, but he returned to Rome in 1642.

PRATT, Matthew. Philadelphia, 1734-1805.
Metropolitan Museum 118.

Pratt, who was described by his contemporary Charles Wilson Peale as "a mild and friendly man, not ambitious to distinguish himself," was a talented and sensitive portraitist. His career was eventually frustrated by a dearth of clients, and his later years were spent painting picturesque tavern signs, none of which has survived. Pratt was the pupil of his uncle, James Claypool. He traveled to London in 1765 and spent several years in the studio of Benjamin West. He returned to Philadelphia in 1768.

PRENDERGAST, Maurice Brazil. St. John's, Newfoundland, 1859; New York, 1924.
Brooklyn Museum; Metropolitan Museum; **Museum of Modern Art** 161; Whitney Museum.

America's most lyric colorist, Prendergast may have been America's first modern as well. He delighted in painting charming processions of calm girls in windblown skirts against backgrounds of trees, sky and water. He translated visual reality into mosaics of rich and glittering color notes. While some of his colleagues adopted Impressionism almost verbatim, he creatively modified its ideas—notably those of Cézanne—to form his own personal idiom. After ten years with a Boston drygoods company, Prendergast turned to painting. In Europe he studied with ultra-conservatives, but he later discovered Cézanne. He exhibited with The Eight—the so-called Ashcan School—in 1908, and in 1913 he was in the New York Armory Show. His brother Charles (1869-1948) is famous for decorative panels, carved screens and magnificent frames.

PUVIS DE CHAVANNES (poo-*veess* duh shah-*vahn*), **Pierre.**
   Lyons, 1824; Paris, 1898.
Gallery of Modern Art 316; Metropolitan Museum.

France's foremost muralist, Puvis de Chavannes shared the conservatives' enthusiasm for portraying literary and "lofty" themes from ancient times. His means of expression, however, were far removed from the banal murals of the academic artists: he omitted naturalistic detail, used subdued but luminous color and tonal harmonies and composed with an eye to essential forms. At its best, his work is tranquil and decorative, with fine spatial feeling and rhythmic groupings. Puvis de Chavannes studied art in Italy and, briefly, with Delacroix. In 1861 two of his murals won medals at the Salon and were acquired by the government. His most important murals were done for the Panthéon in Paris, the Palais des Arts in Lyons, the Sorbonne and the Public Library of Boston. In 1897, after some thirty years of devoted companionship, he married the Princess Maria Cantacuzène.

RAPHAEL SANZIO (*rah*-fah-yell *sahnt*-see-oh). Urbino, 1483;
   Rome, 1520.
Metropolitan Museum 11-12.

In the 19th Century, Raphael was spoken of only in superlatives: he was "in truth the greatest of artists" and the "most beloved name in art." Raphael was, in fact, an extraordinarily gifted virtuoso. His line is sensitive and expressive, and his feeling for figures balanced in space is exceptional. Furthermore, he influenced the course of painting and architecture towards classic poise, proportion and idealization. Nevertheless, his towering rank is today no longer sanctified beyond question. His greatness seems diluted by a glib facility; all but his best Madonnas are softened by an obvious surface charm and sentiment; his color is sometimes dry and lusterless. He is a superb eclectic, a magnificent adapter of the concepts of other artists and a charming illustrator—but weaker than the greatest masters. Son of a minor painter at the court of Urbino, Raphael served as assistant to Perugino and studied the work of Michelangelo and da Vinci. Pope Julius II commissioned him to paint frescoes for the Vatican, including the renowned *School of Athens* (1511), and Pope

Leo X appointed him chief architect of St. Peter's and procurer of antique art for the Vatican. He died suddenly, leaving his *Transfiguration* (Vatican) uncompleted, and was buried in the Pantheon with the simple inscription, "He who is here was Raphael."

REMBRANDT VAN RIJN (*rem*-brant vahn rine). Leyden, 1606; Amsterdam, 1669.
Frick Collection 237-238; **Metropolitan Museum** 58-62.

Like Shakespeare and Beethoven, the name of Rembrandt represents supreme creative achievement. Rembrandt's profound dramas of personality are perhaps the most warmly human, eloquently compassionate, yet enigmatically elusive in all painting. Few can approach his power to penetrate outer matter and portray essence. His use of light and dark, his resonant color, his strong forms and deep space cast spells over the eye and mind, yet his work retains the touch of everyday reality. His style evolved from detailed realism and theatrical light effects to late paintings which were stripped to the essentials. Ironically, his late work proved disquieting to his contemporaries, who lamented that Rembrandt had missed perfection by ignoring the classic Italian tradition embodied in Raphael. Son of a prosperous miller and a baker's daughter, Rembrandt left the University of Leyden to study painting. In 1631 he settled in Amsterdam, gained fame as a portraitist and, at twenty-five, was commissioned to paint the *Anatomy Lesson of Dr. Tulp* (Mauritshaus, The Hague). In 1634 he married a burgomaster's daughter and cousin of an art dealer. (Of their four children, only one would survive infancy.) In 1639 he purchased a large house and taught some forty students—some of whose paintings were later ascribed to their master. In 1642 he painted the so-called *Night Watch* (Rijksmuseum, Amsterdam). After the death of his wife, he took Hendrickje Stoffels, an illiterate country girl, as a mistress. Around 1657 he was declared insolvent and part of his possessions were put up for auction. In 1661-62 he painted his last official commission, *The Syndics of the Cloth Hall* (Rijksmuseum).

RENOIR (ren-*wahr*), **Pierre August.** Limoges, 1841; Cagnes, 1919.
Frick Collection 251; Brooklyn Museum; **Metropolitan Museum** 101-103; Museum of Modern Art.

Renoir's art is filled with glittering light, thrillingly textured flowers and fabrics and charming young girls and firm-fleshed women. "A picture," the artist felt, "ought to be a lovable thing, joyous and pretty. There are enough boring things in life without our fabricating them." Yet Renoir did not exploit appealing themes as a substitute for quality; gifted with a mastery of color and a dazzling facility for manipulating paint, he blended Impressionism's radiance with the glow of Venetian art, something of the zest of Rubens and the grace and delicacy of the French 18th Century. Renoir was apprenticed at thirteen as a painter of flowers on porcelain. He later studied at the Beaux-Arts and met Monet, Cézanne, Courbet and Manet. He was accepted in the 1868 Salon and in 1869 painted with Monet at Bougival. In 1874 he exhibited in the first group show of Impressionists. In 1875, in a disastrous auction sale, some Renoirs sold for 100 francs. In 1880-81 he painted his famous *Luncheon of the Boating Party* (Phillips Collection, Washington). His first solo show was in 1883. In 1892, he became the father of Jean Renoir, now the noted film director. With 1898 came the onset of arthritis. By 1912 he was partly paralyzed and confined to a wheel chair, but he continued to paint. In 1915, with an assistant, he worked at sculpture.

RIBERA (ree-*bay*-rah), **José** (or Jusepe) **de.** Játiva, Valencia, 1591; Naples, 1652.
Brooklyn Museum 323; Hispanic Museum; Metropolitan Museum.

Although he settled in Italy in his early years and never returned, Ribera is considered one of Spain's finest realists. His picturesque beggars and unflinching depictions of martyrdom record the stark reality of the physical world, frequently with spiritual overtones. His work is marked by breadth and simplicity, effective massing of dark and light and skillful execution of solid forms in deep space. Son of a shoemaker, Ribera left for Italy about 1620, lived in Parma, Venice, Padua and Rome and finally settled in Naples, then under Spanish rule. He was eventually appointed court painter to the Viceroy. The Spanish King twice sent Velázquez to commission paintings from him.

ROUAULT (roo-*oh*), **Georges.** Paris, 1871-1958.
Metropolitan Museum; **Museum of Modern Art** 169.

Rouault's sombre pictures, which seem so remote from the restless strife of contemporary "isms," hark back to the Romanesque and Byzantine, to stained glass windows and to painters like Rembrandt. A devout Catholic, Rouault is this century's only major religious painter, not only through his many Crucifixions and heads of Christ, but in the mystic spirit pervading his landscapes and even his depictions of prostitutes, peasants and melancholy clowns. The materialistic and malevolent world he portrayed weighed heavily on his own compassionate spirit: "I do not feel as if I belonged to this modern life on the streets where we are walking at this moment," he once said; "my real life is back in the age of the Cathedrals." Rouault's power of color is matched by rhythmic line, elaborate texture and stark drawing restricted to the most expressive movements. Apprenticed to a stained-glass maker and restorer, Rouault studied painting under

Gustave Moreau, in the same class as Matisse. At Moreau's death, he became curator of the Gustave Moreau Museum. In 1903 he helped found the Salon d'Automne, where he later exhibited and where the Fauves made their debut. In 1913 the important dealer Ambroise Vollard bought all his paintings. In 1929 he designed sets and costumes for Diaghilev's *Prodigal Son,* with music by Prokofiev. He was commissioned in the 1940's to design stained-glass windows for the church at Assy, France. In 1947 he sued Vollard's heirs to recover hundreds of unfinished paintings; he later burned over three hundred of them. He was honored by Pope Pius XII, and one of his paintings was acquired by the Vatican. At his death the French government decreed a state funeral.

ROUSSEAU (roos-*soh*), **Henri.** Laval, 1844; Paris, 1910.
Guggenheim Museum 257-258; Metropolitan Museum; **Museum of Modern Art** 220-221.

Rousseau's story—the tale of a gentle, naive artist whose "child-like" pictures are now cherished in proud museums and the best private collections—has become part of the folklore of modern art. Rousseau is labeled a primitive—a vague term for unsophisticated "Sunday painters"—but no true primitive ever equalled his power to endow a picture with haunting enchantment. His jungle fantasies, his views of streets, suburbs and landscape, his allegories and his glimpses of daily life are memorable in their unhackneyed design, mastery of intricate pattern, control of forms in space and sensitive color. He had the soul of a poet. To Apollinaire, he remarked, "It is not I who paint, but some-one else who holds my hand." Apollinaire declared that Rousseau "had such a strong feeling of reality that when he was painting a fantastic subject, he often became frightened and, trembling, was obliged to open the window." Rousseau charmed the leading painters of his day; sated with the softness of Impressionism and revolted by academic clichés, they found in his unselfconscious compositions fresh new insights. In 1865 Rousseau enrolled in the army, where he played a clarinet in the regimental band. After his discharge, he found a modest post collecting tolls. (He is often called Le Douanier, which means "customs official.") He began to paint late in the 1870's. Shortly afterward his wife died. (Only one of his many children survived; she became a nun.) In 1885 he retired on a small pension and gave lessons in singing, painting, violin and flute. He was issued a copyist's card for the Louvre in 1884. In 1885 he began to exhibit at the Salon of the Independents, where artists could show their work without having to pass a jury; Gauguin, Renoir and Redon admired his pictures, but most others laughed. Madame Delaunay, mother of the painter, commissioned his *Snake Charmer* in 1907 (Museum of Modern Art, Paris). When Rousseau was involved innocently in a check-forging scheme, he received a suspended sentence. The dealer Vollard and a few others began to buy his work, but he remained poor. He died in a charity hospital in Paris. Apollinaire composed a poem for his gravestone, which Brancusi carved.

ROUSSEAU (roos-*soh*), **Théodore**. Paris, 1812; Barbizon, 1867. **Frick Collection** 249; Metropolitan Museum.

Rousseau was a leading landscape painter of the Barbizon School, the famous group of artists whose rejection of the historical and anecdotal in favor of down-to-earth, naturalistic views meant years of exile from the Salon. Rousseau's interest in outdoor light and in the freshness of nature helped to pave the way for greater realism and, to some extent, for Impressionism. To Rousseau, "Light spread over a work is universal life . . . without light there is no creation." Rousseau entered the studio of an academician at fourteen and made his Salon debut in 1831. He was rejected by the Salon from 1836 to 1848, but after the Revolution of 1848 the State bought his *Edge of the Forest at Fontainebleau* (Louvre). In 1850 he auctioned some fifty paintings at a great loss, but in 1852 he was received by the Emperor. He was named president of the French jury of selection for the Universal Exposition in 1867. Under the guise of "an anonymous American collector," he bought paintings from his neglected and poverty-stricken friend Millet.

RUBENS (*roo*-benz), **Peter Paul**. Siegen, Westphalia, 1577; Antwerp, 1640. **Metropolitan Museum** 34-35.

Rubens' art pulsates with sumptuous color, swelling forms and colossal energy. If he rarely achieved profound drama and occasionally slipped into pomp and bathos, he was at his best a great colorist, a great draftsman and a highly imaginative composer. The new life he injected into the waning Venetian tradition inspired Watteau, Boucher and Fragonard by its shimmering color and fluid rhythms and moved Delacroix, who drew on Rubens for his fiery color and dramatic movement, to oppose the dry, greyish art of Neoclassicism. Rubens' influence also appears in Constable's airy landscapes, in the Impressionists' broken-up atmospheric color, in Renoir's flowing forms and jewel-like color and in Cézanne's weighty structural quality and dynamic diagonal groupings. Rubens was admitted to the Antwerp painters' guild in 1598 and spent 1600-08 in Italy, where he painted for Vincenzo Gonzaga, Duke of Mantua. In 1609 he was appointed painter to the court of Archduke Albert in Brussels. He married a lawyer's daughter, established a magnificent home and studio in Antwerp (now a museum) and collected Titian, Tintoretto and Veronese. He employed talented assistants, including van Dyck, Frans Snyders and Jacob Jordaens. He spent 1622-25 in Paris,

met Velázquez in Spain and went to London as envoy to King
Charles I, who knighted him. In 1630 he remarried, to a sixteen-
year-old. In 1638, crippled by gout, he was forced to stop painting.

RUISDAEL (*royce*-dahl), **Jacob van.** Haarlem, 1628?; Haarlem?,
  1682.
Metropolitan Museum 56.

The leading figure of 17th Century Dutch landscape, Ruisdael
explored the changing beauties of sky, clouds and wind and the
melancholy of panoramic vistas. His colors are dark-toned and
brownish, yet fresh. His most famous landscape is *The Mill Near
Wijk by Duurstede* (Rijksmuseum, Amsterdam). Ruisdael probably studied with his father, Isaak, and his uncle, Salomon, both
important landscape painters. He received a degree in medicine
at Caen and in 1676 registered as a physician in Amsterdam. In
1681 he moved to Haarlem.

RYDER, Albert Pinkham. New Bedford, Mass., 1847; Elmhurst,
  L.I., 1917.
Brooklyn Museum 354-355; **Metropolitan Museum** 135-136.

Ryder is America's master of the mystic and the romantic—a
pictorial poet, both brooding and lyric. His thickly encrusted
paintings are small in size but enormous in their sense of epic
space. He evokes unforgettable power through contrast and dramatic tonal nuance. Forms devoid of extraneous detail blend with
strong rhythms to evoke strange emotion in the viewer. His colors
are limited, but tellingly combined. An eccentric, Ryder would
sit in his studio amid a vast accumulation of rubbish and paint
over and over on one small picture for years at a time. Because
of overpainting, and because his materials often included wax,
candle grease and liberal doses of varnish, some of his pictures
have darkened and deteriorated. Ryder moved to New York
about 1863. He studied independently and at the National Academy of Design and exhibited for the first time at the Academy
in 1873. After subsequent rejections, he and four other artists
organized an independent art group. During the early 1880's he
was supported financially by a brother. In 1882 and 1887 he
visited Europe, primarily for the sea voyage. After 1900 he
painted fewer pictures. Ryder was included in the 1913 New
York Armory Show.

SARGENT, John Singer. Florence, 1856; London, 1925.
Brooklyn Museum 353; **Metropolitan Museum** 137-138.

Sargent subverted his high talent to the demands of the wealthy
for dazzling technical dexterity. ". . . portrait painting is a pimp's
profession," he once wrote; "I abhor and abjure [portraits] and
hope never to do another, especially of the upper classes." Nevertheless, among his more than 500 portraits of suave people and

exotic places, a number do evoke delight through their master-fully appealing surfaces, genuine charm and supple, authoritative brushwork. The son of an American doctor, Sargent traveled and studied in Italy, Germany, France, Spain and Holland. During the ten years he lived primarily in Paris, he produced two of his masterpieces, *The Daughters of Edward D. Boit* (1882, Museum of Fine Arts, Boston) and *El Jaleo* (1882, Isabella Stewart Gardner Museum, Boston). In 1884 he settled in England, and in 1890 he visited Egypt and Palestine, absorbing local atmos-phere for his mural commissions for the Boston Public Library (completed 1916). In 1918 he went to France as an official artist for the British Imperial War Museum.

SASSETTA (sah-*seht*-tah), (real name Stefano di Giovanni). Siena?, 1392; Siena, 1450.
Metropolitan Museum 1.

One of the most enchanting "little masters" of the Sienese School, Sassetta came into his own only in this century. He is admired for his archaic pictorial charm. In 1423 Sassetta was recorded as painting an altarpiece for the Sienese wool makers' guild. He worked on the font in the Duomo of Siena in 1427. In 1449 he was commissioned to paint a major fresco for Siena's Porta Romana, but he died before its completion.

SEURAT (sur-*rah*), **Georges.** Paris, 1859-91.
Metropolitan Museum 114-115; **Museum of Modern Art** 157.

By the time of his tragic death at thirty-one, Seurat had painted some of the supreme masterpieces of the 19th Century. The genius of the movement generally known as Pointillism, Seurat used small dots (the French word is *point*) and brushstrokes of contrasting colors to increase the intensity of his light, permitting the blending of the hues to take place in the spectator's eye. Be-yond his striking surface treatment lie less obvious but more pro-found qualities: the great originality of his composition, the sub-tlety of his arrangements, the air of grandeur of his visions and the astonishing quality of his figures—monumental and timeless, yet filled with the warmth of life. Seurat believed that art could be produced by rational and almost coldly scientific analysis; when friends praised the spirit of his compositions, he mused, "They see poetry in what I have done. No, I apply my method and that is all there is to it." Seruat is credited with restoring order to the freedom of the Impressionists and with having in-spired the Fauves by his vibrant, contrasting colors and the Cubists by his near-geometric forms and his non-naturalistic control of space. Seurat studied at the Beaux-Arts, worked two years under a pupil of Ingres and did extensive research into the science of color. In his earlier years he concentrated on drawings; one of them—the portrait of his friend and fellow student Aman-

Jean now in the Metropolitan—was accepted in the Salon of
1883. The next year his first major oil was rejected by the Salon,
and he helped organize the Salon of Independents. Through the
help of Pissarro, his masterpiece *An Afternoon on the Grand
Jatte Island* was in the Eighth Impressionist Exhibition. In 1891
he showed his partly completed *The Circus* (Louvre). He died
suddenly of pneumonia; only after his death did his family and
friends learn of his mistress, Madeline Knoblock, and his infant
son (who died two weeks after his father).

SEVERINI (say-vay-*ree*-nee), **Gino.** Cortona, 1883; lives in
Paris and Rome.
Guggenheim Museum 273; **Museum of Modern Art** 190.

The most lyrical of the Futurists, Severini is known for his lush
color and exuberant rhythms. He was influenced by French color
and Cubism more deeply than the other members of his group.
Severini entered Balla's studio school about 1904. In 1906 he
settled in Paris, where he met Braque, Picasso and Delaunay and
married the daughter of the poet Paul Fort. After World War I,
he painted in a representational and classical modification of
Cubism, using romantic Harlequin motifs; he published "From
Cubism to Classicism" in 1921. In the 1920's and 1930's he
painted frescoes and designed mosaics and churches in Switzerland and France.

SHAHN, Ben. Kaunas, Lithuania, 1898; lives in Roosevelt, N.J.
Brooklyn Museum; Metropolitan Museum; **Museum of Modern
Art** 210; **Whitney Museum** 310-311.

Shahn unites a documentary interest in character and detail with
poetic symbolism. His work characteristically contains irony and
satire, elegiac sorrow and lyricism. He prefers to use media like
tempera in order to avoid "those fascinating accidents you have
with oil." An articulate writer and lecturer, he has stated: "I'm
interested in life, and only in art so far as it enables me to express what I feel about life. . . . You paint something because
you like it a lot or else because you hate it. . . . What is form?
It is only the shape taken by content. . . ." Shahn's family emi-
grated to America in 1906. He worked as a lithographer's apprentice while attending school and had his first one-man show
in 1930. From 1931 he concentrated on social themes, including
the Dreyfus Case, the trial of Sacco and Vanzetti and the false
imprisonment of the labor leader Tom Mooney. He assisted
Diego Rivera on his Rockefeller Center frescoes (destroyed) and
in the mid-1930's worked for the Farm Security Administration
as an artist and photographer. With his second wife, the artist
Bernarda Bryson, he painted frescoes for the Bronx Central An-
nex Post Office. In the 1940's he did murals for the Social Security Building in Washington and posters for the Office of War
Information and for the CIO.

SHEELER, Charles. Philadelphia, 1883; lives at Irvington-on-the Hudson, N.Y.

Brooklyn Museum 362; **Metropolitan Museum** 148; Museum of Modern Art; Whitney Museum.

A foremost exponent of crystal-clear realism, Sheeler believes in "accounting for the visual world with exactitude." His smooth, impersonal technique seeks "to remove the method of painting as far as possible from being an obstacle in the way of consideration of the content. . . ." In a Sheeler picture, a barn, a Shaker table, a factory or a machine serves both as a quiet but intense image and as a subtly calculated element in an underlying structural arrangement disciplined by a keen appreciation of abstraction. Sheeler traveled in England, Holland and Spain and shared a studio with Morton Schamberg (1881-1918), a brilliant young artist whose semi-abstract work explored the "machine as art" theme. About 1912 he began to support himself through photography. He was in the 1913 New York Armory Show and had a one-man show of photography in New York in 1919. In 1929 he painted *Upper Deck* (Fogg Art Museum, Harvard), a key work.

SISLEY (see-*zlay*), **Alfred.** Paris, 1839; Moret, 1899.

Brooklyn Museum 333.

Sisley's airy and lyrical landscapes are more fragile than those of Monet, Pissarro or Renoir, but filled with a sparkling freshness and finesse of handling. Sisley's father, a rich importer, sent him to London to work in coffee and cotton, but the youth studied Turner and Constable instead. Returning to Paris, he became a friend of Monet and Renoir. The Franco-Prussian War bankrupted his family's business. In 1874 he was in the First Impressionist Exhibition, and in 1895 he had a one-man show at Durand-Ruel. Though his last years were spent in poverty, just one year after his death his prices began to soar.

SLOAN, John. Lock Haven, Penn., 1871; Hanover, N.H., 1951.

Brooklyn Museum; Metropolitan Museum; **Whitney Museum** 290-291.

Sloan's glimpses of city life are possibly the finest paintings achieved by the realists among the so-called Ashcan School. In turn bantering and zestful, brooding and poetic, they illuminate Sloan's view of poor New Yorkers: "drab, shabby, happy, sad and human." His later work includes New Mexico landscapes and supple nudes. Sloan was also an important illustrator, teacher, writer, lecturer and general gadfly to the smugness of the fashionable art world. Not until his later years did he earn a reasonable income from his art: "Though a living cannot be made at art," he once wrote, "art makes ·living worthwhile. It makes living, living. It makes starving, living. It makes worry, it makes trouble, it makes a life that would be barren of everything, living. It brings

life to life." After working as staff artist on a Philadelphia newspaper, Sloan joined Henri, Luks, Glackens and Shinn in New
York in 1904. He supported himself with magazine and book
illustration and, with Henri, organized the famous exhibition of
The Eight in 1908. He joined the Socialist Party in 1910, was
the unpaid editor of Masses magazine and ran for the State As-
sembly in 1912. He was in the 1913 New York Armory Show
and had his first one-man exhibition at the Whitney Studio Club
in 1916. In 1932 he resigned as president of the Art Students
League, where he had taught for years, when the school rejected
his invitation to the German artist George Grosz to join the
faculty. (The League later reversed itself.) He worked on the
Public Works of Art Project in 1933.

SOYER, Raphael. Tombov, Russia, 1899; lives in New York.
Brooklyn Museum; Metropolitan Museum; Museum of Modern
   Art; **Whitney Museum** 313.

An avowed enemy of abstraction, Soyer paints with an unmistakably individual poetry, often movingly eloquent. His portrayals
of the unemployed, of dancers, of girls in the studio and on the
street convey a sense of unsentimental compassion which sets his
image of New York at the opposite pole from that of Reginald
Marsh's lusty extravaganzas. At his best, his colors are richly
textured and luminous and his drawing expressive. Soyer received
his first art lessons from his father, a writer and teacher. He emi-
grated to the United States in 1912, studying in New York art
schools at night while working in factories by day. In the early
1930's he began teaching at the Art Students League. Two of
Soyer's brothers are also painters of stature: Moses, Raphael's
twin, is represented in the Whitney with his *Girl in Orange
Sweater* (1953); Isaac, a younger brother, painted the Whitney's
Employment Agency (1937).

STEEN (stain), **Jan.** Leyden, 1626-79.
Metropolitan Museum 64.

A robust and lusty painter, Steen portrayed a happy-go-lucky
world. Everyday scenes were his main interest, but his work also
included keenly observed landscapes. Uneven in quality, he could
be slapdash as well as sensitive and strong. Of his 700-odd paintings, about 500 remained unsold at his death. Steen studied at
the University of Leyden and married the daughter of one of his
teachers. From 1654 to 1656 he managed breweries to earn extra
income. When his wife died in 1669, he gave some of his pictures
as payment for her medical bills. In 1672 he was licensed to
operate a tavern in Leyden.

STELLA, Joseph. Near Naples, 1877?; New York, 1946.
Metropolitan Museum; Museum of Modern Art; **Whitney Museum** 299.

Stella's best work blends variations on Futurism with pioneer semi-abstraction. His style ranges from precise realism and romantic-decorative compositions to abstract collages. He is famous for his epic rhapsodies to New York—romantic visions inspired by the age of steel and electricity. Stella came to America in 1896 and studied art under the conservative William Merritt Chase. In 1908 he was commissioned by a magazine to paint Pittsburgh steel strikers. In France and Italy in 1909-12, he met Boccioni, Carrà and Severini. He exhibited in Rome in 1910 and in the New York Armory Show in 1913. In 1918 he exhibited the first of his Brooklyn Bridge paintings. His later years were spent in comparative obscurity and relative artistic decline.

STUART, Gilbert. North Kingston, R.I., 1755; Boston, 1828.
Brooklyn Museum 344; Metropolitan Museum; New York Historical Society.

Stuart's facility for likenesses made him the leading American portrait painter after the Revolution. His best pictures combine perceptive characterization with suave polish and appealing color. Stuart sailed to London in 1775, painted low-priced portraits and was Benjamin West's assistant for some five years. He scored a success in 1782 with *The Skater* (National Gallery, Washington) and married in 1786. (He became the father of twelve children.) In the early 1790's he returned to the United States. His third and final portrait of Washington from life (1796, Museum of Fine Arts, Boston) was the model for the portrait on the current one dollar bill. He also painted Jefferson, Madison and Monroe.

TANGUY, Yves (eve tahng-*ee*). Paris, 1900; Woodbury, Conn., 1955.
Museum of Modern Art 204; **Whitney Museum** 307.

Tanguy's fancies are unique among the Surrealists: instead of using representational figures in bizarre confrontation, he created a new vocabulary of strange abstract forms and set them drifting on stages of sky, sea and land. His range is narrow, but completely self-sufficient. Line, color and form are handled with finesse and delicacy. As a child, Tanguy saw the dolmens of Brittany—prehistoric stone structures set in open fields—and may have been permanently influenced by them. He began painting in Paris in 1918 and joined the Surrealists. In 1939 he settled in Connecticut. Later trips brought him to Arizona, Rome, Paris and Milan. His wife was the Surrealist painter Kay Sage.

TCHELITCHEW (chel-*lee*-cheff), **Pavel.** Moscow, 1898; Rome, 1957.
Museum of Modern Art 202.

Tchelitchew's love of mystery and fantasy grew from a childhood interest in Russian fairy tales and imaginative illustrations. His work includes sensitive and highly personal portraits and compositions which probe for fresh insight through exaggerated perspective, multiple images and symbolic comment. His mature paintings and drawings are the most important modern examples of art influenced by the study of human anatomy. Tchelitchew studied art in Kiev, lived in Turkey and Berlin, and in 1923 arrived in Paris, where he did designs for the ballet impresario Diaghilev and joined the Neo-Romantic painters. In 1928 he had his first one-man show, in London. In 1934 he settled in Weston, Conn.; the next year he began his major painting *Phenomena* (bequeathed to the Soviet Union). In the 1940's he began a series of transparent figures and heads in spheroid lines.

TERBORCH (ter-*bork*), **Gerard.** Swolle, 1617; Deventer, 1681.
Metropolitan Museum 63.

Among the finest of the Dutch "little masters," Terborch specialized in portraits and scenes of upper class Dutch life. His soft harmonies are enlivened by the lustrous fabrics he depicts with high fidelity. Compared to many of the Dutch painters of genre (stories of everyday life), Terborch's scenes rise above the level of skillful illustration; they have an innate artistic quality and catch charm in casual moments. Son of a minor painter, Terborch visited England, Italy and Germany and was invited to Madrid by Philip IV, who gave him the rank of a nobleman. He later returned to Holland.

TERBRUGGHEN (ter-*brok*-hen), **Hendrick.** Deventer?, 1588?;
Utrecht, 1629?
Metropolitan Museum 55.

Interest in Terbrugghen has increased greatly in recent years. His deeply religious paintings, imbued with Catholic spirit, are unusual coming from a militantly Protestant Holland. He also painted a number of concert groups. Possibly influenced by the powerful realism and stark dark-and-light effects of Caravaggio, his art also has something of the mood and tonality that Vermeer would perfect some fifty years later. Son of a lawyer, Terbrugghen spent ten years in Italy and settled in Utrecht in 1616. In 1627 Rubens called on him and praised his work enthusiastically.

TIEPOLO (tee-*yay*-poh-loh), **Giovanni Battista.** Venice, 1696;
Madrid, 1770.
Frick Collection; **Metropolitan Museum** 19.

With Tiepolo came the end of the great Venetian tradition which included the soulful poetry of Giorgione and Titian, the thunder of Tintoretto and the panoramic splendor of Veronese. Tiepolo's work is vivacious, yet grandiose, alive with zest and spectacle. He seemed to work so easily that a contemporary reported "[he] paints a picture in less time than another painter takes to grind his colors." His clear colors sparkle in sunny air, his rhythms are lively and his handling is dashing. He was a master of illusionistic perspective and the disposition of figures in high space. Young Tiepolo married a sister of Francesco Guardi. He received important fresco commissions in and about Venice between 1723 and 1728. He and his two painter sons, Domenico and Lorenzo, went to Wurzburg in 1740 to decorate the Emperor's new palace and to Madrid in 1762 to paint in the throne room of King Charles III.

TINTORETTO (tin-toh-*ret*-toh) (real name Jacopo Robusti). Venice, 1518-94.

Frick Collection; **Metropolitan Museum** 15-16; Morgan Library.

According to tradition, Tintoretto's motto was "the drama of Michelangelo and the coloring of Titian." His drawing is terse, his lines expressive and his colors iridescent. His light-and-dark effects are explored with startling virtuosity. Tintoretto pioneered in the use of a fluid, ribbon-like brush stroke (in his time he was often attacked for so-called lack of finish) and in the dramatization of action through unusual angles of vision and daring foreshortenings. He is most famous for compositions that burst with colossal energy, but he is equally brilliant in lyric paintings and in brooding, almost Rembrandt-like portraits. His epochal impact can be traced in painters like El Greco, Rubens, Delacroix and Cézanne. The son of a dyer (Tintoretto means "little dyer"), he may have served a brief apprenticeship with Titian. In 1548 he won acclaim with *The Miracle of St. Mark* (Academy, Venice). He married in 1550. (Two sons and a daughter later became his assistants.) In 1560, when leading artists were invited to submit sketches for a painting for the Confraternity of San Rocco, Tintoretto antagonized his colleagues by showing a completed painting and offering it as a gift. From 1564 and 1588 he executed a vast cycle of more than fifty paintings for the School of San Rocco in Venice, for which he was made a member with a fixed lifetime salary. In 1586, commissioned to decorate the Council Chamber of the Doge's Palace, he and his assistants executed the world's largest oil, *The Glory of Paradise,* some seventy feet long and twenty feet high.

TITIAN (*tish*-in) (real name Tiziano Vecellio). Pieve di Cadore, 1477?; Venice, 1576.

Frick Collection 227; **Metropolitan Museum** 13-14.

The central genius of the dazzling century of Venetian art, Titian painted religious masterpieces, bacchanalian festivals, haunting pastorals, voluptuous nudes and portraits which range from keen character studies to absorbing idealizations. In a long and fruitful life, his power never waned; his later paintings startled patrons by their freedom of handling and their dissolution of shapes into a shimmering fabric of color. It was in color, in fact, that he made his greatest contributions. He carried it to unprecedented richness, its golden glow bathing everything in jewel-like splendor. He revealed new potentials by allowing color to by-pass linear drawing and overflow shapes as a means of rendering atmosphere, dramatizing space, creating mood and subordinating detail to total effect. Applied in glazes of layer upon layer, his color makes his best pictures sheer visual delight. Titian had an enormous influence on painters ranging from Tintoretto, El Greco, Rembrandt and Poussin to Cézanne and Renoir. Titian studied with Giovanni Bellini and the young Giorgione (who had a strong influence on him). In 1516 he succeeded Bellini as official painter of the Venetian Republic. He was employed by Alfonso d'Este, Federico Gonzaga of Mantua, the Dukes of Urbino and the House of Farnese. Through Pietro Aretino he was introduced to the Emperor Charles V, who appointed him court painter in 1553 and named him a Count Palatine. In Rome he was visited by Michelangelo. After the abdication of the Emperor, Titian painted for his son, Phillip II of Spain.

TOBEY, Mark. Centerville, Wisc., 1890; lives in Seattle.
Metropolitan Museum; **Museum of Modern Art** 217; Whitney Museum.

A painter of moods and mysticism and one of the most individual of American abstractionists, Tobey combines the inventive audacity of modern Western art with the delicacy and spirituality of the East. His exquisite paintings transcend physical appearance to capture inner values. His work is characterized by fragile linear movements, evocative symbolic forms and over-all patterns. In his own words, his compositions use "Oriental fragments as characters which twist and turn, drifting into Western zones, forever speaking of the unity of man's spirit." A key to his unique art is his interest in the Baha'i creed. Tobey worked in fashion drawing and society portraits, had his first solo exhibition in New York and settled in Seattle in 1922. He studied Chinese bamboo brush technique and traveled extensively in Europe and the Near East. In England in 1935 he painted *Broadway Norm* (private collection), the first work of the so-called "white writing" style. In the 1958 Venice Biennale he became the first American artist since Whistler to win the Grand International prize.

TOULOUSE-LAUTREC (too-*looz*-loh-*trec*), **Henri de.** Albi, 1864; Chateau de Malromé, Gironde, 1901.
Brooklyn Museum 337; Metropolitan Museum; **Museum of Modern Art** 158.

A master illustrator, Lautrec had an extraordinary ability to fix a fleeting gesture or capture the very essence of a personality. He is unsurpassed in his economy and suppleness of line, his audacity of arrangements, his startling contrasts of dramatic color and his swirling, arabesque movement. His subject matter ranged from the salon to the bordello. His perceptive eye avoided both sentimentality and unconcern. Asked by the singer Yvette Guilbert why he often painted sordid subjects, he replied that "everywhere and always ugliness has its beautiful aspects; it is thrilling to discover them where nobody else has noticed them." Lautrec's style was influenced by the flat patterns and color of Japanese art and by the Impressionists, most notably Degas. He scorned landscape: "Nothing," he said, "exists but the figure." A direct descendant of the Counts of Toulouse, the young Lautrec broke both thigh bones in accidents which permanently stopped the growth of his legs. Still in his teens, he studied art under academicians, but by 1886 he was a friend of van Gogh and knew Pissarro, Gauguin and Seurat. Two years later he painted his first major composition, *At the Cirque Fernando, the Ringmaster* (Art Institute, Chicago). In the early 1890's he took up lithography and made the first of his famous posters, *The Moulin Rouge*. In 1895 he visited London, where he did his *Portrait of Oscar Wilde* (private collection). His health began to deteriorate due to hard drinking, long hours and intensive work, and in 1899 he suffered a physical breakdown. He made his famous *Circus* drawings while in a sanatorium. After his release he suffered a paralytic stroke. The artist's mother and friends inaugurated the Toulouse-Lautrec Museum in Albi in 1922.

TURA (*too*-rah), **Cosimo.** Ferrara?, 1430-95.
Metropolitan Museum 2.

The chief painter of Ferrara, Tura was a highly individual artist whose work is characterized by anti-realistic drawing, a supple and sophisticated line and unusual color harmonies. Through slender means he evokes a restless and tense emotion. Very little of his art has survived. Tura presumably spent his early years in Padua and may have known Mantegna. From about 1451 he painted mostly for Borso d'Este, Duke of Ferrara, for whom he also designed decorations for pageants, festivals and tournaments.

TURNER, Joseph Mallord William. London, 1775-1851.
Frick Collection; **Metropolitan Museum** 73.

In Turner's revolutionary vistas, light and color fuse and flow across the canvases so boldly that some of his astonished contemporaries felt he was painting "pictures of nothing." His nebulous shapes and tangible atmosphere anticipated the effects of Impressionism, and his near annihilation of representation foretells some of the most avant-garde effects of American abstractionists. Son of a hairdresser and a mother who died in an insane asylum, the young Turner exhibited his first oil at the Royal Academy in 1797 and by 1802 had become an Academy member and professor of perspective. Shortly afterward he began his almost constant travels. In 1843 John Ruskin, England's major art critic, acclaimed him the "only perfect landscape painter." In 1844 he made his masterpiece, *Rain, Steam and Speed* (National

Gallery, London). He disappeared for long periods and was eventually found dead in a waterfront shack, under the assumed name of Mr. Booth. His will left hundreds of drawings, watercolors and oils to the nation.

VAN DER WEYDEN (van dur *wide*-un), **Rogier** (also called Rogier de la Pasture). Tournai, 1399?; Brussels, 1464.
Metropolitan Museum 23-24.

One of the greatest Flemish painters, van der Weyden is more starkly emotional and less naturalistic than his predecessors, the van Eycks. His colors 'are rich and gleaming, his line crisp and elaborate. By 1435 van der Weyden had settled in Brussels, where he was appointed "Painter to the Municipality." His greatest works include his *Descent from the Cross* of about 1438 (Prado, Madrid) and *The Last Judgement Altarpiece* of about 1446-48 (Hôtel Dieu, Beaune). He traveled to Rome and Ferrara in 1449-50.

VAN DYKE, Sir Anthony. Antwerp, 1599; London, 1641.
Frick Collection 231; **Metropolitan Museum** 36-37.

An exceptionally gifted virtuoso and a master of flattering aristocratic portraiture, van Dyke received so many commissions that he organized something of a portrait factory: the master would sketch in the face; the hands and costumes (often placed on professional models or dummies) were quickly brushed in by skillful assistants; then van Dyke would apply the finishing touches. During his London period alone, van Dyke produced some 350 likenesses, but only occasionally did they do honor to his high talent. His compositions became the prototypes for fashionable English portraits. The seventh of twelve sons of a peddlar grown rich in silk, van Dyke was apprenticed to a painter at ten, had his own studio at sixteen, and at nineteen was registered as a master painter in the Antwerp guild. After several years in Rubens' workshop, where he ranked as the ablest assistant, he was in 1620 summoned to the court of James I of England. He spent five years in Italy and in 1632 returned to England at the invitation of Charles I, who knighted him and gave him a pension and two houses. He married Lady Mary Ruthven in 1639.

VAN EYCK (van ike), **Hubert.** 1370?; 1426?
Metropolitan Museum 21-22.
See Jan van Eyck.

VAN EYCK (van ike), **Jan.** Maaseyck?, 1390?; Bruges, 1441.
Frick Collection 230.

Credit for the founding of the Flemish school is given to Jan van Eyck and his older brother Hubert. Jan van Eyck is one of the greatest technicians in painting and among the most skillful of all realists. His paintings are profound integrations of luminous brilliance, delicacy and grandeur. He was a genius at minute detail, but it is the spiritual intensity of his work that gives it its drama and solemnity. His command of the new medium of oil mixed with egg emulsion revolutionized art, lending painting much greater flexibility. Very little is known about his brother Hubert; in fact, his very existence is in question. In the 1820's, a four-line inscription was discovered on one of the world's greatest paintings, the *Adoration of the Mystic Lamb* altarpiece at Ghent, a work which had been attributed to Jan. The faded text identified "Hubertus Eyck" as the greatest of all painters and stated that he had begun the altarpiece and that Jan completed it in 1432. Hubert is also said to have been buried in front of the altarpiece, but no records have been found to substantiate this or other aspects of one of art's greatest mysteries. Jan van Eyck was by 1422 the official painter to John of Bavaria, for whom he decorated the Palace of the Hague, and was later named court painter and gentleman of the bedchamber to the famed art patron Philip, Duke of Burgundy. He married in Lille and became father to ten children. He was sent on confidential missions to England, Spain and Portugal to seek the hands of princesses for his patron, and in 1434 Philip stood as godfather to one of his children. He settled permanently in Bruges in 1430.

VAN GOGH (van go *or* van gokh), **Vincent.** Groot-Zundert, Holland, 1853; Auvers-sur-Oise, France, 1890.
Metropolitan Museum 69-70; **Museum of Modern Art** 159.

The most popular name in modern art, van Gogh has become a legendary symbol of the despair and ultimate triumph of the misunderstood artist. Van Gogh's scant ten years of feverish painting chronicle the enormous shift from the interest in visual phenomena of the Impressionists to the inner emotion of the Expressionists. In his fervid, swirling visions, broad areas of intense color are juxtaposed in striking and sudden contrasts to express drama, emotion and mood. His forms are animated by twisting linear rhythms. His terse, rough brushstrokes exalt the hand and the heart at the same time that they assault the eye and mind with their crackling tension. Non-naturalistic distortions infuse his canvases with bold vigor. The mystic passion he thrust upon the serene mainstream of 19th Century French art became a potent liberating influence on the art of the 20th Century. The eldest son of a pastor, van Gogh was employed by an art firm in which his uncle was a partner. He worked in art galleries in The Hague, Brussels, London and Paris. After a trip to England and brief employment as an assistant teacher, he studied in Amsterdam for theological college but failed his examination. He spent three months at an evangelical school in Brussels, then he volunteered to serve as lay minister among Belgian coal miners. In 1880 he decided to become a painter; he studied briefly with the well-known painter Anton Mauve, the husband of his cousin. After painting his first masterpiece, *The Potato Eaters* (1885), he joined his brother Théo in Paris and met Lautrec, Pissarro, Degas, Seurat and Gauguin. In 1888-89 he attempted to found an artists' colony at Arles; Gauguin spent two months with him there. On Christmas Eve he suffered a violent mental breakdown. At his own request, he was confined to an asylum at St. Rémy, where he painted and wrote intensively. The only oil he sold in his lifetime, *The Red Vineyard,* was purchased for a modest figure at an avant-garde exhibition in Brussels. He put himself under the care of a doctor who was a friend and a collector of contemporary art, but on July 27, 1890, he shot himself. He died murmuring to Théo, "Misery endures forever." Théo died the following year. The year after that, over one hundred of van Gogh's paintings were exhibited in Amsterdam.

VELAZQUEZ (vuh-*lah*-skiz *or* vale-*ath*-kathe), **Diego Rodriguez.**
  Seville, 1599; Madrid, 1660.
Frick Collection 234; Hispanic Museum; **Metropolitan Museum**
  46.

Velázquez, the unsurpassed master of detached and impersonal realism, has few equals in the art of great portraiture. His profound respect for common humanity is as apparent in his majestic portrayals of royalty as it is in his moving depictions of court fools and dwarfs. His eye seized on the essentials of appearance, and he enhanced them with poise and dignity. He was a master colorist, a composer of magnificent tonal harmonies, a brilliant manipulator of space effects and an innovator in rendering light and atmosphere. With a wizardly control of his brush, he (unlike Hals) avoided virtuoso display in favor of telling simplicity. To Manet, enormously in Velázquez' debt, he was "the painter of painters." At fourteen Velázquez entered the studio of Francisco Pacheco (whose daughter he was to marry in 1618). In 1623 he painted his first portrait of King Philip IV; appointed court painter, he spent his remaining thirty-seven years painting for the King and serving in honorable court positions. In 1628 he painted his famous *The Drinkers* (Prado, Madrid) and met Rubens. In 1648-51 he visited Italy to select paintings for the Spanish Royal Collection, now in the Prado. His later masterpieces include *The Surrender of Breda, Las Meninas, The Tapestry Weavers* and *The Infanta Margarita* (all in the Prado).

VERMEER (vur-*meer*), **Johannes.** Delft, 1632-75.
Frick Collection 239-240; **Metropolitan Museum** 66-68.
Vermeer worked within the Dutch tradition of engaging interior scenes, but he far surpassed even his most gifted contemporaries. His skill and poetic vision put him in that rare company of artists who are admired both by other painters and by the general public.

Every element in his compositions is coordinated into a subtly precise orchestration. He avoids undue sentiment and story-telling appeal. Though a theme is always present, he seems to cast a spell over each scene, and some profound significance appears to hover over his canvases. His light, which flows over objects, blurs or sharpens contours and creates stunning dark-to-light transpositions, is of such quality that the paint seems to disappear, replaced by a magic texture. His control of space and his feeling for the essence of a form or pattern are masterful, and his colors are highly personal. After his death, he was scarcely known until a century ago, and some of his greatest paintings—including *The Artist in His Studio*—bore forged signatures of more saleable artists. The French art critic Théophile Thoré-Bürger launched the rediscovery of Vermeer in 1866 with an article called "The Mysterious Sphinx of Delft." Vermeer's lights, he wrote, "are silver, his shadows the color of pearls." Vermeer's father was a silk weaver, part-time innkeeper and small art dealer. At twenty-one, the young Vermeer married and was admitted as a master painter to the Guild of St. Luke. He apparently sold well but painted slowly, eking out additional income for his eleven children by dealing in art. Promissory notes show that he was forced to borrow frequently, and after his death his wife was declared bankrupt. Antony van Leeuwenhoek, the lens grinder who was the first man to see bacteria, helped administer the sale of the widow's remaining paintings and property.

VERONESE (vay-roh-*nay*-zay), (real name Paolo Caliari). Verona, 1528; Venice, 1588.
Frick Collection 228-229; **Metropolitan Museum** 17.

Veronese is unequalled in his enormous tableaux of sumptuous aristocratic life. His groupings throb with energetic sweep, forceful counterbalance and rhythmic interrelation of movement, yet all is held in control by sensitive and vivid brushwork. Rubens, Delacroix, Renoir, Cézanne and many others were influenced by his masterful use of color to mould shapes and to evoke space and sparkling atmosphere. At thirteen, Veronese studied under a minor painter whose daughter he later married. In 1552 he was commissioned by Cardinal Gonzaga to paint an altarpiece for the cathedral in Mantua. He later moved to Venice, where he painted his *Marriage at Cana* (Louvre) and important frescoes. In 1573 he was called before the Inquisition to defend certain details in his huge *The Last Supper in the House of Simon,* "which the Holy Tribune considered . . . impious and improper and even heretical . . . in a religious scene." He defended himself by declaring, ". . . if in a picture there is some space I enrich it with figures. . . . We painters take the same license the poets and jesters take. . . . I paint pictures as I see fit and as my talent permits." The Inquisition ordered him to make alterations, but instead he changed the title to *The Feast in the House of Levi* (Academy, Venice). He later did paintings for the Doge's Palace.

WATTEAU (vah-*toh*), **Jean Antoine.** Valenciennes, 1684; Joyent-sur-Marne, 1721.
Metropolitan Museum 78-79.

The finest French artist of the 18th Century, Watteau perfected a new style of exquisite, dreamy compositions. Called *fêtes galantes,* they portray romantic groups in park-like settings and are characterized by languid emotion, theatrical masquerade, enchanting outdoor effects and a wistful melancholy. Watteau's lustrous color is soft, his handling firm, and his drawing fluid. Of Flemish ancestry, Watteau arrived in Paris in 1702 and worked for art hacks turning out stereotyped religious paintings. He later studied under Claude Gillot, who specialized in theater subjects, and Claude Audran, the custodian of the Royal Collection in the Luxembourg Palace. In 1717, on the presentation of his *Embarkation for the Island of Cythera* (Louvre), he was granted full membership in the French Academy. The fabulous collector Crozat (who owned over 400 paintings and 19,000 drawings), invited Watteau to stay at his home and study in 1716. Suffering from tuberculosis, Watteau spent a year in England to consult a famous physician, but he died soon afterward at thirty-seven.

WEBER, Max. Bialystock, Russia, 1881; Great Neck, L.I., 1961.
Brooklyn Museum; Metropolitan Museum; **Museum of Modern Art** 168; **Whitney Museum** 297-298.

One of the most important figures in modern American art, Weber was among the first to respond to the influence of the Fauves, Cubists and Futurists. After a period of audacious semi-abstraction, he turned to representational Expressionism marked by poetic and spiritual overtones. Weber arrived in the United States in 1891. In 1905, after teaching art, he sailed for France, where he helped organize a class under Matisse and exhibited with the Independents in 1906. In 1910, back in the United States, his first one-man show aroused violent critical attacks. He published his *Cubist Poems* in 1914. His one-man show at the Newark Museum was the first solo exhibition of an American modernist in any museum. The Museum of Modern Art gave him its first exhibition of a living American in 1930.

WEYDEN, Rogier van der. See VAN DER WEYDEN, Rogier.

WHISTLER, James Abbott McNeill. Lowell, Mass., 1834; London, 1903.
Frick Collection 255; **Metropolitan Museum** 129.

Whistler was a valiant and witty battler against the tradition of evaluating paintings in terms of their subject matter. Influenced by flat Japanese patterns and the simplicity of Velázquez and

Manet, he developed an exquisite personal style of harmonious tonal relationships, striking patterns and novel space arrangements. Son of an Army Major, Whistler entered West Point (then under Robert E. Lee) but three years later was discharged for deficiency in chemistry. ("Had silicon been a gas, I would have been a Major General," he once said.) In 1855 he went to France to paint and met Fantin-Latour, Courbet, Degas and Manet. In 1863 his *Symphony in White No. 1: The White Girl* (National Gallery, Washington) was rejected by the Salon, and he exhibited at the Salon of the Rejected. He settled in London in 1871 and began painting his Thames nocturnes. His famous portrait of his mother was exhibited most reluctantly by the Royal Academy in 1874. In 1878 he sued the famed critic John Ruskin after a scathing review; Whistler was awarded one farthing damages but assessed half of the court costs, forcing him into bankruptcy. In 1888 he married, and in 1890 he published his "The Gentle Art of Making Enemies." In 1891 the Glasgow School Corporation bought his portrait of Thomas Carlyle and he sold his portrait of his mother to the Luxembourg Museum. (A portrait of Whistler by William Merritt Chase is in the Metropolitan.)

WILLIAMS, William. About 1710; about 1798.
Brooklyn Museum 341; **Metropolitan Museum.**

Williams' background is obscure, but he apparently went to sea as a youth, was shipwrecked in Central America and about 1741 settled in Philadelphia, where he was the teacher of Benjamin West. He wrote accounts of the lives of artists and an autobiography in fictional form called "The Journal of Llewellyn Penrose," probably the first novel written in America though not published until 1815. He sailed for England about 1780 and is believed to have died in a Bristol poorhouse.

WYETH, Andrew. Chadds Ford, Penn., 1917; lives in Pennsylvania.
Metropolitan Museum 155; **Museum of Modern Art** 211; Whitney Museum.

Wyeth's sharp-focused realism combines the appeal of minutiae with highly individual dramatic concepts. His work is characterized by understatement, delicate tone and striking space arrangements. "My aim," he declared in 1943, "is to leave no residue of technical mannerisms to stand between my expression and the observer . . . not to exhibit craft, but rather to submerge it, and make it rightfully the handmaiden of beauty, power and emotional content." Son and pupil of the famous book illustrator N. C. Wyeth, young Andrew had his first exhibition at seventeen. In 1947 he was awarded the American Academy of Arts and Letters Merit Medal, given to a painter only once each five years, and in 1963 he was among the first to receive the President's Medal of Freedom.

ZURBARAN (thoor-bah-*rahn*), **Francisco.** Fuente de Cantos, 1598; Madrid, 1664.

Hispanic Museum; **Metropolitan Museum** 47.

Zurbarán's grave, meditative art combines intense realism with an austere and mystic spirit. His figures, modeled with bold light and dark, convey a self-contained, solitary, brooding quality. Most of his paintings portray saints and monastic life, but he was also among the first masters to explore the still life as a self-sufficient theme in painting. The son of peasants, Zurbarán was sent to Seville, where, after apprenticeship to a minor painter, he became a friend of Velázquez. In 1634 he went to Madrid, where he painted *The Siege of Cadiz* for Phillip IV. He received many major commissions for convents and monasteries. In his later years his work took on softness and his creative power declined.

SELECTED LIST OF ART GALLERIES
IN NEW YORK CITY

There are more than 250 Art Galleries in New York City, ranging from some that specialize in ancient Egyptian art to those that present the newest and most avant-garde forms. For listings of current exhibitions, consult *The New Yorker* and *Cue* magazines, or the Saturday or Sunday editions of *The New York Times* and *The Herald Tribune*. Most galleries are closed on Mondays, and all close by 6 p.m.

ALAN, 766 Madison (66th), LE 5-3113, Chiefly American contemporaries. A.C.A., 63 E. 57th, PL 5-9622, American contemporaries, chiefly representational. ALAN AUSLANDER, 1078 Madison (74th), UN 1-5035, European and American contemporaries. BABCOCK, 805 Madison (68th), LE 5-9355, Americans, 19th and 20th centuries. BORGENICHT, 1018 Madison (79th), LE 5-8040, Chiefly American contemporaries. LEO CASTELLI, 4 E. 77th, BU 8-4820, Avant-garde, including *Pop*. CHALLETTE, 9 E. 88th, LE 5-8120, Modern Europeans and Americans. CONTEMPORARIES, 992 Madison (77th), TR 9-1980, European and American avant-garde, including *Op*. CORDIER & EKSTROM, 978 Madison (76th), YU 8-8857, 20th century Europeans and Americans. DAVIS, 231 E. 60th, PL 3-5420, American representational. PETER DEITSCH, 24 E. 81st, RE 7-8279, Modern prints and drawings. TERRY DINTENFASS, 18 E. 67th, RH 4-1580, Modern Americans. DOWNTOWN, 32 E. 51st, PL 3-3707, Americans, Folk and 20th century. DURLACHER BROS., 538 Madison (55th), EL 5-3398, American contemporaries, chiefly representational. EAST HAMPTON, 22 W. 56th, CI 6-3218, Chiefly American moderns. EGAN, 41 E. 58th, PL 5-1825, American moderns. ANDRE EMMERICH, 41 E. 57th, PL 2-0124, Ancient sculpture, European and American moderns. FAR, 746 Madison (65th), RE 4-7287, Chiefly modern drawings and prints. RICHARD FEIGEN, 24 E. 81st, RE 7-6640, European and American contemporaries. FISCHBACH, 799 Madison (67th), YU 8-2755, American moderns. FITZGERALD, 718 Madison (64th), PL 2-1272, Contemporary American realists. FORUM, 1018 Madison (79th), LE 5-6080, Modern Americans, chiefly representational. ROSE FRIED, 40 E. 68th, RE 7-8622, European and American moderns. GALERIE ST. ETIENNE, 24 W. 57th, CI 5-6734, Chiefly European expressionists. GRAHAM, 1014 Madison (78th), LE 5-5767, 19th and 20th century Americans. GREEN, 15 W. 57th, PL 2-4055, American moderns. GREER, 35 W. 53rd, CI 6-1555, European and American moderns. GRIFFIN, 611 Madison (58th), EL 5-3353, European and American moderns. HAHN, 960 Madison (75th), LE 5-3520, Europeans and Americans, 19th and 20th centuries. HIRSCHL-ADLER, 21 E. 67th, LE 5-8810, Europeans and Americans, 19th and 20th centuries. LEOPOLD HUTTON, 787 Madison (67th), AG 9-9700, 20th century Europeans, esp. German Expressionists. IOLAS, 15 E. 55th, PL 5-6778, 20th century Europeans and Americans, esp. Surrealists. MARTHA JACKSON, 32 E. 69, YU 8-1800, European and American moderns. JANIS, 15 E. 57th, PL 9-4241, 20th century Europeans and Americans. KAMER, 965 Madison (75th), YU 8-6920, Primitive and Archaic art. KLEJMAN, 982 Madison, LE 5-5484, Primitive and Archaic art. KNOEDLER, 14 E. 57th, PL 3-9742, Old masters to moderns. KOOTZ, 655 Madison (60th), TE 2-7676, 20th century Europeans and Americans. KORNBLEE, 58 E. 79th, UN 1-4245, American moderns. KRAUSHAAR, 1055 Madison (80th), LE 5-9888, Chiefly early 20th century and contemporary Americans. LA BOETIE, 1042 Madison (79th), LE 5-4865, 20th century Europeans and Americans. LEFEBRE, 47 E. 77th, RH 4-3384, Modern Europeans and Americans. LOEB, 12 E. 57th, PL 3-7857, Modern Europeans and Americans. ROYAL MARKS, 19 E. 71st, UN 1-3400, 20th century Europeans and Americans. MARLBOROUGH-GERSON, 41 E. 57th, PL 2-5353, Chiefly 19th and 20th century Europeans and Americans. PIERRE MATISSE, 41 E. 57th, EL 5-6269, 20th century Europeans and Americans. NIVEAU, 962 Madison, RE 7-1094, 20th century Europeans and Americans. ODYSSIA, 41 E. 57th, HA 1-3690, Modern Europeans and Americans. PACE, 9 W. 57th, HA 1-3292, Modern Europeans and Americans. PARKE-BERNET GALLERIES, 980 Madison (76th), TR 9-8300, Frequent auctions of· art from all periods. BETTY PARSONS, 24 W. 57th, CI 7-7480, Chiefly American moderns. PERLS, 1016 Madison (78th), TR 9-7440, Chiefly 20th century Europeans and Americans. PICASSO ARTS, 1046 Madison (80th), UN 1-0450, Picasso only. REHN, 36 E. 61st, PL 3-4694, Contemporary Americans. ROKO, 867 Madison (72nd), LE 5-7630, Modern Americans. ROSENBERG, 20 E. 79th, RH 4-2340, French 19th century; modern Europeans and Americans. SAIDENBERG, 1035 Madison (79th), BU 8-3387, 20th century Europeans and Americans. SALPETER, 42 E. 57th, MU 8-5659, Modern Americans. BERTHA SCHAEFER, 32 E. 57th, PL 5-3330, Modern Europeans and Americans. SCHOELKOPF, 825 Madison (69th), TR 9-4638, Contemporary Europeans and Americans. SILBERMAN, 1014 Madison (78th), TR 9-6980, Old masters to 20th century. STABLE, 33 E. 74th, RE 7-0100, Modern Americans. STAEMPFLI, 47 E. 77th, LE 5-1919, Modern Europeans and Americans. STONE, 48 E. 86th, YU 8-6870, Modern Europeans and Americans. VIVIANO, 42 E. 57th, PL 8-1030, Modern Europeans and Americans. WILDENSTEIN, 19 E. 64th, TR 9-0500, Old masters to 20th century. WILLARD, 29 E. 72nd, RH 4-3925. HOWARD WISE, 50 W. 57th, CO 5-0465, Modern Europeans and Americans. WORLD HOUSE, 987 Madison, LE 5-4700, 19th and 20th century Europeans and Americans. ZABRISKIE, 36 E. 61st, TE 2-9034, Contemporary Americans.